126

A. J. MUNDELLA

1825–1897

ἌΝθρωπος φύσει ζώον πολιτικόν
(Man is by nature an animal meant for civic life)
ARISTOTLE

THE RT. HON. A. J. MUNDELLA, M.P.

A Portrait in oils by Sir A. Cope exhibited at the Royal
Academy in 1894 and now in the Town Hall, Sheffield

A. J. MUNDELLA

1825–1897

The Liberal Background
to the Labour Movement

W. H. G. ARMYTAGE

LONDON
ERNEST BENN LIMITED

First published 1951

THE AUTHOR

W. H. G. Armytage, a familiar name to listeners to the West Regional Programme of the B.B.C., is a South African. Born at Kimberley in 1915, he came to Cornwall in his teens, and was later at Cambridge where he took a first in history. After serving as a combatant infantry officer during the last war, he returned to a lectureship at the University of Sheffield. He has written a number of articles on nineteenth-century history for British, American, and Canadian journals, and has given several talks on the Third Programme. He is at present working on the diary of A. H. D. Acland.

Published by Ernest Benn Limited
Bouverie House, Fleet Street, E.C.4
Printed in Great Britain by
Richard Clay & Company, Ltd., Bungay, Suffolk

Contents

PART I   MANUFACTURER

Chapter   Page

1   *The Successful Stockinger, 1824–1860*   13

Aliens in England: The Leicester youth: Chartist evangel: Partnership, patents, and prosperity: The end of the factory

2   *The Local Liberal Leader, 1853–1867*   25

Middle-class manufacturers: The war scare and the volunteers: Cobden's Commercial Peace: The Nottingham Board of Arbitration: The Parliamentary Election of 1861: The implications of mass-production: His breakdown: Voices from the hive: The Election of 1865: The Election of 1866

3   *The Champion of the Trade Unions, 1867–1868*   47

Shadows over Sheffield: Hornby *v.* Close: The panic of the debenture-holders: The Government acts: Roebuck found wanting: The Sheffield Election of 1868

PART II   POLITICIAN

4   *Donning the Labour Harness, 1869–1870*   67

Labour's spokesman in the Commons: Eluding the League's grip: The architecture of the 1870 Act: The Voluntaryists fight back: The Education Bill: Another fire: Marginal activities

5   *America, 1870*   84

The rise of Germany: His reception in America: American influence on him

6   *Drawing Away from the Pack, 1871*   92

Venereal Diseases: Army reform: A Charter for the unions: Children of the brickyards: The Scott Russell affair: Closing the public-houses: Peacemaker of the party: The Newcastle lock-out: Keeping the unions loyal

Chapter   Page

7   *Isolation from the Radicals, 1872*   107

    Gas and water: The Nottingham T.U.C.: A Charter for the
    miners: Radical splinter groups: The farm labourers: The
    Mundella Act

8   *Politician among the Pressure Groups, 1872–1874*   122

    Groups as persons: The Nine Hours Bill: The collectivist:
    Plimsoll and the T.U.C.: H. J. Wilson and the Noncon-
    formists: Fawcett champions the employers: The Sheffield
    T.U.C.: The Election of 1874

9   *The Prop of the Party, 1874–1876*   142

    Liberal Disunity: The Nine Hours Bill adopted: The En-
    dowed Schools struggle: The right to picket: The lost leader:
    The Plimsoll story: The Sheffield Liberals re-unite: The
    second step to compulsion

10 *Towards the Front Bench, 1876–1880*   168

    The Bulgarian atrocities: The National Conference: The
    nation galvanised: The Eastern Question Association: The
    National Liberal Federation: Enthusiasm channelled: The
    emergence of Broadhurst and Burnett: Cheap meat: Workers'
    playtime—fishing and fresh air: Essays in political philosophy:
    The Liberal tide rises: The Election of 1880

PART III   MINISTER OF STATE

11 *Vice-President of the Council, 1880–1885*   203

    Impact of a new hand: Warnings from the continent: The
    Mundella Code: The re-organisation of Welsh education:
    Opposition from the voluntaryists: Children and cattle
    separated: Tensions above and below: Signs of work well
    done: New departures in secondary education: The schools
    question in the 1885 election: The Cross Commission:
    Evaluation of his work

12 *President of the Board of Trade, 1886*   237

    Gladstone's third ministry: Expansion of the Board's duties:
    Railway rates: Mundella's Bill: The apathy of the cabinet:
    Its impact on Liberal railway directors: Chamberlain seizes
    his opportunity: The great Liberal split: The Conservatives
    take office: His Bill adopted: It becomes law: Mundella's part

CONTENTS

Chapter   Page

PART IV   ELDER STATESMAN

13   *A Voice in Opposition, 1886–1892*   269

The deficiencies of Britain's industrial army: More trouble
with the voluntaryists: Work for the S.P.C.C.: The Bishop
of Salisbury: Dark clouds: His educational programme:
Child labour: The raising of the school-leaving age: Free
education: Drafting Blue Books: The Election of 1892

14   *President of the Board of Trade, 1892–1894*   289

The railways prove awkward: Further administrative expansion: The great coal strike: Minor reforms: His political
downfall

15   *The Last Phase, 1894–1897*   306

The old man rallies: Arbitration in the air: The school
boards in danger: His death: Valedictions

16   *His Place in the Period*   318

Apostle of arbitration: Administrative reformer: The influence of Sheffield: Commercial agent: Education and the
new clerisy: The trade unions: Taker of tensions

Bibliographical Notes   337

Index   379

Illustrations

THE RT. HON. A. J. MUNDELLA, M.P. *Frontispiece*
A Portrait in oils by Sir A. Cope exhibited at the Royal
Academy in 1894 and now in the Town Hall, Sheffield

THE FIRE AT HINE AND MUNDELLA'S *Facing page 48*
As seen from the Canal Bridge, Carrington Street
[*With acknowledgements to the Illustrated London News*]

THE ELECTION RIOT AT NOTTINGHAM IN 1865 *Facing page 96*
[*With acknowledgements to the Illustrated London News*]

AN ANTI-MUNDELLA CARTOON *Facing page 144*
Circulated before the Parliamentary Election of 1868

MUNDELLA, REJECTED BY THE PEOPLE OF NOTTINGHAM
Facing page 192
Sets off for Sheffield, grasping his staff (Robert Leader)
One of a number of cartoons depicting him as 'The
Wandering Jew'

THE PARLIAMENTARY ELECTION AT SHEFFIELD IN 1874
Facing page 240
A Right wing forecast

THE CANDIDATES FOR PARLIAMENT IN 1874 *Facing page 288*
Robert Leader is admonishing the kneeling Roebuck,
while Leng looks on from the wings

Illustrations in the Text

	Page
MUNDELLA 'RUNS' THE MAYOR OF NOTTINGHAM	27
MUNDELLA 'HORSES' THE CHIEF CONSTABLE 1861	28
MUNDELLA AND NO. 30 RECEIVE A SHOCK IN 1865	42
THE TRIUMPH OF SIR ROBERT CLIFTON 1865	43
LENG BLOWS UP THE WORKING MAN'S IDOL 1868	61

PART I
MANUFACTURER

CHAPTER ONE

The Successful Stockinger, 1825–1860

THE absence of either an iron curtain or an Ellis Island has been both the strength and essence of the English Liberal tradition. With neither barrier nor screen to impede the free flow of emigrants to this island, it has become an asylum for the oppressed from the whole of western Europe. Even the most critical of continental observers have paid tribute to this.

A French historian renowned for his Liberalism acknowledged:

'Hateful as England is, she appears grand indeed, as she faces Europe,—as she faces Dunkirk and Antwerp in ruins. All other countries—Russia, Austria, Italy, Spain and France—have their capitals on the west, opposite the setting sun: the great European vessel seems to float with her sails bellied by the wind, which erst blew from Asia. England alone has hers pointed to the east, as if in defiance of that world—*unum omnia contra*. This last country of the Old World is the heroical land; the constant refuge of the exiled and energetic. All who have fled servitude,—Druids pursued by Rome, Gallo-Romans chased by the Barbarians, Saxons proscribed by Charlemagne, famished Danes, grasping Normans, the persecuted Flemish manufacturers, the vanquished French Calvinists,—all have crossed the sea, and made the great island their country: *arva, beata petamus arva, divites et insulas.* . . . Thus England has thriven on misfortunes and grown great out of ruins.'[1]

The ethos of that greatness was the liberal tradition: a tradition of reasonableness, tolerance, compromise and humanity. It was also a tradition of service and industry: the service which was perfect freedom, and the industry which was life itself. Perhaps it suffered from the interpreters who loved it most; men like Samuel Smiles, who dedicated himself to be its hagiographer. Yet even Smiles, sure and confident exponent as he was, full of pride in the inventiveness and resourcefulness of his age, never hesitated to ascribe to foreign refugees their full credit for the great industrial advances of his own time, and insisted that the subject was one which was 'well worthy of fuller investigation',[2] since the immigrants influenced 'in a remarkable degree' the whole of English economic, political and religious history.

It is a great theme, but before it can be explored in all its fullness, the basic biographies have to be written, for it is only from them that the history can be distilled. Both Michelet and Smiles, like all historians, were writing the history of their own times as they interpreted the past. Their own times witnessed a migration from the continent far greater than any that they had chronicled. Especially was this so in the first quarter of the nineteenth century, when, from the leaden chamber of reactionary Austrian rule in Italy, choice spirits emerged to seek in England a freer vent for their energies. In the expanding industrial economy of post-Waterloo England they found the sanctuary which later generations of their countrymen were to find in America. Intellectual idealism, æsthetic sense and sensitivity were the natural endowments which they brought with them.

Initiator and pioneer of this Italian influx was Ugo Foscolo, who tried so hard to become a British gentleman that he ruined both his health and fortune in the attempt. Others, with greater integrity, retained their native characteristics while conforming to the customs of their adopted country. Thus Anthony Panizzi, whose head looks down on every entrant to the Reading Room of the British Museum (his own particular creation), was a life-long participant in movements for the liberation of Italy, and a generous helper of his fellow-exiles. Less respectable, but equally intense, was Murat's former aide-de-camp, Colonel Maceroni, who extended his political activities from Italian to American and Spanish politics, and wrote a manual of street-fighting for London workmen, in case they might wish to take to the barricades.[3] He was also a mechanical inventor: a steam-coach of his design was tried out in the year after the Great Reform Bill. Yet perhaps the most imaginative of all was the son of Gabriele Rossetti, Dante Gabriel, who owed to his origins the violent intensity of passion that expressed itself in the pre-Raphaelite movement.

These were the distinguished immigrants. There were others, whose accomplishments did not qualify them for admission to the Holland House circle, and whose purses were so short that they had to find a home in the provinces. Obscure as many of these were, the success of their efforts to find a living depended mainly on their ability to teach a foreign language. One of them was Antonio Mundella, a Lombard from Como, who took part in an unsuccessful rising against the Austrians,[4] and escaped, like Panizzi, to save his life. He drifted to Bradford, where he became naturalised.[5] There too he was unsuccessful. So he drifted southwards to

14

the more congenial atmosphere of Leicestershire, where he taught modern languages.

His arrival, in the general labour migration which went on over the eighteen twenties, occasioned no comment. Leicester, where he settled, was already a town dependent for its livelihood on the usual paleotechnic craft: in this case, domestic manufacture of lace and hosiery. This was carried out on frames in the homes of the people. These frames were hand operated, and the operators were known in the trade as 'framework knitters'. The Italian exile met one of these framework knitters—a lady called Rebecca Allsop. She was of Welsh extraction, 'richly endowed mentally, and possessed of some property'.[6] We are also told that she was adept at lace embroidery. The combination of intelligence, industry and a competence proved irresistible, and they were married. On 28 March 1825 she gave birth to her first child, who was christened Anthony John.

I

Mundella's English birth was an undoubted fact, yet during his lifetime it was widely scouted by his political opponents. His long, hooked nose, Italian name and slightly bizarre taste in clothes, led to the natural assumption that he was an Italian. Even a close political friend like G. O. Trevelyan could write to him:

'I never realised that what makes you so much pleasanter than other people was your having been born within sight of Monte Generoso. If the sensibility falls to you and the manifestation of it to your friends, they have all the gain and I doubt if you have much loss. I wish if that is the case we had a little more Italian blood on the Treasury Bench.'[7]

More especially did the taint of alien blood become a taunt as he championed unpopular causes, when it often caused him acute embarrassment.[8]

He went to a Church of England school. It was one of those maintained by the National Society out of voluntary subscriptions to provide elementary education for the poorer classes. Called the St. Nicholas National School, it gave a training based on the teaching of the established church. This is interesting in view of the fact that Mundella's father was a Roman Catholic. Mundella's teacher was a clergyman, who had a taste for natural history. He seems to have left some impression on the minds of his pupils, for Mundella and a friend called H. W. Bates used to go 'groping in the pools'. In Bates' case the enthusiasm sustained him as a man to explore the Amazon.[9]

Mundella was fired by no such enthusiasm. On the contrary, he often said in later life, 'Creeds and catechisms were my especial abomination, and even the beautiful collects of the Church of England were imposed on me so often that they became distasteful'. There is a story, told by a contemporary Baptist minister of the town, that in the year 1832 some 2,000 small boys marched in a triumphal procession to celebrate the passing of the Reform Bill. Each of them carried a small flag and wore a small medal which had been specially struck for the occasion. But young Mundella, aged nine, carried a banner. By so doing he was regarded as sufficiently dangerous to be expelled from school. The severity of the punishment was, however, somewhat mitigated by his subsequent re-admission on payment of a small fine.[10]

His schooldays soon ended. His mother's eyesight, strained beyond capacity by her close work on the lace-frame, began to give way, and he had to start work as a printer's devil, fetching beer for thirsty compositors. This he did for nearly two years.

When he was eleven he was apprenticed to a stockinger. In the hierarchy of the industry such a man stood at the very centre of the community. He owned and rented the frames, and bought and sold the products woven on them. Mundella's first employer was William Kempson, of Albion Street, Welford Road, Leicester, and in these long years of apprenticeship he learned more than the mere mechanics of the hosiery trade.

For, matching his own adolescence, the industry was undergoing a profound revolution. The old paleotechnic process, part hand, part machine, was breaking down. Since the family was the basis of the industry (adults weaving the flat web on the frames and children seaming it into hose), work became more intense as competition increased. So foul was the atmosphere in these cottage workrooms that one framesmith abandoned his craft because of the illnesses he contracted in visiting them. As the screw was turned ever tighter, the hardships intensified. The total earnings of a family, after the rent for the cottage and the frame had been deducted, were often not above three and sixpence a week.[11] Looking back upon it, Mundella was shocked. 'The condition of the framework knitters', he wrote, 'was one of chronic lack of employment and hunger.'[12]

In an industry where the profits were small and the dispersion of frames was great, the renter of frames often tried to snatch the profits of the grocer as well, and pay for the finished article in truck. Food, clothes and raw material became the only rewards of many framework knitters. The system had been intensified by the shortage of cash and small change during the wars. Since a number of frame-owners were outsiders, like bakers, butchers, farmers' sons and others, the temptation on the part of overseers to indulge in this kind of abusive truck payment to the framework knitters was great. 'The wretched framework knitters probably suffered most from truck, as they always had,' wrote Sir John Clapham, and he further pointed out how easily the abuse could flourish in times of bad trade.[13]

Bad trade now hit the industry. Elastic ribbed stockings—the staple manufacture of the town—went out of fashion. Sixteen Leicester firms became bankrupt. Many knitters were thrown out of work. A close contemporary observer reported: 'They were hopeless of improving their condition, and helpless if they attempted it'.[14] A *deus ex machina* was needed.

2

The fiery evangel of Thomas Cooper touched these disconnected discontents. Cooper, a thirty-year-old native of the town, was a self-educated schoolmaster, local preacher and reporter, whose hard self-mastery of the classics preceded an apocalyptic conversion to Chartism. Cooper's chartism was a personal, gnomic creed that was intrinsically his own. The Charter, with its stark assertions of the principles of manhood suffrage, vote by ballot, annual elections and property-less parliamentary representation, served as a framework on which he could embroider a highly coloured biographical interpretation of the past, a new hagiography in which the saints were Philip Sidney, John Hampden and William Tell. He founded a 'Shakespearean Room' in Leicester, where lessons from the poet were declaimed and lectures on the worthies of the past were delivered.

To further the 'good old cause' (as he called it), Cooper founded a newspaper with the apt title of *The Midland Counties Illuminator*. For, like the gentle, melancholy Lovett, who had framed the Charter, Cooper held that education was 'the universal instrument for advancing the dignity of man and gladdening his social existence'. So great was Cooper's hold in the town, that he was affectionately known as 'the General'.

To adolescent Mundella, then fifteen, Cooper's histrionics had a powerful appeal. He attended the meetings, and was inspired by the powerful harangues: on one occasion so much so that Cooper was moved to record it.

'A handsome young man sprang upon our platform and declared himself on the people's side and desired to be enrolled as a Chartist. He did not belong to the poorest ranks, and it was the consciousness that he was acting from a spirit of self-sacrifice as well as his fervid eloquence, that caused a thrilling cheer from the ranks of working men. He could not be more than 15 at the time.'[15]

This was Antony Mundella's first political speech, delivered in a manner he was to perfect as he grew older.

But Cooper over-reached himself. The educator turned agitator, and among scenes of rushlight meetings, flag-tearing and hustings-brawls, he contested Leicester as universal suffrage candidate in 1841. He was defeated. His followers, however, continued to demonstrate. On 8 August 1842 over 100 men left their homes and paraded the town with a band playing and flags flying. Not even the reading of the Riot Act restored order, so the military were called in to deal with the situation. Cooper, ironically enough, was at Hanley, appealing to the strikers there to maintain order. But on his return on 26 August 1842 he was gaoled, and so passed out of the immediate horizon of the artisans of Leicester.[16]

The following year another crusader appeared in the town. On the last Wednesday in 1843, Richard Cobden spoke in his nationwide campaign for the repeal of the Corn Laws. Though his theme was cheap bread for the workers, he was the victim of continuous 'noisy interruptions'. His influence, however, was felt by Mundella, whose later career abounds in allusions to the debt he owed the great reformer.[17]

But neither Cooper nor Cobden could alleviate the lot of the framework knitter. In 1843, 25,000 of them petitioned parliament:

'Your petitioners', they supplicated, 'are suffering severe privations from the low rate of wages to which they have been reduced when employed, and the frequent periods in which your petitioners are out of employ are greater in extent than any other body of workmen similarly situated . . . which suffering your petitioners attribute to the want of protection for labour, by which we are left at the mercy of the unprincipled and competing employers; which system has extended itself throughout all the branches of this trade.'[18]

But no alleviation of their lot was to come from Westminster. Instead it was to come.through a series of technological changes, which were to create a popular demand for hosiery, speed production and thereby raise the wages of those employed in the new factories.[19]   Mundella's employer, William Kempson, was sufficiently opportunistic to take out a patent in 1842 to improve the manufacture of hosiery.[20] Other hosiers, too, were making an effort to popularise their goods and exploit the new fashion of exposed stockings. But the most enterprising firm was that of Collins, which applied the steam-engine's power to work a round frame to spin a seamless tube of hose on a machine.[21]

By 1845 the Leicester operatives were so alive to this change that when the Nottinghamshire and Derbyshire hands passed a resolution to petition parliament to re-establish the authority of the London Framework Knitters Company throughout the kingdom, the Leicester operatives dissented, and called the proposal 'behind the age and impossible to execute'.[22]

This tide of technological change Mundella himself was to take on to a fortune. In that same year 1845 he left Kempsons and became an overseer in one of the two large warehouses set up by Harris and Hamel. His old schoolfellow, Bates, recalls him at this time:

'A tall thin, active, smiling young fellow whom I last saw about the year 1846 or earlier. If I recollect aright, you went heart and soul into business soon after your recovery from the severe illness caused by your growing too rapidly.' [23]

A year before Mundella joined the firm, the senior partner, old Richard Harris, had taken out a patent to improve the manufacture of looped fabrics. So much did they prosper that the average earnings of a single employee jumped to one pound a week.[24] The new machinery responsible for this was so jealously guarded that Felkin remarked, 'This house secured secrecy as to their production by the enclosure of their machinery'.[25]

For the next three years, from 1845 to 1848, Mundella served his novitiate in the new mercantile order. He was paid £200 a year and a commission on profits. He became the superintendent of the large poor Sunday School at which he taught. To complete it, he married Mary Smith, 'a woman of rare strength and sweetness of character',[26] with whom he was to have forty-four years of happily married life. Nor did his association with Richard

Harris [27] end in the firm. He joined him on the political platform, advocating the same cause of universal suffrage that had fired him as a lad of fifteen.

For the Liberals of Leicester were following the lead of the great Richard Cobden, and making common cause with the working class on this question. At a grand meeting of 3,500 people held in the Amphitheatre on 17 April 1848 Mundella delivered a rousing speech from the same platform as the Chartists. His theme was that the middle and working classes should combine to reform the house of commons: 'A Union of the middle and working classes has been hinted at. What are the middle classes waiting for?' he demanded and continued:

'The majority of the present members of the House of Commons, while professing to be representatives of the people, unequivocally exhibit their purely aristocratic character by uniformly opposing all proposals for retrenchment, by disregarding and treating with contempt all petitions for the concession of popular rights, and by assaulting with derision, with hooting and bellowing, those honest and independent representatives who were true to the interests of the nation.' [28]

A week later he sat on the platform at an even larger meeting to pledge support for the People's League, Cobden's national organisation for forwarding universal suffrage on a united middle- and working-class basis. Richard Harris was again with him.

Richard Harris himself was elected to represent the town in parliament after the two sitting whig members had been unseated for bribery. When Richard Harris was elected to parliament, and the People's League had collapsed after its first conference, Mundella decided to leave Leicester. He was offered a partnership in Nottingham by old Jonathan Hine, who, with his son Benjamin Hornbuck Hine and his grandson John Hine, was anxious to embark on the construction of a large new factory. At twenty-three years of age, Mundella was made a partner. In the next twenty years he was to make a name for himself as a captain of a growing industry.

3

As in the rest of Europe, so in Leicester, the year 1848 saw great changes. Mundella's contemporary and schoolfellow, H. W. Bates, threw up his post as a clerk in a Burton brewer's office and, in company with A. R. Wallace, a master at the Leicester Collegiate School, went off to explore the Amazon. They did not return for four years.

Mundella himself went to Nottingham, where there were literally fresh fields to conquer; for two years before he arrived a general Enclosure Act had empowered the Nottingham Corporation to take in 1,200 acres of former common land.[29] In a short time, factories, warehouses, residential estates and parks were laid out. The Hines were determined to be in the van of this expansion and to wrest command of the hosiery trade from the Saxon hosiers, who were at that time marketing for half a crown an article that Nottingham could only sell for ten shillings.[30]

The seven-and-sixpence disparity was a problem which could be solved only by another labour-saving invention, and that was ready to hand. In October 1849 the Chevalier Claussen demonstrated such a machine to a deputation of Nottingham manufacturers, and their comments were rhapsodic.[31] It worked at great speed—700 picks a minute—and enabled twenty pairs of stockings to be manufactured on it in a day. This was ten times faster than the old stocking-frame, and Chambers' *Edinburgh Journal* pointed the moral that this machine meant the end of the old framework knitter.[32] Deliveries of this new machine began in August 1850. But, though fast, it could not fashion the stockings —so there was still some scope for the hand-worker. A machine which could fashion, declared the *Nottingham Review*, would alter the whole structure of the industry.

The firm of Hine and Mundella took the plunge. Planning their firm on the new round frame, they commissioned a large new factory, five stories high, to be built opposite the Midland Railway Station. T. C. Hine was the architect. It was the first factory in the trade built with steam power as its prime mover.[33] Completed on 25 September 1851, its rooms were wide and spacious, and lit from floor to ceiling. Externally it was shaped like a large letter L, 192 feet by 120 feet, and executed in faced brick with stone dressings. The long frontage contained the warehouse, and the shorter one the factory. It excited praise. The guide to the town referred to it as the 'best specimen of the new species of factory yet erected'.[34] Outsiders were impressed. *Eliza Cook's Journal* noted that 'there was not only cleanliness and light, but elegance, about that which I had been led to consider all smoke and uncleanliness'.[35] Here the smells and filthy atmosphere of the framework-knitters' cottages were things of the past.

The association was an ideal one. 'I have never seen,' said old Jonathan Hine, 'one so perfectly united and possessing all the ingredients conducive to a successful issue.' Their employees realised this, and gave a party to the heads of the firm. At the dinner they declared:

'You have already laid before us those rules which you thought necessary to regulate this establishment, and we cannot help noticing the good feeling that is manifested in them towards us, raising as it does a corresponding one in our minds towards you. We hope to convince you that it will not stop here, that our exertions will show that we are resolved to carry out your wise endeavours to make this house as one noted for punctuality and correctness, which we all know tend to mutual satisfaction and prosperity.'[36]

Mundella made a speech in which he declared his faith in stockings, expressing a hope that the bloomer craze would not do away with them altogether.

With this spirit animating the firm, great developments followed, all from further patents. Mundella said later:

'In nearly every case it was the man who stood before the loom and who brought his brains to work upon the loom who had been the means of improving it.'[37]

His tireless search for patents paid dividends. By taking the inventor into partnership with him, he managed to secure inventions which did, as the *Nottingham Review* forecast, alter the structure of the industry. Two years after the factory opened he secured one which enabled them to weave stockings with ribs down the sides. The next year (1854) the firm won the gold medal of the Paris Exhibition from a class of 180 competitors. This was followed by the most revolutionary change of all—an invention which enabled the stocking to be made and fully fashioned by automatic action.[38]

Co-patentee with Mundella in this important innovation was Luke Barton. Its importance was such that it so accelerated the operation of the round frame that stockings could now be made a hundred times faster than they could by the framework knitters. The discovery was a dramatic one. Describing his search later, Mundella said:

'I went into a garret, where I found a poor man working on a circular revolving machine which he had fixed to the bottom of a wooden chair, the only chair in the room. For seven years he had been patiently working at it. It was completed. I purchased it. The poor man had his share, and is now in comfort and independence.' [39]

By 1857 further improvements had made it possible for both inside and outside of the stocking to be woven exactly alike, so that the facings were similar. In the same year *The Times* could refer to Hine and Mundella's as a 'model factory', and rated the number of its employees as 4,000. The Crimean War, with its demand for warm clothing for the troops, led Mundella to clash with the War Office over their antique specifications in the contracts offered to the trade. These antique specifications were powerful in preserving the existence of the hand-frames during this period of great technological change.[40] Mundella protested bitterly that the worst articles were purchased at the highest prices, and brought to the attention of Baring, First Lord of the Admiralty, a typical case:

'A quantity of underclothing had been purchased for the troops under these circumstances. The articles were made at Nottingham and sold to a Dublin Commission agent in Dublin, who sold them to an army clothier in that City by whom they were sold to the War Department at 40% above the original price.' [41]

The expansion of the industry amazed him as he regarded it in retrospect:

'There is no parallel in England of such rapid improvement as in this trade since 1852. In '48 there was not a factory in the town. Yesterday I looked through the wages books and found men earning from £1 to £3.'

It brought prosperity to the factory hands, and, what is more, they themselves realised it. The workers' representatives at their meetings at the 'Dove and Rainbow' inn had, since 1855, enthusiastically endorsed and approved of 'the prices which have been and are so cheerfully paid by large houses in the trade'.[27] The high wages earned Mundella the loyalty of his employees, so that he could boast:

'Why do all the Trade Unions stand by me so firmly? Because I have helped to double and quadruple their wages. I don't want to dwell upon this, but since I became an employer I have carried my feeling for the workpeople to the verge of Quixotism. Had I been less considerate for the good of others I should now have been a very rich man.' [42]

Even more important was the highly organised nature of the factory, which enabled him to grant a nine-hour day.

'In my factory', he told the trade, 'I do not have one man dependent on the other. I have a steam hoist which conveys cotton tops etc., to every room in the fabric, and the men, therefore, have no occasion to wait. Great annoyance is caused by men waiting for each other.' [43]

This intensive production itself raised another issue:

'At the present time', he declared, 'we require in our cotton factories more of brains and less of brute labour than we have ever required. The hours of work have been too long for the operative to work with the vigour and attention which the complicated machinery of the present day demands.' [44]

That was the most pregnant conclusion of all. It demanded the end of the half-time labour of children, and their further education. It is therefore not surprising that Mundella, who saw this so clearly, was to play such a large part not only in advocating, but also in carrying out an ambitious educational programme.

4

This mounting prosperity produced its own temporary check. For while the factory was working overtime to fulfil outstanding foreign orders, someone carelessly dropped a taper which had been used to light the gas. Just after the hands left work the watchman noticed smoke, and gave the alarm. This was at nine o'clock in the evening of 1 February 1859. It took nearly an hour for the horse-drawn fire-brigade to appear on the scene with their hose-cart. They broke a few windows, managed to introduce the hoses, and played on the fire till all became dark within. Thinking that the fire was mastered, they were about to relax, when suddenly the accumulated gases inside the warehouse ignited, and in an instant the whole was a mass of flame. The entire factory, running from Parkinson Street to Station Street, was completely destroyed. The warehouse portion, facing Station Street, was so damaged by water that the goods inside were ruined.

By morning little was left but charred timber, broken shafts and disjointed wheels. Nothing like it for extent of injury and amount of damage had occurred in the town since the destruction of the castle a quarter of a century before. The cost of replacing the machinery was estimated at £35,000.[45] Four hundred employees were thrown out of work. It was the ninth great fire that had occurred in the town since Mundella had arrived.[46]

CHAPTER TWO

The Local Liberal Leader, 1853—1867

THE fire illumined the extent to which Mundella had risen during eleven years. Not only was it recorded in the *Date Book of Memorable Events in Nottingham*, but the *Illustrated London News* reported it together with a graphic drawing. As the annual turnover of his firm had mounted from £20,000 to £200,000, Mundella began to loom more largely in the life of the town.

I

He was not a pilgrim in his ascent up the social scale, for with him mounted others whose industry and opportunism matched his own. Lewis Heymann, a German from Hamburg, did for the curtain trade what Mundella had done for stockings: he literally created a demand, and then so organised his factory that he could not only satisfy it, but whetted still further demands. Heymann specialised in the lace curtain which became such a cardinal feature of the Victorian terraces, building his factory around a team of original and talented designers under the leadership of S. W. Oscroft,[1] whose work showed its genius by the award of the Gold Medal of an International Exhibition. The character, energy, good taste and agreeable manners of Heymann were matched by a capacity for gauging the tastes of foreigners, and by assiduous foreign travel he built up a most flourishing export market.[2] An even closer friend of Mundella's than Heymann was W. G. Ward,[3] who, at the age of thirty, in the year in which Mundella was co-operating with Luke Barton to patent the fully fashioning machine, took over a dark and unhealthy factory in Broad Marsh and transferred it to Besford. There he ran an industrial community, which by his own efforts was paved, sewered and lighted: a veritable model village that would have delighted either Robert Owen or Titus Salt.[4] Both Heymann and Ward rose to power by the imaginative exploitation of the native intelligence of the town, and both signalised their appreciation by attempting to cultivate it still further. Heymann was indirectly responsible for the gift of £10,000 to the University College,[5] and Ward converted the old castle to the first art museum in the country.[6]

2

Association with such men enabled Mundella to evolve a coherent social philosophy in which the necessity for educating workpeople was a cardinal feature. Together they formed a social force in the town which could not be ignored. Slowly they supplanted the old landed feudality symbolised by the duke of Newcastle, whose house at Clumber had long been the centre of social gravity in the district.

A sign of this displacement was Mundella's election to the Shrievalty of Nottingham, which took place on 9 November 1853.[7] It was an eventful year of office for him: frosty, and crisp with portent. It saw the declaration of war with Russia, itself productive of army contracts for hosiers of the town to clothe the shivering soldiers of the Crimea. On 3 July 1854 the Scots Greys set off for the front, and were given a civic send-off in the Square, attended by all the civic officials in full regalia. The rolling of their drums was followed by the mutterings of social discontent— mutterings which, if they did not reach the crescendo of the previous fifty years,[8] were sufficient to result in the breaking of thousands of windows in the surrounding area. But these mutterings were not so much the finale of an old score as the prelude to a new one, in which the tempo was to be greatly accelerated. A boom was on the way.

Signs of that boom were especially prominent during the year. In February 1854 the two railway companies which ran trains from Nottingham to London bid so frantically for passengers on their three-and-a-half-hour expresses that fares were actually lowered to three shillings, a state of affairs which, happily for the shareholders, lasted only for a month. In Nottingham itself the opulent residential centre of the Park was laid out in the same month, and T. C. Hine was commissioned by prosperous manufacturers— Mundella among them—to build elegant villas. As this middle-class residential suburb grew, and fresh culture patterns were formed, the manufacturers really began to dominate the town, and on 30 July 1856 their representative, C. Paget, who had built up a most efficient milk supply for the town, was elected to

Parliament without opposition, and re-elected on 1 November 1858.[9]

Mundella's direct participation in local politics was very un-eventful, as befitted the times. Four months after Paget was first elected to the house of commons, the municipal elections took place. For the new middle-class Park Ward sixty-one-year-old William Felkin,[10] a lace merchant who had already been twice mayor of the borough, was once more returned. A fortnight

BUNDELLER.—" I say Slyvester, if you think this new Mare of yours will win the Mayoralty Stakes, you'r mistaken? I shall neither ride nor back her."

later he was elevated to the aldermanic bench, and at the subsequent by-election Mundella was elected in his place.

He was a councillor for four months before he opened his mouth. Then, on 2 March 1857, he pleaded for better accommodation for bathers in the Trent, who had nowhere to change their clothes. He was initiated into the arduous mysteries of committees: serving on one which conferred with the local justices on the expedience of enlarging the gaol; on a second for dealing with the grievances of the Trent bathers, and on a third which was set up to explore the possibilities of improving the town. His speeches on these diverse subjects revealed that he had not lost his early radical ideas. He wanted bigger schools, not bigger gaols; more co-operation between the middle and the working classes;[11] and more restrictions on the public-houses.[12] His enthusiasm for education was recognised by his appointment to the board of the Nottingham People's College, an institution stemming from a remarkable experiment in popular adult education that had been made at Sheffield a decade before.[13]

His strength lay more in his ability as a wire-puller. The Liberals

'CAPTAIN BUNDELLA SELECTING A STEED FOR THE C.C.'

of the town were a diverse assortment of whiggish shop-keepers (who clung tenaciously to the custom of the local whig magnates) and radical manufacturers (who opposed the heavy ransoms which the local landowners levied on the expanding railway network). Mundella, supple and conciliatory, was elected vice-chairman of the local Liberal party, which began to hold regular policy-making meetings in a room in the Exchange Hall. So regular did these meetings become, and so open were they to the curious stranger, that their decisions became a staple topic of conversation in the town, and the uninformed began to regard them as a kind of cabal. In a happy moment of inspiration, someone hit on the number of the room as a nickname, and from henceforth 'Number 30' became the target of abuse levied by tories, anti-dissenters and local malcontents of all kinds. Not without reason, it was usually coupled with the name of Mundella, and his activities became the subject of much rough banter in the broadsheets which were set fluttering about the town at election time. One of these sheets, which bore the apt title of *The Fish Stall Gazette*,[14] carried advertisements for a book on *Conkology—by Captain Bundella—with portrait and proboscis*: a shrewd blow aimed at Mundella's most prominent facial feature which was to be repeated with deadly insistence for the rest of his political life. Another sheet, bearing the title of *The Extraordinary Gazette*,[15] offered its readers a guide to form in the local election stakes, and included amongst its strong odds 'Mr. Bundell's Proboscis—by Captain Absolute out of Cox's Horror'.

3

These references to Mundella's military rank were inspired by his activities in the local Volunteer movement. The disturbing activities of Napoleon III had caused the flesh of many an Englishman to creep, and a rash of patriotic sentiment burst out over the serene face of Victorian middle-class life. Even the Poet-Laureate was moved to redeem the popularity which he had lost by the publication of *Maud* by hurriedly publishing a jingoist poem called *Riflemen Form*, written on 9 May 1859 with its summons:

> 'Let your reforms for a moment go,
> Look to your butts and take your aims,
> Better a rotten borough or so
> Than a rotten fleet and a city in flames.'

Ten days after Tennyson's poem was written, Mundella spoke at a large meeting held in Nottingham to support non-intervention in the affairs of Europe. He denounced all thoughts of war, but he stressed the necessity of preparedness:

'Let us make ourselves ready for any occasion,' he said. 'Let us make our own war budgets by shouldering our rifles. Let us defend our own shores, and at the same time, tell our own ministers that we are not going to be led abroad to fight the battles of other countries.'[16]

He matched his words with deeds. Since Nottingham was so behind in the national Volunteer movement, Mundella and five others went to the castle grounds at six o'clock in the morning on Monday, 30 May. There, at his suggestion, they fell in as a squad on the terrace overlooking the meadows and received their first drill. They engaged an old regular sergeant-major—Jonathan White—to drill them, and with each succeeding meeting their numbers increased.[17] So rapidly did they grow that the mayor called them to his parlour, where the official resolution for the formation of the corps was proposed by Mundella himself. Today a stone in the pavement of Castle Terrace, near the entrance to Mortimer's Hole, marks the spot where the Robin Hood Rifle Corps was founded.

Mundella was gazetted subaltern in the corps on 15 September, and a month later was promoted captain of No. 1 Company. In their service he could use qualities other than purely martial ones. He used his position on the Town Council to demand butts for his company, a request which the Council were slow to grant. On 25 September 1859 he made a vehement speech at a council meeting against the ridicule to which the Volunteer movement was being subjected, and pointed out its beneficial effects on the young men of the town, who had all been chained to their desks and counters too much. The aldermen were against him.

Fellow-radicals in other parts of the country were displaying similar enthusiasm. Up at Bradford, W. E. Forster had formed a company of his own mill-workers, and was drilling them. Forster, seven years older than Mundella, was later to be one of his most intimate friends. Down in London another radical, Thomas Hughes, just coming into the limelight because of his brilliant account of life at Rugby under Forster's father-in-law, was captain of a corps that numbered over 1,000.

Mundella was as energetic as either of them. At a dinner to the two local representatives of the borough he was chosen to reply to the toast of 'the corps'. His speech, urbane and restrained, was loudly applauded.[18]

4

But peace was preserved by other means than early morning drills. Richard Cobden, fresh from his second visit to America, where he had been much impressed by the mighty hum of peaceful change,[19] went to France in January 1860. His visit, coming on top of his refusal to take office in the government, was none the less official. He negotiated a commercial treaty between the two countries which was a striking precedent in European co-operation. For Cobden, having seen what the new world was doing, spent the remaining six years of his life trying to realise the ideals of free trade which Carlyle so unkindly called 'a calico millennium'.

Yet to the rank and file of English merchants it certainly seemed a millennium. Chambers of commerce throughout the country drew up statements and estimates for their great commercial champion. For Nottingham, Mundella, as chairman of the local chamber, not only drew up a statement on the hose trade, but went to Paris for a month with Cobden's delegation. In the memorandum signed by himself and W. G. Ward they expressed a hope that 'the French tariff might be so arranged as to permit of an interchange of some branches of our manufactures, producing extended commerce, and increasing good will between the nations'. Their exertions were rewarded by Cobden being able to tell the French emperor that three-quarters of the population of France did not wear stockings, so that the admission of a few thousand dozen would be a national boon.

Contact with Cobden had much the same effect on Mundella which an earlier association with Thomas Cooper had done. It gave his politics another turn: widened his outlook, and deepened his social insights. He was often brought to confess how much he was merely the executant of Cobden's ideas. Nine years before this, Cobden called England 'the most ignorant protestant country on the face of the earth', and warned his countrymen that

'the trade and progress of a nation depend not so much on contest of arms, as on the rivalry in science and art which must spring from education. Did any reflecting man walk through the Great Exhibition without feeling we are apt to be under a delusion as to the quality of men in other parts of the world? Did it not make English men feel they had to look about them? And how will you be able to rally, how will you attain to further improvements in arts and manufactures but by improving the education of your people! I don't think we can wait.' [20]

Cobden had failed to arouse the same enthusiasm for national education as he had done for cheap bread because of the difficulties created by the dissenters. He looked to the very class of which Mundella was such a shining exemplar:

'Our mercantile and manufacturing classes as represented in the Chambers of Commerce are, after all, the only power in the State possessed of wealth and

political influence sufficient to counteract in some degree the feudal and governing class of this country. They are indeed the only class of this country from
whom we can in our time hope for any beneficial changes. . . . The future of
England must depend on them.' [21]

The personal contact Mundella had with Cobden was reinforced by reading these speeches. He declared:

'Cobden was the greatest statesman and prophet of the century. His speeches
are an inspiration. A man whose disciple I am willing to confess I am.' [22]

5

Mundella's mission to France and Cobden's treaty only intensified the hardships of the old framework knitters. For, by
increasing the market for hose, they stimulated yet further
the tendency to mass-produce. More mass production meant
increased wages for the factory workers. Thus the framework
knitter was not only outpaced, but outpaid. So, resentful towards
the new inventions, and envious of those who worked them, the
framework knitters went on strike towards the end of 1860.

In the obsolete outwork industry which survived and kept them
employed, their labour absorbed 90 per cent of the costs of production. Four consecutive strikes broke out in the wide-frame
section towards the end of the year, and though the rest of the
industry remained at work, it was known that they were contributing to keep the strikers out. As the fourth strike broke out,
some of the employers were for stern measures. A general lock-
out, they argued, would bring the men to their senses. Mundella
strongly disapproved of this plan. 'It meant throwing the whole
population on the streets. We should have a dreadful state of
commotion. We were sick of it.' [23] The workers were further
inflamed by petty prosecutions—one Henry Bennet was arraigned
before the magistrates for saying 'Ba ba' to a blackleg—and issued
inflammatory placards illustrated with gross personal insults towards the employers.

Mundella therefore suggested that the manufacturers and operatives should hold a round-table conference. On 10 September
1860 he persuaded his fellow manufacturers to agree. So a handbill was issued inviting all those concerned to come to a meeting.
A week later (17 September 1860) a five-hour conference was
held in the committee room of the Chamber of Commerce,
attended by the representatives of either side.[24] To conciliate the

workers, one of their body was appointed chairman of the meeting. The proceedings were momentous. They took place while over 1,000 framework knitters were out of work. One of the manufacturers pointed out that the real cause of the trouble was the great advance in the methods of production, which had materially altered the trade. The discussion degenerated into a wrangle between him and an operative, when Mundella intervened with two suggestions. The first (to solve the immediate difficulty) was that the employers should grant the wage increases demanded, the second (to prevent a further recurrence of the strikes) proposed that a board of arbitration for the industry should be established. This was agreed. One old operative remarked, 'I have been in the hosiery trade since I was ten years of age, and I have never been at such a meeting before'.[25]

The idea of such a board was not new. William Felkin, the historian of the trade, and at this time sixty-five years of age, had been advocating it for many years. Twenty-five years previously he had translated an account of the Conseils des Prudhommes, a French phenomenon which was famous in the thirties for the arbitrament of wage disputes, with the theme in mind that 'their first duty is to reconcile, their second is to arbitrate'. [26] Fifteen years previously Felkin had read a paper to the British Association on boards of conciliation, urging that they should be 'local, cheap, frequent and final'. [27] By 1856 he had been one of the twenty-five witnesses before a house of commons committee which prepared a blue book on arbitration, and the *Nottingham Review* wrote glowingly of his effort to promote such boards, agreeing that such a board in the town 'would have the salutary effect of rendering nugatory the labours of those clever but unscrupulous adventurers who use their arts to misrepresent facts and inflame their fellow workmen against their masters.' [28]

It was Mundella's flair, however, that translated Felkin's idea into a fact. On 3 December 1860 the first meeting of the board took place, with six employers and six operatives, to elect officers for the coming year. Mundella was elected president with enthusiastic unanimity, and the workman who had been chairman at the previous conference was chosen as vice-president. In his presidential address Mundella set the tone of all future meetings:

'I hope you look upon yourselves as judges of disputes, and consider that you are bound to form an impartial opinion on all matters that are brought before you. I hope you will also consider that your object will be to promote the prosperity of every branch of the trade, and of all persons engaged in it.'

6

Business, volunteers, the establishment of the board of arbitration: none of these three weaned Mundella from his perennial interest in the world of politics. As vice-chairman of the local Liberal party he still presided over the committee meetings in room No. 30 in the Exchange Hall.

To the local tories 'Number 30' became the symbol of all that was bad. A political speaker anxious to raise emotion could always rouse a Nottingham audience by a reference to 'Number 30' and its mysterious ways. Evidence of its power was the return of C. Paget and J. Mellor as Liberal members for the town on 29 April 1859. This triumph 'Number 30' confidently hoped to repeat at the by-election caused by Mellor's elevation to the judicial bench in December 1861.

But the tories were ready. With a lively, wealthy fox-hunting young baronet as their candidate, they prepared to challenge the mysterious hold which 'Number 30' had established on the town. A couplet was circulated.:

'If the men of Nottingham are true,
They will make Number 30 look very blue.'

The young baronet, two years older than Mundella, in fact, was young in little but spirits. He was a devoted addict of the Turf, so much so that even the local journal was moved to comment some years later that his connections in that quarter 'led him into extravagance, and involved him in pecuniary difficulties which exercised a baneful influence on his career for many years afterwards'. His name was Sir Robert Clifton.[29]

Certainly 'Number 30' began to look very blue. To begin with, they could not agree as to who should represent them. At first they thought of Samuel Morley, a local hosier, who lived in London. Then they considered Lewis Heymann, who lived in the borough. But both of these were unacceptable; Morley to the left wing, and Heymann to the right. So once more 'Number 30' met, and this time they offered their support to Mr. Cheetham, a Stalybridge manufacturer, but he declined to stand. Confounding their deliberations were the tory supporters, who actually managed to gain admission to a closed meeting held on 6 December 1861.

34

As a gesture of despair they fell back on the son of the duke of Newcastle: Lord Lincoln.[30]

Lord Lincoln was the last person to fall back on. He was frail and weak both in body and spirit. He had been suggested as a possible tory candidate only four days before he was adopted by 'Number 30'. He was also a very sick man: responding to the invitation by sending a doctor's certificate as an excuse for non-appearance. This serious handicap meant that 'Number 30' had to do some vigorous campaigning. So Mundella threw himself into the pre-election battle to save the party. Speaking and organising were his *forte*, and, as a contemporary observed, 'he was at it night and day'.

Under the flickering naphtha flares that lit the public halls and houses of the times, his brassy tones and basso laughter drew Liberal cheers. But Sir Robert was his superior in party warfare. Seizing on the great hooked nose which was Mundella's most prominent facial feature, he asked whether or not Mundella was a German. It never failed: the audience would cry 'No, an Italian', and Sir Robert would conclude in terms of extreme satisfaction, 'I am glad he is not an Englishman'. By these and other means Sir Robert would work his audiences up to a state of lively excitement, till they would chant in unison 'Shame on Mundella! Shame on Mundella!'

To this organised campaign of vilification Mundella could find no effective response. His essays in refutation, however subtly phrased, were now drowned by a chorus of groans and hisses which assailed him every time he rose to speak. He was threatened with bodily violence. Obviously, since further appearances would ruin the cause, an outside speaker of calibre had to be brought in. So Sir Morton Peto, the man who built Nelson's Column and half the railways then existing, seemed the most likely person to obtain a patient hearing. But even when Mundella rose to his feet to propose a vote of thanks, the hostile chorus broke out once more.

Eight days before the poll was taken, Lord Lincoln himself appeared. Still ill, he held a select audience at his room in the 'George' Hotel, and then left. Mundella urged the group to throw off their lethargy and canvass with all their energies, concluding, 'Gentlemen, my name is a little too prominent in Nottingham just now. But it is no small thing to bind the earl of Lincoln to such principles as those upon which he comes here.'

The verb 'to bind' was taken up and distorted. The tory election agent, James Acland,[31] was quick to sense its possibilities, and raised the cry that Lord Lincoln was Mundella's puppet. And just to show how little he cared for Mundella's activities, Sir Robert Clifton staged a lavish entertainment at Clifton Pastures. The occasion was a gay one, and there was much horse-play. It was also a great success, for when Lord Lincoln did appear, two days before the poll, to speak in the Exchange Hall, the same torrent of disapproval greeted Mundella's attempt to put the Liberal case to the meeting.

Finally, on Boxing Day 1861, the poll was held. Thronging the space in front of the Exchange, where substantial hustings had been erected, a crowd heard Lord Lincoln and Sir Robert Clifton proposed and seconded. After a show of hands, the sheriff declared Sir Robert to be elected. But the Liberals disagreed, and demanded a poll. In vain they tried to assert themselves, but Sir Robert's supporters surrounded the polling-booths. In the final count it was found that the first result was handsomely endorsed: Sir Robert was elected by a majority of 1,402 out of a total electorate of 3,690.[32]

It was a crushing defeat for Mundella and 'Number 30'.

7

Meanwhile, the very house of commons to which Sir Robert had just been elected had set up a royal commission to inquire into the conditions of children's employment throughout the kingdom.[33] The hosiery trade, with its 129,000 employees (of whom only 4,063 were, according to the parliamentary return of 11 February 1862, under the protection of the Factory Acts), was among the first to be examined.

J. E. White was sent to Nottingham to report on the state of child labour in the factories. He had long conversations with William Felkin, the local historian of the trade and Mundella's predecessor as a councillor for the Park Ward. From what he both saw and heard, White was able to form a good opinion of the conditions prevailing in the new factories: the routine which prevailed there affording much less opportunity to overwork children. He singled out the factory of Hine and Mundella for especial comment: finding it 'airy and light', with a nine-hour working day, and no cases of bad labour conditions.

But his opinion of the old framework knitting section of the industry was most unfavourable. Here 116,000 out of the 129,000 workers were employed. There was no fixed routine: men took Mondays and Tuesdays as holidays, and would work late on Fridays, to the great hardship of children employed with them. He cited some revealing examples of the manner in which the poor rates of pay for hand-seaming resulted in children being forced to work very early in life. One five-year-old child he found had already been working for two years. Another was so small that she had to stand on a chair in order to reach the work-table. Most of them had to be pinned to their mothers' dresses to keep them to their work and prevent them from falling to sleep. Yet, with all this, an average child could seam only ten legs a day at most, and the rates of pay were ninepence a dozen.[34]

White concluded that conditions in the trade had vastly im-proved since the previous governmental inquiry had been made twenty years before. The reason he found in the better factories, with their superior organisation, intensive output and shorter working hours. His report, together with those of his colleagues, was eagerly read by a German *émigré* who at that time was forty-five years old: Karl Marx. Marx, appreciating with White the rhythm of technological change, wrote some penetrating para-graphs on the way in which factory legislation would itself 'ripen' the capitalist system by hastening the decline of the small masters. For, by imposing conditions and provisions for labour, such legislation would demand greater capital outlays in industry.[35] Not only Marx, but the first professor of political economy at Oxford was similarly provoked to comment on the wasted poten-tialities of these poor child labourers. 'These children', he wrote, '—and there are thousands in their position—have natural gifts and dormant faculties which instruction might lend to develop and call forth if only we could obtain for them the protection of a law of the land.'[36]

8

And Mundella? He disappears from the scene at this period—a sick man.

For the fire, the rebuilding, the volunteers, the board of arbi-tration and the excitements of the election had proved too much. In 1863 the dislocation of the cotton trade resulting from the

American Civil War caused him to break down completely. He went to Italy to recuperate. But his recovery was so slow that his partners, despairing of his ever being able to assume active responsibility again, turned the firm of Hine and Mundella into a limited liability company.[37]

So, on 15 July 1864, the *Nottingham Review* carried the announcement:

'A new undertaking is announced under the title of the Nottingham Manufacturing Company (Limited). The object is to carry out on an extensive scale the manufacture of hosiery and lace with the aid of certain valuable patents.

'The basis of the project is the purchase of the old-established business and connection of Messrs. B. H. Hine, Mundella and Co. of Nottingham & London, with their stock in trade, premises, machinery and patents. The partners in the firm promise to give their co-operation, being members of the company board. The capital proposed is £200,000 in 10,000 shares of £20 each, three-quarters of which have already been subscribed for.'

As a limited liability company, the Nottingham Manufacturing Company went from strength to strength. They took over the business of J. and J. Wilson in Nottingham and Saxony. Further interests were acquired in Boston to secure distribution to markets in Philadelphia and Massachusetts.[38] Though these developments occurred after Mundella had relinquished personal control of the business, they were remembered against him in later years, when he was accused of being a free trader for a sinister purpose.

Mundella was indeed a sick man. His boyhood friend Bates, back from eleven years in the wilds of South America, where he had made his name by exploring the Amazon, chaffed him as a healthy man would chaff an invalid: and tried to make him see himself 'with the gout and a grown-up daughter reading to you'.[39]

It is tantalising to have no record of any of his convalescent meditations. But, curiously enough, it was at this very time that Richard Cobden was writing: 'The manufacturing classes have no interest opposed to the public good.' [40] Mundella's convictions must have been greatly fortified by reading this, and buoyed to take up the political struggle once more; for we find him saying soon after: 'I believe there is one thing more than another wanted in this country, and it is a Cobden for education.' [41] The obvious conclusion which his hearers were supposed to draw was that he intended to fill that role himself.

9

Elsewhere similar opinions were gaining ground. As Mundella lay in his bath-chair listening to his daughter's voice, other more strident tones were catching the ears of the public. The London working men, whose labyrinthine progress had been guided by such a dynasty of organisers since the time of Francis Place, now came out into the open with a great meeting on Primrose Hill. Under the Celtic spell of George Odger [42] they gathered together, ostensibly to celebrate two events: the arrival of Garibaldi in England, and the tercentenary of Shakespeare's birth. But Odger made it quite clear that the demonstration was a sign that a new force was abroad: that responsibility, sound finance and organisation were transforming the world of labour from a collisive into a cohesive force. Odger, then forty-two years old, was the spellbinder who endowed ideas with hands and feet. His able and less demonstrative associates were Robert Applegarth, [43] a Sheffield joiner who had organised his fellow-tradesmen into a powerful union, and George Howell, the thirty-one-year-old prototype of the twentieth-century union official. [44] The three were a perfect team: Odger the speaker, Applegarth the planner, and Howell the executive. Together, they decided that the cellular unit of the working-class movement should be formed not in the public-house, but in the trade hall; that large benefit balances should be built up to subsidise political action; that every opportunity should be taken to secure arbitration of labour disputes; and that, above all, trade unionism should be pre-eminently respectable.

The impact of this new cohesive labour force upon the politics of the year 1864 was immediate and effective. The London *Telegraph* speculated on the occasion of the demonstration at Primrose Hill: 'How then if this same working class were really *worked*?' it asked, and followed with a metaphorical rider which showed that the shadow of the law of diminishing returns was already falling over the writer's shoulder: 'If this mine which turns out nuggets of itself (i.e. Shakespeare and Garibaldi) had shafts of good legislation, galleries of fair franchise, and claims of free and full education driven into it, what might not be expected?' [45]

That question was disturbing others, who were beginning to see that, far from the education of the labouring classes being as undesirable as had hitherto been the case, it was essential for the economic well-being of the country. Joseph Whitworth, the great engineer and gun-founder,[46] as well as William Chambers, the eminent publisher,[47] both pointed at this time to the poor man's utopia across the Atlantic, where the inventiveness and intelligence of every citizen were given the fullest possible scope. But for the almost immediate masking of this serious American threat, due to the Civil War, it is possible that more would have been said on this theme in the same way as Cobden had said it twenty years before. Americans knew it too: not without cause was it whispered that certain Englishmen supported the confederate South because it was embarrassing the pushful Yankees.

Odger's demonstrations of Labour solidarity touched deeper chords than those of mere enlightened self-interest, and the notes that were given off echoed through the rest of the century. The responsive agent was W. E. Gladstone, who on 11 May in this very year made the oracular pronouncement that was to secure him the undivided loyalty of the Labour movement. That pronouncement, which his biographer declared 'gathered up the wandering forces of time, and precipitated a new era', ran: 'Every man who is not presumably incapacitated by some consideration of personal unfitness or political danger is morally entitled to come within the pale of the franchise'.[48] It was a comfort to the timid, and a stimulus to the advanced. It was immaterial that, to Lord Palmerston, exculpatory gloss was subsequently put upon the declaration. Gladstone had spoken, that was enough. By so doing he put himself at the head of forces which were to carry him farther than he ever intended to travel.

Five months later, on 28 September, occurred yet another demonstration of the political symbiosis which had taken place: under the presidency of Professor E. S. Beesly, a meeting assembled in St. Martin's Hall, London. 'Packed to suffocation', one delegate described it, and from nearly a century's distance it certainly seems to have been crowded with personalities.[49] For it was the first meeting of the International Working Men's Association, whose prime movers were Odger and Applegarth. The German émigré Marx, who had been sharpening his dialectic on the *Reports of the Children's Employment Commission* then coming from the press, wrote an address to the delegates.

It was time Mundella got better.

10

He did.

Soon he was out of the bath-chair, for the election of 1865 was at hand. At last it looked as if the union of the middle and working classes was about to be consummated, for on 15 and 16 May a large conference on the reform of parliament was held in Manchester. Out of this grew the Reform Union. Some of its members, like Samuel Morley,[50] did not confine their efforts to helping this, but contributed generously to finance the establishment of the Reform League, which was very efficiently engineered and run by George Howell.[51]

Morley had already been considered as a possible candidate for Nottingham, four years earlier. Cobden had urged him to get into parliament, not only because he had a good radical record, but also because his wealth and influence would carry many manufacturers along with him. This time 'Number 30' chose him to run with Charles Paget in a four-cornered fight for the two seats.

It was a rowdy affair. One canvasser was put in a flour-bin, another had his boots taken off. A mob invaded a committee-room in the St. Ann's Ward and removed the entire staircase. The inevitable *Fishstall Gazette* appeared, carrying such riddles as:

> 'Why is the Number 30 candidate like a bullet?'
> 'Because he's led.' [52]

Bad puns could not hide bad blood, and blood certainly flowed during this election. One local historian sorrowfully acknowledged: 'In no election in Nottingham before or after, had vile slander, personal intimidation and the stirring up of the worst passions been used to such an extent'.[53] Paget's nickname, 'Cow-juice', and Morley's, 'Framerent', showed that a very real animosity had been roused. Mundella tried to appeal to the reason of the electors by issuing a broadsheet 'to assist in the analysation of things in general and of individuals in particular, and to endeavour to show their true origin and bias', calling it *The Political Microscope*.[54]

But both sides lost their heads. Sir Robert Clifton, true to his sporting traditions, challenged Morley to hold a public meeting in the centre of Nottingham. The challenge was accepted. Twenty-nine railway carriages bearing Liberals from the surrounding countryside converged upon the station on a warm summer's evening in June. They emerged from the station to meet a hail of stones and bricks. Mundella, watching from his office window, saw the latent animosity between town and country burst out. The police, even with their reinforcements,[55] could not control the crowds which went surging up the streets. One gang captured the Liberal platform in the Market Square, dismantled it and started a bonfire. Windows were smashed, including those of the *Express* office. To put down the disorder, the mayor sent to Sheffield for a detachment of soldiers, and by one o'clock in the morning quiet was eventually restored.[56]

A POLITICAL BURLESQUE ON THE FORTH-COMING ELECTION.

The Liberals felt that sufficient precautions had not been taken, and that those in authority had connived at the troubles. Mundella, who had seen the trouble begin, led a deputation to the Town Hall to protest. Three days later he again took to the platform to expose the misrepresentations of the tories. Once more he had to stress the fact of his own English birth to rebut the xenophobic jeers at his alien origin.

Part of the bitterness felt at this election was undoubtedly due to the labour question. Sir Robert Clifton had delivered himself of some sharp opinions which were reproduced on placards for the enlightenment of his supporters. In one speech, delivered to the licensed victuallers of Preston, he had expressed the opinion that 'the sooner these trade agitators are put down, the better'. Sir Robert's supporters did not conceal his opinions: for it was one of their strong cards, and too many of the frame-renters in the town thought likewise. Instead they circulated a counter-charge that

Morley had made his vast wealth by sweating his out-workers. To those who remembered the hungry forties, it was quite credible.

DID OVERCOME

HOW SIR ROBERT

NUMBER THIRTY.

N°30

NOTTINGHAM   [1865]   ELECTION.

On 12 July both Morley and Clifton were elected, perhaps because of the practice of 'plumping', whereby the electors voted for only one candidate. Yet the Liberal second string, C. Paget, was so close behind Sir Robert Clifton—a mere twenty-five votes separated them—that Morley wrote to Mundella urging him to institute an inquiry. At the same time, Morley expressed his gratitude for the 'deep and hearty interest in the election' which Mundella had taken.

Mundella did as Morley asked. After collecting evidence of bribery, he organised a petition to the house of commons, which was presented on 7 February 1866. The tories responded by presenting a counter-petition against the return of Samuel Morley. So the house appointed a committee to examine both. The committee first sat on 20 March, and after twenty-seven days declared that neither Sir Robert Clifton nor Samuel Morley should sit, since 'excessive numbers of persons were employed on behalf of Messrs Paget and Morley as messengers, canvassers and protectors from violence', and that in three wards alone out of seven nearly 200 voters were so employed, and received from their agents sums varying from 15s. to £4 10s. 6d.

Naturally enough, Morley was unseated, and Mundella was quick to console him:

'During your election I spoke three times only to our own meetings when our friends were admitted by ticket, but it cost me weeks of the most shameless persecution. My liberties and those of your friends were circumscribed and invaded in a manner which I should have believed impossible in the Queen's Dominions.'

He went on to describe the intimidation which was practised:

'The committee can never know, and never believe, half the barbarity of our opponents. It would be dangerous to tell it, for it would be simply incredible. . . . Besides an attack on my house at midnight, which placed in jeopardy the lives of those dearest to me on earth, I was warned that my property was in danger of being fired. I had to employ men to guard it. I increased insurances enormously. Many of your friends, I believe, have done the same.' [57]

II

From this rowdy election Mundella acquired much political wisdom. Amongst other things, he realised that however progressive a party might be, it was fatal to plant candidates on the constituency without some previous sounding of popular opinion. As he wrote later:

'From experience I have had, the surest way to alarm the jealousy of a constituency is for them to suppose that their freedom of choice is in some way sought to be controlled. Nothing but this feeling, well worked upon by the local Tory papers, handed Nottingham over to Clifton and Toryism. Jealousy of "Number 30"—meaning a clique—destroyed the Liberal Party in Nottingham.' [58]

Hardly had the committee reported, when 'Number 30' were seeking another radical candidate. This time they chose well, and approached Lord Amberley on 22 April 1866. Amberley was the twenty-four-year-old son of Lord John Russell, then convulsing the country with his second Reform Bill. He had advanced views on religious matters, while his politics were more radical than those of his father. He was no career radical, either: as well as being a friend of John Stuart Mill and a person who eschewed luxurious living, he was much admired by Jowett. Brand, the Liberal whip, advised Amberley not to stand, 'as it would be a rough contest'. But the Nottingham delegation were persistent, and Lord John gave his approval, adding that there was 'a fair prospect of a quiet election' unless 'Sir Robert Clifton is to stand on the Conservative side, and bring a mob of ruffians at his heels'.

With Lord Amberley, 'Number 30' chose Handel Cossham, a Bristol coal-owner, whose treatment of his 5,000 Bristol colliers was both enlightened and unique. Both of them travelled to Nottingham on 30 April, comparing addresses, were met at the station and driven in an open carriage to their headquarters, 'The Flying Horse'. The full strength of 'Number 30'—some 150 in all—mustered to pay their respects and conduct them through a groaning and hissing crowd to the Exchange. There Dr. Ransome [59] was in the chair. It looked as if 'Number 30' had at last found the answer.

But the opposition was not to be defeated. Before Lord Amberley and Handel Cossham had time to settle down, the Conservatives invited Ralph Bernal Osborne to stand for the seat. Osborne was twice as old as Amberley, was probably one of the best impromptu speakers without a seat, and had such experience in representing various constituencies that Disraeli once raised a laugh by saying he couldn't remember at one particular moment for which Bernal Osborne actually sat. [60]

This split the Liberals. Bernal Osborne, though he had promised Lord John Russell that he would not stand if it meant that Amberley would have to retire, refused to see Amberley throughout the election. He capped this by inviting Sir Robert Clifton to take the chair at his first public meeting. Lord John lamented that his son had fallen among thieves, but the son was determined to stand by the local Liberals, who he declared 'could not foresee that Bernal Osborne would come'.

Mundella was his busy self. On 4 May he took Lady Amberley round his factory. 'It was most interesting and curious', she wrote in her journal. Later that day he joined the Amberleys in their box at the opera 'and was much hissed', Lady Amberley noted. [61] Her Aunt Louisa did not improve matters by writing, 'There is not so rough and brutal a lot as the Nottingham mob in all England', adding about the Conservative candidate, Sir George Jenkinson, and Amberley's colleague, Cossham, 'I know no one good thing (of either) and I hope with all my heart that both will fail signally'. Lady Amberley's brother, Lyulph Stanley, only three years older than her husband, was nevertheless a great source of comfort, coming post-haste to Nottingham to help them with his fervid radical enthusiasm.

Nottingham was indeed a rallying point of those who were later to play a part in Mundella's own political life. Besides Lyulph Stanley, George Potter, editor of the *Beehive* and an advanced trade unionist, appeared. It was a hectic fortnight. The presence of troops in the town moderated the horse-play, and apart from the usual bouts of fisticuffs and the cries of 'Cow-juice', 'Pump-handle' and 'Baby', Amberley survived to be elected on 11 May. The traitor Bernal Osborne headed the poll, but he only succeeded in getting 211 votes more than Cossham, who was at the foot.[62]

Amberley's return, and the establishment of a political name, were decisive factors in the events of the next two years. It was particularly apt that Mundella's last public act of that year was to take part in the meetings of the British Association which were held in the town. The main theme was Huxley's: realism was needed in the schools of the country. With his old friend Dr. Ransome, colleague since the days when they had together formed the Robin Hoods, Mundella took part in all the soirées and educational meetings. He was grooming himself for his rôle. His old schoolfellow Bates—now a famous explorer—returned for the occasion. After the meetings were over he wrote to Mundella saying how much he had enjoyed the fast life of Nottingham. 'The pace was killing', he confessed. 'All the people I have seen speak of the meeting as a great success.'[63]

That pace was to quicken.

CHAPTER THREE

The Champion of the Trade Unions, 1867–1868

THE rowdies of Nottingham were indeed lambs compared to those of Sheffield. For at Nottingham the issues were clear: framework knitters were being displaced by factory workers; the town was drawing upon the younger generation of the countryside; whigs were pursuing their ancient and honourable feud with the tories. But at Sheffield no such clear issues presented themselves. We at this distance can disentangle them, but very few of those who were living and working in that cramped and smoky aggregation of houses set in the folds of the surrounding hills could do so at the time.[1]

I

Old landmarks were vanishing, old standards were being rapidly re-valued. For Sheffield it was a decade of such rapid expansion that ideals could not keep pace. Since the golden years after the Great Exhibition, when the bright tangs of Hiram Smith's file symbolised the place of that industry among the three greatest of the town, the whole trade had been disturbed and displaced. Some of the file manufacturers, like F. T. Mappin,[2] had introduced machines for the mass-manufacture of files. These machines, like the new hosiery machines at Nottingham, were bitterly opposed by the filesmiths and file-grinders, who threw what remained of the hand-made file trade into great confusion by strikes lasting for three months at a stretch. Mappin was not content, however, to make files, and had established a large new works for the mass manufacture of railway springs. Others, like Charles Cammell,[3] abandoned file-manufacturing to concentrate on the highly profitable rolling of steel rails, and his Cyclops works expanded towards Grimesthorpe with such rapidity that in 1864 he converted it into a limited liability company with a capital of £1,000,000. In that same year John Brown[4] also established a £1,000,000 firm, soon to become not only the largest steel-rail-rolling firm in the world, but a prodigious manufactory of armour

47

plate that was being continuously improved. Completing a formidable quartet was Mark Firth,[5] who also found among the bluebells of Brightside a convenient spot to establish a massive concern which concentrated on the forging of great guns. Firth's upset the file trade in a very literal sense, for, having laid down what was then the largest Nasmyth hammer and the largest anvil in the world, he was sued by his file-manufacturing neighbours, who complained that its mighty vibrations made it impossible for their workmen to keep a steady hand.[6]

The unhappy file-grinders found themselves displaced.[7] So did scores of little men whose pattern of life had been the small community union numbering less than 200 men. Reluctant to surrender their traditional way of life to these new and mysterious masters, whose opulent mansions slowly reared themselves in the west end of the town, they drew still closer together for mutual security. As they foregathered in public-houses to sing the mournful refrain hammered out by one of their own craft sixty years before:

'Wearied bones, despised and daunted,
Hungry guts and empty purse,
Hung with rags, by bailiffs haunted,
Prove the times grow worse and worse,'[8]

it is little wonder that a local publican was able to win their attention by his bold and practical scheme.

This publican, William Broadhead,[9] landlord of the 'George' in Carver Street, proposed to make workers' solidarity a reality. He offered them something more heady than small beer: the power that comes from intimidation. As secretary of the saw-grinders' union—a small union of only 190 men—he knew the masters who were obstinate and the men who refused to associate. Where one employed the other, he proposed drastic action. A letter was sent to Firths:

'Gentlemen,
    'The game works merrily and we brush away all obstacles before us. If we appear to be rather long about it you see we are none the less sure. It is your turn next and the man who hangs back will be the first to get it. If I but move my finger you are sent to eternity as sure as fate. Be advised and take the hint in time.'[10]

Threats like this were not idle ones, for Broadhead meant business. Gunpowder was placed in Firth's boilers, and Helliwell, a work-

THE FIRE AT HINE AND MUNDELLA'S
As seen from the Canal Bridge, Carrington Street

man who would not join a union, was blown up by a home-made bomb. Others suffered similarly. Samuel Baxter had gunpowder dropped down his chimney, Elisha Parker's horse was hamstrung, and Linley, a small master, who was employing too many boys instead of union men, was tracked down and shot.[11]

The terror was all the more effective because it was secret. The mysterious agent struck under the name of Mary Ann. Sheffield became notorious throughout the country. By 1865, when the Social Science Congress met at Sheffield, the secretary of the Organised Trades of the town was forbidden to read a paper which he had prepared in defence of the unions. This secretary, William Dronfield,[12] was a person of spirit and character, and was determined that the plight of the filesmiths and their fellows should be aired in some kind of national assembly. Since the Social Science Congress would not hear him, he would convene his fellow unionists from the rest of the country. So he summoned a national conference of all trade unionists. This met on 17 June 1866,[13] and sat for five days at Sheffield. 187,771 workers were represented by 138 delegates, among whom was George Odger. The meetings were thrown open to the press, and it is from their reports that we can see the issues that preoccupied the delegates. These issues—lock-outs, shorter working hours, the existing and unsatisfactory law of master and servant, and the necessity of establishing courts of arbitration—were discussed in such a manner that George Odger, whose experience of such gatherings was unique, declared that the conference was 'one of the largest that had ever assembled in the cause of labour, and . . . one of the most intelligent and business-like I have ever met with in the whole of my life'. In view of his activities with the International Working Men's Association, this was high praise. It showed that some national expression of the working-class point of view was almost at hand,[13a] and to bring it about a National Alliance of Organised Trades, consisting of all the trade unions of the kingdom, was formed. This National Alliance was to have an annual conference, a standing judicial council and a deliberative committee. Rules of procedure were drawn up for the presentation of credentials, and it looked as if a labour parliament was to be born at long last.

Such high hopes were soon dissipated. Less than three months after the delegates had met, an explosion took place in the house of Thomas Fearneyhough, a saw-grinder of New Hereford Street,

D

which rocked the country.[14] It was caused by a can of gunpowder deposited in the cellar. This explosion, which was obviously the work of the unions, was all the more damaging since it occurred only a week after Dronfield had presented the seventh annual report of his Association of Organised Trades, and urged the workers 'to make overtures to their employers in a respectful manner, and not to be exorbitant in their demands, because if they were, they would lay themselves open to the imputation that they were trying to drive the trade from the town'.

The employers of the town were incensed. On 13 November 1866—a month and six days after the explosion—they accredited a deputation to wait upon the Home Secretary asking for the appointment of a Royal Commission to examine the legal position of such lawless bodies, whose disrespect for the elementary rights of property had now extended to the fundamental right of life itself.

2

Nor was this the only threat which the trades had to face. The treasurer of a Bradford union had embezzled a few pounds from the local cashbox. These funds, in the days before the Welfare State, not only supported the members during a strike, but provided sick pay, superannuation, insurance against loss of tools, and funeral expenses. In some districts where workmen were struggling against a living death they even afforded an emigration bounty by which means these men could escape to a great new world across the Atlantic.[15] Money was the very life-blood of the new unions which were being organised on the plans of Applegarth and his associates: never to be wasted unnecessarily, and jealously conserved to make the unions strong. The Bradford treasurer was a thief, and, as such, should have been punishable under the normal processes of the common law.

But that common law did not apply to them. The Bradford magistrates decided that inasmuch as the constitution of the Bradford union contained rules contrary to that law, they could not recognise its right to hold property. The case was taken to the Court of Queen's Bench, but they, on 6 January 1867, only confirmed the decision of the Bradford magistrates. What was even more dangerous, their judgment fixed the law on this subject. As a result of this decision, known henceforth as the case of

Hornby *v*. Close,[16] the legal position of all trade unions through-out the kingdom was now prejudiced. They either had to dissolve, or secure a modification of the law. There was no middle way.

3

To the average middle-class Victorian the picture was not painted in colours which showed the attitude of the trade unions to be anything but threatening. In spite of the efforts of their literary hero, Thomas Hughes, to gloss the ugly writing on the wall,[17] they were liberally plied with information which was calculated to make them react away from any appeal by Dron-field, Odger and company. Living as they did on the invest-ments which an earlier generation had made in the railways, in manufactures and in overseas trade generally, their flesh was prone to creep at the very mention of foreign competition.

Yet at this very time, when Overend and Gurneys, Peto and Betts and the British Joint Stock Bank had crashed around their drawing-rooms,[18] another International Exhibition had been held in Paris. Following the £20,000,000 deficits which caused the Stock Exchange to panic on 10 May 1866—a shock which one contemporary compared to that of an earthquake, because it was so sudden, so unexpected and so devastating—came the disturbing news that British exhibits in Paris were no more than 'slovenly intruded heaps of raw material mingled with pieces of rusty iron'.[19] Prone as they were to look for the moral in any tale of woe, the temptation to regard the unions as the cause of it all was strong. Those who had a taste for economics pointed to the Wages Fund theory, where it was explicitly stated that wages could be raised only at the expense of prices or the lowering of quality. Unionism, by this theory, was not only irrational, but wicked and futile. Even John Stuart Mill said so, until he changed his mind two years later. The *Edinburgh Review* tolled the bell over the corpse of British industrial supremacy with sickening sanctimony, declaring that the exhibition showed 'evidence of our decline upon the largest possible scale'.[20] Even at South Kensing-ton, home of what scientific instruction there was in the country, Belgian iron girders were being used by the contractors, and similar stories came in from Glasgow and Sheffield.[21]

Amateur diagnoses of the economic malaise were essayed by everyone. But it was not until the Conservative government appointed a parliamentary committee to examine the technical education of English workpeople, and followed it up by a systematic inquiry as to the nature of labour combinations in other countries, that any real light was shed on the problem. Mundella gave evidence before the committee, which was placed under the able chairmanship of Bernhard Samuelson,[22] an enterprising ironmaster who was to become his close friend. In his evidence, Mundella did not mince words. He had been a juror at the Paris Exhibition, and had travelled extensively in Germany, besides having business interests in Saxony. He said:

'By the aid of principals of large establishments, I have tested large numbers of people employed in various trades in our locality. We had a uniform form, asking whether such and such people could, for example, read and write, or do any arithmetic; and with regard to their general intelligence, taking the most simple tests possible; and I can assure the committee that the failures are almost incredible.'

And in response to further questions:

'The ability to read a simple paragraph is not possessed by nearly fifty per cent of the people employed in our large establishments in Nottingham and the immediate neighbourhood. I am almost afraid to tell the committee the state of things, for nobody believes these things when he is told.' [23]

He also committed these views to paper in a memorandum which he drafted for the government in response to a questionnaire sent out by the Committee of the Privy Council on Education asking what trades were being injured by lack of good technical education. He pointed out the inherent weakness of the hosiery trade in this respect, and urged that good, cheap, accessible technical schools should be established immediately, as continental competitors had already established them.[24]

This theme he elaborated to a number of audiences, embroidering it with meaning. Before good technical schools could even begin to function, he argued, elementary education should be made compulsory. The social consequences of this policy, he continued, stretched far beyond the mere reviving of Britain's flagging industry. The working classes would be made more responsible, more capable of participating in courts of arbitration, less criminal, less subject to the debauching effects of an urban environment. He appealed to the cupidity of his middle-class hearers, and urged them to consider the great saving which an enlightened educational policy would effect in rates alone.

At the same time as he preached this educational evangel, he was active in advocating the establishment of courts of arbitration. The two were complementary. Trade unions were part of his general policy for social peace. Their leaders—Applegarth, Odger, Dronfield, Pickard and Normansell—responded by urging their unions to accept arbitration wherever possible. Odger's remark that 'strikes are to the social world what wars are to politics . . . they become crimes unless prompted by absolute necessity', was quoted by Mundella when he was invited to address a public meeting in Sheffield on 'Boards of Arbitration'. He was accompanied on that occasion by George Kendall, secretary of the Three Counties Trade Union of Hosiery Operatives, and by a representative of the lace-workers. Both of them testified to the efficacy of the Nottingham board, and at the conclusion of the meeting William Dronfield was loud in his advocacy that a similar board should be established in Sheffield.[25]

4

Dronfield's anxiety to show how co-operative Sheffield workmen could be was very real. On 25 March 1867, eight months before this meeting took place, the bill setting up the Royal Commission to examine the affairs of trade unions had passed the house of lords. On 3 June three lawyers began specific inquiries at Sheffield into the real identity of 'Mary Ann'. Slowly the curtain was drawn aside on the full scale of the crimes which had been inspired by the landlord of the 'George', as one by one various unionists told their tale. The commissioners had a two-handed engine for extracting confessions: they were empowered to punish the obstinate who refused to give evidence, and pardon the frank who told all. That they did not have to use the first illustrated their good faith and the belief of the criminals in the second.

On the thirteenth day of the hearing William Broadhead, wearing his gold eye-glass, broke down completely and confessed to a long number of such intimidatory acts. His categorical disclosures of the time, place, agents and results of these acts horrified his hearers, and, when published, nerved many unionists to dissociate themselves from such a monster. It is to their credit that his union refused to expel him, maintaining that what he had done was entirely on their behalf.

But the rest of the unions rallied to Paradise Square—then the forum and focal point of Sheffield's political life—to demonstrate against him. On 8 July, under the chairmanship of the Rev. R. Stainton, a Congregational minister, a resolution was adopted in which they professed to 'view with deepest shame and abhorrence the systematic crimes which have disgraced the trades of the town' and declared their 'readiness and determination' to do all in their power to redeem the character of the town.

A week later, to the day, a chamber of arbitration was formed as a token of their sincerity.

A similar series of disclosures had been made at Manchester, where the Royal Commission on Trade Unions had detached another body to obtain information, as the Sheffield body had done. In Manchester it was the Brickmakers' Union which had set a bad tone: arson, machine-smashing and the placing of thousands of needles in clay worked by non-unionists were all laid bare. Clearly the unions would have to fight hard for their rights, since so many of them seemed anxious to show that they had no conception of their duties.

And in London this was precisely what Applegarth was doing. He summoned a standing conference of the secretaries of the major unions. This became the general staff of the unions in their hour of peril, a high command to which the Webbs have given the name of the 'junta'. Its leader was Applegarth. He made himself responsible for the summoning of witnesses. He gave evidence himself before the commission, answering no fewer than 655 questions that covered all aspects of union policy and finance. His activity was pressurised by the recent decision in the case of Hornby *v*. Close, by the sensational disclosures at Sheffield and Manchester, and by the long-felt need of all unionists that unions should be at least equal to friendly societies. He was encouraged by the support of two members of the Royal Commission, whose sympathies enabled them to frame suitable questions. These two, differing widely as they did on the basic philosophy of human existence, were united in their determination that the unions should have a chance to establish their place in the public confidence. One was the young positivist Frederic Harrison,[26] who saw in such groups the only logical means by which labour could obtain its economic ends. The other was the Christian Socialist, Thomas Hughes,[27] who fondly hoped that through these groups the labour movement might be led towards a co-operative New

Jerusalem. Equally sympathetic, though not as vocal, was the earl of Lichfield. When the time came for the report to be written these three dissented from the conclusions of their seven colleagues.

5

One of these seven colleagues was John Arthur Roebuck, M.P. for Sheffield. Concerning his sympathies, both his constituency and his colleagues were left in no possible doubt: for he went to Sheffield to deliver a searing philippic on the authors of the outrages and the tyranny of the trade societies in general. He compared their attempts to limit child labour to the barbarous practices of the Chinese, who, he said, murdered their offspring.[28]

Applegarth and Howell were quick to respond. Applegarth came to Sheffield and addressed a public meeting, accusing Roebuck of being 'the only member of the Royal Commission whose sole object was to make out a case against the unions'. Howell followed this up by forwarding a petition from the London Trades Council that Roebuck be removed from the Royal Commission.

Though Roebuck could not be removed from the Royal Commission, he could be removed from the house of commons. The year 1868 was a golden opportunity to do so, since by the Reform Bill of the previous year all town artisans had been given a vote. The local leaders of the unions, especially Dronfield, showed themselves very much alive to this possibility. As possible opponents to Roebuck they toyed with such candidates as Ernest Jones, the ex-editor of the *Northern Star*, Auberon Herbert, the son of the earl of Carnarvon, and Richard Whiteing, a mystical radical. None of these seemed acceptable.[29]

The deliberations of the Sheffield artisans were given a new turn by the discovery that the dissenters and whigs of the town had also been considering the possibility of opposing Roebuck at the forthcoming election. Robert Leader,[30] the fifty-one-year-old editor of the local radical newspaper, the *Sheffield Independent*, had shown signs of great dissatisfaction with Roebuck's waspish attitude to public affairs. Such deviations from the Liberal party line as supporting the Austrians in Venetia and the Confederate South in the American Civil War had not passed without adverse comment in the *Independent*. Leader had supported Roebuck for twenty years with all his journalistic resources, but that loyalty had now worn thin, especially as Roebuck was going out of his normal way to insult the nonconformist element in the town, ridiculing their teetotalism and sabbatarianism as 'one foaming muddy river which it is very difficult to stem, and very disagreeable to see and smell'.

One of the leaders of nonconformity in Sheffield was the same Mark Firth whose industrial empire was taking shape in Brightside. Firth's devotion to his faith led him to sustain a college which had been built by his family for the training of ministers for the Methodist New Connection, as well as acting as treasurer for their foreign missions. Firth's hold on the town was very real, and in the numerous chapels which sprang up at this time his opinions were respected. He had also a great enthusiasm for education.

It was this enthusiasm which also inspired Mundella. On 15 and 16 January the Manchester Education Aid Society convened a conference to discuss an Education Bill which W. E. Forster and H. A. Bruce were to introduce in the house of commons that session. Among the 500 delegates who attended was Mundella, who spoke very strongly on the second day. His theme was that the recent Factory Act of 1867 did not go far enough in prohibiting the half-time labour of children, and he proposed that the conference should amend the bill to provide for compulsory attendance. 'As a large employer,' he said, 'I believe the conference and England generally expect far too much from the education clauses of the Factory Acts. The half-time system is of little value in the way of education.' He went on to describe his own experiments and experience in the matter:

'I have been engaged for some time in making enquiries as to the educational condition of people in factories, and I have found that only 41 per cent educated under the half-time system can read tolerably well. In Saxony every child from six to fourteen is in daily attendance at school for sixteen hours a week, and surely, what can be done with Saxons can be done with Anglo-Saxons? We are so afraid of trenching upon our liberties that we will soon have no liberties left at all.' [31]

This was strong meat—too strong for the conference, and far too strong for *The Times*. He found only one supporter out of the 500, and that was the inspector of schools for Nottingham. W. E. Forster challenged his criticism of half-timers, threatening to withdraw from his position as sponsor of the bill if the conference supported Mundella's amendment. *The Times* applauded Forster's action, and called Mundella's suggestion 'a serious error', reminding him at the same time that in England there were 'formidable objections unknown in Saxony'. In a special editorial, in which the conference was described as 'the most representative gathering for educational purposes that has ever been brought together', *The Times* regretted that 'proposals otherwise deserving at least of consideration should be clogged with the dead weight of a visionary scheme'.[32]

To earn the displeasure of *The Times* for being the apostle of a 'visionary scheme' was in certain quarters a recommendation rather than a disqualification. At Birmingham, where a young and energetic screw manufacturer called Joseph Chamberlain was busy galvanising the National Education League to extend its activities over the whole country, Mundella seemed to be an admirable ally. He was invited to address their national conference too, and here he was even more categorical. He told a simple story to illustrate his theme:

'I found on the steps of my counting-house door a number of lads and coaxed them upstairs to my counting-house. There were nine of them, and some of them very ragged specimens indeed. They thought I had some sinister motive, and it was with some difficulty that I induced them to go with me. I examined them separately on their educational requirements. Not one of these poor boys could read the simplest word. I had *The Times* newspaper before me. Two of them could manage "The", but not one of them could spell "Times". Their ages ranged from eleven to sixteen.' [33]

Applegarth was present at this meeting. He fully agreed with Mundella's argument, and told his own union: 'Opposition of masters and men does not arise from a desire of either to oppress each other, but rather from ignorance. . . . I look to education to teach all parties better.'[34]

6

Nothing has hitherto been said of the colliers of Sheffield, a large and powerful group organised within the framework of the South Yorkshire Miners' Association.[35] Had Mundella confined his activities to addressing educational gatherings, it is very likely that they would never have heard his name. But in the spring of 1868 their attention was riveted on a particularly ugly strike in

South Lancashire, where their fellow-colliers had been asked to accept a cut of 15 per cent in their wages. The South Lancashire colliers refused, vowing that they would rather eat grass than accept the reduction. So the coal-owners locked them out. There were the usual incidents. At Wigan the managers of the coal and iron company brandished revolvers when beset by an angry mob, and actually fired shots. Troops were moved into the town. On 24 April, following a week of riots in the streets, the strikers lost patience. Arming themselves with anything that came to hand, they marched in a body to the pits, determined that if they could not work, nobody else should. They attacked the forty police who were guarding the pithead machinery, overcame them, started up the engine, and were just about to draw up the cage to smash the winding gear when they were stopped by a large body of police and soldiers.

Mundella was called in to arbitrate. He was completely successful. On 4 May it was announced that the men were going back to work, that the owners had bowed to the inevitable, and that the strike, which had cost half a million pounds, was quite unnecessary in view of what could be achieved by discussions round a table. If any proof were needed of the efficiency of arbitration, here it was.

A month later, as Mundella was travelling to Manchester by train, he opened a letter from William Dronfield. It contained a formal invitation to address a joint meeting at Sheffield of the Organised Trades and the Reform League. Mundella replied that he would return the following day, and would meet them in the evening. His address was regarded as so satisfactory that they offered him their support if he would contest the seat at the forthcoming election. Mundella hesitated, writing to Robert Leader to sound him on the opinions of the local Liberal party. The labour leaders urged him to accept. Robert Applegarth travelled to Nottingham to persuade him. In June, Mundella was invited to address the first meeting of the Congress of the Trades, to be known from now on as the Trades Union Congress, but, owing to a previous engagement at Liverpool, he had to refuse. Leader was enthusiastic. On 24 June a circular was issued, proposing Mundella, and on 20 July he was formally adopted at a meeting in Paradise Square.

Frederic Harrison was delighted and wrote to Beesly on 25 July:

'Mundella's evidence is first rate. He is a thorough trump—a regular unionist by nature, who, like Pisistratus or someone "has taken the demos into partnership" and made a joint union of masters and men which at any rate keeps quiet within the field and bullies outside employers savagely. Mundella said "If we find an employer underselling us by cutting down the wages, we interfere". How? "Oh," said he coolly, "we arrange to take on his hands ourselves!! and we just leave him to the men's union." He will turn Roebuck out for Sheffield, who now is very uneasy. *That* is Applegarth's doing.' [36]

7

The summer of 1868 was one of the hottest on record. Temperatures of 91 and 92 degrees in the shade made harvesters rest at high noon. During the sixteen weeks of drought an extraordinary number of fires raged on the hills and moors outside the town. At Handsworth, Norton Woodseats and Redmires they caused considerable concern. The supply of water in the town was restricted.

Political meetings were held in cool and pleasant places. On 31 August Samuel Plimsoll threw open the shaded grounds of Whiteley Woods Hall to the South Yorkshire miners. They came in great numbers to hear Mundella and other Liberal white hopes, with such enthusiasm that the omnibuses were overloaded. The wheels of one, carrying seventy instead of its normal load of thirty, collapsed at Leavygreave, injuring seven passengers.

The Organised Trades of Sheffield rallied strongly behind Mundella, determined to disprove Roebuck's jeer that the British working man 'could bark, but he could not bite'. On 3 September they staged a demonstration in Mundella's favour. Mundella himself was tremendously active, addressing meetings daily for four months preceding the actual election. Applegarth came to Sheffield to fight for him, accompanied by Lloyd Jones, the old Chartist, and Goldwin Smith, the radical Oxford history professor. Goldwin Smith's appearance was virtually his last before he left for Cornell. Howell was in communication with him, stimulating the local branch of the Reform League to rally round the nominee of the Organised Trades.

Though there were four candidates in the field, contesting the two seats, attention was riveted on the struggle between Roebuck and Mundella. Eighty-one-year-old George Hadfield,[37] who had been sitting with Roebuck since 1852, was so sure of his seat that he did not appear till two days before the election. His dogmatic sectarian opinions (uttered in a shrill, incisive voice) and his consistent generosity to the local chapels made him an obvious choice of the local nonconformists. The fourth candidate, Edwin P. Price, Q.C., had no possible chance whatever.

The Roebuck–Mundella contest assumed an importance that was almost national. Well it might, for it was the first example of the newly enfranchised town worker exercising his vote. Applegarth tried to allay the suspicions of many doubting Liberals: 'The workers will not launch their votes in one compact mass against the institutions and property of the country,' he declared, 'but will support one in whom they believe they have a faithful representative of their interests.' [38] 'Mundella and Moderation' might well have been his cry. For the issue of Applegarth's fight would have important repercussions in the trade union world. Should his nominee prevail, the sectionalist, opportunist policy of George Potter would be finally defeated. Moreover, Mundella's candidature was a challenge to the whig element in the Liberal party itself. For when Applegarth appealed for Gladstone's blessing on Mundella's candidature, Gladstone replied:

'As I understand the matter there are three candidates in the field for Sheffield in connection with Liberal opinions and the Liberal Party; two of them are in direct opposition to each other, Mr. Mundella being one. Now it appears to me it is for the people of Sheffield to decide between them, and that any opinion given by me at the moment respecting the ability, character and services of any one of the candidates would constitute a virtual interference, and would carry me beyond the line of duty.' [39]

Mundella was alive to the rebuff, and commented, 'The fact is they are frightened out of their wits lest Roebuck get in, and dare not do anything to help me'.

The two chief protagonists were the cartoonist's joy. Roebuck, small, hunched and frail, had a ferocity of manner that had earned him the nickname of 'Old Tear 'em'. Mundella, tall, forbidding, with a large black beard from which protruded his majestic nose, was a complete physical contrast. Once more the nose got him into trouble. Attacks were levelled on his ancestry as well as his commercial morality. He was accused of using 'Saxon serfs' to the detriment of British labour. Cartoons, picturing him as a dark, sinister, Semitic figure, selling patent medicine inscribed 'cheap labour', were sedulously circulated.

He wrote to Robert Leader on 7 August:

'Dronfield keeps writing me that emissaries are employed to go about and prejudice the working men by asserting that I am "a bad master". And our workmen here keep hearing of it and are dreadfully indignant, and without any knowledge on my part, I hear they are getting up protests etc. etc. in all the Trades. I feel the more the *Telegraph* plays this game the better, as without ever bidding for popularity, and often battling against the ignorance and prejudices of the workmen, I have, by straightforward dealing and strict impartiality, won their respect, and they are too anxious to show it.'

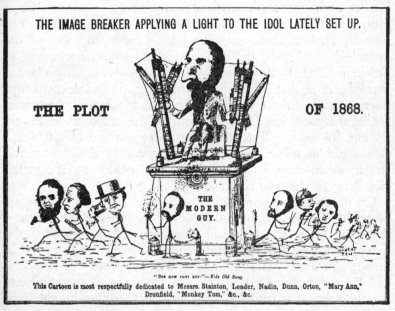

THE IMAGE BREAKER APPLYING A LIGHT TO THE IDOL LATELY SET UP.

THE PLOT   OF 1868.

THE MODERN GUY.

" See how they run!"—*Vide Old Song.*

This Cartoon is most respectfully dedicated to Messrs. Stainton, Leader, Nadin, Dunn, Orton, "Mary Ann," Dronfield, "Monkey Tom," &c., &c.

Both Nottingham workers and Nottingham manufacturers rallied to his defence, and wrote to both the *Independent* and the *Telegraph* to refute the slanders which were being loaded on their fellow-townsman. Meanwhile Mundella was campaigning with great energy, and was able to write to George Howell on 25 September:

'I am working at Sheffield like a horse and feel confident that I shall defeat my opponent. Do all you can outside me, as I am a strong Radical and they tell me that the moderates are afraid of me. I hope that nothing will be left undone that will tend to secure the victory. I believe that it will be one of the greatest in England if carried on with energy and discretion.'

His energies were drawn outside the constituency in October, the month before nomination, in order to lecture to the Social Science Congress at Birmingham. There he proved to his audience that trade unions were beneficial to the working classes and the nation. He cited the 'mental activity and progress' of the trade unionist as contrasted with the 'stolid, stagnant and depressed condition of the non-trade-union artisan'. His detailed appreciation of the three leading trade unionists of the time—Applegarth, Odger and Guile—was the eloquent testimony of one who knew their reputation for conciliatory dealings with employers. On the last day of the month the national journals began to take notice of him. The *Spectator* advised Liberal electors to vote for him. The *Saturday Review* abandoned Roebuck's cause 'in view of the organised hostility of the trade unions'. Most effective was an article in *Good Words* written by J. M. Ludlow, in which he expressed a hope that Mundella, as the energetic and devoted supporter of trade unions, would soon be able to advocate their claim for legal recognition from the floor of the house of commons, adding, 'In no way can that town wipe out the blot which a Broadhead has stained her with more effectively, than by sending to Parliament one who has been so true a missionary of conciliation between class and class and man and man'.

On 16 November nominations were made. Mundella was proposed by Thomas Dunn and seconded by William Dronfield.[40] After the other candidates had been proposed and seconded, the mayor ordered a show of hands—and declared the result to be in favour of Hadfield and Mundella. The supporters of Roebuck and Price demanded a poll. So, on 17 November, as dull and drizzly a day as it could possibly be, forty polling-booths were opened in various parts of the town. From eight o'clock in the morning these were jammed by hundreds waiting to cast their votes. Arrangements were bad. Thieves took advantage of the crowding to rob and pick pockets. By eleven o'clock all attempts to continue normal business were abandoned—shop-keepers put up their shutters, and honest folk made for their homes. A band of young men with sticks and brooms decorated with strange emblems went about the town tossing people's hats in the air and breaking windows. The official declaration of the poll was proclaimed on 18 November. It read:

GEORGE HADFIELD	14,797	Elected
ANTONY JOHN MUNDELLA	12,212	Elected
JOHN ARTHUR ROEBUCK	9,571	
EDWIN PLUMER PRICE	5,272	

Mundella returned to Nottingham on 19 November. When he arrived at the Midland station there was a crowd of 20,000 people and a sax-tuba band playing to greet him. The greatest excitement prevailed. As soon as he stepped out of the carriage the vast crowd gave one huge shout of welcome, the warmth of which seemed to surprise him. Outside the station a carriage drawn by four grey horses waited to convey him to his warehouse, where a workman presented him with an address. A broadsheet was circulated in the town celebrating, in rustic couplets, the triumph of the man who had made good. Two of the verses ran:

> 'Mundella is the poor man's friend
> And Sheffield people may rejoice,
> There's none more able to defend
> Them, than the man they've made their choice.
>
> 'His interest is the poor man's cause,
> And all their rights he will maintain;
> His aim will be to make good laws,
> Success and honour to his name.' [41]

He was visibly affected:

'You cannot, I assure you,' he told them, 'realise how much I feel affected by the splendid reception which you have quite unexpectedly given me. (*Cheers.*) Throughout a contest unprecedented for rancour, extending over four or five months, my fellow townsmen have always spoken out nobly and handsomely on my behalf.

'Not a paid canvasser, not a glass of beer, nor any alliance of any kind of an illegal or improper character—fighting only for principle, for Gladstone and Liberty—and yet I have achieved a great and glorious victory.

'I go to Parliament to represent Sheffield, but if I know myself, I shall with all my heart and soul and energy, represent the working men of England. (*Applause.*) Labour, I trust, will have in me a good and honest representative of the perfect and equal rights of both.'

Entering the carriage, with the sax-tuba band playing as it proceeded, he was escorted by an immense crowd along Station Street, Lister Gate, Albert Street, Wheeler Gate, Beastmarket Hill and up Derby Road to his residence at the Park. 'Never', wrote the *Nottingham Express*, 'was a reception more hearty and generous. Everybody seemed anxious to excel everybody else in shouting out congratulations.' [42]

PART II
POLITICIAN

E

CHAPTER FOUR

Donning the Labour Harness, 1869–1870

AMONG the other members of that vast Liberal majority of 272, Mundella soon assumed a position of considerable consequence. His natural confidence of bearing was such that Robert Lowe, the autocratic albino who became chancellor of the exchequer, hailed him in mistake for the King of the Belgians. There were others among the back benchers who regarded him with more substantial respect as a pioneer in the field of industrial arbitration. Outside parliament, thirty-three-year-old Henry Crompton, then the legal advisor of the trade unions, asked his help in compiling an article on labour relations which he was then writing for the *Fortnightly*. Arbitration was much in the air: soon the North of England Board was to be set up for the iron industry, a precedent as the first board in a basic industry.

I

No pressure group wooed him more assiduously than the trade union leaders. The bonds forged between himself and Applegarth in the hot summer of the previous year now began to bind him. It was imperative that the unions should be allowed to hold their funds under the security of the law: for on such security depended the whole structure of the pacific and conciliatory policy of the junta. A bill, prepared for that very purpose, was in existence, thanks to the efforts of Frederic Harrison, who, with Thomas Hughes, had drafted the minority report of the Trade Union Commission. This bill had been presented in the previous parliament by Sir Thomas Fowell Buxton, the M.P. for King's Lynn, and George Dixon, the M.P. for Birmingham, 'very much at the instance of Mr. Mundella', as Applegarth acknowledged.[1] But in this parliament Sir Thomas Fowell Buxton had no seat, and George Dixon was engrossed in the promotion of the National Education League.

So the duty of presenting the bill devolved upon Mundella. He realised how impatient the labour leaders were, but he was determined to 'wait patiently and investigate carefully before committing myself to one side or the other. *I am resolved to bring in no bill the first session, but to feel my way to the temper of the House.*' [2] He followed this up by a letter to Henry Crompton, suggesting that Tom Hughes should be entrusted with it. Crompton agreed, and in his reply of 8 January 1869 expressed his 'satisfaction' that Mundella's view was the right one, and that Harrison was wrong. 'Beesly', he added, 'takes the same view as you do that Hughes is the man for the bill.' [3]

In the meantime, Mundella was saddled with the honour of seconding the reply to the Address from the Throne. Speaker Denison wrote to him on 6 February advising him as to procedure: the dinner before the speech, when it would be read over, and the duty of the seconder to handle certain special subjects. Mundella made his debut on the 16 February in a black court dress with a sword tickling his undraped legs. He spoke on his special subjects, arbitration and education, in a short and undistinguished speech, unrelieved by a single anecdote. Though Gladstone and Bright regarded him steadily throughout, he felt that he had been a failure, and he told Leader so.

The plunge once taken, however, he felt much easier. By 13 March his confidence was such that he could write:

'I am getting more accustomed to hearing my own voice in the House, and to stating my own opinions with deliberation and without flurry. I have no hope of ever being a brilliant success, but I am sure I shall not be one of the silent and useless men which I find make up two-thirds of the House.'

In this very week his stock rose considerably: for two days after this letter was written the Report of the Royal Commission on Trade Unions was published, and in it Mundella's Board of Arbitration was warmly recommended. The report acknowledged the usefulness of such boards, and seems to have influenced David Dale, the great Northern ironmaster, when he decided to set up his board in that very month. [4]

By the 23 March Mundella felt confident enough to support the bill which Hughes was to introduce. 'Whether it is introduced by the Government or Hughes', he wrote, 'I must, from my position, stick to it, and I wish rather that the House should desire to hear me, than that I should crave their indulgence, as I must speak for an hour at least.' [5] For in his own constituency there was a serious colliery strike. 'I cannot feel but that Huntsman and others', he wrote of the owners, 'are behaving very ill, and whatever may be the result of present strikes, the further consequences will be serious.' He wrote to Normansell,[6] the secretary of the South Yorkshire Miners' Association, urging him to follow up the Report of the Trade Unions Commission and press for the establishment of a Court of Arbitration. Unfortunately, however, J. A. Roebuck, in spite of the fact that he had been a member of this self-same royal commission which had recommended that unions be legalised and treated with, now launched out into another of his famous diatribes, urging the Sheffield masters not to receive any representatives of the unions or 'gentlemen' speaking on their behalf. Roebuck followed this up with another speech, referring to the newly enfranchised electorate of Sheffield as 'an ignorant foreign body'. Mundella warned Leader, 'It is plain that Roebuck's friends intend to ally themselves with the Churchmen and Tories'.[7]

Pricked in this fashion, Mundella spent the month of April in the planning of the bill to legalise the unions. On the first of the month he expressed himself confident that its moderation, though 'it would not please the anti-Unionist masters nor the extreme Unionist leaders', would nevertheless 'place all *equal before the law*, and protect Union funds on one condition, viz. publicity'. He concluded, 'This I think will give an altered tone and character to the local Unions—when all their regulations, movements, bye-laws, and expenditure, come to be published and subjected to severe criticism, the mischief will gradually disappear'. Three weeks later he and Hughes convened a conference of from twenty-five to thirty M.P.s, when Mundella's plea for a moderate bill again won the day.

His moderation brought sharp criticism from the left wing of the unions' advisers. Henry Crompton was among the critics. 'He is not very discreet, and regards the whole question from the Unionist point of view,' confided Mundella to Leader. 'Political Economists and Philosophers are not practical men, and their sympathies are too one-sided for men who want results, as I do. He and some others are just as unfair to the masters as Roebuck is to the men, and I don't mean to do or say anything *unfair to either*.' [8] He got his way. On 10 April, on Mundella's advice, Crompton withdrew a contentious clause from the draft bill, and on 12 May the bill, as amended, secured the unanimous approval of the assembled trade delegates of Sheffield.

Yet, in spite of its moderation, the bill made no headway in the house of commons. So, to accelerate its progress, a deputation waited upon the home secretary, who expressed his firm conviction that the government would take no part in the promotion of the bill. Bruce's uncompromising attitude was a setback. The only course of action now left was a public demonstration. This was staged on 23 June at the Exeter Hall in London, and organised with great skill by Robert Applegarth, who produced two letters, one from John Stuart Mill, the other from Disraeli, wishing the meeting well. Mundella was still 'moderate and conciliatory towards the masters, and', to quote his own words, 'against all rules and proceedings among the men that savoured of an unlawful, irritating or restrictive character'. With Hughes, he pledged himself to go forward with the bill as drafted. The London *Telegraph* commented, 'Mr. Mundella stood forward last night as a champion of organised conciliation, which, thanks to his efforts, has been practised in some towns with signal success'.

At last they secured parliamentary time for its second reading. Mundella made a speech in which he stated, with moderation and reason, the arguments for legalising the unions, adding the opinion which would warm his hearers:

'It is purely a question of free trade in labour. A master is a corporation and can deal singly with his men if they go to him singly. But if they go to him as a Trade Union they are a body equal to himself and a bargain can be made on equal terms.'

Following him, Samuel Plimsoll made a long and irrelevant speech which both the London *Telegraph* and the *Daily News* reported as exhausting the patience of the house. Mundella, commenting on the whole proceedings, wrote:

'I was purposely kept in reserve to answer objectors. I have been greatly complimented on what I said, which certainly produced a great effect, but I never feel satisfied. Plimsoll disgusted the House, our Liberal friends abuse him roundly for his impudence and *rot*.'

Again, in retrospect two days later, he wrote:

'It is surprising how the House of Commons, the Peers and the country, have come round to our views on the right way of legislating for the Trade Unions: even Mr. Potter and the opponents have quitted and thrown up the sponge. The Speaker and many of the leading men in the House have been exceedingly complimentary to me on my speech. The House was very full, and listened with breathless attention, and applauded constantly. But I am wretchedly reported: I think however it was my own fault, for I was very rapid. Plimsoll was absurd and spoilt the whole thing.'

His self-importance can be forgiven. The *Birmingham Daily Post* thought that 'the speech of the afternoon was Mr. Mundella's —it was a bold, powerful and practical defence of strikes, and earnest throughout. He rose at times to eloquence when vindicating the rights of workmen to the freedom of labour.' But Howell, the watchful chronicler of events, had eyes only for young Thomas Brassey, son of the great railway contractor, who made a classic speech which was subsequently published and expanded as *Work and Wages*. In it, Brassey argued that trade unions, far from raising the costs of production, lowered them, since the increased self-respect and intelligent industry of the worker were worth more to an employer than any effort forthcoming from one who was depressed and downtrodden.

The *Economist* was full of praise for Hughes' and Mundella's bill, calling it 'by far the best attempt ever yet made to settle by law that long and complex controversy'. They endorsed two of the three principles of the bill: that men might consent to work or not work, employ or not employ as they like; and that, trade unions being lawful, their property should receive protection. But the *Economist* disapproved of the way in which Hughes and Mundella proposed to realise these principles by allowing trade unions to register their funds. 'The registrar cannot be a detective,' pointed out the *Economist*—'for vouchers could be manufactured for the most subversive or personal ends by an unscrupulous treasurer.' With the third principle—that the offences arising out of trade union membership should be left to the ordinary criminal law— the *Economist* was in emphatic disagreement.[9] *The Times* was more cynical, saying that the only marvel was that the debate 'should have sustained the attention of the House through a series of elaborate speeches, on a theme which, as everyone knew, is to be dropped for the rest of the session'.

It was not dropped without having a positive result, however. For the following Tuesday—13 July—the home secretary introduced a special temporary bill which afforded to trade unions that protection to their funds which men like Applegarth and Odger had so long been demanding. This bill, which was rushed through both houses, did not escape fierce criticism from Lord Cairns, the recently ennobled Conservative peer. When it received royal assent as 32 and 33 Vic. c. 61 on 9 August 1869 it was scheduled to remain operative until the end of the following session. It gave at least a temporary remedy in case of an embezzlement of funds. Howell praised Bruce for his 'prompt and prudent action',[10] but in Sheffield they regarded it as a triumph for Mundella. When he came to the town to speak, on the day Bruce introduced the bill, his enthusiastic supporters removed the horses from his carriage and dragged him in triumph to his hotel.

2

The most vehement opponent of the Trade Unions Bill in the house of commons was Edmund Potter, M.P. for Carlisle, who wound up his long attack with a novel plea in favour of yet another demand of the trade union leaders: 'Many of the trade unionists', he said, 'are uneducated men. The government must therefore not only legislate next year for trade unions; they must bring in a strong education measure; for it is only by a very strong compulsory education bill—I do not care how strong—that we can hope to make much impression on trade unions.' [11]

This novel argument was appreciated by many other manufacturers whose sympathies did not lie with the trade union world. It was very convenient to Applegarth and his colleagues, too, that there should be such support for their own ultimate objectives. So it is not surprising that a common platform was soon created on which these divergent interests could appear in order to promote the cause of national education. This platform was the National Education League, whose provisional committee met in February 1869 at Birmingham. With forty-eight-year-old George Dixon as chairman, thirty-eight-year-old Jesse Collings as secretary and thirty-two-year-old Joseph Chamberlain as vice-president and driving force, the League aimed at making education secular (to remove it out of the hands of priests of all denominations), compulsory (to overcome the tendency of squires and small manufacturers to keep children away from school), and free (in order to overcome the artisan's objection to losing the labour of his children). The League began to press for the establishment of local authorities, empowered to levy a rate, in order to establish schools throughout the country. When the Reform League was dissolved on 16

March, after four years' continuous agitation, many of its members joined this new body. Within nine months from the committee meeting of February 1869 nineteen branch committees were established, forty M.P.s enrolled, and a large fighting fund was built up. Applegarth was seventh on the list of Dixon's original members, and Edmund Potter was to move the appointment of the officers at the first general meeting.

Between the first committee meeting in February and the first general meeting in October 1869, Mundella himself kept the education question well to the forefront of parliamentary attention. The solitary anecdote of his maiden speech was one where the parishioners had appointed a road-mender as teacher of the village school only to find that he was not only incompetent, but irremovable. In an unpremeditated speech on the Poor Laws he made a plea for the 'better employment of those charitable funds, which are sufficient in amount to provide for the education of the whole country', urging Forster to go farther in establishing his endowed schools commission (set up to consider misapplied educational endowments) by empowering them to nationalise non-educational endowments as well. This ambitious suggestion came to nothing. During the recess he spoke at Loughborough on the wretched state of education in the town. He pointed out that 40 per cent of the local children did not attend school—an accusation which infuriated Lord John Manners, the sitting M.P. for Loughborough. Lord John Manners replied that one-seventh of the population was at school. Mundella made an examination of the writing and arithmetic of Loughborough children, in order to present them for public comparison with similar work done by school children in Saxony and Switzerland. 'The contrast', he concluded, 'is something to make an Englishman blush for his country.' His blackening of the educational picture was resented by the Conservatives, who conducted an erasive campaign of denials. But, encouraged by similar statements from members for other industrial areas, W. E. Forster ordered a statistical return to be obtained from the four large towns of Leeds, Liverpool, Manchester and Birmingham. Mundella went back to Sheffield, and in the first of his annual addresses to his constituents in Paradise Square told them:

'The more you educate, the more good you have done, and the more poverty and wretchedness you put an end to. As much money has been wasted over the

73

war in Abyssinia as would educate every child in the British Dominions at the moment. I am not a convert to the League. I have been a convert to national compulsory education for years when many of my friends thought I was going mad.'[12]

Naturally, the League tried to enlist him under its banner, but Mundella was wary. He distrusted their secularity, and told Leader on 20 September 1869:

'Dixon and others are pressing me hard to attend the educational meeting at Birmingham. I am a member of the League, but not in agreement with them in detail. I don't believe we can afford to set aside existing agencies in England. I am not in favour of free schools, and I am sure the word "secular" would not go down at present. They are anxious that I should speak on the general question at the town hall meeting [on 13 October]. I could not do this without explaining how much I differed from them. I want the education. I want enough schools, and sufficient pressure to bring the children to them, but I really don't care how this is accomplished if it is done in fairness to all classes and all creeds.'

Nevertheless, he attended the general meeting on 12–13 October 1869. It was mainly concerned with the discussion of a bill which was to be presented to parliament based on the League programme. When the discussion degenerated into a wrangle between Professors Fawcett and Thorold Rogers as to what constituted a 'secular education' (Fawcett was for reading the Bible without comment, and Thorold Rogers was not), Mundella brought it back to earth by producing a copy of the new North German Labour Act. This prescribed that no child should be allowed to work before he was twelve years old, and then only if he had been to school for six years. He pointed out the extensive provision made therein for half-time attendance at school until the child was sixteen, and that through the length and breadth of Saxony he had not found one illiterate child. He poured scorn on the 'complete failure' of existing Factory Acts in England, pointing out that 'to neglect a child until he is eight, nine or ten years of age, and then, when he first commences work, to insist on his going to school is the most objectionable and unreasonable form of compulsion I think it is possible for the human mind to devise'.

He spoke out strongly against the doctrinaire secularists like George Holyoake: 'The word secular has been scandalously abused. All truth is holy. The order, system and cleanliness of a school are the most religious influences that can be brought to bear.' He forecast that to tamper with the religious suscepti-

74

bilities of the people would be most dangerous for the future of education, and closed his speech with a telling verse:

> 'So have I seen a country on the earth
> Where darkness sat upon the living waters
> And Brutal Ignorance and Toil and Dearth
> Were the hard portion of its sons and daughters.
> And yet where those who should have op'd the door
> Of Truth and Charity to all men's finding,
> Squabbled for words upon the altar floor,
> And rent the Book in struggles for the Binding.'

Forty-nine years later, Robert Applegarth could still remember his prophecy, and wrote to Mundella's daughter, 'He was perfectly right'.[13]

3

Two days before this conference, Forster began to sketch the outlines of an education act which he intended to submit to the cabinet on 21 October. In the memorandum he outlined the courses that lay before him. Two of these plans stressed that the districts should rate themselves; another two that voluntary effort should be induced and tempted to supply such deficiencies as there were. On 24 November he was told that the cabinet had agreed to the preparation of an education bill along the lines of his memorandum.

At this very time Forster was seeing much of Mundella. He had made references in the house of commons during the 1869 session to Mundella's zeal for the Saxon schemes. 'Forster urged me', Mundella told Leader on 7 November, 'to work away at this question, and to stir up the public mind as much as possible. I told him I had doubts about going to Birmingham, as I did not agree with all of their programme.'

Mundella sent Forster copies of his speeches. Forster replied on 5 December expressing his hope that 'the question will be settled this year', and on 9 December urged Mundella to lunch at the Reform Club and 'have some talk'.[14] At one such meeting Mundella brought Applegarth along with him, to confirm his own statements about Swiss education which Forster questioned. Mundella descanted upon Applegarth's observations, adding that he had supplied the data on which they were based. The upshot of this meeting was that Applegarth, who was about to attend a meeting of the International at Basle, prolonged his stay in order to make an educational report for Forster.[15] Mundella was delighted at being the recipient of Forster's confidence, and breathed to Leader: 'All that is known of the Education Bill outside the cabinet, I know, and he [Forster] tells me only, and I am bound to strictest confidence. He has consulted me constantly and relied on my assistance.'[16]

Mundella also carried out an independent investigation on his own account, in order to obtain a complete picture of the average standard of education reached by industrial workers. He examined the employees in his own mill, and persuaded his friends to examine theirs, sending to Stockport, Manchester and Sheffield the forms on which results were to be recorded. On 2 December he received replies from Stockport. Out of 154 children employed (ninety-five of whom were half- and fifty-five full-timers), thirty could not write at all, eighteen wrote wretchedly, and ten only moderately.[17] He sent some of these forms to Leader on 3 January 1870, expressing the wish that Sheffield would take stock of its educational provision, as Birmingham and Manchester had done.

'If say Mr. Allott, Messrs. Cammells, and a few other large establishments,' he wrote, 'would allow someone to test the acquirements of the young persons of eighteen and under, I think it would give a better idea of what remains to be done than volumes of statistics, and would help me in the work that is before me. No one realises it until it is tested in this manner.'[18]

He sent similar forms overseas to Saxony, where H. Felkin, the representative of the Nottingham Hosiery Manufacturing Company, had them completed for him. The replies showed that the sixth standard in English elementary schools was below the lowest Saxon, Prussian or Swiss standard in similar schools.

4

Meanwhile, the inevitable reaction against the aggressive policy of the League set in with the establishment of the National Educational Union, an organisation of all denominations which aimed at 'judiciously supplementing the present denominational system'. The only rate aid envisaged by the union was for pauper children. In this body one of the twin moving spirits was sixty-nine-year-old Edward Baines, the Leeds newspaper editor, whose consistent hostility to any form of state aid to education had broken the back of Cobden's attempts to promote it. The embodiment of the 'very Dissidence of Dissent and the Protestantism of the Protestant Religion', he stood, in Matthew Arnold's eyes at this time, as the perpetuator of social anarchy.[19] With him was the seventy-year-old earl of Harrowby, who earlier in the year [20] had moved the rejection of Gladstone's bill to disestablish the Irish church. Now, with Baines, he initiated the union's counter campaign by meetings at Manchester on 1 October and at Leeds on 6 December. As their programme they put forward a bill which proposed to extend the work of the two societies then undertaking the elementary education of the country 'with such additions as may be needed to complete the education of the working classes'. The union managed to get the support of the earl of Shaftesbury, who, twenty years before, had written in his diary:

'I dread, sadly dread, the schemes for national education. A scheme for local rates to maintain the education of the people is a death warrant to the teaching of the evangelical religion. It had better be called "a water rate to extinguish religious fire among young people".' [21]

5

When, on 17 February 1870, W. E. Forster introduced the government bill, he acknowledged the help he had received both from Dixon and Mundella.

'What is the principle relied on by the hon. member for Birmingham and the hon. member for Sheffield, to whom so much credit is due for stimulating educational zeal in the country?' he asked. 'It is the education of the people's children by the people's officers, chosen in their local assemblies, controlled by the people's representatives in Parliament. That is the principle on which our bill is based; it is the ultimate force behind every clause.' [22]

Forster's bill proposed to fill up the gaps in the existing framework by allowing a year's grace to the two societies in which to make provision for schools. If there was still a deficiency in any district or town after that date, school boards were to be formed to establish schools maintained from a local rate. He steadily set his face against secularism, realising that it would involve his own ostracism.

Mundella's criticism of the bill was directed against the permissive character of the compulsion to attend school. The school boards, he insisted, should be invested with full powers to compel this attendance. Of this the *Economist* wrote, 'We know nothing in the history of English opinion more strange or more suggestive'.[23] On 9 March 1870 Mundella, with Dilke and forty other

M.P.s and 400 members of the League, headed by Joseph Chamberlain, waited upon the Prime Minister at three o'clock in the afternoon. After Chamberlain and Dilke had presented the case for universal rate-aided schools, Mundella described the application of compulsory laws in foreign states.[24] But privately Mundella was annoyed with the doctrinaires and sceptics of the League itself, and wrote to Leader the following day:

'A very indiscrete thing has been done tonight. The secularists in the League are pushing the Nonconformists into antagonism about the religious question. I, and members of the League generally, had arranged for amendment in committee *on compulsion, separation of religious teaching, and universality of school boards.* And we hoped to carry all these. But the secularists in the League, hoping the Nonconformists would support them, have raised a question for a decision on the second reading, which, if carried, *would kill the Bill,* and prevent the question "that this Bill be read a second time" from being put.' [25]

Consequently, when the second reading began on 14 March, Mundella was ready to back Forster against any amendment the League might propose to torpedo the bill. On 18 March he spoke against Dixon's secularising amendment as 'a miserable religious squabble', and urged those participating in it to realise the deplorable state of secular education as it existed. He declared that the religious difficulty existed more in the house than out of it, and urged the members to consider the real essentials of the bill: a conscience clause and compulsion. He quoted extensively from Saxon and American practice.

His speech was very well received. The speaker sent for him to offer his congratulations, telling him that Disraeli acknowledged it as one of the most effective and sensible speeches that he had heard. Gladstone himself referred to it as 'a pre-eminent addition to debate', adding 'I freely and frankly own that it was not without an effort I myself accepted the principle that compulsion must be applied in some effective manner to the control of education'. Dixon withdrew his amendment.

By common consent of members and non-members of the League, Mundella was nominated to move the case for compulsion when clause 65 (which dealt with the attendance of children at school) was discussed on 8 July. Great distrust was expressed of the 'continental system', for which Mundella had such admiration. Mundella advised one of his critics to take a return ticket to Germany in order to see for himself:

'It is said', he continued, 'that compulsion is un-English; but many of the
things which are un-English today become English tomorrow. Slavery was
at one time English, but it had ceased to be so, and I hope to see the time
when pauperism and ignorance would cease to be so too.'

After arguing that England was one of the most paternal
countries in Europe with regard to legislation, yet in compulsion
they were behind the rest, he continued:

'Under the protection of the police I have recently explored some of the
crowded parts of London, and the sights which I have seen were of the most
horrible character. I saw courts in which children, poor, miserable, squalid and
neglected, were as thick as flies in a sugar cask. In one court the children were
so thick that I could hardly help putting foot upon them. Their parents were
in the gin shop. Within a few yards of this House there are thousands of
children who never come in contact with human love, who never hear a virtuous sentiment, who never have any teaching but that of the streets, whose
parents are to be found in the gin-palaces and the public-houses; and yet the
state neglects these children because, forsooth, it respects the "liberty of the
parents". Yes, this is tolerated in the name of civil liberty, of paternal liberty
and of paternal rights; and the results are such, in twenty districts of London,
that no language can describe them, and that none can see them, except under
the protection of the police. I tested dozens of these children, and I did not find
one in twenty who could say the Lord's prayer, or make out words of one
syllable.' [26]

W. E. Forster was moved, acknowledging that he agreed with
Mundella on the question, but that it was impossible to fully
adopt the principle until they had the schools. Accordingly, the
school boards were given the power to enforce compulsion, but
the 1870 Act did not make it obligatory that they should do so.

On 15 July Mundella remained in the house of commons for
seventeen hours in order to press the adoption of the ballot in
school board elections. As he told Leader:

'Without the ballot, the poor ratepayers in the rural districts dare not vote
against the nominees of the squire and the parson. With the ballot, the nonconformists will get a share in the representation. It was the bitterest fight in
which I was ever engaged.'

It was well worth it. Though it is possible to agree with John
Morley, and see in the 1870 Education Act 'nothing better than a
small reform, secured by a sacrifice of principle, which by its
presence on the statute book prevented the Liberal Party from
subsequently accomplishing a bolder measure more in accordance
with Liberal traditions', yet full credit must be given for the
balance which it did retain between the existing schools and those

which were about to be created. This balance it was to be A. J. Mundella's particular function to preserve as the years went on. Indeed, as he grew older, his support of the board schools tended to blind him to other and more suitable vehicles for carrying along his own ideas.

Nothing presents an apter architectural embodiment of the ideas of the Liberals of 1870 than the old board schools, which, blackened now by three-quarters of a century of soot, stand gauntly above the drab Victorian streets. Solid, stone-built structures, they are often compared to prisons. But the more discriminating will notice that the windows were many and large, and there were invariably tiles of good Hanley pottery half-way round the walls. They represented 'the order, system and cleanliness' that were to be brought to bear upon a generation that otherwise would have been dwarfed by the factories. This was the most efficient factory act yet passed, for it did bring the children into schools for part of their lives.

6

In the middle of the debates on the Education Act, Mundella suffered a grievous personal loss. On 16 March 1870 another fire broke out in the buildings of the Nottingham Hosiery Manufacturing Company. It started, like the previous fire in 1859, with a gas explosion, and did most damage in the factory itself. The steam fire-engine, when it arrived, could only play for five minutes at a time, so the firemen had to use the manual pump. Stones were thrown at the windows to get the water through the flames. At a critical moment, just when the fire seemed to be under control, a hose burst, causing great confusion. At eight o'clock the roof fell in. When the fire was finally put out, two stories were gutted, and a large quantity of machinery and cotton destroyed. Fortunately, however, the warehouse was saved.

Three days later Mundella confessed that the fire was a serious loss, not only in destroying stock, but in delaying business. 'The damage will be not short, I think, of £20,000—all machinery. It was a great shock to many,' he wrote to Leader.

7

His main activities of the two sessions had been to give the trade unions some financial security before the law, and his part in the architecture of the 1870 Education Act. There were other marginal activities of his first year which brought him into wider parliamentary circles. One was his attack on the sinecure colonelcies at the War Office and the antiquated system prevailing there for issuing army contracts—'a disgrace to us for years past'.[27] The operations then proceeding against Theodore of Abyssinia he denounced as a great scandal, 'a war of gold reflecting the greatest discredit on all who took part in it'. He told a story to illustrate his meaning:

'A ship was chartered to take out compressed hay at so much the voyage and so much per day demurrage. When the Captain arrived out with his cargo he was kept waiting for months charging demurrage, the mules on the shore dying meanwhile. He was then ordered away to an Indian port, where he was kept waiting for months. He was then ordered out to sea to throw the cargo overboard. That being countermanded he was told "we don't want your hay, take it away, and do what you please with it", and he, knowing where he could find a good market, went and sold it and brought the proceeds home to his owner.'[28]

He capped it with several others. As a result, he was made a member of the select committee to inquire into these and similar abuses.

As a hosier who had profited by invention, he naturally took part in an attempt to modernise the Patent Laws. As then existing, they debarred inventors from seeking the most profitable field for the exploitation of their inventions. This, to Mundella, accounted for the fact that Great Britain had only 2,000 patents a year compared with the 11,000 patents registered annually in the United States.[29] Another abuse against which he spoke was the absurdity of the postal rate, whereby it cost less to post a circular from Palermo to Aberdeen than from the house of commons to the Strand. Here again his naïve linking of the commercial and the educational motive can be seen.

'The cheap penny newspaper is no longer the privilege of the wealthy, but the comfort and relaxation and to a great degree the education of the working classes, and cheap papers have really no circulation through the post.' [30]

He sponsored the County Courts Bill enabling a creditor living more than twenty miles from his debtor to bring an action in the court nearest his home.[31] He roundly denounced the obsolete Game Laws,[32] whose savage punishments kept between 10,000 and 20,000 potential breadwinners 'confined in dungeons'. So, by jolts and goading, and sometimes by concerted action, reform was got under way.

Such efforts brought him to the notice of John Bright (shortly to resign the only Radical seat in the cabinet), who wrote to him asking for some names of 'men whose opinions will carry weight' for nomination to the Ballot Committee.[33] Three months later he was chairman for the second session of the first national congress of the co-operative movement. It lasted for four days, and Thomas Hughes, A. J. Mundella, W. Morrison and Auberon Herbert took the chair in turn. This congress set up the first central board for the movement, to which Mundella was appointed, with Applegarth, Holyoake, Auberon Herbert and T. Hughes. This congress had a great effect on the co-operative movement, and was repeated in succeeding years at Manchester, Birmingham and Bolton. All this activity impressed Gladstone, who 'looked to co-operation as the new influence which should reconcile the mighty powers of capital and labour'.[34]

Mundella vigorously propagated Cobden's principle of free trade. This involved him in a correspondence with Sir Louis Mallet (himself the grandson of a refugee), then secretary of the board of trade. Mallet had been assistant commissioner to Cobden in drawing up the Chevalier Treaty in 1860. He was an ardent disciple of the master, seeing in the extension of these treaties a real hope for the solution of social disorder. Mallet and Mundella met at Nottingham in September 1869, and Mallet was so absorbed in conversation that he left his overcoat and note-book behind. Letters shuttled between the two in November. Mundella insisted that the time was critical, and that the sooner a policy of full free trade was adopted the better, as the 'opening of new markets is one of the most urgent duties of the British Government'. Mallet's reply shows how the permanent official saw the government of the time:

'I quite agree with you that we are on the eve of a movement which, if not absolutely retrograde, will be a dreadful waste of force. I cannot but think that our Government is to a great extent to blame for this untoward combination of adverse circumstances. No one knows better than I how cold and apathetic every Government has been on this subject since Cobden's treaty, and I have always told them that unless you considered that treaty as part of a great policy it was an act of empiricism and deserved the fate with which it is threatened. But Gladstone never regarded it in this light; he never took the slightest interest in the policy, if indeed he ever understood or accepted it.' [35]

Mallet was right. Gladstone, though a great European, seemed to miss the real portent of Cobden's gospel. For as far back as

1835, Cobden had drawn attention to the 'silent and peaceful rivalry of American commerce, the growth of its manufactures, its rapid progress in internal improvements, the superior education of its people and their economical and pacific development'. It was the U.S.A, and not 'the barbarous policy and impoverishing armaments of Russia', which constituted the real menace to the commercial and national prosperity of Great Britain. He staked his reputation that the people of England generally would discover the truth of this before he died. They would have done, too, had the Civil War not taken place.[36]

As a good Cobdenite, it was high time for Mundella to go to America and see things for himself.

CHAPTER FIVE

America, 1870

AS the wrangles over the Education Bill drew to a close, Mundella was aware that his political stature had increased. He posed an imaginary case to Leader:

'Suppose for a moment I had the chance of succeeding Forster or of being the Baxter of the War Office, do you think my constituents would be offended or flattered thereby?'

He himself was rather doubtful:

'I am bound to say I have no faith in our mode of dealing with social questions. I am somewhat of an idealist in politics: I believe we might achieve grand results with a more vigorous government. I should like to see some of my ideas in practice.' [1]

Business weighed him down. He complained:

'The war is a personal trouble to me. It is shutting up our business in Saxony and subjecting us to war levies etc. etc. However, if Germany is victor, and I cannot believe in her being vanquished, I shall be content.' [2]

A week later he continued:

'A depressed trade, a falling market, a terrible loss by fire and a failure in America will, I expect, sweep away all the earnings of the year. To be in Parliament, a man ought to be independent of business. This horrible war is a new and increasing source of anxiety to me.' [3]

A short visit to the war areas in France did nothing to restore his spirits. 'The scenes I have witnessed of butchery and misery make these days [of travelling there] seem like months or years.' His visit, with its inevitable account, provoked Bunce of the *Birmingham Post* to accuse him of 'morbid curiosity'. Mundella was angry, and told Leader:

'The editor is a very low fellow and is angry because I acted independently of the League. Singularly enough, Dixon preceded me on the same route by one day, and is about to visit the German schools with my introductions and accompanied by my friends.' [4]

I

On 3 September 1870 he and Tom Hughes sailed for America. As their ship was in the Channel, the Emperor Napoleon was surrendering his army. A feeling of suppressed excitement had gripped England which it did Mundella good to escape. His visit had a definite purpose. He himself said:

'I resolved before leaving England to make myself acquainted, as far as time would allow, with features of the American social and political scene bearing upon questions in agitation in Great Britain with a view to proximate legislation.'

The major part of his time was spent in New York and Boston. In the three months at his disposal he worked to a plan, and did not indulge in the normal run of sight-seeing. By contrast, Tom Hughes saw the Middle West from the private saloon of an American railway magnate,[5] and entertained readers of the *Spectator* with his accounts.

The American correspondent of the *Glasgow Herald* (which had no political connections with Mundella at all) was moved to write about him in almost lyrical vein:

'So many Englishmen who visit us, skim over the continent as much as a bird skims over the surface of a lake, never understanding our people or our institutions, and returning to misrepresent us, that we have more than a kindly feeling for one who is not led astray by his first impressions.'

At the first school which Mundella visited in New York he met Thomas Hughes. Mundella arrived at the school ten minutes late to find Hughes addressing more than 900 girls, and was himself called upon for a similar task. He visited the Girls' High Normal School in Fourth Street North, and marvelled at the competence of the women teachers and the attractive and healthy appearance of the pupils. The normal schools, as opposed to the Latin schools, made a great impression on him. It is tempting to think that he regarded them as possible models for imitation in England, where, apart from the endowed grammar schools and public schools (counterparts to the American Latin schools), no secondary education for the masses existed.[6]

Mundella was regarded as a person of sufficient consequence to be introduced to the President.[7] The *New York Tribune* of 1 November recorded the fact that:

'A. J. Mundella Esq., M.P. for Sheffield, England, called on Secretary Boutwell[8] to-day, and was by him introduced to the President, with whom he had a very pleasant interview. He examined the Treasury Department thoroughly, taking especial interest in the system of examination for appointments so recently adopted.[9] He afterwards called on Secretary Cox[10], General Parker of the Indian Bureau[11], and General Eaton, Commissioner of Education.

'Mr. Mundella thinks our school system the most liberally endowed and sustained of any in the world, and declared that our educational buildings, interior arrangements and apparatus are unequalled, although there are serious defects in our system of teaching, qualifications of instructors, and in want of laws enforcing attendance. He is surprised to find so little attention paid to technical designing, and other special schools intended for the industrial arts and sciences.'

His outspoken appreciation of the merits and defects of American schools was not the only occasion when Mundella delivered himself of his opinion, or learnt something to his advantage. At Boston he was so impressed with the school furniture of the Rice School that he begged a chair and desk to bring to England and exhibit to his hearers. Philbreck, the local director of schools, accompanied him. Mundella was struck with the truly democratic nature of the schools, and said later:

'. . . there side by side in school sit the child of the governor of the state, the child of the Irish immigrant, the young gentleman with his gold watch and chain, and the child of the negro, all receiving the same education. It makes me more disposed than before in favour of free education.' [12]

There was a lighter side. At a party given in Boston by James T. Fields (then resigning from the editorship of the *Atlantic Monthly*), a notable company assembled to meet Mundella. Emerson, Lowell—who ten years later was to become ambassador to England when Mundella was a Minister of State—R. H. Dana and Oliver Wendell Holmes were present. Mundella surprised them all, especially Holmes, when he drew out of his pocket a letter from his daughter Polly, in which she expressed her fervent wish that he should meet the author of *Autocrat of the Breakfast Table* and *Professor at the Breakfast Table*. Holmes was nonplussed by such demonstrative admiration, thinking that Mundella must have been 'run away by his amiable feelings'. He quickly realised his mistake, however, and wrote to Mundella on the 20 October:

'But I assure you I believed every word you said before I had been with you five minutes, and I know I need not assure you it gave me a pleasure, which I hope I did not betray too visibly. You must remember I know you as a public man who has a perfect right to know nothing of his transatlantic neighbours, except their loyal interest. I did not think my thoughts had found a nest so high up.' [13]

Mundella was delighted with the success of his visit, and on returning to New York wrote to Robert Leader:

'I am worked as hard as in our Parliamentary session. . . . I don't know how to describe my visit here.

'I never received so much lavish hospitality in the whole of my life. The very best possible people here (and there are some splendid specimens of the Anglo-Saxon) vie with each other in honouring me and contributing to my pleasure and to the objects of my journey. All the public institutions are open to me, and the commissioners of the schools go with me everywhere and explain everything. I have already accumulated about a library of useful reports on Education, Charitable Institutions, Liquor Laws, Patents, Prisons, etc. etc. My brain is in the condition of a sponge that cannot absorb more without squeezing out something.

'I have seen our old friend Goldwin Smith, and am going to, I think, spend a day or two at Cornell University. Sumner, David Wells, Wilson, Clapton and the really eminent politicians have opened their minds to me freely. I shall be spending my time with the Hon. D. A. Wells when you receive this. He is the Political Economist and Free-Trader of America and the coming man.

'The most intellectual and influential club of New York, the "Century", gave a magnificent banquet to Hughes and myself last Tuesday, W. C. Bryant the poet being in the chair. Speeches of the most friendly character to England were made by the most influential and ablest men in the city.

'At Boston I made the acquaintance of dear Longfellow, Russell Lowell, Oliver Wendell Holmes, Dana, Wendell Phillips, Sumner and many others. I spent all my time with them and felt like leaving dear old friends on parting with them. They have written and said the kindest and most flattering things about me and have made me feel that Sheffield has conferred upon me the greatest honours. Not a little of this, however, results from my having defeated Roebuck. I can never convey to you how bitterly his words are remembered by this people. His name above all others is most offensive to them. His power of stinging seems to have exceeded our English estimate of it.

'I have taken every opportunity of acquainting myself with the elementary and high schools systems here, together with the working of the Prohibitory Laws, Patent Laws, Ballot, Tariff, etc. etc., and have derived a mass of information and new light that I hope to turn to good account in the future. I am also "en rapport" with the parties in the "Sheffield" steel difficulty and have communicated with Mr. W. Smith about it, and hope to be of some service in facilitating smooth working in future. But not a word of this at present.' [14]

Two days before he returned to England, Mundella lectured in New York 'to the largest audience their largest hall could contain'. The platform was filled with eminent men.[15] He gave an address which the radical newspapers in England eagerly recorded.[16] In it he sketched the main lines on which he expected English legislation to run for the next ten years: compulsory education, justice in Ireland, the abolition of the religious tests for universities, the repeal of laws affecting trade unions, state control of educational endowments, protective legislation for factory workers and miners: all of which he was himself to play such a

87

great part in promoting. He pointed out how such measures impinged on the general education of England and America, where illiteracy and ignorance underlay the 'war of classes' which was causing so many strikes. He returned to his familiar theme:

'We are an old country, where all the resources of nature are already appropriated. We have old wrongs to redress, old neglects to repair, old class prejudices and distrusts to remove. . . . Labour can only stand on equal terms with capital when it is associated.'

2

The speech certainly had an effect not only on those who heard it, but also on the country at large. Some of Mundella's sentiments did not please a section of the American working men, so the New York Working Men's Union took action. On the 18 November 1870 they held a meeting, and a Mr. O'Keefe asked the chairman, Nelson W. Young, whether Mundella had given this address in the interests of capital or labour. Mr. Young temporised, and suggested that perhaps Mr. Mundella did not understand the working of labour unions in the United States. The meeting then unanimously adopted a resolution that:

'We condemn that part of Mr. Mundella's address delivered on the 14th inst., which says "every man has a right to decide for himself whether he will or will not be a member of a trade organisation", as the doctrine put forward by that gentleman has already done the trade unions of America the greatest amount of injury.' [17]

The meeting went on to engage the Cooper Hall for a discussion of the labour question and Mr. Mundella's views upon it.

Others were not so critical. Ten years later, R. H. Dana wrote from Rome asking if he had a copy of it for the Italian Prime Minister. 'For', wrote Dana, 'I wish him to see it as it struck me at the time, as one of the striking presentations of the great dangers and defects of our present system that I had ever seen.' [18] C. R. Fay has endorsed the effect of Mundella's advocacy of social peace, pointing out that of the threefold choice which faced American workers in the seventies—i.e. Marx and Trade Unionism; Lassalle and Politics; or Mundella and Arbitration—they chose the last.[19]

Oliver Wendell Holmes wrote to assure him that 'you have left an impression of your intelligence and character among us such as few visitors whom I have met have left, or others are like to do'. [20] John Eaton, Commissioner of Education, and zealous crusader for free schools, wrote to Mundella to congratulate him on 'the good you accomplished among us by your visit'.[21] He enclosed the annual reports of his department, an honour he reserved for only three other English politicians: W. E. Gladstone, W. E. Forster and John Bright. Another prominent American educator, Birdsey Grant Northrop, who, as secretary to the Connecticut State Board of Education, had established free schools and compulsory attendance, came over to England to testify to Mundella's good work in America. In 1872, just before Northrop went to Japan to 'westernise' that country's educational system, he visited Mundella in England. He was invited to the Trades Union Congress then assembled at Nottingham, where he told the delegates:

'The people of my state are very grateful to Mr. Mundella for spreading the truths of the grand principle of arbitration there. I have by tongue and pen often given circulation to the views expressed by Mr. Mundella, and I am happy to think that by this means he has contributed greatly to the welfare of the working men of Connecticut.' [22]

For Mundella's outlook in industrial affairs had impressed many Americans. David A. Wells, the great free-trader adviser to Presidents Garfield and Cleveland, was then chairman of the New York Tax Commission. He and Mundella kept up a correspondence on the latter's return, exchanging statistics and commercial information.[23]

3

America certainly impressed Mundella. Like all returned travellers, he was inclined to dilate upon his visit.

'In America', he wrote to Leader, 'I have been treated with distinction and hospitality far beyond any merits of my own. I have been honoured with the confidence of the most distinguished men of the country. . . . I possess some knowledge of schools and scholastic institutions which will be of value to the new school boards. . . . I have exercised considerable influence in public and private on the future relations of the country, and have some information for Mr. Gladstone.' [24]

He was not exaggerating. The school boards did use his information and help. The London School Board invited him to confer with them on the subject of their compulsory bye-laws, and he attended on them for an hour and a half for that purpose.[25]

In Sheffield a meeting was arranged, to which Mundella brought along the chair and desk he had begged from the Rice School in Boston. He spoke for two hours to a good crowd, and impressed his political opponents in the town. One of them confessed that though he had voted for Roebuck in 1868, his next vote would be for Mundella. Another, wiser than he knew, prophesied that Mundella would be Minister of Education in the future.[26]

Still more satisfactory were the results of his talks with Gladstone and Forster. 'Both of them', he exulted to Leader, 'are struck with my suggestions and information.'[27] Three months later he again wrote:

'After a long time with Gladstone I went to Forster and we spent two nights in succession at the club, and discussed the position of the American Question, and the possibility of International Arbitration. He told me he had not been able to sleep for thinking of it and he would go to work on it in the Cabinet.'

Mundella's help was not confined to exhortation. 'I have been engaged with Forster getting out a list of leading names in America, with their characters and opinions, for Earl de Grey's guidance,' he told Leader, announcing that de Grey had sailed for the States in the *Cuba*.

The impress of this visit can be seen in his speeches in the house of commons, where his steady advocacy of American material assets weighed with Forster. Perhaps most important of all was the sense of mission it gave to him, as it had given to Cobden twenty-five years before.

The *Spectator* speculated as to whether he would get a position in the government. Mundella duly noted it, but commented to Leader on New Year's Day 1871: 'I will not be a silent official, and I know already that aristocratic influence is as yet too strong for Gladstone to resist.' This hard core was very visible to those who, like himself, stood on the periphery of office. He observed three months later:

'We have in Osborne, Peel and other hungry but disappointed place-seekers, a bad lot of half Tory whiglings. The government has not been so wise and firm as it might and ought to be, arising really from Gladstone's susceptible conscientiousness.'

In spite of rumours in the *Standard*, he was firmly of the opinion that he would never be offered anything. 'I have let them under-

stand that I could not support their extravagant policy', he wrote.
'I am better out of office, I think, during this parliament.'

He was. The session was even more active than the two preceding ones. It needed all his close application both inside and
outside the house to keep pace with what was afoot, and abreast of
what he and others intended should be done.

CHAPTER SIX

Drawing Away from the Pack, 1871

I

ON his return from America, Mundella was plunged into the examination of what was perhaps the most distasteful aspect of Victorian life—the increased incidence of venereal disease. So rife had this become in the armed forces that the Contagious Diseases Acts had been passed to segregate garrison towns from the rest of the country. In these garrison towns the police were given power to effect an examination of any woman suspected of carrying infection. Passed first in 1864, and later extended in scope, these acts provoked great resentment, since they embodied no higher conception of womanhood than that of safe fornicating instruments for the armed forces. Hostile feelings were voiced by Josephine Butler (herself the daughter of an anti-slavery crusader), who devoted herself to working for their repeal. In 1869 she founded, and acted as secretary to, the Ladies National Association for Repeal of the Contagious Diseases Acts. On her side she enlisted a number of important provincial politicians, among them H. J. Wilson of Sheffield. So successful was her agitation, that by 1870 a Royal Commission was appointed to examine the efficiency of the acts.

From 14 December 1870 to 13 May 1871 Mundella sat as a member of this commission. He has left the best extant account of the remarkable change of heart which came over it. The majority started by being strong supporters of the acts; only Mundella and three other members were not hostile to Josephine Butler. As the ghastly, sordid details were elicited from the eighty-four witnesses who testified in favour of the acts, the contradictions inherent in their enforcement became apparent. So much so, that Charles Buxton (who was vice-president of a society for extending the scope of the acts) ended by coming out strongly in favour of their repeal. Others similarly affected were F. D. Maurice, and Dr. Bridges.

'We fought clause by clause, and word by word over the report as if it were a battle in parliament,' said Mundella. The struggle was, however, so indecisive that their report was confused and contradictory. It recommended that the periodic and compulsory examination of women should cease, but that the acts should be further extended to cover certain districts. Mundella, disgusted by the whole affair, bitterly regretted having assented to its publication. He maintained that the acts were wrong, and signed a declaration to that effect. Furthermore, he and others urged that power should be vested in a central sanitary authority to institute proper means for the effective treatment of venereal disease in every large centre of the population, not only in the eighteen garrison towns.

From this time onwards he became one of the firmest and foremost opponents of the acts, and fearlessly spoke out for their repeal. Nor did he confine his attention to occasions when they were the specific topic of discussion, but carried on his campaign in the debates on the estimates.[1] He urged that the acts, if necessary, should apply to men as well as women, and that a celibate army should be abolished. He pressed for the raising of the legal age of seduction to sixteen, since over 25 per cent of the victims of venereal disease were under this age. Though he never sacrificed as much as James Stansfeld in the cause, he was fearless in upholding it.

2

Such evils were aggravated by the armed forces. As 1871 saw the biggest army estimates since the year of Waterloo, it is not surprising that Mundella severely criticised any further expansion of the forces which might end in yet more demoralisation. Others were at hand to help. Sir Charles Dilke held a breakfast on 4 March at his house [2] to discuss ways and means of assaulting the estimates, which were to be discussed sixteen days later.

This brought Mundella still farther into the open. He proposed the adjournment of the debate, and persuaded Gladstone to agree to it. Disraeli jeered at Mundella's persuasive powers, and Gladstone wrote telling him 'not to mind the opposition bluster, which merely indicates the absence of substantial grounds of attack'. A day later he moved that 'the army be put in a state of efficiency without increasing the estimates'.

His long speech was so laced with fact that Lord Eustace Percy wondered where he got his figures.[3] He called for the abolition of sinecures, the pruning of the Horse Guards' influence and the abolition of the 'old lags'. The remedies he advocated were simple: short service, more volunteers and better organisation. He quoted:

> 'More men? More men? that's where we fail;
> Weak things grow weaker still by lengthening;
> For what's the good of adding to the tail,
> When it's the head's in want of strengthening?'

The extra £3,000,000 should be spent on making the people more intelligent. He pointed to the significant words of the German Emperor and the coming contest that they foreshadowed: 'Henceforth it will be the task of the German people to make themselves victorious in the universal competitions of the nations in time of peace'. This, to Mundella, implied yet further educational reform.

No chance came for taking action in this matter for the next four months, during which the debates on the Ballot Act had served to enhance the urgency of the education of the working classes. The day after the house of commons had gravely discussed the ability of the average British citizen to mark a cross on the ballot paper, Mundella delivered a vehement speech in favour of making the compulsion of the 1870 Act a very real thing. So carried away by his argument was he that he cried, 'I believe there is no good elementary school in the country'. Undeterred by cries of 'Oh! oh!' from members, he went on to demand German teaching and American buildings. He pointed out that the problem affected not only industrial success, but also the maintenance of social peace: 'As long as the people are kept in ignorance, we shall have difficulty in settling social questions and questions of capital and labour, and we will have wages eked out by poor relief in the country.'[4]

His speech stung more than one to reply. Among them was C. B. Adderley—a wealthy Conservative ex-Vice-President of the Council—who strongly disapproved of Mundella's continued disparagement of his own country. Adderley (later ennobled as Lord Norton) was to become one of Mundella's sternest critics.

3

In the midst of such grisly and arduous business, none the more palatable for being unpopular, Mundella was called in, as the faith-

ful ally of the trade unions, to help them fight a government bill
introduced as a result of the lapse of the 1869 Act which had given
them temporary security for their funds. Introduced five days after
parliament had been opened by the Queen in person, the bill was
prefaced by a dreary account of past legislation in favour of trade
unions. The bill itself (described by the *Economist* as 'suited to the
present temper of men's minds') abolished the common law super-
stition that trade unions were not to be recognised because they
were 'in restraint of trade'. It proposed to give the unions the
same rights as were enjoyed by joint-stock companies—i.e. to
join together for legal objects and to act together in legal ways.
It further proposed to establish a system of legal registration
which would safeguard them from absconding treasurers. As a
charter of existence it was considerable, and a great advance
on the temporary act of 1869, which had lapsed at the end of
1870.

But, for the labour leaders, the bill carried a sting in its tail.
This was embodied in the third clause, which enacted that no
workman should use violence to anyone, or venture to molest
anyone for trade union purposes, under penalty of being sent to
prison for three years. This 'intimidation and molestation' (to use
the words of the bill itself) was given such a large and expansive
definition that it extended to punishing a trade unionist for
'persistently following a fellow workman about from place to
place'.

So they rallied to agitate for the curtailing of this obnoxious
third clause. On 1 March (a fortnight after the bill had been
printed), delegates of the London Trade Societies met under
George Odger's chairmanship in the Sussex Hall, Bouverie Street.
Applegarth read the report of the 'junta', in which the removal of
the obnoxious clause was recommended. When Odger moved
that the meeting 'deeply regretted such an illiberal obnoxious
clause should have found its way into an otherwise Liberal bill',
he got a unanimous vote of support. Preparations were therefore
hurriedly made for an emergency Trade Union Congress to meet
as soon as possible.

When Mundella met the delegates to this congress in the Port-
land Rooms on 6 March he was given a tumultuous welcome,
which, if anything, redoubled when he agreed to head a deputation
to the home secretary in order to protest against the offending

clause. He followed this by advising them to have a clear list of the amendments which they required. When he withdrew, Odger told the congress:

'If we picked the House of Commons through, we could not find two more earnest men with regard to Trade Unions than Mr. Mundella and Mr. Hughes. They are prepared to attend our meetings, to consult with us and to learn our opinions, to understand our especial considerations, and to arrive at conclusions which they believed would be calculated to benefit the future conditions of our societies. These two gentlemen are strongly of the opinion,' continued Odger, 'that the third clause ought to be struck out, and they are willing to make a statement to that effect in no uncertain terms in the House of Commons.'

So, on Thursday 9 March, Mundella took the deputation to the home secretary. Bruce defended himself and his bill, yet promised to consider their grievances. In the few days that followed, a more extreme party among the unionists, led by George Potter, editor of the *Beehive*, wanted the second reading of the bill to be deferred, professing themselves entirely dissatisfied with it. Mundella, in a letter to Leader, written two days after the deputation, showed a way out of the impasse:

'The unionists complain of the third clause on account of its very complicated and obscure chapter of offences, and its implications that they ratten. They are willing that the offences as described by Mr. Bruce shall be severely dealt with, but that interference with the freedom of Labour shall be dealt with by the Criminal Law and apply equally to all classes.
'I think they are right, but if the objection were only sentimental, I think it would be wise to take them at their word, and by the simple expedient of dividing the bill, settle the question.' [5]

That was done. On 26 March Bruce divided the bill into two parts. The first part consisted of the original bill, minus the obnoxious third clause. The second part was re-christened the Criminal Law Amendment Act.

On the 1 April, Mundella wrote to Leader:

'This has come on twice in succession after twelve o'clock. I have spoken repeatedly, but the reporters run away at midnight. The bill has really been modified *at every stage*. In committee several alterations were made to relax the stringency of the third clause—*none* to increase it. I am waiting the reprints of the bills (promised for Monday) to see if anything further can be done. I feel bound to fight for the most liberal measure that can be obtained, and really it will place Trade Unions on a very different footing to the old law. The *Beehive* seems determined not to understand the bill. *Everything is legal* except certain offences named in the third clause and they are illegal only when done with a *view to coerce*.'

THE ELECTION RIOT AT NOTTINGHAM IN 1865

The first part of the bill, giving the trade unions the right to exist side by side with joint-stock companies as states within the state, became law three months later.[6] The junta was satisfied with it as a measure, and remarked, 'If this was all the government had done and nothing more, they would be fully entitled to the gratitude of the working class for fully and faithfully redeeming the promises they have made.' With that pious expression of gratitude, the junta dissolved. It had been in existence for four years as the high command of the trade union movement. It had assumed power in the dark days when the unions were fighting for their existence before the law. Its dissolution was inevitable when that existence was guaranteed.

Its successor was the Parliamentary Committee of the Trade Union Congress, which took violent exception to the Criminal Law Amendment Act.[7] This, the second part of the original bill, stemmed from the original clause three. It was to be the thorn in the trade union flesh for the remainder of the life of the ministry. As a manifesto issued on 7 October ran:

'Instead of the spirit of fairness, the same class bitterness and prejudices as of old characterise the passing of this measure, which for unjustness and one-sidedness exceeds the old law which it supersedes. When the bill left the House of Commons, it was in all conscience arbitrary enough; but on its return from the House of Lords, its worst features were intensified a hundredfold; and in this form, in spite of the appeals of the government, it was passed into law.'

4

Mundella had been eagerly forwarding a measure of his own, for which he secured the enthusiastic backing of the trade unions. This was to curtail the employment of children in brick and tile yards. Labour support was reinforced by the names of Lord Sandon, Thomas Hughes, Auberon Herbert and Bernhard Samuelson. Lord Shaftesbury gave his blessing to the movement, and wrote to wish Mundella 'success and a crown of laurels', offering to move an address to the Crown if Mundella was not successful.[8] Such action was not needed. After the bill had been read a second time, Lord Morley incorporated it in his own Factory and Workshop Act. This effected Mundella's aim. The employment of girls under sixteen and boys under ten in brick and tile yards was now prohibited. No fewer than 35,000 were thereby given the opportunity to attend school.

G   97

But not all Mundella's measures had this success. He remarked to Leader on the changed temper of London political circles:

'London Society', he wrote on 28 May, 'is horrified and alarmed at the news from Paris and is leaning to the opinion that all Liberal progress means the confiscation of property and the cutting of throats. Sorry reaction seems likely to follow and the bad management of our own government comes in opportunely to assist it.'

5

By the middle of the year there were troubles in the labour world. George Potter, the restless editor of the *Beehive*, was dissatisfied, and it was not long before Conservative opportunists began to fish for him. Their agent was, singularly enough, a sixty-three-year-old marine engineer called John Scott Russell. Scott Russell had a flair for technical invention. He had developed the wave-line system of ship construction, and had also built road-carriages to be driven by steam. As secretary of the Society of Arts, he had won the regard of the Prince Consort. This regard seemed to influence his life profoundly. Scott Russell imbibed the Prince's conception that the national welfare depended on technical education. Not only was he one of the joint secretaries of the 1851 exhibition, but he was also one of the nine purchasers of the building when the exhibition was finished. In 1871 he was engaged in designing the great rotunda for the exhibition at Vienna.[9]

One of his minor engineering triumphs had been to design a ship that would carry trains across Lake Constance. This conception he applied to English politics by essaying to carry the labour leaders over to the Conservative party. From Westwood Lodge, Sydenham, he launched 'The New Social Movement'— the inspiration of which he attributed to the late Prince Consort, who, said he, 'had furnished him with letters of introduction' by which 'I was able to study all that wonderful organisation for the culture and discipline of the people, which in the case of the Prussian nation has produced such a result'. With a man Friday— P. Barry—he conceived the Disraelian idea of dishing the whigs by forming a 'Council of Legislation' (consisting of peers) and a 'Council of Workmen' (consisting of the labour leaders). These, he alleged, had agreed on a seven-point programme: self-government for the counties, an eight-hour day, a homestead law, technical education for the masses, the establishment of public markets and public recreation places, and the purchase of public undertakings (like the railways) by the state.

Among the so-called members of the Council of Legislation were a formidable galaxy of Conservative peers and commoners: the earls of Lichfield and Carnarvon, the marquis of Salisbury, Lords Henry Lennox and John Manners, Sir John Pakington, Sir Stafford Northcote and Gathorne-Hardy. The duke of Richmond, the earl of Derby and Disraeli were said to be sympathetic.[10] The Council of Workmen embraced, in addition to Potter, the names of Daniel Guile and that of the chairman of the Labour Representation League. The focus of the enterprise on their side was the *Beehive* office.

After a socialistic speech by Sir John Pakington at Leeds on 6 October 1871, the papers were full of the scheme. In the flood of comment on the disclosures of an alleged pact that was said to have been signed at Carlton House Terrace, the *Observer* soberly remarked that 'the story was substantially correct in so far as the preliminary negotiations were concerned'. This struck a chill in many a Liberal heart which remembered 1867 and the dishing of the whigs.

At first Mundella was inclined to scoff at the idea, and told Leader on 13 October:

'The story about an alliance between Toryism and the leaders of the working men is all nonsense. I will answer for Applegarth. He is sound and true to the government and Liberal principles. I am quite sure from my conversations with Pakington that there is no danger of his side going in for reduced hours, but they are willing to take up social questions and ride them.'

Leader, however, remarked in the *Sheffield Independent* the following day: 'The novelty of the idea has electrified the old party managers, who are beginning to feel that the end of the world is at hand'. The presence of the name of Lord John Manners in the group of signatories gave grounds for believing that this was indeed the materialisation of the ideas of *Sybil*, and that the Liberal thunder would be stolen by dreamy patrician reformers. This in turn prompted Mundella to reply on 18 October:

'Potter is a humbug, and lives pretty much on *doles*. What *The Times* can be about to make so much of such a weak fellow I cannot understand. The Tories mean trying to get some hold on some of these men, but they will not pay the price.'

But bit by bit evidence appeared. Mundella, having found that Applegarth had been working for the alliance, admitted that 'it is not such a myth as the Tories wish to make it out'. It provoked him to write on 23 October:

'I have no doubt but the *fools of the party* have left a loophole to escape through, and I doubt if Scott Russell on his return from Vienna will find himself able to produce the signatures of the peers, etc., but I am convinced that Pakington and others of Disraeli's tools have been bidding for the working men through a socialistic programme. The worst feature of modern politics is, to my mind, the absence of a really honest opposition. It is dangerous work when the professed advocates of Conservatism are prepared to go to all lengths for the attainment of power. Applegarth admits the whole thing, and admits they will have a complete showing up of the intriguers on Scott Russell's arrival.'

By the 29 October, Mundella was firmly convinced that a tory plot to capture the working-class vote had been afoot, and that the *Daily News* was on the right scent. He took good care to see that Applegarth did not sign the propositions, and was present when George Potter published the official trade union repudiation of the whole affair, commenting, 'These fellows are very foolish and ignorant, after all'.

So significant did the movement appear in official Liberal circles, that Gladstone in his first public address since becoming prime minister to his constituents at Blackheath on 28 November devoted some time to criticising it.

'Those who propose to you—whoever they may be—schemes like those seven points of which I have spoken,' he told them, 'those who promise to the dwellers in the towns that every one of them shall have a house and a garden in free air, with ample space; those who tell you that there shall be markets for selling at wholesale prices retail quantities—I won't say they are impostors, because I have no doubt they are sincere; but I will say they are quacks.' [11]

6

There were more serious threats to the party than 'the New Social Movement'. The licensing question, which was to provide the Conservatives with the support of publicans and brewers for the next generation, first appeared on the legislative programme of the government in this year. In the summer Bruce introduced a drastic bill, and from that moment onwards Mundella, in common with many other Liberal members, knew no peace. On 25 April he forecast:

'The Licensing Bill will be a source of violent agitation. The brewers and publicans are behaving like madman, and I have had several letters equivalent to notice to quit. I shall certainly support the second reading of the bill, and amend it as far as I can. I should be unworthy of a seat in the House if I hesitated on this question, and I have faith enough in the energy and devotion of my friends in Sheffield who care for national morality that they will be able to counteract the influence of the drink seller.'

When the government withdrew their bill, Mundella was critical, and at midnight on 17 May he wrote: 'I think the government behaved ill in withdrawing their bill just as the country was arousing itself to push it through'. He objected to prohibition, and preferred a good system of licensing. To that purpose, he, together with Sir R. Anstruther, Tom Hughes, Bernhard Samuelson and Sir Harcourt Johnstone, introduced a suspensory bill. On this, Mundella wrote to Leader on 25 May:

'All this is in favour of respectable houses, and will increase their value. I need not tell you that it is not at all a pleasant thing for me to vote for the Permissive Bill. I knew it would prove vexatious and disappointing. Still, it is only the fear of this that has brought "the Trade" to reason.'

A torrent of abusive letters descended upon him, warning him that the next election in Sheffield would be decided on the licensing question. He sent some of them to Leader on 23 June as 'specimens of polite literature, of which I receive more, I think, than the whole House of Commons. You have some very original people in Sheffield.' As its effects became visible, he remarked on 10 November, 'I expect the Licensing Bill will wreck us and be the forerunner of dissolution'. Twelve days later he moaned again, 'The publicans will unhorse a good many of us'.

7

But, as if that were not enough to embarrass the government, the younger radicals started a republican movement. Mundella had no sympathy with them, and complained, 'I cannot go after all sorts of political hares with the madcaps of the Radical Party'. [12] He warned Auberon Herbert (who in most matters was content to accept his guidance) that 'such conduct merely widens the breach between class and class, divides the aim of the Liberal Party, defers needful and attainable reforms to grasp at shadows and tilt at windmills'. [13] Of Dilke he confessed:

'Dilke has surprised me by his folly. These extremists are doing the work of reaction better than a hundred Tories like John Manners. They drive away both the timid and extreme men from our party, and will land us in a minority before long.' [14]

On 23 October he wrote again:

'School fees promises to be another wedge into the Liberal Party. I wish the critics would provide a solution. They evidently forget all about *Education*. I met Dilke last week; he and Fawcett sneer at the School Fees and Conscience Question, but glory in what they believe to be the advance of secularism. Forster will not yield an inch, and really I cannot see how he could if he would.'

Consequently, he turned his own attention to wooing the labour groups for the Liberal party. Applegarth, who had been ejected from the secretaryship of his union for consenting to serve on the Contagious Diseases Commission, was given a useful part-time post with the Capital and Labour Committee of the Social Science Association. He wrote to tell Leader: 'I am working him as a settler among the working men in forming Boards of Conciliation. Hence his visit here. He will be true to me. At any rate, he can say no ill of me.' [15] Applegarth did remain loyal. A month later, 'plodding about in the rain, snow, hail and blizzards of Lancashire', he wrote asking Mundella to write a circular for a board of arbitration in the cotton trade, adding, 'You can write such a circular better than anyone I know. I will give you the ground-work . . . if issued promptly, this will have an important bearing on several disputes in the Burnley district.' [16]

8

At Newcastle, 9,500 engineers under the leadership of John Burnett, despite the disapproval of the secretary of their trade union, stayed out on strike for a nine-hour day. Mundella's old Chartist mentor, Thomas Cooper, happened to be passing through the town in the course of his self-appointed duty as a Lecturer in Christianity. Writing to Mundella from Newcastle on 13 September, he enclosed one of his little tracts, with the inscription, 'I mark the patriotic course of my old Chartist pupil with no little pride and joy'.

At the same time, Mundella received a letter from Thomas Brassey (who served with him on the Capital and Labour Committee of the Social Science Association) urging him to offer his services as a mediator. This Mundella did, and replied to Cooper, suggesting that in this position he might be of service to the men in their negotiations with Sir William Armstrong. Cooper answered on 19 September :

'I have called thrice on my old disciple Joseph Cowen Jnr. today and cannot see him. Give me another day and I will see what can be done. He knows what the men will be likely to do far better than I. As for the masters, I fear there is little hope of them. They have now brought several of the men before the local Magistrates—after 16 weeks absence from work!—and got them convicted of "breaking contracts"!! I assure you that the feeling is so bitter among the men that I see little chance of their taking any part in *proposing* arbitration.

'But as I have already said, give me another day (for I leave Newcastle for South Shields on Thursday) that I may see Joseph Cowen, and if possible, *with him* see some of the strike committee.'

The following day Cooper had further progress to report:

'I have had an hour's conversation with Burnett, the chairman of the Nine Hours League, and Joseph Cowen Jnr. I may assure you *at once* they rejoice at learning your proposal and *feel sure* that a visit from you must be productive of good—if it did not issue complete success. They are decidedly of the opinion that the sooner you are *here*, the better.

'They wish me, however, to tell you that you must *not* come, as being sent for, or in any way desired to come *by the Men*—for, if you do, Sir William Armstrong and Co. will *not* listen to you. But Joseph Cowen suggests that as you are Vice-President of a Committee of the Social Science Association for enquiry into the practicability of arbitration &c. you should appear in *that* character. Your *first* step therefore will be to write *personally* to Sir Wm. Armstrong & also to "John Burnett, President of the Nine Hours League, Westgate Inn, Newcastle-on-Tyne", stating that in your character as said Vice-President, you wish for an interview with Sir William & with Mr. Burnett, in order to ascertain whether the strike cannot be ended, and perfect concord be restored.

'It would be better that your notes should be dated from the Station Hotel, Newcastle-on-Tyne, and that you should come over, at once, and send your notes from thence—telling Sir Wm. Armstrong that you will call upon him in an hour—or two hours, if you think it better. And also sending the note to Burnett to the Westgate Inn and desiring him to call on Joseph Cowen at the Chronicle Office and come to you immediately.'

He then went on to relay the suggestions of Burnett and Cowen:

'Mr. Burnett & Mr. Cowen wish you to have a *prepared* mind when you see Sir William.

'1. They suggest you should propose that 3, 4, 5 or 6 of the Employers should meet 3, 4, 5 or 6 of the men, and discuss the questions between them fully and without reserve; and that the men should then *report* to the Hands on strike, what has been concluded upon! *Not* that the delegates who thus meet the Employers are to promise anything without consulting the body of the Men— but it may be pretty safely asserted that whatever conclusion be come to at such meeting, the great body of the Men will be almost sure to accord with it if the Delegates recommend it.

'2. You may suggest that the Employers agree that the Men shall go back to their work on the *Nine Hours* system—and leave the matter of wages to a Board of Arbitration chosen half by themselves and half by the Employers. It is thought the Men would agree to this *at once.*

'If you cannot leave home at once—please write to:—

        Joseph Cowen, Junior Esq.,
        Chronicle Office,
        Newcastle-on-Tyne,

and say when you will come. Mr. Cowen is the best friend the Men have.' [17]

Mundella did not go at once, for he was pressing Forster to admit German cattle. But a week later, on 27 September, he could tell Leader, 'I go to Newcastle today. I do not go very hopeful. I shall keep it very quiet if I can, if any good results I will let you know.' On 1 October he was at Darlington with David Dale, where he met the officials of the Board of Arbitration which settled all wage questions for thirty miles around the town.

'What a contrast to Newcastle!' he exclaimed. 'It is one of the most remarkable strikes I ever witnessed; although I can express no opinion publicly, I may say *to you* that the masters are *all in the wrong*, and this struggle has changed the rate of wages throughout the North of England. I have nothing to send you as yet. Tomorrow morning I return there and receive Sir W. Armstrong's ultimatum. I am not at all sanguine. Frigid, hard and proud, nothing but defeat and humiliation lies before them.' [18]

He went to Sir William Armstrong with the proposal that the nine-hour demand of the men should be accepted, balanced by a wage reduction, which was to be fixed by a board of arbitration comprising six workmen and six representatives of the employers. The men were enthusiastic about his suggestions, but Sir William Armstrong was not. By 4 October, Mundella was back at Nottingham, exhausted by his efforts, and his daughter had to write her father's customary letter to Leader. She said, 'Papa is nearly run to death, and has no time for anything approaching rest. I was dreadfully sorry about Newcastle, but trust some settlement may still be effected.' It was. Before the end of the fortnight the men obtained their demands, after staying out for five months. On 15 October, Mundella said:

'The Newcastle masters have paid dearly for their folly. They have conceded double what would have originally satisfied the men. They have been deficient in honesty, tact and temper, and well deserve what has followed.' [19]

Their success was followed by a similar concession in all the engineering works in the kingdom.[20]

9

At the end of the year Mundella was ill. The Central Press Agency put out the story that he was 'seriously ill', but he told Leader:

'Of course you will say it is overwork: so says the Doctor; between ourselves this is all gammon. I should probably have had a similar attack if I had been the idlest fellow in the world. I have taken a cold which has got to my kidneys and back, and as this is a weak spot I am obliged to lay up and be careful. I am still in bed with some grinding pains, but the worst grind is to be here helpless and idle. However, I can read, write and think, and I hope I shall turn my enforced leisure to some account.' [21]

Part of his leisure was spent in exhorting Leader:

'Pray induce every good man you can to enter the town council. I fear you will have it full of publicans before long, unless our friends stick to it. I cannot tell you in the limits of a letter how difficult it is to keep clear of their local affairs; both sides write all sorts of letters in order to drag me in.' [22]

Others besides local politicians worried him at this time. George Howell, now the convenor of the forthcoming Trades Union Congress, sent Mundella a bill to be presented in the following session. Its purpose was to establish boards of arbitration throughout the country. Mundella was cautious. He replied that he did not approve of compulsory arbitration, but would present Howell's bill if it left the initiative to the districts and industries themselves.

But he hastened to draw the Trades Union Congress to his side by adding:

'My friend, Mr. Ward, the Mayor of Nottingham, intends giving the Congress a hearty reception, and I hope it will not end without some *really more efficient steps* being taken to promote arbitration than the mere passing of a resolution.' [23]

The marriage of the T.U.C. and the provincial politician was noticed at this very time. On 9 December, *Vanity Fair* published a full-page coloured cartoon of him; wagging an admonitory forefinger before his great hooked nose. Under the hirsute face and flashing smile, the caption read '*EDUCATION AND ARBITRATION*'.

He realised that he must take a bold decision and cut his ties with Nottingham. So he abandoned his connection with the Nottingham Manufacturing Company, and persuaded the directors to transfer the merchant side of the business to Morley's. He told Leader, 'From now on I shall go in for unprofitable politics exclusively'. From baying with the radical pack, he was about to lead a little hunt of his own. That he might establish himself in London, he rented a house in Stanhope Gardens for a year.

CHAPTER SEVEN

Isolation from the Radicals, 1872

I

'I AM a nice kettle of fish, cooking by means of water and gas,' Mundella remarked ruefully to Leader, as the heat of the Sheffield Borough Council was turned upon him to promote their acquisition of the local gas and water companies.[1]

It was a sad position. Both companies straddled the town with monopolistic powers which nothing had so far broken. The gas company, having crushed the attempts of its consumers to form a rival concern by obtaining injunctions to restrain them from laying pipes, now controlled the entire illumination of the town. The water company, secure in the possession of parliamentary powers, supplied with water on their own scale such consumers as could pay the rate. Matters came to a head when, in 1864, one of the main reservoirs burst, and millions of gallons swirled down the Loxley Valley towards the industrial area of Sheffield, causing loss of life and damage which official assessors estimated at £262,844.[2] To meet this huge indemnity, the water company sought, and obtained, further parliamentary powers enabling them to increase their charges, and to be relieved from the obligation of supplying the town with a constant supply at a constant pressure.

So the borough council determined to seek authority to take over both undertakings. In June 1869 they set up the necessary committees, but found that neither the gas nor the water company would part with their shares, even when offered very favourable 9 per cent debentures. In an attempt to stop the water company raising their charges, the borough council undertook to fight them before the magistrates' court, and won.

But the water company were led by a man of talent and resource: forty-six-year-old Ralph Blakelock Smith, who, as their legal adviser, sought to restrain the borough officers from spending the ratepayers' money in promoting such activities. They failed to find a sponsor for the parliamentary bill which they drafted, so sought an injunction at the Court of Queen's Bench to restrain the borough from using public moneys in such an unauthorised manner. They were successful. The corporation were now in the unhappy position of having to pay the costs of the case before the magistrate, together with the costs of promoting a bill in parliament, out of their own pockets.

In despair, they turned to Mundella.

Mundella was in a quandary. He realised that it was quite evident that 'the great majority of the people of Sheffield' were 'in favour of purchasing the gas and water companies' properties', but warned Leader, 'It will be a severe and costly fight for both sides'. He had neither confidence in the mayor nor in the officials who were entrusted with the promotion of the project, and told Leader:

'The Town Clerk and his satellites haunt me on the most frivolous pretexts. They seem to me to be such weak fussy people that I regard it very probable their case, however strong, will fail under their management.' [3]

This was the position by 10 March 1870.

All that session he was preoccupied with the Education Bill and his trip to America. The mayor,[4] embittered by the failure of his plans, roundly accused Mundella of bad faith in not attending to the interests of the borough. Furthermore, he alleged that Mundella could have given evidence before the Parliamentary Committee which sat to consider the Sheffield Bill. Mundella's supporters in the council were furious. They demanded that the charges should be substantiated. Leader himself was threatened with a writ for libel by the town clerk.[5] With both the mayor and town clerk of Sheffield faced with a huge bill of costs, both utterly unable to draw upon the public funds to meet it, things looked black indeed for future good relations between burgess and burgery.

But in 1871 an ally appeared in the person of George Leeman,[6] the sixty-two-year-old mayor of York, who in that year was elected to the house of commons. In his dual capacity as M.P. and mayor, Leeman decided to deal with this new and distressing state of affairs. He allied himself with Mundella, and the two prepared a Borough Funds Bill, the aim of which was to allow municipal corporations to use public money in pursuit of parliamentary powers to take over public utilities. Mundella rallied to his side, and the two of them enlisted the support of a number of corporations who sought to relieve themselves of the disabilities which the judgment invoked by the Sheffield Water Company had brought upon them. The bill was duly presented, but, as Mundella told Leader, 'the Gas and Water Companies have the most perfect organisation that can be devised for opposition'. In spite of persistent pressure by Leeman and Mundella, the bill had but little chance, and by 6 August that year Mundella was again lamenting, 'The opposition of the Tories and the Companies is very strong and bitter'. He added three months later, 'The water company should sell out. . . . The corporation must be forced from their past expenditure. It is that which has driven them to extremes.'

By the 1872 session, however, things wore a better complexion. C. B. Adderley, the Conservative M.P. for North Staffordshire, an authority on and pioneer of town planning, was as keen an advocate of local government as he was of self-government in the colonies.[7] His chairmanship of the Sanitary Commission had resulted in a report which threw bright lights on the dark alleys of the northern industrial towns. Gladstone had to pacify the enthusiasts for local government after dropping Goschen's farsighted plan. So on 25 July the bill was almost through the committee stage: the critical clause was the sixth, which contained retrospective rights, especially for the Sheffield Borough Council to recoup its losses. Mundella was almost savage as he wrote:

'We have sat up till daylight for three months over it, and unless it goes to the Lords at once, its chances are nil. Hibbert, Leeman, Dixon and myself held a conference at six o'clock. Beach and Goldney succeeded in withdrawing all amendments on condition of our withdrawing the 6th clause. The arrangement was completed 15 minutes before the House rose, and the Bill went through Committee.

'However, there was a great running to and fro in the lobby . . . the Tories hate big Borough and Municipal Corporations. The former return Radical M.P.s, the latter petition for Ballot and other obnoxious Bills and are always wanting sewage farms or interfering with the fishing by polluting streams, or doing some other disagreeable thing. The number of Landlords who have some grudge against, or litigation pending with Boroughs is really surprising, and *they hate them*. Of course Blacklock Smiths and possessors of monopolies in general entertain similar views and the result is—what you see.'[8]

Posterity was to see more. For this small and apparently unimportant measure literally unlocked the municipal coffers to enterprising corporations which wished to run their own public utilities. Dixon's own constituency of Birmingham was, during the next three years, to undergo great alterations under the leadership of its energetic mayor, Joseph Chamberlain.[9] But poor Sheffield, crippled by the voluntary rate which had to be levied to pay past debts, and smarting from reverses not only over the gas and water bills, but also over the successful opposition by the two local landlords to any further improvements, lagged far behind.[10]

2

Those other corporations, the trade unions, also faced the session of 1872 in a far different order of battle than before. Applegarth was eclipsed. The junta dissolved. Himself no longer secretary of the Carpenters and Joiners, a widower with five children to support, Applegarth was on the periphery of labour politics rather than at the centre, where he had been when the parliament had opened four years earlier. He became a private secretary to one of the Education League politicians, and ran errands for Glyn, the Liberal whip.[11]

Generalissimo of the new general staff of the army of labour was Alexander MacDonald. A shrewd Scots miner, he had trodden the hard path from the pit to the university, and thence, by successful speculation, to a position of independence. Never forgetful of his origins, he organised a national union of miners which by 1869 had become a reality. Though it split in that year, his enthusiasm was such that within the two years that followed he was able to draft a miners' charter, intended to secure a standard of economic justice which had long been lacking in the industry. Typical of the man was a design which he drew for a Yorkshire branch of his union. It showed a miner pointing to a number of boys and saying, 'They must and shall be protected and educated and only work eight hours a day'.[12]

MacDonald was determined to press the claims of the miners to the utmost. He was elected chairman of the new Parliamentary Committee of the T.U.C. in this year. Whereas Applegarth lost his initiative in trade union politics with the passing of the first of Bruce's acts in 1871, MacDonald took it up with the failure of his second in the same year. MacDonald's demands were open and forthright: the unions should possess the right to enforce their own strikes by peaceful picketing.

Mundella was sensitive to the change that had come over affairs. He offered to get Applegarth a post at the board of trade, but

Applegarth refused it, and on the termination of his private secretaryship became a commercial traveller for a French firm of mining-appliance manufacturers. With MacDonald's fierce independence, Mundella was uneasy: with his criticism, Mundella was exasperated. 'That rascal MacDonald, a dishonest but clever and unscrupulous miner's agent,' he described MacDonald to Leader, 'that bad fellow who is "Elcho's Limited". He is acting on the instructions of his Tory masters.' [13]

The meeting of the Trades Union Congress was purposely brought forward to the week beginning the 8 January 1872, in order to hammer out the programme which was to be put through parliament. Worthies of the town of Nottingham spared no pains to fête the seventy-seven delegates—so much so that George Howell recorded that 'Nottingham holds the place of honour in this respect'.[14] It was a momentous assembly, for, with deliberate consciousness of what it was about, the congress constituted itself as a non-party vent for the aspirations of labour, giving an American observer a message to convey to his countrymen that British labour was not hostile to the interest of capital, but desired to live beside it on terms of equality.

Mundella participated in the proceedings, being toasted at the soirées arranged for them. He confessed to Leader:

'The Trade Congress falls very heavy on me, but I am doing my duty, and marvellously good is the apparent result. Much more forbearance and moderation characterises all their proceedings.'

The 'forbearance' which Mundella observed in the delegates was very real. They listened courteously while he harangued them on the necessity of thinking of child labour as well as their own. They promised him support for his Factory Bill and his Truck Prevention Bill. They were silent when he chided them like an angry father:

'From what I have observed from the way some of you have dealt with each other during the Congress, you would not make better employers than some that I know. The whole root of the matter is treating each other with courtesy on a basis of equality.'

Throughout the whole duration of the congress, Mundella stressed the necessity of a close alliance between capital and labour. In a farewell speech he compared the former to a tree planted by the latter, which could only bear fruit as it was nourished. Nor was this the only analogy which was drawn before the assembled eyes of the delegates. The vicar of Nottingham preached at a farewell service which was organised: his text could serve as a commentary on their efforts for the next decade. It ran, 'Friend, go up higher'. Well might a later historian of the working-classes complain that Mundella's 'subtle art . . . of fostering and shaping the opportunist ideology of the proletarian movement' now began to bear fruit. For Nottingham set a precedent: receptions to these annual gatherings of labour delegates became part of the accepted civic folk-lore.[15]

3

A close observer of the Nottingham Congress would notice that the influence of Alexander MacDonald was paramount. His Miners' Charter—the Mines Regulation Bill—stood high on the agenda. So did the motion for repeal of the Criminal Law Amendment Act, with its restrictive interpretation of picketing, which had been passed so recently. The congress also pledged itself to support the Factory Bill which Mundella was to introduce, a Truck Bill which he was to sponsor, and an Arbitration Bill, which was drafted by Rupert Kettle.

MacDonald's influence was, if anything, increased by the new disposition of the Parliamentary Committee of ten. George Odger was now unrepentantly republican, two articles of his on this subject in the *Contemporary Review* being widely quoted. He was, like MacDonald, an open advocate of labour representation, of land nationalisation and of political expediency. Neither of them ever subscribed to the middle-class doctrine that labour should follow the lead of enlightened Liberals: a doctrine so energetically maintained by Mundella. Also supporting MacDonald was John Normansell, a fellow miner-worker and organiser, who was his right-hand man in the hierarchy.

Just how exacting the new high command of the union world was prepared to be, can be seen from Howell's analysis of the voting on the previous 19 June, when the lords' amendments had passed the commons. In this analysis, 130 representatives of the leading centres of industry were specifically named as voting against giving the unions the right to picket. Of these, 101 were Liberal M.P.s. 'We posted their names,' recorded Howell, 'and left further action to the several constituencies which the aforesaid members represented.'

The cap-in-hand attitude, which the Parliamentary Committee had hitherto adopted, was now dropped. Before 1872, in going to the house of commons, MacDonald as president, and Howell as secretary, had to send in their names to Mundella, or another sympathiser, who would then come out and take them into the lobby, where they could solicit support for their particular measure. That was now changed. From 1872 onwards they were given the freedom of the lobby, which made their work immeasurably easier.

In fighting the parliamentary battles of the committee, Mundella often stood alone. Until labour representation was a reality, he was truly indispensable: his zeal in their cause gave little ground for complaint, and much for enthusiasm. Night after night he would sit on the benches, waiting for a chance to speak. Frequently he would be there till the small hours of the morning when members were fast asleep. On such occasions the house presented a sorry spectacle—for of the few who remained to hear each other speak, each one had a particular radical axe to lay at the foot of some particular upas-tree.

In the service of the trade unions, Mundella plied their measures with the energy Gladstone expended on the trees at Hawarden. Their main aim—to amend the Criminal Law Amendment Act of 1871 so that they might picket—kept him very busy.

For precedents illustrating the wide interpretation which the magistrates were prepared to give to the word 'intimidation' began to accumulate almost daily from the day the act became law. One celebrated case concerned George Turk, was who summoned at Hammersmith Police Court for distributing, while he was on strike, a handbill on which was printed advice to other workers to do the same till they got a nine-hour day. The court ruled that the advice on the handbill was 'intimidatory'. This judgment hit the Trades Union Congress as they were assembled at Nottingham in the January of 1872.

The other cases, equally unjust from the trade union viewpoint, were collected by George Howell, and incorporated into a memorial. On 21 March, Mundella led a deputation to the home secretary, only to be reminded that such severities as the act engendered were due entirely to the amendments which had been inserted in his bill by the house of lords. They left the home office with the cold and comfortless assurance that the vigour of the law would be applied in a more uniform manner.

In April 1872, when the appeal against the Hammersmith judgment was due to be heard, the prosecution withdrew their case, leaving Turk's Committee to pay the costs and Turk himself still a convicted man. On 29 April, at a further conference of the trade union leaders and their two lawyer M.P. sympathisers— Henry James and W. V. Harcourt—Mundella gave his opinion that a bill to amend the Act of 1871 should be introduced. With great speed it was drafted, and presented by 18 May.

The speed with which this plan was conceived was in striking contrast to the wearisome days that followed. For a month and a half the little group waited for their chance to introduce the bill, and their chance came only after midnight on 5 July. In a thin and drowsy house the bill was presented. Lord Elcho, however, was ready. He moved the adjournment of the debate, and secured it by two votes. In spite of the greatest vigilance for a loophole in parliamentary time, the bill had to be withdrawn on the last day of the month.

More encouraging, however, was the success of the Mines Regulation Act—an official bill introduced in response to MacDonald's agitation. During the passage of this measure the proprietary interests were so strong that they almost succeeded in emasculating it. To begin with, they formulated and carried the amendment that no owner, agent or manager should be made responsible for breach of the provisions of the act unless it could be shown that he had 'knowingly' done so. Mundella put up a gallant fight for the protection of girls and boys. The committee, however, not only rejected the sweeping motion against the employment of female labour at the pit-head, it also refused to accept an amendment which he supported restricting such employment to girls under sixteen. Nevertheless, he did have the satisfaction of securing some concessions. By pleading the case of the boys employed underground, he managed to prevent a retrogression to the mine-owners' demands that they should work 112 hours a fortnight. MacDonald was quick to give honour where it was rightfully due, and told a vast gathering of South Yorkshire miners: 'He has acted nobly, and his conduct deserves for him the lasting gratitude of the entire population'. [16]

The passage of the Mines Regulation Act illustrated the rifts that were growing in the Liberal lute. Blind Professor Henry Fawcett, whose interest in Indian finance was earning for him the title of 'the member for India', did not agree with Mundella's collectivist notions of the power of the state. For when Mundella spoke out strongly for curtailing the labour of women at the bank-top 'with coal-heavers' hats, smoking pipes with the men, and drinking with them in public-houses', Fawcett was quick to seize on such implications of the inequality of women. Mundella's response, crude as it was, shows that he was prepared to stretch the concept of state control till it embraced a collectivist compass:

'The function of the State', he told the House, 'is one to protect human life, to protect children and to facilitate the administration of justice. If it is not the duty of the government to do anything but protect society against the thief, as Herbert Spencer maintains, what will be the result but anarchy plus the policeman?' [17]

4

Nor was Fawcett the only Liberal whose doctrinaire radicalism ruffled Mundella. His hopes of a middle and working-class alliance against vested interests seemed to be particularly frustrated at this time. To begin with, the nonconformists held a great conference at Manchester on 24 January 1872 to insist upon 'united literary education by the State, and separate religious education by parents, or the voluntary agency of religious committees'. In a paper on the political relation of his co-religionists to the Liberal party, Henry Richard, a former Congregational pastor in the Old Kent Road, and now M.P. for Merthyr, categorically said:

'If it comes to a question between allegiance to a party and loyalty to a principle, we cannot hesitate. We are willing to exercise patience, to make concessions; but to adopt a course which will involve the sacrifice, or the surrender, or the serious compromise of these vital principles for the sake of any man or party is what we cannot, what we ought not, what we must not, what we dare not, and by God's help, what we will not do.' [18]

This was the language of revolt. Mundella was thunderstruck.

'How Richard can have the face to make his speeches I cannot imagine,' he wrote to Leader as he read the reports of Richard's speech. 'If you have the Crosby Hall lectures by you, look at his and Miall's [19] on education. They are exactly the very reverse of all they are now saying. Imagine the Sheffield School Board having to arrange with all our sects for Religious Instruction after school hours!'

Others were equally roused. The Church Defence Association, scenting the Liberationist pack, took fright.[20] They decided to challenge every Liberal who supported Miall. The nonconformists, quick to follow, retorted that they would fight every Liberal who voted for school fees. 'Betwixt the two, with the certain opposition of publicans,' lamented Mundella to Leader, 'things look pleasant for men of my opinions. . . . Alas! I fear the children will be the sufferers after all.'

Just when he should have been able to rally a group of moderate men around him, they fell away like flies. Hughes took fright at the determination of the T.U.C. at Nottingham in January, and wrote to Mundella:

'I am sorry that the Trade Unions ran amok at the Criminal Law Amendment Act. I warned them not to do so. . . . I, for one, won't go in for total repeal, and have so written to the *Co-operative News*.' [21]

Mundella was worried about Hughes, who had taken silk three years before: 'I am anxious about Tom Hughes,' he wrote; 'he is poor and has a large family, and his earnings are dependent on his health.' [22] The truth was that Hughes was still sufficient of an idealist to believe that he could carry the trade unions with him towards the New Jerusalem of a co-operative state, and the frank secularity of the MacDonald regime revealed at Nottingham led him to steer clear of an alliance with them.[23] The consequence was that Mundella was left in closer, because more singular, contact than ever before. Before long Hughes was to become quite isolated from the union parliamentary committee.

Hughes' place as a middle-class ally of the unions was taken by Henry Crompton, whose positivism only served to drive Hughes still farther into the arms of the Church Defence Association. To the positivists, Hughes' attachment to the principles of the established church were an aberration, for positivism stressed the fact that both metaphysics and theology were but preludes to the theme of what they called 'positive knowledge'—knowledge which was established on the certitude of observation and experiment.[24] Crompton was only thirty-six years old, and his mentor, Frederic Harrison, only forty-two. Yet both of them exercised a profound influence over the Parliamentary Committee of the T.U.C., which welcomed them for their industry and eminent practicality. But to Mundella, Crompton was a thorn in the side.

'These academic radicals', he complained to Leader, 'are half cracked. Crompton is the son of the late judge, his wife is the daughter of Lord Romilly, they are related to peers all round, yet they are always railing against the privileged classes.' [25] Crompton returned the compliment: 'It is high time that Mundella's monstrous and absurd pretensions to educate the nation should be checked', [26] he wrote to Auberon Herbert, and ground away at his pamphlets in the intervals of working as clerk of assize in North Wales.

More distressing still was the defection of Mundella's old political ally Samuel Morley. By now, Morley was a real power in the Liberal party. He was a convert to state education, he owned in the *Daily News* what was then the most effective Liberal organ, he was secure in his representation of Bristol, and he was showering his wealth upon the nonconformists. Yet Morley at the age of sixty-three was displaying all the dissatisfaction of men half his age. In June of this year he invited trade union and radical leaders to rally at the Cannon Street Hotel. Sixty or seventy responded, and by 17 July three meetings had been held and a twenty-one-point programme had been adopted. This was even more ambitious than Scott Russell's New Social Movement of a year before. The county franchise, payment of members of parliament, and abolition of the property qualification for election both to councils and parliament, showed that he had a definite labour programme; while categorical demands for freeholdings for the poor, revision of the civil list, universal school boards, state purchase of railways, county boards for local government, a nine-hour day, and repeal of the Criminal Law Amendment Act showed that he mistrusted the good faith of Gladstone's ministry to bring these things to pass. Some of the men who listened to and elaborated these proposals were significant. Cremer, Odger, Lubez and the shambling Eccarius all attended, the latter fresh from his rupture with Karl Marx. They represented such organisations as the Bradlaugh Republicans, the Land Tenure Association, the Working Men's Club and Institute and the International. Well might Mundella lament to Leader on 23 July 1872: 'Poor Morley is up in the clouds, drinking tea with all the irreconcilables in London, and persuading them they are of some importance'. [27]

But of all the errant Liberals, none gave Mundella greater pain than Auberon Herbert, the Liberal M.P. for Nottingham. He and Sir Charles Dilke, M.P. for Chelsea, were both young men, full of promise. Herbert was only thirty-four, Dilke twenty-nine : both had seen the world, and formed a bright constellation of wit and daring on the lower gangway. Unfortunately, both of them chose to move for an inquiry into the Civil List in order to air their republican principles, an action that was both untimely and unnecessary. For a most disorderly scene ensued. Both were greeted by such a chorus of cat-calls and hoots that *Hansard* was unable to record their speeches. The motion was swamped by 276 votes to 2. Mundella made a speech full of wisdom, just after order had been restored:

'The scene which has taken place will have a most unhappy impression on the country. It cannot fail to give rise to the suspicion that the House dare not listen to the arguments in favour of the motion.'

He continued:

'The system of persecution and suppression of the right of free discussion which have been adopted this evening, will tend to raise the mover and seconder of the resolution to the rank of heroes and martyrs, and give a factitious importance to their proposition.' [28]

He confided to Leader, 'Herbert is politically dead, and I am grieved and disappointed at his extravagant folly'.

Another of Mundella's old Nottingham associates, Lyulph Stanley, brother-in-law of Lord Amberley, who contested the representation of the town in 1866, was also experiencing the drawbacks of being too 'advanced', for he failed to win a by-election at Oldham. Mundella saw the reason:

'He threw it away. . . . He is a sceptic and something of a doctrinaire. His expressions about the Bible, and his desires to open Museums on Sundays lost him two or three hundred Wesleyan voters.' [29]

And again:

'I doubt if these doctrinaires have any principles. They worship themselves and each other, and their violence is only equalled by their bitterness and conceit.' [30]

Two months later he was again writing:

'I am utterly wearied and disgusted with hobby riders, and am becoming the sworn enemy of all abstractions. What you will do with me at the next election I know not, but I am almost in the mood to hit out right and left at Fawcetts, Mialls, Herberts, Dilkes, "et hoc genus omnes".' [31]

He looked with a jaundiced eye on the whole complexion of the party. Its leader he regarded as insulated from the rank and file by 'a mass of half-tory whiglings'. Gladstone's political aberrations at this time have been explained by his latest biographer on the grounds that 'he was a sick man, with all a sick man's petulance and obstinacy'. As for the party itself, Mundella could only use the adjective 'disgusting'. He continued:

'It has done its work and is demoralised. . . . Everyone who is disappointed, who fancies himself fit for office, who wants to control his tenants, or has a secret hatred for the Ballot, contrived to give it a slap. Childers surprised everybody, and his speech was attributed at once to his non-appointment to the Chancellorship of the Duchy. Harcourt is a Tory who plays the game of radical brag. Fawcett hates Gladstone, and would vote in the teeth of his principles to spite him.' [32]

5

With the planks of the party platform being carried off by those who should have nailed them together, the Liberals were incapable of facing the Conservatives with a resolute front. Disraeli scented mischief, and told a large audience in the Free Trade Hall at Manchester:

'It may very likely be the game of the Radical party to try and turn out the present ministry if they can, and put a Conservative Government in its place, that Conservative Government being in a minority, hoping that by so doing they shall be able to reconstruct their own party upon a new platform, pledged to more extreme and more violent measures, and then to have a Cabinet formed of the most thoroughgoing Radicals. These may be their tactics. But just because it is their game it ought not to be ours.' [33]

It was at this juncture that a distraction came to save the Liberals. The authors of this were the farm labourers, who in the pouring rain tramped from their farms to listen to Joseph Arch [34] urging them to organise into a trade union. Mundella wrote to Howell on 7 April: 'Look at what the landlords are doing in Warwickshire! Evicting labourers for joining a union, whereas if a unionist threatens a non-unionist, he gets three months imprisonment.' [35]

The country squires acted swiftly, assisted by many country parsons. A bishop advised them to throw Arch in a river. Here was the golden opportunity for Mundella. Farmers had long opposed his policy of importing cheap German livestock—sheep and cattle—to lower the price of meat, while he, for his part, was

becoming more and more convinced of the necessity of dis-
establishing the church. Here was an opportunity to hit out at
both farmers and parsons, by assisting the movement to become
a national one. Mundella took it.

He made preparations for a monster meeting to be held in
support of Joseph Arch on 2 May at Willis' Rooms in London.[36]
He personally undertook to circularise the leaders of the party to
attend and give a national blessing to what was, in origin, a provincial movement, fostered by the Birmingham politicians like
George Dixon.

Of the many replies he received, some saw in this movement a
stick with which to beat the tories in the county elections: votes
for the farm labourer meant the end of the tory predominance in
the counties. But others were less politically blinkered. Baldwyn
Leighton wrote to him:

'This movement, *if wisely directed*, may be a great opportunity of perman-
ently improving the condition of the farm labourer and at the same time
benefiting his employer by improving the quality of agricultural labour. For
the labourer ought to rise and improve with his wages, and I think I could show
that the average labourer might be worth fully 25% more with increased
alacrity and zeal.' [37]

The meeting went with a swing, and obtained a good report in
all the papers. It is not surprising that the new movement spread
like a fire among dry grass. Before the end of the year it embraced over 100,000 members, with half as many again organised
in other unions. One of Applegarth's pupils became its secretary
to compensate for Joseph Arch's complete lack of, and love for,
administration. As Mundella saw the movement gathering
strength, he exulted:

'The government have played a trump card. We are going to enfranchise
the rural population. The Tories listened in horror to Forster's speech. They
talked out the bill in sheer despair. . . . I think this is the turning point in our
career as a party, and we shall soon recover ourselves.' [38]

6

The aberrations of his colleagues strengthened his own position
in the party hierarchy. In this very session he had introduced a
bill, much against his will, for the promotion of courts of arbitration. It was the first of two acts out of the many which he introduced as a private member to bear his name. Known to the

lawyers from this year until 1896 (when it was repealed) as 35 & 36 Vict. c. 46, the Arbitration (Masters and Workmen) Act 1872, it has come down to us as 'Mundella's Act'. It was intended to supplement Lord St. Leonard's Act of 1867, which was passed to establish 'Equitable Councils of Conciliation to Adjust Differences between Masters and Workmen'. Mundella held no high opinion of this: once describing it as well meaning but absurd.[39] The absurdity lay in its elaborate provisions for elected councils, and it was never effective.

Mundella's Act was passed on 6 August. It was intended to facilitate and encourage the system practised by Sir Rupert Kettle (its draftsman) whereby a set of rules was posted up in the workshops after being agreed upon by representatives of the masters and the men. These rules were to be binding, and a workman could reject them only by giving forty-eight hours' notice. The drafting committee of masters and men were to act as a Court of Conciliation, and, failing them, any other representative body similarly constituted. Their decision was to be enforced by distress or imprisonment. Though the act was as big a failure as its predecessors, it caught the imagination of the T.U.C., which three years later was petitioning for local boards to be established throughout the kingdom.[40]

A week after this act became law Mundella went to give his annual address at Sheffield. To do him justice, he barely mentioned the act, concentrating on the major legislative work of the year. He received a great ovation. By a curious coincidence, unrelated to anything that had taken place in parliament, he and his supporters, when they arrived in Paradise Square, were unable to ascend the platform, as it was too high to vault. So a ladder had to be fetched, and one by one, Leader, Clegg, Stainton, Birks, Nadin and the other worthies of the Liberal cause ascended in a dignified Indian file. The meeting chaffed them good-humouredly, and accorded Mundella a great reception.

He had won their hearts.

Two months later he told Leader that he intended to settle himself in London. He left Stanhope Gardens and took up residence in 16 Elvaston Place, South Kensington.

CHAPTER EIGHT

Politician among the Pressure Groups, 1872–1874

H E was not alone. He had found the secret of political success: attachment to a pressure group. These groups were the political life of the time, overlapping parties and classes, aggregating, re-grouping and splintering in a dialectic which stimulated the political philosophers of the next generation to endow these groups with a 'real personality'. For no sum of persons who have come together to promote a political object can remain together for long without developing a permanent character as group persons. So argued Maitland and Figgis, whose impressionable years were spent just at this very time.[1]

We have seen the impact of these groups, both in chrysalis and imago, on the politics of the sixties—a period when, as Dicey has shown, the collectivist phase of politics and ethics began.[2] It is now, as the seventies began to wear down the Gladstonian ministry to its roots, that the groups interpose themselves between the individual and the state. The artisan had no longer to be dynamited to break his individuality: the union claimed him by its tradition. Even within the churches—traditionally the one great group that interposed between man and the state—sub-groups proliferated, each claiming its aggregate of loyalties. Clergy like J. C. Cox and Canon Girdlestone could help the farm labourers, while Bishop Ellicott could advocate that all such agitators should be thrown in the river. Similarly, the Central Nonconformist Committee could deliberately set out to break W. E. Forster, while thousands of their co-religionists swore by Mr. Gladstone and his ministers. The old labels did not fit: the new ones had still to be written.

I

One of these pressure groups was the Factory Workers' Short Time Committee. This group was composed of unionists and non-unionists alike. It was pre-eminently labour in outlook, yet it did not affiliate itself with the T.U.C. Indeed, it was so little considered by the congress assembled at Nottingham, that Mundella had to speak strongly on its behalf:

'I wish you working men of England', he told the Nottingham Congress in January 1872, 'would think a little more upon the question of child labour and consider how it bears upon your own. For the honour of humanity, I beseech you to educate your children that they may grow up strong, intelligent, and healthy. It is your duty to see that your children are kept at school for a proper length of time, for it is not to be thought of that a father should work nine hours a day, while a child is employed for ten.'

So, independently of the unions, Mundella set about fighting to remove the children from the factories and bring them into school. Had a poll of labour opinion been taken, many would have been found to be against this; for it meant, in the days of large families before Bradlaugh's neo-Malthusian propaganda had taken effect, that the sooner children worked, the larger the meagre family incomes would be. 'Happy is the man who has his quiver full of them', they sang in their little chapels, knowing well enough that each child represented an addition to earning power. As the standard of living rose, fathers would count their blessings. That children should stay at school, and get ideas above their station, was inconceivable.

The Webbs have insisted that in this matter the trade union leaders were being deliberately cynical in preferring to fight for shorter working hours for themselves behind the petticoats of their womenfolk.[3] Such a view, based on a *post-hoc* gloss of the facts by old-guard unionists of the nineties, is untenable. The fact is that the trade union leaders had far more pressing matters in hand: amendment of the Criminal Law affecting their power to strike, regulation of the miners' working conditions, wages boards and union politics. Odger at this time was flirting with Dilke, MacDonald with Elcho, Cremer with Morley, and Howell with his own political ambitions. The children were a minor concern, left to the prosy middle-class philanthropists.

Forster saw the importance of the question, and encouraged Mundella to go ahead with his plans.[4] The seventy-one-year-old Lord Shaftesbury emerged once more to take the chair at a meeting which inaugurated a Factory Acts Reform Association on 7 January 1872. But Shaftesbury was too old to undertake the rigours of another campaign, so the choice fell on Mundella. At a further meeting, held on 20 March at the Westminster Palace

Hotel, Mundella was formally asked to undertake the presentation of a bill to shorten the working hours of women and children employed in textile factories.

It was a particularly congenial task. For eighteen years past he had been consulted whenever an amendment to the Factory Acts was contemplated. His ideas were fortified by experience and strengthened by conviction. He replied to the invitation in a speech which was both responsible and portentous. In it he advanced the argument that such a measure was necessary if Great Britain was to increase the quality and quantity of her manufactured goods. He cited the experiences of enlightened employers like Hugh Ashton of Oldham, which showed that more intensive production involved shorter working hours.

But there were many, not only on the Conservative side, who questioned his integrity of outlook. Shorter working hours, said these critics, meant economic suicide. Mundella was known as a forthright apostle of free trade, a true Cobdenite. They hastened to point out to the public that Mundella owned factories in Saxony, which worked twenty-two hours a day on a shift system. Shorten the hours of labour in English factories to nine hours a day, they prophesied, and Saxon goods would flood the country, crippling those manufacturers who had not Mundella's foreign interests.

It was a telling blow. Mundella felt it keenly, and hastened to address a public letter to the secretary of the movement, rebutting the charge.

'The business with which I am connected', he wrote, 'employs two factories in Nottingham, and one in Loughborough, all working under the Factory Acts. If the Fifty-four Hours Bill becomes law, there is no firm in the hosiery trade that will be so largely affected by it as the one in which I an interested.'

He added that such Saxon interests as the firm possessed amounted to only 10 per cent of the total interest embraced by the Nottingham Hosiery Manufacturing Company.[5]

The reform was indeed part of a much wider movement which was taking place at the time as society progressed from the paleotechnic to the neotechnic phase. The whole system of apprenticeship was breaking down as the machine grew more complicated and the prime mover of society became more complex. But apprenticeship, as a custom, was invested with all the sanctity of a tradition. Craftsmanship could not exist without it. The machine was regarded by many social reformers of the time as an evil which destroyed the individuality of the worker. Mechanisation was a term of reproach.[6] For the safe and comfortable acquisition of artisan techniques, apprenticeship was infinitely more desirable than attendance at any technical training-school, where an unwary workman might disclose the trade secrets of his master. It went with rule of thumb.

The decay of apprenticeship had another aspect too. For nearly a century and a half it had been the only outlet for children of the poor—the industrious poor, as the contemporary euphemism ran. Now, however, the spectacle of a new kind of poor was seen: the displaced poor, who had drifted to the margins of society because they had neither the wit nor the flexibility to adapt themselves to a changing economic pattern.

2

'We rise like partridges from a covert,' Mundella told Leader, describing the attempts the private members made to catch the Speaker's eye. His Factory Bill, printed on 15 April 1872, waited three months for its second reading. On 29 July he led a deputation to the home secretary. Coming out, he met a counter deputation from the Yorkshire mill-owners, who had come to plead for its non-consideration.

Gladstone took refuge in an old device: appointing two inspectors of the Local Government Board to make a report on the situation. These inspectors were to examine the working of the existing Factory Acts and the effects of factory life upon the physical condition and social position of the workers.

Mundella's pressure group were very disappointed. On 1 August they held another meeting, and thanked him profusely for his efforts. He replied by promising them that he would devote the next session to the effective promotion of their cause.

In the meantime he busied himself collecting more ammunition. He wandered down to the East End of London, and into the slums of Bristol. He wrote to J. T. Brunner, who was then starting his great alkali works at Winnington with Ludwig Mond. Brunner replied:

'As you know, the great effect of the Factory Education Act has been that a mere register of attendances has been required at a place called a school, with little or no guarantee as to the fitness of the master. The Act should have required a certain amount of attainment before the child became a full-timer.'

He made contact with Fitzjames Stephen, then advocating in the pages of the *Pall Mall Gazette* a considerable extension of the powers of the state over children.[7] Stephen offered to draft a supplementary bill dealing with the rights of children whose guardians were unscrupulous.[8] Mundella encouraged the publication of a history of factory legislation, and himself wrote a preface in which he openly advocated action by the state. Harmony of the education and labour laws, he pointed out in this, was essential to check national degeneracy. The whole tone of the history was one of special pleading: the bias being that the 'marvellous advances in the direction of compulsory education' and the intervention of the state in favour of the working classes removed the dangers of a social revolution.[9] So great was his activity that the Comte de Paris, author of the first history of the English trade unions, wrote a long letter of inquiry at this very time, knowing that from Mundella he could obtain the necessary references to the bluebooks on problems of labour and juvenile employment.[10] He also supplied information to Frederic Harrison for an article which appeared in the *Beehive* on 18 January 1873 on 'Misinterpretation of Strikes'.

3

Had the trade union leaders been solidly behind him, Mundella might have stimulated the government to take some action. But at the very time when they should have been in their most cooperative mood, they were badly stung by the case of the stokers at the great London gas producer at Beckton.

They had cause to feel aggrieved. The men at Beckton Gas Works (500 of them) were all summoned on 5 December 1872 for refusing to work. They had formed a Gas-stokers Reference Committee to demand the reinstatement within ten days of an employee who had been dismissed: twenty-four gas-stokers had been sent to prison, each for six weeks hard labour, for alleged breach of the Master and Servant Act. So frightened were the rest that the committee took to their heels and the strike collapsed. Six were tried for conspiracy on 18 December 1872 at the Old Bailey, where Mr. Justice Brett ruled that they were privy to a conspiracy to molest the employers, and sentenced them to a year's imprisonment.

The Trades Union Congress which met for parliamentary discussion at Leeds in January 1873 was therefore in a suitable mood to hear the counsels of the radical doctrinaires like Henry Crompton, who urged upon the delegates the policy of 'no compromise'.

Crompton suggested that the parliamentary committee should undertake a comprehensive programme, embracing repeal of the Criminal Law Amendment Act of 1871, abolition of imprisonment for breach of contract, repeal of the Small Penalties Act, reform of the Conspiracy Laws, a royal commission to inquire into the summary jurisdiction of magistrates, and an amendment of the Jury Laws.

Mundella was unfortunately unable to attend this congress. He was intermittently ill for the first half of the year, his household was moving and his brother lay dying. But he suspected that there would be wild talk, and wrote to Leader: 'I am sorry not to be at Leeds. I have so little confidence in the wisdom of these men. They are deplorably deficient in tact and knowledge.' [11] His worst forebodings were fulfilled. For not only did the congress empower the parliamentary committee to press ahead with Crompton's programme, but they also enthusiastically endorsed Samuel Plimsoll's agitation for ensuring the safety of lives at sea. George Howell, Mundella's associate in politics, now consented to act as secretary of the Plimsoll Committee.

This, for Mundella, was very trying. He not only did not like Plimsoll's emotional, histrionic poses, but he dreaded appearing on the same platform. 'I sympathise with the cause, but not the man,' he told Leader—'and I don't like being on the same platform with him. His wretched vanity and reckless talk make it painful and undesirable to be associated with him.' [12]

There was more than personal dislike in his aversion for Plimsoll. Plimsoll's crusade was seized upon by the opposition as a useful means of causing embarrassment to the government. The Plimsoll Committee contained the names of such Conservatives as Lord Elcho, Lord George, Lord Claud and Lord John Hamilton, in addition to that of Lord Shaftesbury. Much help was afforded it by the Conservative *Sheffield Telegraph*, so that Mundella complained:

'Plimsoll has been coarsely abusive of Gladstone and laudatory of Roebuck. Roebuck has indeed fallen low when he needs the recommendation of that poor creature whose head is cracked with vanity and whose character is tainted with bankruptcy and meanness.' [13]

A week later he was equally angry:

'Our friend Plimsoll will catch it in a day or two. I have sent Gladstone a memorial of the meeting with a copy of Plimsoll's speeches, and he will send a reply for publication.'

Nevertheless a temporary bill was rushed through the session to ensure that ships were registered before leaving port, in order to prevent cases of the kind described in *Our Seamen*.

Mundella, for his part, was still active on the matter of the Beckton gas-stokers. The Defence Committee of the labour leaders, set up to look after the imprisoned gas-stokers, received a telegram from Mundella on 1 February 1873 telling them that the home secretary had reduced the stokers' sentences by eight months. Mundella was pleased to write to Leader the following day: 'I think I did the gas-stokers good service. The memorial sent by the trade unions was so offensive that it could not be noticed.' [14]

But his efforts to amend the Criminal Law Amendment Act had no success whatever. No sooner had Mundella consented to sponsor a bill, than on 13 March 1873 Gladstone announced the resignation of his ministry. For seven days there was a paralysis of business. When Disraeli refused to take office on 20 March the Trade Union Parliamentary Committee decided to press their bill upon Gladstone. Mundella sponsored, and spoke at, a meeting of M.P.s at the Westminster Palace Hotel. The bill was read a first time on 12 May. On 15 July Auberon Herbert gave notice of a motion for the appointment of a select committee, which was defeated by four votes. Meanwhile the bill to amend the law of conspiracy, which was in the hands of Sir W. V. Harcourt, had suffered a similar fate.

4

Of all the galling burdens which Mundella had to bear during this year the hardest were those imposed upon him by his non-conformist supporters. Sheffield was particularly rich in the sharp and rugged self-supporting chapels which sprang into life with each fresh acre of red-brick dwelling-houses. [15]

They goaded him to press Forster and stop the disbursement of public moneys to the established church. Such was their inter-pretation of the 25th clause of the Education Act, which allowed the Guardians to pay the fees of necessitous children. Their wrath was fed by the youthful editor of the *Fortnightly Review*—John

Morley—who roundly trounced the 'holy army of misologists' whom he professed to see behind Forster. This 'holy army' was held to be responsible for permissive compulsion, permissive school boards and, above all, the 25th clause. For everyone the 25th clause became, as Disraeli percipiently observed, a symbol of the struggle. Those who favoured denominational education defended the 25th clause; those who opposed denominational education wished to see the clause repealed.[16]

A leader of the anti-denominationalists was H. J. Wilson,[17] whose zeal for good works had previously led him to Josephine Butler's platform. A gold-and-silver refiner who professed radicalism in its purest form, he had refused to pay rates if the odious 25th clause should be sustained by the Sheffield School Board. His awkward conscience gave Mundella a good deal of pain and embarrassment during these two years. On 8 April 1872 he sighed to Leader:

'I have had an active exchange or two with H. J. Wilson, who is bent on mischief, and does not hesitate to avow it. He is full of disappointments and hatred, and will disappoint me if he does not prove a marplot. I never read such angry letters as his, and a circular issued by him anent the Mundella Committee is full of bitterness and charges of bad faith.'

Into this rich field of discontented dissent Joseph Chamberlain turned the machine of the National Education League, now organised on a purely secular basis. By doing so Chamberlain reaped a rich harvest. He himself saw the nonconformist revolt as an expression of something wider: dislike of governmental equivocation, and the discontent of the working class. In the *Fortnightly Review* for September 1873 he began to talk of a new party which should assault the hitherto impregnable quadrilateral to secure a free church, free land, free schools and free labour. He compared the working classes to the Governor of Barataria. Their dishes of political power, set before them with such pomp and ceremony, were instantly removed before they could touch them.[18] Three months earlier one of his lieutenants, Edward Jenkins (Applegarth's employer), came out in the *Contemporary Review* with a strong article against Fitzjames Stephen, entitled 'Bismarckism in England'. It held up the ideas of Fitzjames Stephen to the severest criticism as an expression of continental centralisation, dangerous for England to follow.

Chamberlain's other lieutenants had been moving against the

Liberal party in the by-elections too. Before Jenkins had stood at Dundee against Fitzjames Stephen, Cox had stood at Bath, and Langley at London. Mundella told Leader:

'I appealed to Dixon to stop Cox's proceedings at Bath, but he is weak and powerless. Chamberlain and the fanatics have the mastery, and mean to gratify their vanity and magnify their importance by showing their power to do mischief.' [19]

Mundella tried hard to soothe the outraged nonconformists and combine them on a common platform. Two days before the end of the year 1872 he told Leader of a recent visit to Bristol, where, at the invitation of Dr. Caldecott, he and Samuel Morley had met Dr. R. W. Dale of the League: the four of them had tried to find a *modus vivendi* in which all friends of education and all friends of religious teaching could combine. On 17 January 1873 he outlined the plan: denominational schools were to pay one-sixth of the cost of the school in order to provide their own religious teaching; school boards were to arrange such teaching either before or after the hours of secular teaching.

'This once accomplished,' he wrote, 'there is no need for the repeal of clause 25; the objections to that clause at once disappear, compulsion is rendered easy, and the religious difficulty solved. I hope the advocates of religious teaching will accept this compromise to which Dale has assented. If they do not, they will push the advocates of nonconformists and Education into secular teaching, to the statutory exclusion of religious teaching, a result I for one should deplore.'

On 30 January 1873 he foresaw 'the education question will raise a breeze. I shall steer an independent middle course. I stand by the programme arranged by Morley and myself, and will take from the government what I can get.'

It hinged, of course, on the government.

'I believe a really plucky educational policy would be the very best policy they could fight and fall on, but the Government and the House are not yet educated up to it.'

So, going about on another tack, Mundella tried to rope in Dixon and Fawcett to back a bill to secure compulsory education. Fawcett proved awkward, and replied:

'I feel very strongly that it would be very undesirable to have it presented to the House as a League bill. I am quite sure that if Dixon has charge of it, it will never be considered on its merits. You would be a far better person to introduce it, and Dixon might of course have his name on the bill.'

Dixon was equally antipathetic to Fawcett, and wrote to Mundella:

'Fawcett does not sufficiently appreciate the point that our agitation could not be carried out unless we ourselves took action in the House. . . . I cannot expect Fawcett to put his name to our bill and I should not desire it, because he has spoken against us in the House and is no longer a friend of ours. But he must not expect us to abdicate our position or cease to perform what we conceive to be our duty, because we share the fate of all advanced political sections, viz. that we cannot carry all our friends with us.' [20]

In Sheffield itself, H. J. Wilson and the nonconformists would not be reconciled. Mundella told Leader on 9 May 1873: 'One thing is certain, the publicans will not forgive us, and we may as well fill our sails with the enthusiasm of the other side.' This he assiduously set out to do. 'I am going to write to H. J. W.,' he continued, referring to the question of a second Liberal candidate to succeed Hadfield, 'and urge unity and a prompt selection of a candidate. If we mean to win we must work hard for it.' A fortnight later he could report, 'I think you will find H. J. W. moderate by degrees. I took the opportunity of last Wednesday's debate and division to read him a good lesson, and he accepted it more kindly than heretofore. I told him to go home and try to agree upon a good Liberal, and agree to carry him.' [21] But by 9 August, H. J. Wilson was flirting with the National Education League, and Mundella heard that he was trying to get Cox (who had upset the party apple-cart at Bath earlier in the year) as the second candidate. Leader wanted Allott—a local accountant with strong dissenting connections—to stand, but H. J. Wilson continued to oppose this.

So by the end of the year there was nothing more that could be done. Joseph Chamberlain, as chairman of the League executive, himself decided to fight the second seat, so Mundella found himself fighting with Chamberlain, Allott, and Roebuck for only two seats. To such lengths were the nonconformists prepared to go.

5

Having aggravated the artisans, the government could scarcely be expected to aggravate the employers. So Mundella's Factory Bill received a chilly reception. Yet its provisions gave little cause for alarm. They merely aimed at bringing the small workshop under supervision, and continuing the state protection of child labour begun by Lord Shaftesbury.

It proposed to raise the half-time age from eight to ten; to continue half-time employment from thirteen to fourteen; to reduce the hours of labour for children, young persons and women from sixty to fifty-four a week; and to abolish the custom prevailing in silk factories, where children of twelve were allowed to work sixty hours a week. Such provisions were not only necessary to prevent the physical deterioration of the race, but were economically desirable in view of the increased tempo of production.

A number of employers agreed with Mundella, and gave him their active support. Among them was William Fison, the Bradford business associate of the Vice-President of the Council. He, Sir John Ogilvy, Sir D. Wedderburn and others accompanied Mundella's deputation to the home secretary on 17 May 1873. With them went workers' delegates from Bradford, Dundee, Glasgow, Blackburn, Preston and Chester.

Mundella, as spokesman, referred to the report of the inquiry instituted in the previous year after his bill had failed to pass the house, and pointed out that his Nine-Hour Bill, which had lain before the house of commons since 11 February, embodied the main findings of that report. He reinforced his argument by naïvely suggesting that shorter working hours in the morning would actually save gas, steam, power, and wear and tear, since under his bill employees would be able to breakfast before they came to work. Fison gave him strong support.

But opposition was soon forthcoming. Making a stand against Mundella on grounds of pure principle were Henry Fawcett and his wife Millicent. Henry spoke vehemently in the house, and his wife wrote letters to The Times. Both opposed Mundella's bill on the grounds that it would restrict the freedom of women and hinder the movement towards their emancipation.[22]

More formidable was the reaction of the large employers of labour who sat in the house: men like Sir T. Bazley, whose cotton-spinning factories at Helliwell were the largest in the kingdom. Bazley's baronetcy had been ostensibly earned by his provision for the intellectual and bodily needs of his workpeople—he had been the first employer to introduce the system of paying weekly wages on Friday. He and others waited on the home secretary on 11 June 1873 to point out that a measure which so intimately affected

849,000 textile workers and would prejudice such large interests should not be subjected to the theoretical experiments of a few enthusiasts. They denied that Bridges and Holmes (the two Local Government Board inspectors who had been commissioned to report the previous year) had made a convincing case for further legislation to cover textile workers; and demanded a proper royal commission to examine the whole question. Banding together as the Association of Employers of Factory Labour in the Counties of Lancaster, York, Chester and Derby, they set about the propagation of their point of view with all the resources at their command.

In the face of such formidable opposition, Mundella and his supporters were by no means immobilised. John Middleton of Dundee, William M'Weeny of Bradford, and T. Birtwhistle of Accrington, drew up a document for circulation to the house of commons. In this they refuted the arguments of the employers, taking as their text a report which had been published four months previously, in which Her Majesty's Secretaries of Legation reported on spinning and weaving factories overseas. Far from injuring the textile trade and its export trade, they concluded, it would actually have the reverse effect.[23]

Mundella himself took up the challenge in the house of commons on 11 June, when he tried to secure a second reading of his Nine-Hours Bill. Though his customary brassy and jocular eloquence was muted by a throat infection, he retailed his statistics in such a telling manner that the Factory Acts Reform Association were delighted. Meeting fourteen days later, they tendered their best thanks 'to Mr. Mundella for the most effective manner in which he introduced his Bill, and for his bold and judicious advocacy of the claims of women and children employed in the textile manufactures of Great Britain and Ireland'. At the same time they thanked Disraeli for supporting Mundella's appeal to the government for a special day in which to discuss the justness of such factory legislation at this time.

Looking back at the scene, the then secretary of the Parliamentary Committee of the T.U.C. wrote in retrospect:

'Never before, no, nor since, were employers of labour in all the great industries so well organised, so united, so powerful in wealth, influence and numbers, as then. It was not merely an organisation to resist advances in wages, reductions in the hours of labour, or other labour movements; but a combination to impede, frustrate and obstruct progressive legislation.'[24]

Mundella felt the full force of this: in July he again appealed for time in which his Nine-Hours Bill could be discussed; yet by the 28th Gladstone's promise on the subject was still unredeemed. When he rose yet again on 4 August to press its consideration, Fawcett delivered the *coup de grâce*, and the bill was withdrawn.

Mundella was not depressed, however, and wrote to Leader:

'My Factory Bill has had no end of ill-luck. Still, even that gives it prominence, and I shall come out right in the end. Fawcett's speech was simply dishonest. He made coarse personal attacks founded on misrepresentation.' [25]

By contrast, Mundella's speeches were consistently, though perhaps not wilfully, misreported. He asked Leader:

'Can you tell me who furnished you with the report of my speech on the Factory Acts? It is precisely the same word for word as supplied to the Manchester papers and the *Sheffield Telegraph*, and without exception is the grossest and coarsest caricature I ever read. I can give you whole sentences so changed, not only to deprive them of their point and meaning, but to render them into coarse and vulgar language.' [26]

For Mundella felt the importance of the bill and told Leader: 'It will be one of the leading measures before long'. The *Beehive* thought so too. On 9 August 1873 it remarked on the failure of the bill to reform the Criminal Law Amendment Act and Mundella's Nine-Hours Bill. 'The workmen', it declared, 'cared more about these than about all the measures put together for which Gladstone takes credit since his accession to office.' .

The opposition to the demand of the labour groups banded together with greater force as the year 1873 drew to a close. To supporters of the existing Criminal Law Amendment Act and the Master and Servant Act, the attempts made by Mundella and the T.U.C. to secure their repeal were dangerous. To a large body of Liberal manufacturers, the Nine-Hours Bill was part of a wider system of trade union demands, and so they decided to make common cause to resist them. The original nucleus of the Association of Employers of Factory Labour expanded into the National Federation of Associated Employers, in which the great textile manufacturers took a leading part. Seventy-year-old Henry Ashworth, the lifelong friend of Cobden, a Quaker, and, like Cobden, a firm opponent of the pretensions of the trade unions, together with Sir T. Bazley, represented the cotton-spinners. Seventy-year-old Sir Titus Salt and fifty-six-year-old Sir Francis Crossley represented the extensive textile manufacturers: Sir Titus, worsted and alpaca at his own town of Saltaire near Bradford; Sir Francis, carpets, which he mass-manufactured at Halifax.

When these four, and many others of lesser calibre, were banded together in the National Federation of Associated Employers they became a formidable political force. This happened early in April 1873, when Howell, who had got wind of what was afoot, told George Potter, with the result that the *Beehive* warned its readers on 19 April and again on 12 July, urging them to sink their individual aims and meet national organisation with national organisation. During the summer, as Mundella pressed the consideration of his Nine-Hours Bill, the secretary of the National Association of Federated Employers (Henry Whitworth) published three pamphlets. They were: *Observations of the Employers upon the Report of the Local Government Board* by J. H. Bridges and J. Holmes; *Observations of the Employers upon the Speech of Mr. Mundella M.P. made in the House of Commons on the 11 of June 1873*; and a third pamphlet containing the speeches of Professor Fawcett and Sir Thomas Bazley. The newspapers reviewed the contents of each pamphlet.

After 11 December 1873 the Employers' Association redoubled their activity. Four days later, led by Sir Thomas Bazley, M.P., and Edmund Potter, M.P., they sent a deputation to Robert Lowe, protesting against the power of the trade unions, which they claimed would increase when they obtained the coercive power of picketing. On this issue the Employers' Association took their stand, claiming that the trade unions did not really represent the world of labour. They claimed that the repeal of the Criminal Law Amendment Act, for which the unions were fighting, would not enable them to protect men who were unwilling to strike. As one of their members, W. H. S. Aubrey (later the editor of their journal *Capital and Labour*), wrote to *The Times*:

'Should they [the Trade Unions] be successful in these changes [the proposals put forward at Nottingham the year before] a period of legislative change adverse alike to the employers and to the liberty of the individual workmen and to the interests of the whole community will be brought in with the next Parliament.'

So, to afford a centre of action, to instruct public opinion and to conciliate electoral support, the Association bent its resources. A manifesto was issued, denouncing the organisation and growing political power of the trade unions, together with 'the active members of parliament who are energetic in their service'. This manifesto evoked rebukes from both *The Times* and the *Economist*. In a main leading article on 16 December 1873 *The Times* commented on the presence of Bazley, Ashworth, Salt and Crossley among its members, but nevertheless remarked that it was 'a movement tending politically to put asunder forces which have long been allied, and tending socially to draw capitalists and labourers into two hostile camps'. Eleven days later the *Economist* hoped that it would 'content itself with being small and useful, and not large and mischievous'. They, too, called attention to some expressions in the manifesto which, as they said, 'alarmed' them. The offending passage ran:

'Should the industrial civil war waged by the Trade Unions continue to gather head and increase in intensity—it will be the office of the council of the association to guide and lead them in the use of such measures as shall appear necessary to defeat the organised aggression that threatens the national prosperity.' [27]

Mundella saw which way the tide was flowing even in Sheffield, where there were no textile factories. Replying to Leader's suggestions as to probable candidates for the town in the pending general election, he wrote:

'That will give the Tories, Church and Publicans against us, and numbers of the middle-class Liberals will join them or refrain from voting out of dislike to the attitude of the artisan class. I think this distrust of the workmen has more to do with Liberal defeats than Toryism, Teetotalism or the 25th Clause.' [28]

6

So, as preparations were being made to hold the annual Trades Union Congress at Sheffield in the second week in January 1874, Henry Crompton made a startling suggestion to George Howell. 'Have you asked Chamberlain to the Congress?' he wrote. 'It might be very desirable to do so. If he were there it might end in his being pinned down to our programme.' [29] The suggestion did not bear fruit. Mundella busied himself to secure for the delegates a reasonable reception in Sheffield, and wrote to Leader on the last day of the old year:

'I think it highly desirable that the members of the Conference should not be left in a state of isolation. Liberal and sensible employers should manifest their sympathy with this labour parliament in all efforts of a reasonable and laudable character tending to improve their class. I am afraid the Sheffield Middle Class are very antagonistic towards them and will resent my appearance among them.'

A week before it assembled he wrote again:

'I don't expect the old "nobs" of Sheffield would welcome Trade Unionists. I did and do hope that they would find the same kindly feeling that has characterised their reception in other towns. However, rather than it should be wanting, poor as I am, I will do it myself. I can give them breakfast at the Victoria without any great extravagance.' [30]

On 12 January 1874 Sheffield was invaded by 'elderly persons laden with carpet bags, wearing that equivocal smile peculiar to strangers anywhere'. The local Conservative organ noticed 'nothing remarkable about them but their garments'. [31]

The academic radicals were there in force: red-cheeked Frederic Harrison 'looking as if crops and harvest would interest him more than Trade Unions and practical philosophy'; Goldwin Smith, fresh from America, 'cold, clerical and silent', and the unions' attorney Henry Crompton. In the eyes of the press they were merely 'Mr. Mundella's friends'.

Mundella himself, 'smiling his harsh, Dombey-like smile, and twirling his double eyeglass with an air of modest self-approval', was invited to bring them on the platform after the opening address. In one sense it was his finest hour, for only a fortnight before the opening of the congress, 300,000 iron-workers (embracing all the industry south of the Tweed) had accepted a reduction in wages pioneered through a board of arbitration. Mundella refused to accept the vote of thanks which Congress accorded him for his labours, asking them to reserve it for their Parliamentary Committee, 'which had spent hours, both night and morning, in the lobbies of the House of Commons'. He endeavoured to prevent the trade unions making open war against Fawcett, on the grounds that he was misguided.

He argued for the harmonisation of the laws affecting labour. He urged them to consider the needs of their children. He begged them to support his Factory Bill. He pointed to what happened when a mother went to work, leaving her child at a 'shop' where it was either irregularly fed, or else dosed with Godfrey's cordial. George Howell backed him up and urged the delegates to wait upon their M.P.s to secure the passing of this 'sanitary and humane measure'.

So the Sheffield Congress drew up a consolidated programme. The first five items all illustrated the continued baulking they had suffered since the adoption of the Nottingham programme. The catalogue of their grievances showed how specific they now were:

(i) Repeal of the Criminal Law Amendment Act of 1871.
(ii) Alteration of the Master and Servant Act so that breach of contract should be an offence.
(iii) Alteration of the Conspiracy Bill on the lines of Sir William Harcourt's Bill.
(iv) Imprisonment to be used only as a last resort.
(v) Limitation of the summary jurisdiction of magistrates.
(vi) Eligibility of workmen to serve on juries.
(vii) A Workmen's Compensation Bill.
(viii) Mundella's Nine-Hours Bill.
(ix) A bill to prevent truck by weekly payment of wages.
(x) A Merchant Shipping Act on Plimsoll's model.

A week later, Gladstone dissolved parliament. His manifesto alluded to labour questions and labour legislation as fitting subjects for consideration by the next parliament. Such promises, however, rang hollow in the ears of those delegates who had heard the report of the parliamentary committee at the Sheffield T.U.C. Howell himself succinctly remarked, 'It was too late for confidence to be restored':[32] circulation of his own table of questions to candidates showed that the forthcoming election would be fought on the promises of individual members rather than a mass endorsement of the policy of either Liberals or tories. A number of labour leaders decided to go to the polls themselves: notably Alexander MacDonald (who was elected for Stafford) and Thomas Burt (who was returned for Morpeth). With liquor, labour and capital against them, reinforced by a large number of outraged dissenters, the prospects for the Liberals looked glum indeed.

7

At Sheffield there was a four-cornered contest for the two seats. The employers, the liquor trade, and the church backed Roebuck once more, and his searing condemnation of the late government for removing the Bible from the schools and the beer from the public-houses won him large and appreciative audiences. As if that were not enough, Mundella found himself running with Joseph Chamberlain.

Chamberlain's entry into Sheffield politics was not welcome to the moderates.

'I have talked with Allott about Chamberlain looking elsewhere,' wrote Mundella to his chief supporter, 'but it is not easy to do. He is obstinate and impractical to the last degree. I got to the very heart of the League last week, and it was shown to me clearly that Chamberlain is the sole dictator.'

This was two months before the election. A month before he was still lamenting, 'Chamberlain cannot be removed. He is too thorough a creature for the whip to handle. He is master of the League rather than the League of him.'

Chamberlain was prepared to go much farther than Mundella. He 'earnestly reprobated' the educational policy pursued since 1870. He proposed that education should be made free by the simple expedient of utilising the revenues of the established church. By these and other flourishes which his later political career was to make so familiar, he warmed the hearts of those who were most opposed to the blind reaction of Roebuck and his sponsors. Nor was Chamberlain's principal supporter, H. J. Wilson, any less compromising. To each rhetorical flight he would nod assent.

In the great gulf that yawned between Roebuck and Chamberlain it looked as if Mundella's moderation would indeed be lost. For his programme was the essence of caution. He approved of Gladstone's address, with the exception of its inadequate treatment of the educational question. He essayed no flights, nor new departures, but stolidly maintained the platform which he had made so familiar to the readers of the *Sheffield Independent*: the Nine-Hours Factory Bill, and 'the necessity of a complete revision of the laws affecting juvenile labour, which', he added, 'at present override and obstruct the successful working of the Education Act'. It was, in all its mundane and prosaic quality, practical politics.

The differences which appear so startlingly clear to us were not so visible as Mundella and Chamberlain rode about Sheffield in the same carriage. They made a good pair: Chamberlain with his top hat and monocle, and Mundella with his great black beard and hooked nose. They were too good a target to miss. Red herrings were thrown at Chamberlain, and a piece of brick at Mundella, as they appeared on a platform together. At one meeting in Paradise Square a group of roughs sang and booed in the centre as they tried to speak, while from a public-house floated jeers at the Liberal teetotalists. Stung to frenzy, a body of Liberal supporters attacked the public-house and poured all the beer down the sewers. Leader struck shrewd blows for the cause in another direction by masterly cartoons of Roebuck, seated astride a barrel of beer, and clutching a Bible, being dragged to the polls by clerics and publicans.[33]

In the heat of the contest, Chamberlain's extravagant language made Mundella's friends despair. James Stansfeld, brother-in-law of George Dixon, who knew the man of whom he was writing, addressed Polly Mundella in tones of commiseration:

'I felt sure it would be a bad day for your father if Chamberlain were chosen. The least he could do now would be to fight for your father as well as himself, as colleagues ought always to do. I am glad you are with him to help him and cheer him. Don't admit for a moment that he can be beaten. And if he should be, then think on this, that he might easily now find a much more convenient and safer constituency than this big turbulent one, with a considerable Irish taint in it, I presume.' [34]

The result was a victory for Roebuck. But, as a consolation, Mundella was also elected as the junior member. Chamberlain, in spite of a last-minute exhortation to voters to plump for him, was third, and the local man, Allott, was at the bottom of the poll. The figures were:

ROEBUCK	14,193	elected
MUNDELLA	12,858	
CHAMBERLAIN	11,053	
ALLOTT	621	

All over the country similar results told the same tale of Liberal defeats. Fawcett lost his seat at Brighton, as did Tom Hughes at Frome. In all, 176 Liberals failed to get back, thus enabling the Conservatives to obtain a majority of fifty-six. Mundella, sitting in the Reform, wrote a letter to Chamberlain in which he commiserated with him: 'Here in this club', he went on, 'I am surrounded by an army of martyrs, and I should have felt no chagrin to be one of them.' But to Leader, who had also felt the discomfiture of Chamberlain's candidature, he opened his real mind:

'We are about to enter on a period of Tory Rule which will prove a wholesome discipline to the Liberal Party. One class of politicians hope that it will strengthen the weak-kneed Liberals and develop a new and advanced party. A very distinguished man of the moderates said to me today, "the next five years will be spent in educating the Nonconformists". He meant in teaching them to be tame and submissive. I don't believe this. I look forward to an advanced and practical party with larger views and fewer crochets.'[35]

He was ever the good party man. So when Frederic Harrison wrote to him, 'Have you no party in the House and can you not form one?' he never even mentioned the matter to anyone,[36] much less took any action on it.

CHAPTER NINE

The Prop of the Party, 1874–1876

I

COMPARED to the solid tory front, the Liberals seemed in a sorry state. Mundella noted that Gladstone was 'quite discouraged by the aspect of the party', and commented:

'We have a host of men who are disloyal, crochety and unpractical—Harcourt, Dilke, Dixon, Lawson, Jenkins, Leatham and, very shortly, Fawcett. Many others that I cannot enumerate are all bent upon their personal questions or their personal ambitions, and Gladstone will not lead to be stabbed in the back by these men.'

He pointed to the undercurrents of intrigue which were washing away the very foundations of the party:

'There is a great deal of intriguing going on to make Hartington leader. The Non-Cons. will not have Forster, and I hear Lowe and the secular party will not follow him, including Bright, Stansfeld, etc. . . . So you see we are not only weak but disorganised and disunited. I decline to take part in any intrigue. I have let it be known clearly that I regard Gladstone as our only possible leader *as long as he remains in the House.* . . . I shall continue to play the role of mediator and urge unity and courage.'[1]

Gladstone's attitude was condemned by some as 'anarchic', for, as he wrote, 'the real battle is being fought in the world of thought where a deadly attack is made with great tenacity of purpose and over a wide field, upon the greatest treasure of mankind, the belief in God and the gospel of Christ'.[2]

On the other hand, Disraeli was far from withdrawing to the world of thought.

'Dizzy is as cool as a cucumber and his face immovable as wood,' wrote Mundella. 'He is more of a sphinx in office than out, and has attained a mastery over expression and emotion such as I never before witnessed.'[3]

2

This mastery was reflected in his social legislation, which, piloted by Cross, the Lancashire banker whom he made home secretary, gained headway with help from the left wing of the

Liberal party to redeem the hopes of the tory democrats, to make the prophecies of *Sybil* come true.[4]

'There is now a total absence of concert on labour questions in the House. I have my Factories Bill down for second reading on 6 May and shall take my own course on that and other labour measures until things assume a different shape.'

So Mundella saw the political situation in a letter to Howell written after the election. That course lay with the Factory Acts Reform Association, which now rallied to give him formidable backing. Large demonstrations at Blackburn on 24 January and at Leeds on 2 February were followed by lesser ones in Dundee and other textile-manufacturing towns. On 20 March his bill went through the formality of yet another first reading.

Five days later, Mundella introduced to the home secretary a deputation, composed of members of parliament, manufacturers and workpeople. He made an effective and notable speech, which was reported in *The Times*. He quoted the opinion of British consuls in various parts of the world to the effect that his bill would not prejudice British overseas trade, since most foreign countries already had a fifty-four-hour working week. Mundella's own argument was that it would probably improve it: for by improving the quality of the workmen, it would also improve their skill. Mundella's strongest arguments were reserved for raising, not only the age at which children could begin half-time labour, but also the standard to be attained before they left school. Hitherto ages had varied and standards were evaded. He wanted the age raised to ten, and the standard raised to four. Moreover, he wished to see the scandalous exemptions of the silk industry entirely abolished.

Perhaps his finest speech in support of the measure was delivered in the house of commons on 6 May 1874, when it was read a second time. When printed it filled twenty-six columns of *Hansard*, and even today sustains interest by reason of its closely knit argument. Mundella denied that the trade unions 'had anything to do with the bill'. They supported him, just as they supported Plimsoll. He also regretted that his bill applied only to the textile trade, but his excuse was: 'Parliament has legislated upon the subject piecemeal, and it would be impossible for any private member to pass a bill that would deal with all the industrial employments of the United Kingdom, since it would only multiply opposition'. Much as he would like to see a consolidation of the

Factory Acts, he realised that it was beyond the province of a private member.

His arguments were based on the beneficial effects of past Factory Acts, which had saved a considerable proportion of factory workers from becoming cripples. He tried to spike Fawcett's objections by pointing out that in opposing their bill, Fawcett was acting inconsistently, since he had done much to secure the passing of the Factory Act of 1867. Pointing to the universal movement for restricting the hours of labour, Mundella urged that 'the cheaper people work, the longer hours they work, the more wretchedly they live, and the easier it is to compete with them in the foreign markets of the world. This is my experience everywhere.' He claimed that his measure, far from blighting the foreign trade of the country, would give it new life: 'It is said that trade follows the flag—I believe it follows the man—the man who has intelligence, the man who has a knowledge of languages, that is the man who is successful.'

Diplomatically, he claimed to see the innate goodwill behind the opposition of the rich Manchester men who opposed his bill. 'My hon. friend sitting beside me', he said, pointing to Sir Thomas Bazley, 'is a living refutation of his own arguments.' Of Bazley's fellow resisters he continued:

'I am bound to give them the credit of being the most energetic and persevering men I know. They opposed Lord Ashley, they opposed the late Mr. Fielden, and they are opposing me, but they remind me of nothing so much as a stage army where a dozen or two men are representing the contending hosts . . . and ever appearing as a new force.'

To this eloquent appeal, Cross replied that the government already had the intention of introducing a bill on the lines of Mundella's measure. Mundella was delighted.

'I have done very well with my Factory Bill,' he told Leader on 9 May, 'and am in receipt of most gratifying acknowledgements from employers and employed. Mr. Fison [Forster's partner] has written me a very handsome letter of thanks, and my old antagonist, Hugh Mason, begs me to dine with him on Monday next. The Government are, however, very anxious to reap the fruits of my three years work. They will undoubtedly be able to embrace a wider scope in their bill than mine, and, as my object is practically assured and completely successful in the clauses relating to ages and education of children, I am content.'

So the Conservative bill was formally introduced, and the initiative passed from Mundella to Cross.[5] But there was still

AN ANTI-MUNDELLA CARTOON

Circulated before the Parliamentary Election of 1868

work for Mundella to do, in defending the government's measure against attacks, both from the Conservative and the Liberal benches. On 5 June the Glasgow Chamber of Commerce strongly condemned such legislation as injurious to foreign trade. On 12 June Mundella told Leader: 'I am simply worked off my legs with the Factory Bill. I pounded Fawcett last night in such a way that Forster, Lubbock, and others came to congratulate me when I had finished my speech.'

Throughout the last week in June the bill was hammered into shape as it lay before the house. The employers were anxious not to surrender too much children's labour, and Mundella rallied to support Cross against the critics of both parties.

'Everyone is much pleased with the debate on the Factories Bill as to raising the ages of children,' he exulted. 'I resisted Crossley, Ripley, and other *millionaires*. Forster, Cross, and Sandon stood firm, and it is intended, I believe, to raise the age and educational qualifications throughout the country.'

Leader was quick to take any opportunity to fill the columns of the *Sheffield Independent* with his triumph, and Mundella was most touched.

'I am very grateful to the *Independent* for the article in yesterday's issue on the Factories Bill,' he wrote on 26 June. 'Cross made his tardy acknowledgements to me, and the men in the House who can appreciate the whole scope of the measure have been very warm in their congratulations. Very few, however, in the House or in the country, are able to discern that it is the beginning of a scheme to secure the health and education of the entire puerile population, and necessitates a measure of general compulsion. Forster, Lowe, Sandon, and Cross have admitted this in their remarks in the House, and in conversation with me have acknowledged that it is inevitable. It is no small thing to have brought the workpeople themselves to acquiesce in this.'

The workmen were most grateful for his efforts. Meeting on 24 June the assembled delegates from Lancashire, Yorkshire and Scotland unanimously passed a motion 'that the best thanks of the factory workers now assembled are due and hereby given to Mr. Mundella for his most able and generous advocacy of the Factory Bill'. They did more. After discussing the clauses of Cross's Act, they resolved 'that the representatives of the factory workers now assembled do adjourn to the residence of Mr. Mundella, to thank him personally for the liberal spirit he has displayed in resigning his bill on the introduction of the government measure, and for the able and generous support he gave to that measure in all its stages'. To their tribute was added that of Lord Shaftesbury, who spoke in the house of lords on 9 July. As Shaftesbury was in full flow, Mundella went to the bar of the lords, and found himself 'the subject of much attention'.

His work in this sphere was recognised by his election to the Political Economy Club on 3 July 1874. Goschen was disgusted.[6] But Mundella was delighted. For amongst its closed circle of forty members were Gladstone, Lowe, Bagehot, Newmarch, Hare and Fawcett. The death of John Stuart Mill had left a vacancy, which was filled by him on a ballot. He really felt as if he had achieved something.

3

The warm adoption of the Nine-Hours Bill by the government was followed by their equally fervent rejection of the Endowed Schools Commission. This body, set up by W. E. Forster in 1869, had, under its energetic secretary H. J. Roby, succeeded in producing schemes for one-third of the existing endowed schools of the country. These schemes included the setting up of popular governing bodies, the introduction of science and modern languages as teaching subjects, and the creation of special schools for girls. It was, in effect, a state authority controlling secondary education.[7]

But they had inevitably irritated the vested interests. To Thring, the reforming headmaster of Uppingham, they were a 'witches cauldron' in which everything that was good and individualistic was boiled down. Determined that he would not be cast into the cauldron, he organised his fellow headmasters into a powerful body, and soon had the biggest schools working with him. With Eton, Winchester and Shrewsbury behind them, the Headmasters' Conference formed a powerful pressure group which the Conservatives could not ignore.[8]

Lord Sandon, Forster's Conservative successor, therefore took action. As the son of the president of the National Education Union, he was more than ever inclined to look on the trespass of the state upon the rights of private educational foundations as unwarranted and unnecessary. He introduced the Endowed Schools Bill, which proposed to restore the state of affairs that had existed before 1869. It provoked an uproar.

Upon Mundella fell the duty of opposing such a reactionary measure. He told Leader on 24 July 1874:

'In three or four days we have been working night and day to defeat the Endowed Schools Bill. I have done so much of the work that our men come and say to me, "This is a great triumph for you". So do our Whips. I have arranged with Forster the amendments, provided the speakers, and kept the whole debate going, never leaving the House from 3 in the afternoon till 3 in the morning. The defeat of the Tories is complete, and their rage unbounded. The Ultra Tories are at this moment furious. They are cursing their leaders, and would eat a few of us without salt. They have tried howling and dodging, and every kind of strategy, but we have fairly thrashed them and here is the strong Tory government caught in its nefarious designs, exposed and defeated, after a few months of office.'[9]

The vigour of the Liberal attack was minimised by the Conservatives, who accused the Liberals of trying to gather together their scattered forces by this manœuvre. Mundella vehemently denied this. 'I for one', he exclaimed, 'have lost some political capital by my adherence to my educational principles.' Mundella turned the edge to where it bit deepest:

'If one of the City Guilds considered itself attacked, if its members thought they were about to be deprived of one spoonful of turtle soup, a similar cry would be raised.
'Where the endowment has been rich and the school good, it has been appropriated by the rich, but where it had been comparatively poor, and the school good for nothing, it has been left to the poor.'

He pointed to Christ's Hospital and asked, 'The Blue Coat was founded for city arabs, but how many of that class were to be found within its walls?' He wound up his speech with a plea for a really effective state agency for controlling secondary education. This Disraeli was not prepared to set up. So the following day, supported by Gladstone, Mundella moved that progress be reported. Confusion and disorder reigned in the house, and Mundella rose to ask 'whether Mr. Cavendish Bentinck was warranted in skulking behind the chair and there lending his voice to the noise and confusion which prevailed?' Such vehement language provoked a demand that he should apologise.

But in spite of all Mundella's efforts, the ministry won the day. The Charity Commission supplanted the Endowed Schools Commission, and for the rest of the century Gwydr House became a third educational authority overlapping and confounding both the Education Department at Whitehall and the Science and Art Department at South Kensington. Both *The Times* and the *Economist* were disgusted. *The Times* declared:

'It is difficult to find a precedent for it—a Bill proposing the wholesale delivery to one religious body, of schools which, founded for national purposes and endowed with national property, have been set free for the use and education of all Englishmen.' [10]

The *Economist* was much more strongly condemnatory, calling it 'one of the worst measures of modern times', and adding:

'It was moved in a speech that, if anything, makes the measure worse than it otherwise was, since it shows the reactionary sense in which the Education Department wish the measure to be administered.'

It essayed a strong rebuke too:

'If we are to have much of this spirited retrogression under cover of Conservative tranquillity, we do not think that the new regime will last long. Lord Sandon is doing the worst thing he could do, in the worst way.'

But Sandon's work was not yet finished. Two years later he was to stir yet another hornets' nest.

4

But on the most vexed question of all—the right of the trade unions to picket in order to make their strikes effective—Disraeli's strategy was masterly. He appointed a royal commission to examine the question.[11] A kindly interpretation is that Disraeli wished to educate his party on the question in order that they might take action; an unkind view (held at the time) was that he wished to avoid legislation altogether, and chose this way of doing it.[12]

As a political stroke it was a great success. It split the forces of the labour world. Mundella suspected that MacDonald (now a member of parliament) had 'sold the trade unionists' by accepting a seat on the commission. In that belief, he introduced his own bill to reform the Criminal Law Amendment Bill on the same night as he had introduced his Nine-Hours Bill. Immediately afterwards, on 21 March 1874, he wrote a hot, indignant letter to Leader:

'It is evident that the government succeeded in obtaining their Commission just as they had abandoned all hope of doing so. At the eleventh hour, before the paragraph in the Queen's Speech was expunged (as it was certain to have been) Hughes and MacDonald gave a qualified assent to join the Committee. In Hughes' case it was weakness; in MacDonald's, worse. Hughes actually assisted the day before in drawing up the protest against the Commission, and even strengthened the words they proposed to us. There is but little excuse for him, and yesterday he met the working men from all quarters of England, Rolley amongst their number, and Hughes' defence was his worst accusation. He and MacDonald are now reconsidering what course they shall pursue. They both express regret at having been trapped by intrigue on the part of the Government, and that they assented to the Home Secretary's proposals. The way the thing was managed was singularly ingenious and crafty, and Burt's account of the whole story and Hughes' and MacDonald's subsequent relation was as good as a play. Indignant as the men were at finding themselves betrayed, they screamed with laughter at the clever trickiness of the whole thing. Hughes was put in one room at the Home Office, Burt in another; one was played off against the other, and both against MacDonald till two had given their assent.

'Disraeli's promise of legislation this session is all nonsense. Nobody believes him, even his own side think it is all a mistake, and shake their heads over it. See Fitzjames Stephen's article in the *Pall Mall* of Wednesday night, and the paragraph in the *Spectator* today. You may be assured so far as the working men are concerned, they will oppose the Commission and abuse the Government.'

Mundella was inclined to blame Hughes for the whole thing.

'Cross had been trying all in his power to get at the workmen's representatives through Sir Wm. Harcourt, and *had failed*,' he wrote to Leader on 11 April 1874; 'he succeeded only at last through this ingenious trick. . . . Had he failed with Hughes, the Commission would have fallen through.'

With his own measure he was determined to persevere. 'I shall hold it over the government to compel them in June to say something or *legislate*. I hold them to the latter course.' [13]

The Parliamentary Committee was at first embarrassed that its chairman, Alexander MacDonald, had agreed to serve as a commissioner: doubly so since Thomas Burt, the only other labour member in the house, approved of MacDonald's action. On 20 March 1874, MacDonald tendered his resignation as chairman of the Parliamentary Committee, which was accepted. The committee then went on to call for immediate legislation, urging all local unionists to press it upon their members.[14]

When the secretary of the royal commission wrote to George Howell, as secretary of the Parliamentary Committee, asking him to give evidence, Howell refused. For this refusal he was excluded from the lobby of the house of commons. Mundella was invoked to help, and wrote on 22 June 1874:

'I am working away at Lord Charles Russell about your exclusion from the lobby. I hope I shall succeed in getting it revoked and your right of entry at any time established. Come and breakfast with me on Wednesday morning at nine o'clock and let us talk over matters.'

Mundella's help, reinforced by that of Gladstone, Harcourt and Henry James, enabled Howell to be readmitted once more. The episode showed how touchy the government had become upon the question of the Royal Commission.

Cross converted them to a belief in his sincerity after his excellent stand on the Factory Bill in July 1874—so much so that by the following January 1875 the Trades Union Congress were converted to MacDonald's viewpoint. Conversion made them give short shrift to anyone who might even imply that MacDonald had 'betrayed' the workers. W. R. Cremer,[15] who attacked certain members of the commission, was expelled for accusing them of 'treason to the cause of labour'. He had to leave, clutching his hat and umbrella, speeded by the hisses of the delegates, nor was he re-admitted as a member of the congress till he had published a full apology.

The confidence of the unions was justified. Cross brought in two bills: one to repeal the civil disabilities under which striking trade unionists laboured, the other to amend parts of the Criminal Law Amendment Act of 1871 which had given such a wide interpretation to the term coercion. Political strategy, as the trade unionists conceived it, was directed from 27 Villiers Street, the tiny headquarters of the Parliamentary Committee, that lay just off the Strand. Under George Odger's chairmanship, a series of conferences, which Mundella attended, resolved to approve and support both bills of the home secretary, fighting them only in committee in order to introduce minor and more favourable amendments.

So, just as Mundella had been occupied in the previous summer of 1874 with the Factory Bill, now in 1875 he was heavily involved with both trade union bills. In the ding-dong struggle as they passed through committee he succeeded in paring the tentacular malice of the word 'coerce', by carrying an amendment that a fine should be as adequate a penalty as imprisonment. Some onlookers, like W. A. Hunter in the *Fortnightly*, thought that this was the only significant alteration to what were two badly drafted bills. As Henry Crompton claimed with truth in a later number of the same journal, it was a workmen's victory. Mundella was so pleased that at 1.30 in the morning of 15 July he sat down in the house of commons and poured out his joy to Robert Leader:

'It has been the best night for the Liberal party this Parliament. I was teller and leader in the first two divisions, and brought the majorities to 20 and 19 respectively. The Tories were confounded and amazed, and we amended their Bills and we abandoned their clauses right and left. The workmen are delighted, and our front bench are most grateful to me. It is a fact that the House followed me on Labour questions when it would follow nobody else, and at twelve o'clock (midnight) Cross dare not face Lowe's proposition to repeal Section 1 of the Criminal Law Amendment Act.

'He proposed to remodel the act himself by words not on the paper, and he had to yield and report progress till Friday at two. Last Friday night, he declared to the workmen's Parliamentary Committee and myself in conference with them that nothing should induce him to *touch* this act. Tonight he has been compelled to re-open the whole question and you may look out for fun on Friday.'

Three days later he was still jubilant:

'How angry Leng is', he wrote after reading the *Sheffield Telegraph*, 'that Cross has adopted my amendments, and falsified all his prophecies. The report in both papers makes it appear that I said Cross had pursued his way through obloquy and misrepresentation. I said how it encouraged Liberals to pursue a just course through obloquy and misrepresentation when we find a Conservative Government compelled to adopt our measures.'

He rode happily on the thanks and good words of his allies, writing on 18 July:

'You make kindly allusion to my recent successes. It is a fact that is a little flattering and has been remarked upon a good deal that the House of Commons will follow me upon labour questions before anybody else. My amendment and Lowe's are the only ones on which any good fight has been made, and on which Cross has given way, and they have given a new character to his Bills. The Liberal M.P.s and some Conservative (Borough members) came to me and asked how they should vote.'

On 7 August 1875, after a six-hour session, he wrote:

'The Employers and Workmen's Bill and the Conspiracy and Protection of Property Bill have employed me very actively and we have run the Government very close, and certainly *beaten them in arguments*. The Lords have substituted a new clause for the old Criminal Law Amendment Act and have made the Bill *worse* than when it left this House. We have been trying to amend this, and have had a series of fine divisions, when the Government majority has fallen to eleven and never rose above fourteen. I moved to permit men to persuade peaceably by the insertion of the words in the margin of enclosed amendments. This Cross was disposed to concede, but Hardy would not allow him, and they led their blind followers against this most *reasonable provision*. I hope you will show them up.'

So, at last, the Nottingham programme had been translated into law. Symbolising this, George Howell relinquished the secretaryship of the Parliamentary Committee; the Trades Union Congress ceased to meet before the parliamentary session; and the new leaders concentrated on widening the avenues of advancement for the working classes. The new secretary, Henry Broadhurst, was mindful of the services which Mundella had rendered, and forwarded to him an official resolution of thanks from the Parliamentary Committee:

'We owe more to you than to any other single man in the House of Commons,' it read, 'but in addition to what you have done publicly, we owe to you perhaps more for what you have done quietly for our relief and benefit.'[16]

So Mundella might well tell Leader:

'The representatives of Labour in London (at least all the best of them) are so complimentary to me as I never dreamed they would be. They have sent resolutions of thanks for my services with the most grateful letters.'

5

Such a personal triumph stands out all the more starkly in view of the almost total collapse of the Liberal party at this time. Gladstone still evoked Mundella's greatest admiration. In a typical transport of enthusiasm, he told Leader on 8 October 1874:

'Gladstone is, taking him for all in all, the most wonderful man I ever met, and it is difficult to say to which his greatness is most to be attributed, his natural genius or his power of work. What do you think of him walking sixteen miles the other day to inquire after a young lady three weeks after her first confinement? Mrs. Gladstone had walked with him, and was told that the mother was then engaged in taking the first lesson in washing the newborn infant, whereon Gladstone prayed that they might be allowed to be present, and, with the purity and freshness which characterises him, he showed his delight and delighted everybody else by his expression of sympathy and joy.'

All who struck at Gladstone earned Mundella's deep suspicion. He singled out two men who were actively promoting the disintegration of the party.

'Unfortunately for us', he complained on 10 August 1874, 'we have that ambitious and pompous Harcourt always striking at our Leader, caring nothing for the mischief he inflicts on the party or anybody else, caring only in fact for —Harcourt.'

Two months later he singled out Chamberlain:

'He, of all men, has been the most disloyal to the leaders and workers of the Liberal Party, and his attacks on Gladstone during our joint candidature were so bitter and unjust that I will not soon forget them.'[17]

He supported Gladstone throughout 1874 on personal grounds, writing on 15 October:

'His manner of life is exceedingly simple and modest and he seems of late more than ever to inculcate this in others, deprecating all extravagance in dress, expenditure, etc. The fact is, he looks upon the excessive wealth and ostentation which is too common as a great source of danger socially and politically. Everywhere the tendency is to worship money, and his manner of life is all against it.'

But by the beginning of 1875 the fragmentation of the party became so bad that Gladstone formally resigned the leadership. Having earlier described the new parliament as 'the most apathetic, the most reactionary, and the least independent' in which he had ever sat, he now confessed himself bewildered by the Liberal party's apparent lack of purpose. He listed nine points of policy (suffrage, disestablishment, land laws, retrenchment, colonial policy, local government reform, secular education, denominational education and Irish affairs) on which there was not only no plan, but no clear majority in favour of a plan. With his acute sensitivity to public demands, he now thought that he could best serve by promoting some understanding outside the state and world of politics.[18]

Gladstone's retirement was not made easier by Lord Hartington's proposal that the party should have three leaders—one for the whigs, one for the radicals and one for the Irishmen, since 'there is hardly an important question on which the Whigs and the Radicals will not vote against each other'.[19] But Hartington's suggestions did not meet with approval from the others. Goschen observed, 'It seems to be absolutely impossible that things can go on as in the last session'. John Bright thought the same: 'I am in the midst of discord—no one yielding, only chaos. Could I have foreseen what was coming, I should have retired at the election.'[20]

Mundella took the lead in trying to persuade Gladstone to reconsider his decision. 'It seems strange that I should be selected as the medium,' he wrote to Leader, 'but it is thought that the work should be begun by independent members.'[21] He drew up a memorial and canvassed members for signatures. Gladstone was, needless to say, adamant in his refusal even to reconsider his decision. So the little group which Mundella had got together—G. O. Trevelyan and Bernhard Samuelson amongst others—turned to W. E. Forster as their potential leader.

Six months previously Mundella had given his opinion that—

'Forster is the strongest man on our side, and in every way the best in the absence of Gladstone. Our Non-conformist friends are virulent in their dislike of him, and the aspirants on the Front Bench are jealous of him, and trade on the dislike of the Non-cons. Lowe, Harcourt, and Goschen are especially antagonistic to him, but the real Liberals are more and more giving in their adhesion to Forster. I wish all Non-Con. questions were settled, or in a fair way for settlement.' [22]

Now in January 1875 he was assiduous in trying to overcome Forster's scruples. He breakfasted with him a fortnight after the New Year had begun, but failed to make much impression. He confessed :

'Now who is to be leader? One thing is agreed—Harcourt is impossible. It really lies between Forster and Hartington. I suspect the Whigs will make a tremendous attempt to retain it in the hands of the latter. I dislike the man. I distrust his character and I don't think that I shall be one of his followers. Forster is to my mind the only man, but I hear the Non-cons. are bitter and his opposition to the Disestablishment movement will not tend to reconcile them. Not that Hartington and the Whigs will ever disestablish. There is no chance of yielding in that quarter.' [23]

In spite of such goodwill, however, Forster had no desire to lead the Liberals, and wrote to Mundella on 21 January:

'I am anxious lest I should become a bone of contention. The kind and generous way in which my name as possible leader of the party in the House has been advocated, has surprised, and I may say, touched me, and it is impossible not to feel gratified as well as grateful. But you know that I do not desire the post, and I most earnestly desire not to be a cause of contention. If, therefore, you, and others who think with you, have reason to believe it will be better for the party to get me out of the question, I must beg you at once to do your best to do so. Please show this note to Playfair and Trevelyan if he is in town, and to anyone you think fit.' [24]

Mundella was the only prominent member of the anti-whig group left in London, and even he had to rush to Sheffield to attend a meeting to promote a University College there. Nevertheless, he corresponded both with Trevelyan [25] (who was at Stratford) and with Fawcett (who was at Cambridge). The crisis grew as the deadline for the scheduled formal election at the Reform Club drew nearer. Lord Granville seemed willing to listen, and fixed a preliminary meeting for 26 January. But the scheme—if scheme there was—went astray : Trevelyan was thrown from his horse and left at Stratford with a bad feverish attack, while the wobbling of Lyon Playfair led Lord Granville to abandon the idea.

From three totally different quarters opinion appeared to mass against Forster. The *Beehive* voiced what passed for the labour viewpoint: Beesly, writing on 29 January that 'it would be better to stand still under Lord Hartington than to march forward with Forster'. Beesly's tactics were too subtle. He hoped to destroy the Liberal party in order to make way for one which was more advanced: Forster's election as leader 'would prolong the life of the Liberal party as at present constituted'. Most trenchant were the forthright, almost savage, articles of Joseph Chamberlain, in which he scathingly denounced the Liberals, with their 'rough arbitrament of strikes and lock-outs'. These articles, printed in the *Examiner*, followed up a blistering attack which he had delivered the previous October in the *Fortnightly*. To Chamberlain, Hartington was 'the least objectionable leader'. The third anti-Forster group was, in essence, the most powerful of all, since it energised and animated John Bright, who took the chair at the fateful party meeting on 3 February at the Reform Club at which the formal choice was to be made. John Bright, the hoary tribune of nonconformity, had been steadily fading from the political picture since his illness had led to his withdrawal from the Gladstonian cabinet. He re-entered it with great force, expressing in forthright epithet the profound distrust which his co-religionists felt for the man who had passed the 1870 Education Act ('the worst measure passed since 1832'), an act which was 'instrumental in preserving and extending indefinitely the system of voluntary schools'.[26]

But, as Dilke observed, 'at one moment it looked as if Forster might win, in spite of Chamberlain and the non-conformists'.[27] Playfair again began to wobble when Hartington made a speech at Lewes which, according to Fawcett, 'damned his chances'.[28] Even *The Times* professed uneasiness about the outcome of the party meeting. Dixon, now drawing further and further away from Chamberlain, was more than inclined to favour Forster, and G. O. Trevelyan, writing to Mundella, praised him as 'honest and judicious'. Trevelyan, indeed, recovered from his fall, and wrote to Mundella on 30 January:

'The violence of the other side is a good card for us and a good indication. Brogden, who declares for H., is *just* the sort of man I should expect to do so.

The Howard lot are and always were, trumps. I will be at the club at 4 on Tuesday 2nd February.'

Stout counsel came from old Robert Leader, editor of the *Sheffield Independent*:

'I am disappointed that you will have to give up Forster in deference to Birmingham dictation. I shall be very sorry if you do, far better defy them even if they do their worst. But what could they do? They would be simply ridiculous in their separation and I feel sure that they would soon be made to feel that they do not represent Nonconformity but only its noisy fraction.' [29]

Mundella was urged to undertake embassies on behalf of the independents. Fawcett asked him to write to Granville and explain that most of the independent Liberals who sympathised with him were in favour of Forster. He was also asked to arrange for a private meeting of Forster's friends to take place just before the big Liberal party meeting on 3 February. In the midst of it all Forster was constantly reminding him that leadership of the party 'was so untenable that none should be asked to take it'. He earnestly asked Mundella to consider whether he and his associates would not promote the common object 'by withdrawing me and making terms, such terms being the understanding that you would not be considered as acting contrary to party discipline by the fullest advocacy of the principles and measures which you have at heart', confessing that he would rather be an advocate of such measures than a leader.

Mundella himself was sanguine. On 26 January he told Leader that things were going against Hartington 'among the more prominent men on the Liberal side'.

'Dixon's speech at Birmingham was decidedly against Hartington and for Forster,' he continued, 'and Bright, whom the Leaguers had hoped would smite him, *carefully refrained*. Chamberlain was expected to do it, but even he was silent, and the leading Noncons. in the country, men who, like yourself, are practical politicians, are indignant at the course that has been taken in their name. You see J. C. Cox, one of the leaders of the League and of the Liberation Society, has declared for Forster, so has John Morley of the *Fortnightly*. The old whigs, however, are using the social forces at their command for Hartington, and they may succeed.'

Four days later things were still in the balance. He wrote:

'I have nothing to communicate about the Leader. I have seen Mr. Adam's private list; thus far Lord Hartington slightly leads in numbers, but Forster is supported by the strength of the party. I think on Tuesday we shall reach a crisis, and one will probably be withdrawn; when this is done you shall have first news. If I telegraph that "Bradford is scratched" you will know Forster is withdrawn, and may use it, if Hartington, I shall say *"Cavendish".*'

The issue was really decided two days before the party meeting. All through the afternoon of 1 February 1875 Mundella and Playfair were in conference at Forster's house. Bradford was scratched. Mundella told Leader why:

'It has been made clear that there would at once be a *whig cave* with Lowe at its head, and that his old colleagues, with two or three noble exceptions, would be apathetic if not hostile. Bright, under the influence of the League, would be hypercritical, perhaps antagonistic, and the non-conformists of the extreme section would be laying traps for him so that they might alienate from him the more moderate and sensible non-cons. Under these circumstances he would be so hampered as to have little chance of promoting principles which are far dearer to him than position, and he therefore decides to be a free man. . . . We have urged everything that could be urged in opposition to these views of Forster's, but, at bottom, we feel he is right. His exclusion can only be temporary, and we shall either drag the Whig party along with us or leave them to bear the brunt of their unpopular procedure.'

So at the meeting on 3 February Hartington became the leader of the Party. But Mundella was convinced such an arrangement was only temporary, for on 19 March he expressed himself:

'Gladstone will assuredly return some day. He cannot resist the temptation of a good fight.

'It is hopeless getting up meetings to influence the government. They must go on filling up the measure of their iniquity for a little longer, till the country is fairly roused. Pray don't attempt any demonstration till we can do it on a grand scale. They will give us plenty of opportunities hereafter.'

6

With such demonstrations as there were Mundella had little sympathy. Plimsoll's histrionics were especially galling at this time. Plimsoll had drawn off much of the enthusiasm of the trade unionists: his speech at the Liverpool Congress in January 1875 had been greeted with acclamation. Secure in such support, he staged a demonstration in the house of commons itself. On 22 July 1875, having heard that Disraeli meant to withdraw the government's Merchant Shipping Bill, Plimsoll (speaking, as *Hansard* says, 'with great excitement') begged the prime minister 'not to consign some thousands of living human beings to undeserved and miserable death'. His appeal receiving no response, he became still more agitated, and, naming members of the house (he actually shook his fist at one on his own side), he declared that he would 'unmask those villains who would send those sailors to their death'. Walking up the floor of the house, he threw a paper on the table, and though he withdrew his person, he refused to withdraw his remarks.

Mundella's comment was caustic.

'The Plimsoll scene', he told Leader, 'was wild and extravagant in the extreme, the general opinion being that he would soon be in durance as a lunatic. I don't think so. It was clearly premeditated. He told Sullivan *privately* that morning, that he should be in a dungeon that night for the course he was about to pursue. He showed his toothbrush, etc. in his pockets as in readiness. After the scene, he gave Sullivan a letter ready prepared to deliver to his wife; and further, Sullivan stated, that Mrs. Plimsoll dropped copies of the protest out of the ladies' gallery on to the reporters' desk.'

Plimsoll's capacity for embroiling both his cause and himself in expensive libel suits threatened the very peace of the party. On one occasion he had accused C. M. Norwood, the Liberal M.P. for Hull, as the owner of a coffin-ship. Norwood rightly decided to sue, considering it the only way of saving his reputation. To have a libel action of this nature would have been fatal to the party. Mundella had no love for Plimsoll, whom he regarded as a mountebank. When he was served with a *subpoena* as a witness for Norwood, he turned to Applegarth in order to crush the libel action altogether.

Applegarth was accordingly induced to travel to Hull and to endeavour to persuade Norwood to withdraw his suit. Norwood refused. The spectacle of Plimsoll in prison failed to move him. So Applegarth resorted to a species of blackmail. He told Norwood that when the trial did come off, evidence of such a character would be given concerning Norwood's ships that Norwood would repent having pressed the case. A specific instance was mentioned of a ship being lengthened by eighty feet, and a hole in the plating being covered with a stroke of a tar-brush. The tactic was successful. Norwood gave Applegarth a note to the solicitor instructing him to withdraw the case, which Applegarth handed to the delighted Mundella. Plimsoll made a mild apology, and the Liberal façade remained unshattered.[30]

Though Mundella continued to support the cause of merchant seamen, he had but a poor opinion of Plimsoll's promotion of it. 'Plimsoll is, well—not a gentleman,' he told Leader, adding:

'He has a good cause but manages it very badly. The fact is that the cause sustains him rather than he it, and when the question is partially settled and the interest subsides, he will be the least influential member of the House.' [31]

7

The effective sustentation of the Liberal cause and party in Sheffield exercised both Mundella and Leader in the dark days following the Chamberlain–Allott debacle. Heading a break-away group of disaffected Liberals, H. J. Wilson continued to promote Chamberlain's candidature. On 21 October 1874 Chamberlain appeared at Mundella's side at the Sheffield Trades Council annual dinner. H. J. Wilson's busy, dynamic, almost fanatical nature kept a Liberal club going in opposition to the official club presided over by Robert Leader.

With the passage of a year, however, the sores healed. By the end of 1875, Robert Leader and H. J. Wilson had agreed to abandon their cross purposes and to form a Liberal Association in the town. This was to be inaugurated at an impressive meeting. Mundella was called in to secure a judicious mixture of great names in the party, headed by Hartington himself. On 11 October 1875 he expressed his hope that 'the meeting would end in a large organisation'.

'We must *trust to the democracy*,' he told Leader on 11 October 1875; 'they are hearty, unselfish, enthusiastic, and, what is more, numerous. With good management we can make the borough representation secure, and H. J. W. will put plenty of steam into it and work like a horse.'

Indeed, Leader's efforts were well supported by others in a way that Mundella had cause to rejoice over. 'I am glad to have so good a report of H. J. W.,' he told Leader on 21 October. 'I think work and co-operation will keep him in the traces, and by and by he will be your henchman.' A day later he wrote: 'Phillips is a capital fellow. He goes in for organising the working men. He says "I don't care a d—— for the gentlemen." Really, I think he is in the right. The gentlemen will come in in time.'

As the launching of the Association approached, rumours got about that it was intended to promote Chamberlain's candida-ture. This discouraged Leader and others. Mundella wrote to keep them in good spirits. On three successive days he wrote to Leader at length. On 1 November 1875 he wrote:

'I quite understand Mr. Mappin's [32] apprehensions, but the power and in-fluence of men of your class do not consist *in numbers*. Only mix with the people, go amongst them and gain their confidence, and everyone of you counts for a thousand.

'I thought the paras in the London papers preclosing the decision of our new organisation in favour of Chamberlain very mischievous, but it might have been done by an enemy or by an ardent friend of C's.'

The following day he continued urging Leader to base it on popular support:

'Should I get two Rt. Hons. we will billet them on Mappin and I will give them their cue to enlist him. Immediately I saw that Chamberlain's name was associated with the new organisation, I knew mischief would follow. *Now don't be disheartened*, go on. The swells will come in hereafter when we have made it a success. No Association can influence or bind them. This is not the case with the working men and the lower middle class, they are loyal to their party and their friends. Let us only *get enough* of them and we shall soon have our share of the upper crust, and if not, we must do without them. Pray don't despond. This is our darkest time, and dawn follows close upon it.'

And on 3 November he urged that unity should be real:

'I believe in working up some enthusiasm among the people. I am not surprised at Mappin and Smith's reluctance. The separation of classes in Sheffield is wider than in any other place I ever knew, and there will naturally be reluctance on the part of such men to break through the traditions of their order.

'Let us go on, it will come out all right.'

Comfort was needed, for on 24 November 1875 Chamberlain addressed a meeting sponsored by the Liberation Society in Sheffield, voicing the anti-clerical sentiments that so warmed the nonconformist consciences of Wilson and his associates. Mundella did not approve of it, and told Leader: 'C's speech was bitter, rancorous, illogical and eminently indiscreet. I met the editor of the *Daily News* who thinks the same.'

So preparations were pressed on for the great reunion meeting to be held in Sheffield's Albert Hall on 15 December. Robert Leader took the chair; the speakers who blessed it were headed by the Marquis of Hartington, M.P., James Stansfeld, M.P., Henry Richard, M.P., S. D. Waddy, M.P., and Mundella himself. All pleaded for the strength that lay in union. The meeting was so successful in bringing over the nonconformist section under H. J. Wilson that *The Times* felt sure that the object of the whole Association was to promote Chamberlain's candidature.

A week after the meeting had been held Mundella wrote to congratulate Leader:

'Since my return home my right arm has been tied up as my old boil gathered again, and I was obliged to cease writing in order to get it well. Your management of the meeting was *perfect*. Everybody that I spoke to agreed on that point, and no one was more impressed by it than Stansfeld, who told H. J. Wilson the next morning that your speech was simply *admirable*. Of one thing I am clear, no other man in Sheffield could have done it as well, and we all owe you, and wish to render you, grateful thanks.

'The meeting was undoubtedly a great success. Hartington's speech was most discreet, indeed, all the speeches were. Stansfeld's peroration about the destructive party seemed to me to be exceedingly effective, and H. Richard did exactly the right thing, and did it in good temper and spirit. . . .

'I was sorry to see *The Times* take the line it did in assuming Chamberlain's candidature as the object of the meeting. I had a letter from Dixon asking me if this was true, and I told him no second candidate had yet been thought of, and that until the Association was complete no selection would be made. I think Waddy would be glad of a safer seat than Barnstaple. He is a very decent fellow, and behaved well to us.

'You will find many other towns following our example. Southampton and others are about to do it. . . .''

On Christmas Eve he wrote again:

'I think your Fabian policy is right. I am sure great good will result from a closer union of various sections of our party. The meeting itself will moderate all sections. Nothing else could have brought H. J. W. and his friends to listen to such good advice as Lord Hartington's, and Richard's speech would do just as much good to the same party as it would to Smith, Mappin, and the moderate section.'

Thanks to Leader, the Liberal Association of Sheffield proved an exemplar to others, and was to give a lead to them in a great cause before the next Christmas came round.

8

'The Conservative Party will have to be educated on the education question as they were on the Reform Question.' So, on 9 June 1875, Mundella commenced a eulogy of the work of the London School Board. Service on school boards, he asserted, was socially as valuable as service in the house of commons itself. School boards, for Mundella, were the answer to many things: to inefficient enforcement of the Factory Acts, to poor attendance of children at school, nearly half of whom (1,300,000 out of a total school population of 3,000,000) were virtual absentees. Through school boards he hoped to beat the squires, the unenlightened factory-owners and the inefficient inspectors. Therefore, he urged, make school boards compulsory. Sandon was unconvinced. He replied that he could not 'shut his eyes to the fact that an uneasy feeling existed among the ratepayers at the burdens they imposed'. When figures failed he held up the very real bogey of foreign competition. Even then the government were not daunted. One member was amused at Mundella's 'eloquent and characteristic speech', and declared that he 'must be contemplating some system of national decay, or else he would have shrunk from the arbitrary measures he has suggested'.

For compulsion was still unpopular. Mundella and Dixon were still voices in the minority, and, as they told their defeat, they prepared for a fresh attack next session.

As a correspondent wrote to Mundella on 14 July of this year:

'You would have had an easy victory if it were not for the gross hypocrisy that prevails on this subject. But what can you do when at least eight tenths of your opponents pretend to agree with you and then deliberately and designedly go off on a side issue for the purpose of defeating you? The great bulk of the Conservative party, as you say, hates education in itself, but because they have just sense enough to see that a certain amount of education may make their serfs more useful workers for them, they are desirous to give them just that modicum of teaching. Such teaching as would make them men and not machines, our friends on the other side, and not a few of our friends on our own side, will not endure.' [33]

Nevertheless, the question of child labour had begun to tease the minds of many on the government benches. Cross had responded to a motion on 19 February 1875 to set up a royal commission which should examine the advisability of consolidating the Factory Acts. This commission, under its president, Sir James Ferguson, travelled throughout the country, hearing evidence from employers and workmen alike. Mundella was called before it to give evidence. His testimony was important; for not only had he pressed for the appointment of the commission, but the implied terms of reference with which the commission was charged was to see how far the Factory Act of 1874 might be extended to industries other than textiles.

He went before it to give evidence just after he had returned from a fact-finding mission to Switzerland. His argument was simple: the age limit for half-timers should be raised from ten to thirteen, and the standard reached should be higher than three. He added that if pupil teachers were superseded by schoolmasters they would ensure attendance far better than factory inspectors would. His testimony was reported in *The Times* and other papers.[34]

His attention turned to the working of the educational system.

He had long abhorred 'private-venture schools', kept for the express purpose of evading the Factory Acts. He began to give more detailed figures of their prevalence in the country, statistics difficult to obtain, since these schools neither kept registers, gave instruction, nor were subject to inspection. He revealed that in one large town over 20 per cent of the children attended them. He questioned the vice-president as to the attendance and finance of the voluntary schools as well, to ensure that the 1870 Act was having a good effect.

His enthusiasms now became more specifically educational. Matters like the proposed reduction in the government grant towards the Bell Chair of the Theory and Practice of Education at Edinburgh University met with his detailed scrutiny. He protested against the withdrawal of the grant, declaring:

'I look forward to the establishment of a chair of pedagogy at the University of Edinburgh. Professor Huxley in one of the ablest lectures ever given says that the science of teaching is one of the utmost importance, yet from this science the government wish to withdraw the shabby grant of £200.

'It is notorious that our system of teaching in England is not a good one. It involves much waste of power. Children do not make as much progress as they ought, and do not make beneficial use of their time at school.' [35]

It was a problem that could be answered only by some method of ensuring that every school had a means of enforcing attendance. Even the supporters of the voluntary system were coming to see that some form of compulsion was necessary. Now, with all the controversial issues that had agitated the politics of the last five years settled in favour of the radicals, the question of compulsion lay before the government demanding solution. At Accrington, on 11 November 1875, Mundella repeated that only by compulsory education could American competition be met. 'With it', he declared, 'we could import coal from Nova Scotia and still beat them.'

Well might Mundella write to Leader four days before the year 1875 closed:

'I know from my own study of the Education and Labour questions how difficult it is to make the truth penetrate even the most Liberal minds. Forster never fully grasped the idea of a national system because he never thoroughly studied it, but I see it steadily making progress through all difficulties.'

This steady progress was seen in 1876, when for the third time he and Dixon introduced their bill to secure compulsory attendance at school. Mundella was in excellent form this session, and confessed to Leader that he had never spoken with such ease. As soon as the session began, he was on his feet asking why the educational clauses of the Factory Acts were not being complied with—for children were being passed out as fit to commence half-time employment without a certificate being given. Cross, the Home Secretary, promised that the regulations governing the issue of these certificates would be better understood in future, and that arrangements would be made to examine persons in large centres of industry 'immediately'.[36]

The Queen's Speech at the beginning of the session contained the promise that a measure would be introduced. Nevertheless Dixon and Mundella persevered with their own in order to stimulate Sandon's action in the matter. Mundella argued that four out of the six members of the committee on the Employment of Children in Agriculture and Manufactures were in favour of his bill. The rate difficulty he swept aside: the sewer rate was twice as large as the school-board rate, which itself cost as much as a walk in the horticultural gardens. His speech in parliament on 5 April was very effective. Sandon asked him to withdraw his measure to make way for an official draft. Mundella did so.

Sandon's bill, however, was half-hearted. It proposed to set up permissive compulsion—i.e. if the non-school-board districts petitioned, they might be allowed to make bye-laws enforcing attendance. School boards remained with the same powers as Forster had given them—i.e. that they could make attendance bye-laws if they wished, but were not compelled to do so. Fees for very poor children were now to be paid by the guardians and not by the school boards. Labour passes were to be necessary before any child under ten could be employed. It lay before the house from 18 May to 14 August, and aroused such bitter and acrimonious debate that Disraeli thought that it symbolised the rancorous breaking up of the Liberal party.

Its proposals were viewed as half-hearted by the executive committee of the Liberal party. But, what is more important, the prime mover in opposition was Mundella himself. He opened the Liberal case in the second reading by moving for direct compulsion and the adoption of the principles contained in his own measure, which did not envisage any freedom of choice for the districts to impose compulsion.[37] He pointed out that the 1874

Factory Act was in itself an incomplete measure, since it prohibited employment, but did not compel attendance. His argument gathered force from the fact that a further extension of the franchise was envisaged, and the argument for an educated electorate was as strong as ever. Among the names that he cited to support him were Patric Cumin, assistant secretary of the Education Department, and Dr. Bridges, with whom he had worked on the Contagious Diseases Acts Commission. Though the motion was lost by 146 votes, he was not dismayed, and returned with redoubled intensity to the attack when the measure reached the committee stage.

It was at this stage that he carried all the back-bench opposition with him. He was very proud of this, and wrote to Leader:

'I organised the whole opposition, arranged the speakers, and carried it on without leaving my place in the House except to snatch refreshment until twelve on Monday night, and again yesterday. Between ourselves, we have made it very difficult for them to accomplish their object. Bright, Adam, and Forster, and all the men below the gangway are delighted, and some of them have said "you ought to lead us below the gangway".' [38]

For Forster was adopting a more cautious attitude, having roused a hornet's nest by sponsoring the 1870 Act.

'I shall form one of a little knot of Liberals who mean to fight this bill in detail,' he wrote to Robert Leader a week later, 'and if it perishes by delay I shall not grieve over it, neither will Forster, though he is anxious not to imperil his reputation with the moderates by seeming to oppose the bill.' [39]

So clause by clause and word by word the debate continued. From the Conservative back-benchers came amendments which the Liberals fought, and once more the paradox was repeated of the opposition supporting the minister against the amendments of his own party. One amendment aimed at reducing the age of half-time labour from ten to nine years,[40] another proposed that agricultural areas should be excluded from the provisions of the bill.[41] The Liberal opposition was just as cunning. In one amendment a suggestion was made to delete the words 'may if they think fit' from a clause empowering the school-attendance committees in non-school-board areas to make bye-laws. The deletion would have implied that an obligation lay on those bodies to make bye-laws to enforce compulsion. Sandon noticed it, however, and remarked, 'The government start from this position. They do not think the principle of direct compulsion would be a good thing in itself.' Mundella then moved that bye-laws could be framed without a requisition from the local inhabitants being first received. That, too, was defeated.

As the summer wore on tempers rose, and at times exhibited signs of fraying. One Conservative member proposed a clause that school boards should, in certain circumstances, be dissolved. Mundella rose to defend them and used 'such acrimonious and hostile language' that Lord Sandon complained. Mundella had to withdraw remarks which were personally offensive, but declared that he stood by the substance of his speech.[42] Shaftesbury wrote to congratulate him on being a great success.

Mundella's last protest was against boards of guardians being substituted for the school boards as the responsible authorities for paying the fees of necessitous children. He insisted that it was a matter for national decision.[43] Privately, he held that this removal of the 25th clause from the political arena 'was not such a bad thing'. But he believed the time was not yet ripe for the fees themselves to be abolished, and though he agreed with Chamberlain, he wrote to Leader:

'Free schools will come, but the country is not ready for them. As to *fees* being a *tax*, that is all nonsense, but we have gone so near making the schools free that the fees only delude people into the belief that they are paying for education when they are only paying about ½ of the charge.'[44]

After the conclusion of the second reading he wrote again on 30 July:

'Had there been twenty men below the Gangway like-minded with myself, the Bill would not have passed. This is not boasting. I know it, and nobody can know what the strain has been, both of body and mind, to maintain the fight as I have done, and how I have besought (in vain) those who ought to have aided me, and who failed me, to my utter chagrin. (I will tell you more when we can talk quietly.) It requires as much pluck to stand up and be hammered in Parliament as in the Prize ring, and I have taken my own punishment, and other people's. The reaction is dreadful, but I shall be ready again for Report and Third Reading. I am satisfied on reflection and investigation that in the contest betwixt Sandon and myself I am wholly in the right, and I will yet prove it upon him. I thank you for your defence of me, but *pray don't apologise for me*. I mean to continue thrashing both him and the Government.'[45]

As the bill emerged with the Royal Assent, contemporary comment regarded it as highly denominational. Mundella accused Sandon of breaking his promise to introduce a full measure of compulsion, and described him as 'the mildest-mannered man who every scuttled a ship or slit a throat'—the ship being the promised content of his bill, and the throat being that of the body of dissenters. For the contemporary historian of the new fast-dissolving National Educational League it was 'an act for compelling attendance in denominational schools supported out of rates and taxes'.[46]

For the dissolution of the League was imminent. Other pressure groups were drawing off its heads of steam, other causes were moving men's minds. George Dixon, the devoted and faithful founder, was retiring more and more into the shadows of private life. His wife was seriously ill, and to comfort her he applied for the Chiltern Hundreds. Mundella told Leader on 20 June:

'Muntz tells me *confidently* that Chamberlain has warned Dixon out of his seat and that he had thrown it up rather than lead such a *dog's life*.' This was in accord with Stansfeld's comment six months earlier: 'There is no doubt he is *King* in Birmingham but whether there will be a vacant seat is another matter.'

Chamberlain professed himself well enough satisfied with what had been accomplished:

'If properly carried out', he wrote to G. J. Holyoake, 'it will do a great deal for education, but it is a tremendous blow to the Dissenters and to the secular party. This is an issue which the League was not formed to try and it is questionable whether we must not leave the battle to others. We shall have a kind of universal compulsion and universal education and there remain only two things:

(i) Free schools—for which this country is certainly not yet prepared.
(ii) to wrest this education out of the hands of priests of all shades.

The last is really a branch of the Disestablishment movement to which I am more and more convinced that the efforts of all Radicals should now be directed.'[47]

Disraeli congratulated himself that the 'burst of factious fight' over Sandon's bill had shown up 'the utter demoralisation and rancorous breaking up of the Liberal party'. 'It seems split into fragments,' he wrote to Lady Bradford, 'all working against each other. Goschen answered Forster, and Rylands, Mundella.'[48] Disraeli crowed too soon. At the very time he wrote this, his own actions had initiated another 'burst of factious fight' that was to lead to the eclipse of his own party by the end of the decade.

CHAPTER TEN

Towards the Front Bench, 1876–1880

I

'THE Balkan mystery is evidently more interesting than the
Education Debates,' wrote Mundella on 30 July as the debates on the Education Bill proceeded.[1] He was referring
to the situation which had developed since Disraeli had refused to
co-operate with the rest of the European powers subscribing to the
Berlin Memorandum of 13 May: an instrument for pacifying the
rebel Christian subjects of the Sultan of Turkey on condition that
Turkey accepted certain reforms.

Disraeli's rejection of the Berlin Memorandum raised Turkish
hopes and Turkish temper. Two sultans were successively de-
posed. Vigorous action was taken against the rebels of Bulgaria,
in whose fate Russia had expressed such profound interest. And
when Disraeli sent the British fleet to Besika Bay, it looked as if
these acts were endorsed by a pro-Turkish British government.
This revival of Turkish confidence might have achieved its ends
had not the Turks adopted, against the Bulgarian rebels, the policy
of letting loose armed bands of irregular troops known as Bashi-
Bazooks. These, in the month after Disraeli had rejected the
memorandum, carried fire, rape and slaughter into the innermost
parts of Bulgaria. Such atrocities were quickly revealed. The
Liberal *Daily News* carried full accounts by 23 June. Disraeli, well
aware that the Liberals lacked a good stick with which to beat his
government, and also influenced by Sir Henry Elliott (the British
Ambassador at Constantinople) in favour of Turkey, considered
the stories as mere 'coffee-house babble' and 'inventions'.[2]

2

As the parliamentary front displayed the ragged cohorts of the
Liberal party at their most ineffective, the local newspapers took
up the hue and cry. Among those who splashed their columns
with grisly details of the massacres were W. T. Stead, editor of the
Darlington Echo,[3] and Robert Leader, Mundella's own political

adviser. Mundella heard from Dr. Washbourne, of the American Missionary College at Constantinople, and Humphrey Sandwith, who twenty years earlier had been a surgeon in a corps of Bashi-Bazooks: both supplied him with ample confirmation of the atrocity stories. He was shocked, and in a long letter to Leader in late June declared his intention of raising the matter in parliament. On 7 July, three days after Lord John Russell had called for action in the matter through the correspondence columns of *The Times*, the radical group led off. G. Anderson, Mundella, Joseph Cowen and P. A. Taylor all spoke. Mundella told Leader: 'If these atrocities go on I think our government ought to intervene to put a stop to them'. Though the 'Nasmyth hammer' of the Conservative majority prevented anything being accomplished, outside the house indignation gathered strength. On 16 August, Dilke had an enthusiastic reception at a meeting at which he roundly denounced Disraeli. On 4 September, Mundella, at a meeting which had already been postponed because of bad weather, roused a large audience at Sheffield.

Meanwhile, Gladstone himself had been energised out of retirement by such currents of popular feeling. Though ill, he finished and published *The Bulgarian Horrors and the Question of the East*, which appeared on 6 September. Three days later, in the pouring rain, his constituents swayed before him in a meeting which he described as 'the most enthusiastic by far that I ever saw'.[4] His pamphlet, no less than his emergence, added strength to the anti-Turkish movement. On 11 September a working-class deputation waited on Lord Derby to protest against the foreign policy of the government, but they were only treated by the noble earl to a spirited defence of it. A week later the Lord Mayor presided over an anti-Turkish meeting held in the Guildhall, followed by another, the same evening, at the Exeter Hall, under Professor Fawcett. Robert Leader hit upon the idea of embodying these local protest meetings into a national conference upon the Eastern Question. On 4 October, Mundella agreed:

'I think your idea of a great National Conference on the Eastern Question a good one', he wrote. 'Meetings seem to have done all that could be expected of them, and further efforts ought to take the new form you have wisely indicated. A large representative Conference, to be held in London (or in some central place in the country) would speak *once* for all and speak *unanimously*. I shall be glad to hear what you have done in the matter.'

He added:

'Don't let them work you too hard. I have a vested interest in your life and health, in addition to an affectionate regard for the best friend I ever had in public life. I beseech you, therefore, to let your judgment guide you, and not the entreaties of your friends.'

Mundella adopted Leader's idea, and began to think of translating it into action. On 6 October he wrote:

'People here are getting *anxious*, and seem to think that we are drifting into war. The government is weak, the Turks infatuated, and Russia cunning and designing. I have no idea of allowing Russia to profit by the change. I want the Christians of Turkey to be placed in a way of governing themselves, and not to substitute one despotism for another. By supporting Turkey, our Government has played the Russian game, and it now requires great boldness to lead the very movement we have opposed.

'I quite believe your Conference will be a good thing. Pray make your resolutions clear that we are not going to play into the hands of the Russians.

'I think the "Great Guns" should *hardly be Parliamentary*. Get clergy, ministers, representatives of great bodies, Mayors of towns, etc. I am glad Sheffield has the honour of this movement.'

And the following day:

'If we have no Autumn Session, it will be the best means of keeping the Government up to the mark. The localities should, I think, appoint representatives and *request their members* to attend the Conference.'

By 10 October he was 'more strongly' convinced than ever that the Conference should go on', since Forster had made 'a very bad business' of his resolutions; so he saw Howell and Broadhurst, and tried to rope in Joseph Chamberlain. Chamberlain was not enthusiastic. 'Nothing seems to go down with Birmingham that is not of *home manufacture*,' Mundella complained to Leader. Even though Leader followed it up by making a visit to Birmingham, their attitude remained unchanged.

As well as Chamberlain, Harcourt and Dilke also looked coldly on the idea. Harcourt wrote to Dilke on 10 October 1876 deprecating the possible return of Gladstone: 'There is no fear of a return from Elba,' he said, speaking of his late leader's anti-Turk crusade. 'His recent conduct has made all sober people more than ever distrust him. He has done two good things: he has damaged the Government much, and himself still more.' [5] Dilke agreed: 'If Gladstone goes on much longer', he wrote, 'I shall turn Turk. Hartington is the best man for us Radicals.' [6] Hartington opposed the conference because 'it would get into the hands of men of extreme opinions', and professed himself 'in daily dread' of seeing Gladstone's name added.[7] His brother, Lord Frederick Cavendish, wrote to Mundella on 24 November:

'I entirely agree with you in the feeling which you tell me Lord Beaconsfield's speeches have been looked at throughout the country, but I feel much doubt, viewing my connection with my brother, whether it would be advisable for me to take a part in calling the conference and whether indeed my doing so would not tend to prevent some joining in your movement who might otherwise be inclined to do so.[8]

Yet, despite all this weight of opinion against him, Mundella persisted, not only in organising the National Conference, but also in endeavouring to persuade Gladstone to take part. As chairman of the committee for convening such a conference, he wrote to Gladstone on 25 November—the day before Hartington had expressed his forebodings. Gladstone was sympathetic:

'Continued reflection much confirms me in the belief that we are greatly in the dark about Turkey and that we greatly want organised information and methods of spreading it.'[9]

So was James Frazer, Bishop of Manchester, who wrote on 27 November:

'I am right glad to hear of this moment. I was afraid the Country was going to sleep again and that we should awake to find ourselves plunged into the middle of a scandalous and unnecessary war.'[10]

Yet there were deeper motives in the anti-Turk agitation than those of mere opposition to Disraeli. As William Morris confessed:

'I joined the agitation on the Liberal side because it seemed to me that England risked drifting into a war which would have committed her to the party of reaction. I also thoroughly dreaded the outburst of Chauvinism which swept over the country, and feared that once we were amusing ourselves with a European war, no-one in this country would listen to anything of social questions, nor could I see at that time any party more advanced than the Radicals.'[11]

William Morris wrote to Mundella on 15 November enclosing a list of names, and vouched for them as feeling 'strongly and rightly' about the matter. 'Their letters to me all express the desire that something should be done as quickly as possible. Money will be wanted soon, and both of us are ready as soon as it is wanted.' Among the names he sent Mundella was that of W. T. Stead, editor of the *Northern Echo*, 'who says expressly that he must not be put down so'.[12] Fawcett, too, stirred. He wrote on 19 November: 'I do wish something could be done in the way of a protest against Lord Beaconsfield's Guildhall speech.' [13]

The Parliamentary Committee of the T.U.C. were most active. Broadhurst held a conference with the object of considering the 'progress of the Eastern question through the concert of the powers', and particularly of 'diffusing through the country sound information on various branches of the question'. A circular was prepared, and sympathisers were asked to sign. Fifteen thousand signatures to a petition were obtained, and it was conveyed to the house of commons in a four-wheeled cart.[14]

All turned on the appearance of Gladstone. He, and he alone, could give voice to the moral indignation which was felt. He was the symbol of outraged Liberalism, the guarantor of peace. To get him, however, demanded patience. On 25 November Mundella wrote to Hawarden:

'W. P. Adam sees life in our movement and wishes to help us *quietly* although we would not accept it as exclusively party help. I believe we shall have such a demonstration as England has not seen since the Anti-Corn Law days. Carlyle's letter will be the first blow, our demonstration of names the second. Then the conference and meeting, to be followed up by literature and public meetings throughout the country. I wish you would give your assent to the meeting, as we wish to announce the speakers as soon as possible.' [15]

From now on he persisted almost daily in his attempt to land Gladstone on the platform. Gladstone dallied. Mundella pointed out to him the success that the movement was already enjoying, with

'associations and committees organising all over the country, and our move-ment will be national in spite of all opposition. But how can we make it national and omit the most important factor. Our committee meets tomorrow and I am sure will address you with a view to its publicity which will hardly leave you with any other alternative than to assent.' [16]

Gladstone's hesitancy was noticed by Shaftesbury, who had con-sented to act as one of the chairmen for the meetings. Mundella, as self-effacing as ever, wrote to Gladstone:

'I am very careful to keep myself and other politicians out of sight and hear-ing as much as possible. Our friend Adam [17] rejoices in our work, *and in the prospects of your joining us* at the conference. There must be no hesitation I venture to say about this. We leave all political leaders out, but we cannot play Hamlet and omit the Prince of Denmark. Kindly telegraph me your assent on Monday morning so that I may proceed to the Committee meeting and make the needful arrangements.' [18]

Among the scores of literary men who rallied to this cause were J. R. Green, Stopford Brooke, James Bryce and Thorold Rogers, to say nothing of Lecky, Ruskin, Mark Pattison and Browning. The sponsors alone were a formidable list. To cheer Mundella, the victories of the Liberals in the London School Board elections, announced on 30 November, were themselves a striking triumph of the power of organisation. Howell wrote to Mundella commenting on the fact, and adding, 'We have worked in some tune'.[19] Fortified by the result, Mundella was able to triumph over his old bronchial trouble which was making him 'as weak as a cat'.

Gladstone replied on 30 November:

'Many thanks for your various communications. I expect F. Cavendish here in 10 days and I will then speak to him. If, upon full consideration, it is thought that my appearance at one of your meetings on Friday, 8 December is desirable, and more desirable than at a later time, I am ready to say that as at present advised I will come. I hope the Duke of Argyll will actively testify his good will in one way or another.' [20]

Shaftesbury was doubtful of the prudence of Mundella's move, and wrote to him on 5 December: 'In confidence, were you prudent in asking Gladstone to speak?' [21]

On 7 December, however, he could rest. On the night before the national conference he wrote:

'What a work it has been. I was put in the chair the first meeting and I have sat on it the best hours of daylight for three weeks past. It is work as hard as a general election.
'I found that my first business was to extinguish the irrepressibles. A. Herbert, etc., would have damned the whole thing. I extinguished them to begin with partly by extinguishing myself. I have not allowed my name to appear on a single note or document. I don't intend that any Radicals shall speak *if I can help it*. I want to fire off the Bishops, the Parsons, the Peers, the Literati, etc., not those who have been the actors heretofore but *a new set*.
'I have been twice with Gladstone giving him his role. It is like a moth going to the candle to go near him; he is all light and flame.' [22]

3

This 'light and flame' played round the audience assembled at St. James' Hall on 8 December. The marquis of Salisbury had been sent to Constantinople, where the powers had gathered to consider Turkish schemes of reform. He had arrived in Constantinople on 5 December. Four days earlier the Grand Duke

Nicholas had assumed command of Russian armies concentrated on the Roumanian border.[23]

So it was a tense audience that awaited the speakers at St. James' Hall. Two meetings were held: one in the afternoon, and one in the evening. At the afternoon meeting the chair was taken by the duke of Westminster, who earnestly deprecated any intention or desire that the meeting should prove the occasion for any attack upon the government. His remark was received in silence. But when he continued, 'There are many opportunities for doing this at other times and in other places', vociferous applause broke out.[24] After him, speaker after speaker drew up a grand indictment of the Turk. Sir George Campbell vied with Anthony Trollope in testifying that the Turk had neither the power nor will necessary for self-reformation: sentiments echoed by Sir T. F. Buxton, George Howell, Sir Henry Havelock and Dr. Allon. Also on the platform were Lyulph Stanley, G. O. Trevelyan, Henry Richard, James Stansfeld, Henry Fawcett, Samuel Morley and H. Broadhurst. *The Times* remarked, 'We have never known any association for a political object which has obtained support over so large a part of the scale of English Society'.[25]

The alliance of the working-class leaders and the Liberals on this issue was complete. Broadhurst had organised a working-men's committee of the association, and personally conducted its operations.

The afternoon meeting was, for its time, most carefully organised. Admission was by ticket only, and there was a large staff of stewards. To maintain fervour a choir sang hymns, written for the occasion by William Morris. A sense of participancy of the whole audience in the meeting was induced by the community singing of these hymns, conducted by a volatile Irish clergyman by the name of Murphy. He would read out a verse, the choir would sing it, and then the whole audience would join in. It had the emotional stimulus of an American camp meeting.

At the evening meeting the chairman (Lord Shaftesbury) also tried, with indifferent success, to deprecate attacks on the government. His gentle remonstrance was but an overture to thunder. Canon Liddon set the rhythm by advocating armed intervention against Turkey. E. A. Freeman was more outspoken, ' Will you fight for the integrity and independence of the Empire of Sodom?' he demanded. 'Perish the interests of England, perish our dominions in India sooner than we should strike one blow or speak one word on behalf of the wrong against the right.'[26]

A letter from Carlyle was read in which he expressed his high admiration for the Russian national character and policy, and his firm conviction that the Turk must be expelled from Europe.

The sensation of the meeting was not only the appearance, but the speech of Gladstone. Mundella had scored a great success here. For when Gladstone had finished his rousing denunciation of the Turkish Empire, he ostentatiously offered his arm to Madame Novikoff. This was the symbolic representation of conference hopes: Russia and England guaranteeing the freedom of the Christian subjects of the Turk.

That the St. James' Hall conference had no immediate effect on Disraeli, since he had already briefed Salisbury for the Constantinople Conference, we now know. But, by increasing the heat of popular opinion, its effect was incalculable. The galvanising of the Liberal party had begun.

For Gladstone the meetings were 'great, notable, almost historical'.[27] To the tory, Henry Chaplin, they were 'packed ... a barefaced, audacious sham and imposture, so far as national character and name were concerned'.[28] To Lord Shaftesbury, himself a tory, they were, 'God be praised, a grand success. Their effects will be sensible and lasting.' Shaftesbury wrote again to exult how the members of the government were 'smarting under the effects of the congress', and naming Northcote and the duke of Richmond as being the chief sufferers.[29] P. W. Clayden, the free churchman, was impressed, and declared that not since the days of the Anti-Corn Law League had so various and distinguished an assembly been gathered together.[30] A young historian, then on the threshold of a brilliant career, was similarly impressed and wrote, 'The meetings told powerfully on the country'.[31]

Mundella's associates thought so, too, and arranged a breakfast in his honour. 'His efforts', wrote the duke of Westminster, 'were worthy of all praise.'[32]

4

To sustain this heat of public opinion, and if possible to increase it, the Eastern Question Association was founded. Ostensibly its purposes were 'to watch events in the East, to give expression to public opinion, and to spread useful information' from headquarters at 28 Canada Buildings, Westminster.[33] But behind the titular officers of the Association, like the duke of Westminster, the marquis of Bath and Lords Shaftesbury and Cowan, were the effective heads: A. J. Mundella as chairman of the executive committee, and William Morris as treasurer.

Mundella found that it was hard work propelling his committee along the line of vigorous propaganda. He wrote to Gladstone on 17 January 1877:

'I did my utmost to induce them to start a weekly organ of the association and I brought in Mr. Arthur Arnold to help me, but he proved the reverse of Balaam. I brought him to help my scheme but he joined the committee in banning it whereupon I fell back on the next best thing, i.e. large issues of popular tracts. I enclose a sketch of those already in hand. These will be printed at least 10,000 each and distributed gratis (by Cassells I expect) through agents throughout the country.' [34]

Hammer-like, a series of events drove the issue deeper into men's minds. The Turkish government rejected the proposals of the Constantinople Conference, which as a consequence broke up on 20 January 1877. The Russians circularised the powers in February, but with indifferent success. In March Gladstone wrote a further pamphlet—*Lessons in Massacre* for the Eastern Question Association—while another pacificating instrument, known as the London Protocol, failed to achieve its purpose. So, as a climax, on 24 April, Russia declared war on Turkey.

It was in the excitement following on the declaration of war between Russia and Turkey that Gladstone announced his intention of moving five resolutions, condemning the government's policy and Turkish promises of reform. The effect on the party was yet further to aggravate Hartington and Harcourt, and to strain the loyalty and friendship of even Granville. Harcourt 'boiled over with rage', and wrote to Hartington that 'the thing really in its mischievous egotism and folly is past endurance'.[35]

Even when Gladstone had deprived them of their sting, by removing the suggestion that the Turks be coerced, he was still to face the government alone. He noted in his diary, 'Such a sense of solitary struggle I never remember'. Mundella wrote to Leader just before the debate describing his complete sympathy:

'This is after the front bench had decided *all but unanimously* to do nothing. He has taken the bit in his teeth and done it on his own responsibility. Forster was the only other minority member of the late Government who was in favour of moving. Gladstone has done this in great pain: it looks like separation from his colleagues, and will split us up a good deal. His convictions, however, are too strong for him and he is weary of their apathy. He took my arm on Thursday and walked me up and down, evidently in much perturbation. His great heart chafes against considerations of political expediency. I am sorry to say a lot of our men are raging against him, and I almost quarrelled with Harcourt about it yesterday. I hope when the resolutions are out you will be prepared to hold a big meeting in Sheffield in support of them.' 36

The debate on the resolutions began on 7 May and continued for five days. During this time Mundella was incapacitated by boils on the back of his neck: so bad that he could neither hold up his head nor put on a collar. The doctor supplied him with caustic and other remedies to enable him to get down to the house. On top of this came a bad cold and bronchial attack, keeping him in bed while Gladstone was fighting alone. He told Leader on 11 May, 'The work of the House, of the City, and of the Eastern Association, has been too much for me, and the last has broken the camel's back'.

Three days later he made no secret as to where his real political allegiance lay:

'Gladstone, by his single courage and patriotism, is saving the country from a most wicked and disgraceful war, and one which would have found us without a single ally except the Turk, with perhaps, the three Northern Powers against us. . . . I am disgusted with Forster, Bright, Richard, and the peace party. They would have slumbered until the country was inextricably involved. . . . They are so timid as to be frightened of their own shadows. However Gladstone's resolution has saved them.' 37

5

There was another radical politician who saw as clearly as Mundella the great moral value of Gladstone's return. Chamberlain regarded Gladstone as 'our best card', and wrote to Dilke that 'if he could be induced formally to resume the reins, it would be almost equivalent to a victory, and would stir what Bright called "the masses of my countrymen" to their depths'.38

Chamberlain took up the mobilisation of Liberal opinion from where the Eastern Question Association left off. Writing in the *Fortnightly*, he pointed to the influence of the St. James' Hall meeting and others to ask:

'The initiative which the opposition in parliament has failed to take has been seized by public meetings. The assembly has been directed by the Conventions. How long is this to last, and to what lengths is it desired that it should go? ' 39

For him, the answer lay in the National Liberal Federation. This, organically, was the old National Education League, which was dissolved in the early part of 1877 and supplanted by a federation of the Liberal associations of various towns, with its headquarters at Birmingham, and the League officers (to use his own words) 'as chief cooks'.[40]

Under his direction they cooked to some purpose. On 16 April, two days after the debate on Gladstone's resolutions had ended, Gladstone received a formal invitation to address the assembled Liberal associations at Birmingham at what was virtually the inauguration of the Federation. The bait held out to attract him was that he would be able to make his views on the Eastern Question better known. Gladstone, writing to Granville the following day, rejoiced that 'from the Birmingham meeting there will be a ramification through the Liberal delegates assembled there, stretching all through the country'.[41]

Two people, however, were not present. One was Mundella, and the other was Robert Leader. Mundella was on holiday in Antwerp and Amsterdam in late May and early June, while Leader, though chairman of the Sheffield Liberal Association, was still smarting under Chamberlain's actions in the Sheffield elections three years before, and stayed away.

'I agree with you', wrote Mundella on 5 June, 'as to Chamberlain's object. Birmingham is to pull the strings of the Liberal Boroughs, and the puppets are to dance in response to the wires. I don't fear them however. Gladstone is by no means so simple as to fall into Chamberlain's trap. He does occasionally over-estimate men and credit them with higher motives than they merit, but this arises from the generosity and nobleness of his nature. He soon finds out the weaknesses of designing and pretentious people.'

He added:

'Bright is evidently not over well pleased with Chamberlain, and the latter is chafing under Bright's lecture. He said to me yesterday, "Bright is not generous, and doesn't like others to share the applause of his constituency".'

A fortnight later he wrote again:

'As to Chamberlain, he is a born wire-puller and intriguer, and, I suspect, from a conversation that I had with him last night, that he has been at work in Sheffield. He wants to have as many puppets as he can get in the House in order that he may manipulate them. This is a very general opinion, and his movements are watched with a good deal of jealousy.'[42]

On 22 June, Mundella and Chamberlain dined together at the

Reform Club. Chamberlain had evidently received some un-pleasant reminders from M.P.s that they would resent any inter-ference in their constituencies, and he had been forced to deny that he had any intention of so doing. Mundella seemed inclined to believe him, but expressed a doubt to Leader's son:

'The Federation is to appeal to all affiliated associations at suitable oppor-tunities, and, although it may be sometimes very useful, and arouse the associ-ations to simultaneous action, still it seems to me that appeals to the associations will be made or neglected as Birmingham deems desirable, and Chamberlain moves Birmingham. Hitherto they have exhibited nothing but indiscretion. They got up the League, the 25th clause agitation, the bitterness (first against Gladstone, then against Forster) and there is a narrowness, pettiness, and want of generosity in them which disqualifies them for leadership and deprives them of success. I hope for the best but I have not much faith in them.' [43]

On 22 July, he wrote to console Leader:

'What cool impudence of the Birmingham people to expect you to run over at such short notice. I await, with much curiosity, the report of your visit. There is a good deal of jealousy and uneasiness among Liberals in the House about it, some of whom have been mulcted in large subscriptions for they know not what: Adam does not relish the Federation, and is watching it suspiciously. Already some of the subscriptions which ought to have gone to the central association, have been diverted.'

Later, in September, when Mundella was holidaying in Switzer-land with John Gorst, George Dixon and Lord Edmond Fitz-maurice, he heard Lord Edmond's view of Chamberlain: 'Full of overweening ambition, destined to a considerable degree of dis-appointment, but so clever and intriguing withal, that he will sacrifice party interests to his own'. Mundella commented, 'I am disposed to agree with him, and to wish Gladstone had kept out of it'. When Chamberlain came to a meeting at Sheffield, Leader did not even report him in the *Sheffield Independent*.

But in spite of party tensions he confidently asserted on 1 October:

'The Liberal party has never done a greater service to the country than in influencing the government and the nation in favour of neutrality. It would have done still better had it stimulated them to active interference which would have prevented war.'

6

But the surge of anti-Turkish feeling began to subside as the Russian hordes battered in vain at the Turkish fortifications of

Plevna. Opinion reacted in favour of the Turkish David facing the Russian Goliath. The able generalship of Osman Pasha and Suleiman Pasha against great odds swung many to a pro-Turk point of view.

This reaction of feeling had eight months to accumulate. It was further intensified as the strength of the Turkish David showed signs of failing. This was apparent at the close of 1877, when a winter session of parliament was ordered. As the Russians wound their way through river and mountain, drawing nearer to Constantinople, so the threat to British interests in the East (made more important than ever by Disraeli's purchase of the Suez Canal shares) appeared to increase. On 18 November, Kars was captured by the troops of General Melikoff, and the shadow of the Russian began to loom over the Bosphorus.

Mundella wrote to Gladstone a week later, on 25 November:

'The attitude of the association for some time past has been that of watching and waiting and I feel sure that we must not prematurely take action but reserve all our strength and influence for a supreme effort when it is clear that the danger is becoming evident.' [44]

That time was now very close. On 20 December he wrote to Leader:

'We are drifting and the position may become dangerous and lead to war. We are planning a blaze of meetings all over the country for the first and second weeks of January. War will prove unwise to business so we hope to see the commercial bodies move.'

Two days later, in a letter to Gladstone, he revealed the preliminaries:

'Enquiries have been set on foot to gauge the feeling of the Country. The movement on the part of the Chambers of Commerce is entirely spontaneous . . . and is valuable as proceeding from non-political bodies.

'I wrote Mr. Chamberlain as to the Birmingham organisation and he telegraphs me that they have already taken vigorous measures and that I shall have full particulars on Monday.

'We *must* move and we *shall* succeed. I don't think we ought to ask anything of you till we have shown what we can do ourselves. Let us take the responsibility of it too if it fails. Pray give a line of council where you can.' [45]

His urgent wish was that the country should not succumb to war fever. He hastened to deter Auberon Herbert from holding a meeting 'for the free navigation of the straits'. Herbert had drawn off in his orbit Freeman, Canon Liddon, Carlyle, Froude, Browning and John Morley. Writing to him on 28 December 1877, Mundella opined:

'I have no doubt that times have been critical but *are they not growing worse?* If we have only *one* friend left the game is up and we shall soon be *at war*. You will think me a *wet blanket* but I wish you had not called your meeting about the opening of the Dardanelles. The *one* thing now before us is to keep this country out of war. It is quite premature to discuss terms of peace till the danger of war is averted.' [46]

Meanwhile to Leader he opened his heart; writing on 22 December:

'Gladstone writes a noble letter, full of self-sacrifice and readiness to discharge a painful and disagreeable duty. All agree the country *must speak out*.

'Beaconsfield is trying to commit his colleagues to war expenditure and warlike acts, and we can only be saved from dishonour and disaster by the country denouncing war.

'Will not Sheffield Chamber of Commerce follow the spontaneous act of other Chambers such as Manchester, Bristol, and Edinburgh, and petition against an entanglement on this Eastern business? The political uncertainty is exercising a most depressing influence upon trade, and, if we are dragged into wars, the trading and industrial classes will *have to pay*. I could have wished for rest and quiet till Parliament meets, but it is impossible—not a moment to call my own, even in my own house. I expect on Monday, our Eastern Question Executive will call upon you from one end of the country to another to hold meetings and prepare for peace and neutrality.'

A week later he wrote from the distractions of the work of the Eastern Question Association to call attention to Britain's offer of mediation to Russia, made the day before:

'You see, the government has shown its hand. Our people say we have forced it, but that is perhaps arrogating too much to ourselves. The general distrust and consequent depression, has probably done this, and compelled them to do something to allay it.

'I don't think the situation is at all improved by this attempt at negotiation on the part of the Turk. Layard has, for some time past, pressed the Turks to place themselves in our hands, and to some extent,—after all Europe has declined to say anything to their overtures,—they have done it. I *hope* it is not the first step towards war, but I greatly *fear* it is. It gives the government a good pretext for interference, and if they get a rebuff—no matter how much they have provoked it—it will be represented and regarded as an insult to the country.'

A day later he was even gloomier:

'Where it will all end, heaven only knows!

'So far as I am able to judge, there is nothing for it but that the country should speak out, carefully avoiding the peace-at-any-price policy, declaring its readiness to protect British interests whenever they are threatened, but not to maintain Turkish rule. For my part, I don't think that any danger to any single British interest has arisen or is likely to arise.

'I think I must come to Sheffield and bring myself face to face with my constituents. I am able now to do it, and I feel I shall be neglecting my duty if, at this important crisis, I allow personal considerations to stand in the way. I, too, shall be refreshed for my work if I find that my constituents will support me. I want to see whether the country is with us or not.'

So he came to the Albert Hall on 7 January 1878; protesting the good intentions of Russia with such fervour that the *Sheffield Telegraph* attacked him as 'the member for Moscow'. His pro-Russian views began to get more and more unpopular as the Russian advance continued. Three days after he spoke, the Russians captured the Shipka Pass; on 20 January they occupied Adrianople. The Queen's Speech showed that the government were going to prepare for any eventualities, for it contained the ominous sentence, 'Should hostilities be unfortunately prolonged, some unexpected occurrence may render it incumbent upon me to adopt measures of precaution'. Such measures could not be effectually taken without adequate preparation, so parliament was asked to vote a supplementary vote of £6,000,000 to increase preparedness. This was followed by the resignation of Lord Carnarvon—'our watchdog in the cabinet', as Mundella had called him.

On the day of the Queen's Speech (17 January 1878) Mundella presided over a huge meeting of working-men held at the Exeter Hall, London. It was an entirely working-class audience, and the hall was crowded to the doors. Hymns against the Turk were sung to drown the noise of possible interruptions. A young girl recorded her impression of it in her diary:

'17 January 1878. Gertrude Astley and I went to a frantic and gigantic meeting at the Exeter Hall, where the working man under the guidance of Mr. Mundella protested against being dragged into war for the Turk. The Hall was crammed. We sang with great enthusiasm a sort of Anti-Turkish hymn and cheered vigorously between each verse to prevent the enemy singing "Rule Britannia".' [47]

Agitation reached fever point in this month. As Professor Seton-Watson has observed, 'Rarely, if ever, has opinion been so keenly roused and so deeply divided on a question of foreign policy.' [48] Against the activities of the Eastern Question Association sprang up 'The National Society for Resistance to Russian

Aggression and Protection of British Interests'. Satellite organisations to the Eastern Question Association, like the City Neutrality and Peace Committee, the Workmen's Neutrality Committee, the Nonconformist Committee of Vigilance on the Eastern Question and the Midland Arbitration Union, grew up, each with their monster meetings, resolutions and demonstrations.

Mundella urged Gladstone to speak. Gladstone replied on 3 January 1878:

'My construction of the appeal in *The Times* was different. I do not think they regard me as, nor am I, one of the leaders. I think it was an appeal to Lord Hartington and men who have acted regularly with him.

'You cannot, I think, doubt from the moment I take a more active part the whole parliamentary forces of the Tories will be set to work against us.

'But pray continue to write as you see occasion and be assured that every word will be weighed.' [49]

Gladstone enclosed a copy of a letter he sent to Chamberlain in which he feared he 'might unintentionally contribute to throw the question into the arena of party'.

But Mundella was not content—he bombarded him with telegrams at Hawarden. Gladstone replied to one on 24 January discussing the possibility of Derby resigning and the advisability of an attack on the government's war estimate.

'For my part I should be quite ready to back up the preliminary ground of confidence and attack the Government from first to last. But this is a point on which I should probably be guided by leaders of the party, who I hope will meet the occasion with a good heart.' [50]

But the Liberal chiefs got cold feet. As the Russians began to advance towards Constantinople, the debate on the estimates collapsed. The marquis of Hartington and W. E. Forster walked out of the house before the vote was taken.

Nor was Mundella inclined to show fight. A meeting held in Paradise Square on 29 January to discuss this very question had been broken up in complete pandemonium. Hoots and cat-calls drowned the Liberal speakers, and the result was blazoned as a stinging defeat for the Eastern Question Association. Mundella was very depressed when he heard of it, and wrote to Leader on 29 January:

'The Conservatives are *wild with joy* at telegrams from Sheffield stating that a meeting of twenty thousand inhabitants of Sheffield carried an amendment in favour of the Government by ten to one. I am since in receipt of your telegram, and all I can say is that it is the worst news that has reached me since I have been member for Sheffield. It is utterly discouraging to our side, and damaging to my influence on the Eastern Question. Personally, I can bear it and suffer any consequences that may result from it, but I grieve for the sake of the cause and party, and the country. It is more important than you can well believe it to be *at this end*.'

And on the following day he told him:

'Gladstone was grieved at the news. So, indeed, was Forster, and everybody else. I have had a sleepless night, and feel a weaker man in *every way* this morning, but I shall put a good face on it, and go into the fight following my own convictions regardless of all consequences.'

The reaction had indeed set in. The jingo mobs and societies used all the ammunition known in political warfare. Pamphlets, counter demonstrations, direct charges of lack of patriotism, were capped by the breaking of windows (Gladstone's among others). H. J. Wilson shrewdly attributed much of it to 'organisation and drink'. Auberon Herbert declared that Mundella was 'discrowned',[51] and advised him to hold another meeting straight away. Two days after it had occurred, Sir Michael Hicks Beach twitted Mundella for supporting a motion demanding some security for order and decency at public meetings.

Goldwin Smith wrote sage advice on 17 February:

'When this game of brag is over and it is settled that the conference shall meet, would it not be a good thing to move a resolution to the effect that the House will not support any policy having as its objects the curtailments of the liberties of the Christian Provinces. Evidently the fears and jealousies of Austria will lead her to curtail those liberties, and the Jew will, no doubt, second her.

'I am sorry you think the war agitation has damaged you at Sheffield. Rowdies make a great uproar when intriguers set them in motion, but their interest in political questions is not sustained, and the Conference will soon shed over all this turmoil the calm influence of diplomatic dullness. How marked the alliance of Toryism and Rowdyism has been on this occasion. It is one of the great facts, not only of English, but of general politics. Your Leaders made a sad mess of it as people who are half-hearted usually do. Don't try your health by doing too much.'[52]

The flare-up of pro-Turkish feeling did little beyond add the word 'jingo' to the English vocabulary. Though the British fleet and the Russian armies lay within sight of each other, Disraeli had no intention of being so pro-Turk as to allow a war to develop. On 19 February an agreement was reached whereby the Russians undertook not to occupy Gallipoli, and the British in turn undertook not to land troops in Turkey. Though it looked in March as if this *entente* might be upset (Russia and Turkey signed the Treaty of San Stephano on 3 March, to which Britain and Austro-Hungary objected), the appointment of Lord Salisbury to the foreign office in place of Lord Derby (who had resigned) restored the concert of the powers. A congress at Berlin was agreed upon. Disraeli surged to the greatest heights of his career when he returned from this conference exclaiming that he had brought back 'peace with honour'. Mundella was caustic: writing on 11 June, two days before the congress met, he was of the opinion:

'It is humiliating to see the temper of the English people with respect to Beaconsfield. The peace will be made because there is nobody who can and will fight but ourselves, and I believe the terms of the peace will be practically those which Russia has concluded. Whether there should be *one* Bulgaria or *two*, or whether a port in the Aegean should be added or not, was never worth the expense and suspense of the last few months, and the importing of Indian troops, together with infraction of the constitution.'

Four days later, when a copying clerk at the foreign office sold the terms of the Anglo-Russian Treaty to the *Globe* newspaper, Mundella was jubilant:

'The terms', he wrote, 'are really a triumph for Gladstone. The one danger now is lest Beaconsfield, to please his jingoes, should involve us in obligations and guarantees on behalf of Turkey. Something he must do to extract a triumph out of it, for, thus far, it is a victory for Russia. The *Observer* today admits it, and the *Telegraph* is dreadfully uneasy. You see they are taking the word of the Emperor about future aggressions.' [53]

The Congress of Berlin ended on 13 July. Mundella wrote in great haste to Leader as news came of Disraeli's guarantees to Turkey:

'What are we coming to? Beaconsfield, without consulting Parliament, or giving the slightest hint to his policy, has committed the nation to the gravest moral and material responsibilities, and reversed the policy of the last half century. How long will our people tolerate this charlatan? There is something like *consternation* here among serious men. . . . I think a dissolution inevitable.' [54]

7

In the excitement and exertions of the Eastern Question Association, Mundella was supported by the leaders of the working classes. Indeed, his incandescence would have been impossible without their strong pressure behind him. This made meetings like that of 17 January possible. Organisation was provided by Henry Broadhurst, an Oxfordshire stonemason, who had succeeded George Howell as secretary of the Parliamentary Committee of the Trade Union Congress in 1873. Broadhurst, then only thirty-five years old, had the conservative and powerful Stonemason's Union at his back: indeed, his own efforts in the craft had been such that he had worked as a craftsman on the building of the house of commons in the sixties, the tools he used on that occasion still being treasured in the house of commons library.[55]

Broadhurst, a constant visitor at 16 Elvaston Gate, Mundella's London home, began to entertain hopes of being elected as a Liberal member: in 1878 he was chosen to contest Stoke-on-Trent. Also on the Parliamentary Committee of the T.U.C. was another close ally of Mundella's, an ally who later obtained office at his hands. This was John Burnett.[56] Two years younger than Broadhurst, he had, through Thomas Cooper, invited Mundella, as we have seen, to arbitrate in the nine hours strike at Newcastle in 1871. Burnett's victory in this struggle led him, three years later, to succeed William Allan as secretary of the Amalgamated Society of Engineers. In 1876 he had joined the Parliamentary Committee. Both Burnett and Broadhurst believed in the establishment of conciliation machinery and in the concession of democratic privileges to those of their own class. Both of them, in spite of the fact that there were two working-class M.P.s (Alexander MacDonald and Thomas Burt) in the house, looked to Mundella for help in the matters that concerned the unions.[57] Broadhurst was so mindful of Mundella's services that, on behalf of the Parliamentary Committee, he had forwarded an address in which the trade unions formally acknowledged that they owed more to him than to any other member of the house of commons.[58]

8

So, while Auberon Herbert continued to rouse the crowds in Hyde Park, and Charles Bradlaugh got his own and his supporters' heads cracked by outraged supporters of Disraeli's foreign policy, Mundella turned to fighting the Conservatives on the home front. He soon found an issue which affected the stomach of every working man in his constituency—that of cheap meat.

On 25 March 1878 he, together with W. E. Forster, led a deputation to the Duke of Richmond to protest against the ministerial bill then lying before the house which made provision for the compulsory slaughter of all foreign animals entering the country. The issue was a sore one both with farmers and with working men. In 1877 a select committee of the house of commons had been set up to examine the incidence of cattle plague (rinderpest especially) among imported cattle. Mundella had served on this committee, and when its report had appeared in the previous July he had written to Leader:

'Pray don't overlook the Report of the Cattle Plague Committee. *It is monstrous*. All day on Tuesday last, Forster, Chamberlain, myself and a few others were fighting and dividing in Committee against the majority in this question. We shall have meat a tremendous price if they legislate in the spirit of the report.' [59]

This the ministry proceeded to do. So the deputation which waited on the duke of Richmond represented not only the interests of twenty-seven northern towns, but included the chairmen of the steamship companies from nine of the great ports. Mundella pleaded that meat from the United States should be allowed to come into the country without being slaughtered at the point of disembarkation. Speaking for a town which he said consumed more meat per head than any other in the United Kingdom, Mundella made a strong case against the slaughter of meat from the United States, as opposed to the rest of the deputation, which pleaded for a lifting of the proposed slaughter clauses from continental meat.

Mundella regarded it as the main business of the 1878 parliamentary session. Writing to Leader he said:

'After the Whitsun holidays we shall make a serious fight against the Cattle Bill. The government mean to pass it to placate the farmers, who are not, at present, too well pleased with their "friends". What with Agricultural Holdings Act and other shams, they [the farmers] are a little sulky, and *dear meat* would, it is said, sweeten them a good deal.'

This was on 7 June. Five days later, expecting that a general election was imminent after the Congress of Berlin, he wrote:

'I think it would be quite premature to commence *open* electioneering at present. The Session must last for nearly two months longer, and, in the meantime, preparations should be made and all details settled. Every elector should be allotted to the care of somebody, and all the machinery well arranged so that it can be set in motion at a moment's notice. I think the first beginning would be *a lively meeting in the Square*, about the Cattle Bill. It should be a Town's meeting, convened by requisition, and the members invited to be present.'

Three weeks later, as Leader replied that it would not be advisable to try Paradise Square, Mundella confessed his disappointment: but he was able to have the next best thing—a meeting under cover in the Albert Hall. Held on 26 June, it showed that the Sheffield Trades Council were solidly behind Mundella in his efforts against the Cattle Bill. Memmott, the secretary, spoke after Mundella, who had stressed (to the accompaniment of cheers) that the cattle question was 'of greater importance than any juggling about south of the Balkans'. 'It is the one great stand made by the Liberal party on any question of importance this session,' he boomed, pointing out that the report of the select committee, on which the ministerial bill was based, was a report compiled from the testimony of farmers and landowners who hoped through this act to secure some protection against foreign meat.

On 28 June, two days after the meeting, he arrived back in the house 'just in time to run the debate through'. He proudly confessed to Leader:

'By general assent the conduct of the opposition has been committed to me. I arrange for the speakers, etc., etc., I shall speak myself on Monday night, and I hope, before dinner. Take notice it was the Liberal Peers *that got America exempted.*'

By 10 July he could crow:

'Since the government introduced their Cattle Bill in the Lords, the Liberals have succeeded in removing from the compulsory slaughter clauses, America, Sweden, Denmark, Norway, Spain, and Portugal. The Bill as it now stands is absurd. The Privy Council will have *discretion* with regard to the foregoing country, but *none* as to any other. France, Holland, Germany, Belgium are all healthier than ourselves already: should they become entirely free from disease by the time the Bill comes into force, the Privy Council would be unable to admit a single head of cattle inland, however much we require them. We have made a *wide rent* in the Bill, and we shall open it still wider in Committee.'

9

In addition to amending the Cattle Bill, Mundella championed the favourite recreation of many of the town artisans. Typical of this activity was a bill he sponsored for instituting a close season for fresh-water fish, which became law in 1878. After it had passed through the commons for the last time he confided to a friend: 'I am worn out, and at the end of every session it is the same. I am spending my strength. I am on the treadmill every day of my life.'

But in spite of his efforts, his appearance in Paradise Square to give his annual account of himself was the signal for an outburst of hostile feeling. Before the meeting took place on 27 August, the town blossomed into a rainbow of hostile placards exhorting the inhabitants to assemble in their thousands in order to extinguish 'the member for Moscow'. Near the platform from which he addressed the crowd a brewer's dray had been parked and the horses taken away. Just before the meeting began, the dray was occupied by some of the tory bloods of the town, while a number of high-spirited youths elbowed their way through the crowd, singing 'Rule Britannia'. When Mundella began to speak, the windows round the square were packed to capacity. His first few sentences were immediately drowned in uproar: shouts and the singing of 'Rule Britannia' mingled with the cheers of his supporters. For a time he struggled to make his brassy voice heard above the din, but it was too much for him. When the chairman of the meeting tried to propose a vote of confidence, the occupants of the brewer's dray raised placards and passed a negative vote. Hands fluttered for both motions, but in the sea of upturned faces nothing could with certainty be ascertained.

Mundella was more successful a week later, when the meeting was held in the Albert Hall. Speaking there to a crowd of 2,500 (the back seats had to be removed to get them all in), he received an enthusiastic and unanimous vote of support and encouragement for his efforts. In the chair was the man who had stood by him for the past ten years, whose name has occurred so often in these pages: Robert Leader.

A fine example of Leader's service to Sheffield, and the way Mundella co-operated with him, occurred the following year over the threatened enclosure of Maltby Common—the last of the green and pleasant places left to the town after the enclosures of three-quarters of a century before. Having lost 7,385 acres of their intimate greens through enclosure, one might have expected that the merest threat of enclosing Maltby would have roused Sheffielders at once. Such, however, was not the case. The first proceedings were commenced before the commissioners in 1869, and they were revived again in 1877. Even then, when an assistant commissioner, Mr. Leach, came down to see the common, he was handed a petition with only thirty-seven signatures—and with no other delegate to hand it to him but the common hangman! Naturally, Mr. Leach did not take such a protest seriously.

Nor, as the threatened enclosure did not immediately materialise, did the Sheffielders take Mr. Leach seriously, if they knew anything about his mission. It was nearly two years later, in February 1879, when he reappeared to obtain the consent of the 'interested parties'. This time only fifty of the inhabitants could be found to sign the petition, which was presented by a local solicitor. Naturally enough, Mr. Leach returned to the commissioners, who drafted the scheme, and laid it before parliament to await their assent.

It was at this point, when the town was on the verge of losing Maltby Common for good, that Robert Leader acted. He told the town what was afoot. Soon petition after petition rolled in against it—among them weighty ones from the mayors and corporations of Rotherham and Sheffield. The commissioners forwarded the scheme to parliament on 6 May 1879, to be turned into law, but a fortnight later they held another meeting and adopted a special report in which they declared that if the scheme were not passed there was a danger that the interested parties would come to terms and enclose the whole common: 'Persons might arbitrarily enclose the common land, on the chance of nobody interfering'.

Mundella himself saw that things had gone too far. On 9 May 1879 he had written to Leader: 'We don't expect that we shall succeed in doing more than in making a fight. The House is a Landlords' House and in all for Enclosure.' He pinned his hopes on delaying the second reading of the bill till after 17 June, this being the last day, according to standing orders, for sending such bills to the lords. In such filibustering he was helped by Dilke and Shaw-Lefevre (himself the moving spirit of the Commons Preservation Society). The three of them made long speeches on other subjects until the time for discussion had passed. The manœuvre succeeded. The government wanted to pass their estimates, so the Maltby Bill looked as if it would require special facilities.

The proximity of the general election in the following year took Lord Cranbrook to Sheffield to address the electors on behalf of the Conservatives. Robert Leader seized his chance. A deputation

was presented, indicative of so much feeling that Cross reluctantly
gave permission that the bill should be discharged on 4 July.
Mundella secured the consent of the under-secretary in charge
of the bill at 3.20 a.m. in the morning. Maltby Common was
saved.[60]

10

Apart from the histrionics of party warfare, Mundella was
deeply concerned in the promotion of industrial peace and universal education. On 19 February 1878 he read a paper to the
Statistical Society in which his steady optimism was forcibly expressed. *What are the conditions on which the Commercial and Manufacturing Supremacy of Great Britain Depend, and is there any reason
to think that they have been, or may be, Endangered?*—ran the title.
His answer was an emphatic negative. Periodic alarms, extending
over the previous thirty years, had proved similarly false. He
scouted the opinions of M. de Lavaleye and M. Beaulieu, that the
crisis would continue, because all the plant and machinery called
into existence by modern civilisation had been supplied, with the
result that the future field of employment for both capital and
labour would be restricted. He based his optimistic outlook on
the abundance of England's coal and iron resources, her money
power, and the inventive genius of the working classes. He
quoted Americans as saying that they did not so much fear the low
rates of wages prevailing in England as the low rates of interest.
In his opinion, the labour conflicts both in America and Germany
were 'far worse than anything we have yet experienced in our own
country'. In the industrial conflict with these countries, he was
emphatic that

'If the comparatively high price of English labour is adduced as evidence of
our inability to compete with our neighbours, I must repeat that it is on the
increased efficiency and greater energy of labour that we must rely, rather than
on low priced labour',

and urged employers and workmen alike:

to hold fast by the principles of free trade. To strive each in your own way to
promote a good understanding betwixt capital and labour. To develop as much
as possible the scientific knowledge and technical skill of all engaged in the
manufacturing industry; and with the growth amongst us of greater intelligence, temperance, and thrift, I see no reason why the people of the United
Kingdom should not reach a higher state of material prosperity and social well
being than any they have hitherto attained.'

In the discussion that followed, Professor Stanley Jevons said that Mundella's paper seemed to him to be 'one of the most suggestive he had ever heard'. Discussion on it was postponed for a fortnight. When it was continued on 5 March, it inevitably digressed into a criticism of the trade unions. R. Rawlinson thought that unless trade unions could come down to common-sense principles, the country was on the high road to ruin. But Mundella would have none of this. He rejoiced in the fact that colonial dependencies were becoming increasingly prosperous. This, he argued, increased their purchasing power, and enabled them to enjoy a higher standard of living by buying English goods.[61]

So he seized the opportunity of Lord Sandon's departure from the Vice-Presidency of the Council to worry his successor, Lord George Hamilton, on behalf of the teachers in elementary schools. Under Sandon's Act of 1876 the teachers had twenty-seven new regulations to observe, and school boards had a total of sixty-three returns to submit per year. This left the teachers little time for personal culture or recreation. Even more, he criticised the complete lack of stimulus offered by the profession: the inspectorate was a closed road to even the best of them. He challenged Lord George Hamilton to name one of the 118 inspectors and examiners of the department who had been promoted from the ranks of elementary school teachers.[62]

From many platforms he expounded his thesis that only through education could social mobility be established and the war of classes brought to an end. As he told the university extension students at the inauguration of that movement in Sheffield: 'It is impossible for ignorant and educated men to associate together, just as it is impossible to mix oil and water'.[63] He strongly supported all university extension schemes, calling them 'the greatest educational movement of the time after elementary education'. He found the most hopeful sign to lie in the fact that 'the trade unionists are studying political economy and constitutional history and are carrying their text-books about with them, and have their proficiency tested by examination and recognised by certificates'.[64]

The basis on which he wished to build was an educated working class. Without it, wage bargaining, conciliation machinery and all the other apparatus for maintaining social peace would break

MUNDELLA, REJECTED BY THE PEOPLE OF NOTTINGHAM
Sets off for Sheffield, grasping his staff (Robert Leader)
One of a number of cartoons depicting him as
'The Wandering Jew'

down. Only by educating the working class could a sufficient moral sanction be obtained for the tribunal edicts. The system had succeeded at Nottingham. Emile de Lavaleye, one of the great advocates of the right of the state to interfere with private interests where they ran counter to the interests of society (he carried on a famous argument with Herbert Spencer on the subject), was impressed at the way it *did* work at Nottingham. In a letter to Mundella he explained why :

'J'ai été étudier la question a Nottingham ou votre nom est resté tres populaire, et plus, été frappé de l'intelligence de vos ouvriers et les notres sont a la fois isolés et ignorants.' [65]

He was a juror at the Paris Exhibition in 1878. His experiences there reinforced the conviction fostered by a lifetime's observation of the continental and American industrial scene, that the apprenticeship system had broken down. The growing complexity of the modern manufacturing process had supplanted rule of thumb. Unfortunately, however, many manufacturers refused to accept the logical corollary, that the state should provide technical education to remedy this. Technical education, to the unenlightened manufacturer, meant the sharing of his trade secrets. So Colonel Donnelly, of the Science and Art Department, found to his cost.[66]

Mundella was prepared to move with the advanced guard of collectivist opinion to promote technical education. It was partly his wider grasp of the functions of the state that led to his rift with Auberon Herbert, whom he regarded as 'lost to name and fame' for having absorbed the 'crudities and flatulences of Spencerism'. So, in 1878, he worked hard to help the government to consolidate the factory legislation of the country. He had pressed Cross on 20 March 1877 to introduce such a measure, 'so that due time may be given for its consideration'. When it came up early in 1878, Mundella spoke on it no fewer than thirty-seven times, with great care and moderation. Indeed, the only time he essayed a reproof was to warn Henry Fawcett not to allow the discussion to degenerate into a vapid declamation of farmers or any other class.[67] Its provisions are a tribute to his activity, for they extended the principles of his 1874 act (i.e. that the half-time age in textile factories should be raised from eight to ten) to all factories. When half-time did begin, it was to be only twelve hours, with an interval of two hours for meals. What, however, was very important was the definition of a factory. It emerged from the 1878 Factory Act as 'premises where mechanical power was employed in the business of manufacture'. Thus the old distinction which had clouded the administration of earlier factory acts was removed (i.e. that it was a building where more than fifty operatives were working). Lastly, the educational certificate for intending half-timers was defined as standard 4 of the 1876 code (Mundella had complained that his own standard 3 in the draft bill he presented in 1873 was too low), or, of course, the 250 attendances at school required by the 1876 Act—which had become jocularly known as 'the Dunce's Pass'.[68]

As a corollary to the wider extension of education among the working classes, Mundella sponsored a measure for enabling them to play their part in local affairs. Hitherto this had been denied them, for adoption as a candidate both for school board and town council elections necessitated either a financial guarantee or a property qualification. So in 1877 he presented for the first time a measure to abolish this property qualification. In moving the second reading, he pointed out that in his own constituency 80 to 90 per cent of the voters were disqualified from offering themselves for office, yet they were the first class to feel the pressure of the rates. He concluded with the telling argument that it would be most desirable that they should receive the best political education possible (i.e. that of taking part in the conduct of national, affairs). But both in 1877 and 1878 his argument fell on ears which were not attuned either to J. S. Mill or to the T.U.C. point of view. When his measure reappeared for the third time, in 1879, *The Times* offered some crumbs of consolation, and congratulated him on the narrowness of his defeat.[69] Ironically enough, the Conservatives finally passed the measure in the short session of 1880, when, from its first reading on 6 February to its receiving the Royal Assent on 19 March, it encountered scarcely an adverse comment. This was a sign that the centre of gravity in local, as in national, politics was slowly shifting.

About this time his family was 'adopted' by London's intellectual world. R. H. Hutton, editor of the *Spectator*, became very friendly with Mrs. and Miss Mundella, and in one letter wrote:

'I begin to think your family are all—well, I will not say "perfection" lest I should be thought to talk extravagantly and to flatter, but nearer the exact mark politically, socially, and in all points of feeling than almost any I know.' [70]

Browning began to correspond, and Maria Theresa, Mundella's younger daughter, began to build up a small network of acquaintances like Anne Thackeray Ritchie, J. H. Shorthouse, Jean Ingelow, and others. It was at 16 Elvaston Place that Frederic Harrison met R. B. Haldane, and Juliana Ewing her illustrator Caldecott.

II

The legacy of Disraeli's policy towards Russia was a war with Afghanistan. Nourished since 1873 by Russia, the war finally broke out in 1878. It provoked widespread criticism both in India and at home, and gave a tremendous fillip to the anti-jingo agitation. Liberals leaped to criticise the mounting expenditure which the war entailed.

Mundella was quick to seize his opportunity. He approached Hartington to send a leader of the party to Sheffield, in order to run a simultaneous meeting with Birmingham. Harcourt came down on 16 April 1879, and was in his happiest vein. He made a speech in which he coined the phrase 'prancing pro-consuls', to hit the character of the new imperialism, and this became a slogan in the Liberal crusade. Mundella sent him a canteen of cutlery. Harcourt, volatile and humorous as ever, thanked him with a promise that he 'would use its trenchant edge against H.M. Government'. The meeting was a great success. In the middle of the proceedings Mundella produced a telegram from Birmingham:

'Mr. Bright (*cheers*) is addressing with undiminished force (*cheers*) a densely crowded and enthusiastic meeting (*loud cheers*). We wish you success in your attempt to promote the triumph of Liberal principles in Sheffield.'

He then asked the crowd whether he might send a return greeting, and the following was unanimously approved:

'A crowded and enthusiastic meeting of Sheffield Liberals welcome Sir William Harcourt and determine to return two thorough-going Liberals to the next Parliament. We send cordial greetings to, and an expression of hearty admiration of, Birmingham, its veteran senior member, and his worthy colleagues. Hearty thanks for your greeting.' [71]

At the same time, Mundella urged Leader to fight the growing cry for protection or 'reciprocity', as it was called:

'You are quite right in working away at *Machinery*. It is not low wages that is beating us but *high wages* and improved machinery. The fortunes that American workmen make by successful patents stimulates them as a class, and makes them ready to attempt anything. With them, nothing is surprising and nothing impossible, and they are perpetually adapting themselves to changes for the better.' [72]

Two days later he suggested:

'I wish it could be arranged for the Chamber of Commerce to invite an address on "Reciprocity". I think I could explode that nonsense.'

On this rising tide of Liberal strength rode Gladstone. Emerging from Hawarden on 24 November 1879, he began a journey which was unprecedented in the annals of parliamentary democracy in this country. His progress was a triumph. All the way to Midlothian (which he had selected as his constituency) he had to satisfy the urgent devotion of large crowds who clamoured to see him. At Edinburgh a huge assembly waited for him, and bore him to Dalmeny (Lord Rosebery's home) by torchlight. He delivered a sober address as Lord Rector of Glasgow University, and began an equally triumphal return journey, punctuated by the presentation of addresses.

Meanwhile Mundella had been working in similar fashion. Roebuck's death and the increased intensity of feeling in the city made the contest one of more than local importance. The Liberal party thought so much of it that a sitting member, S. D. Waddy, resigned his seat at Barnstaple in order to contest the vacant seat at Sheffield. The *Sheffield Telegraph* warned Mundella not to interfere, but he came from a sick bed to speak for Waddy. Intimidation spread farther than this. Handbills were issued with vague threats about the safety of his seat at the general election. An organised body of roughs under a prize-fighter known locally as 'the Derby Lad' came to Liberal meetings, took up central positions, and caused disturbances. The intensity of the contest can be judged by the fact that Waddy won the seat from C. B. Stuart Wortley by the narrow margin of 487 votes.[73] Commenting on the result, P. W. Clayden remarked, 'It gave evidence of the fierceness of the struggle, and may possibly indicate its end'.[74]

The situation in the inner councils of the party was a delicate one. Hartington wanted Gladstone to be offered the leadership 'in such a way that he will not be able to refuse, or, if he does, that the responsibility of leaving the party without a leader will again rest on him'. On the other hand, W. E. Forster and Lord Granville were against any such premature action. Indeed, Forster, in a review of the situation, opined that the 'best possible result' would be if Gladstone 'might pledge himself never to resume, or at any rate so positively to decline, as to stop the mouths of those who cry out for him'.[75] The counsels of Forster and Granville won the day, and at a meeting of Liberal leaders on 16 December the decision was taken to make no formal communication to Mr. Gladstone.[76]

But among the voices that cried out for Mr. Gladstone was Mundella. He wrote to Leader on 25 November 1879:

'The reaction for *Gladstone* is very remarkable. As I passed a Stationer's shop in Queen Victoria Street, in the city (this morning) the window was crowded with Gladstone's photographs, and there was printed up in large letters "The man for England". This would have been impossible a year and a half ago. In Portsmouth, people went almost mad at the mention of his name. I have some capital popular Liberal songs sung at the Portsmouth demonstration. The effect was most inspiriting. I am sure we shall do well to introduce them.' [77]

At the beginning of 1880 Mundella was in earnest communication with Gladstone, writing on 9 January to ask him to take the chair at a dinner to be given on 14 February to honour Lord Harting-ton's services to the Liberal party. The dinner was planned to emphasise Liberal unity; and Mundella wrote 'at the earnest and unanimous request of the committee' to say:

'The committee is thoroughly representative of the Liberal Party, and comprises every section of it, indeed it is stronger in everything but its chairman, which is the capacity in which I am now addressing you. 240 members of the party have joined in the invitation, and many Home Rulers will come in later, who, while friendly, did not venture (for reasons which you will understand) to sign the enclosed invitation.' [78]

But Hartington told Adam he wished to discourage the idea. A day later he wrote to Mundella and asked him to call at Devonshire House to discuss the whole affair. On 16 January he once more wrote to Mundella hoping that the question of Gladstone's attendance 'might be satisfactorily arranged'.[79]

The 'satisfactory arrangement' was precipitated by the action of Gladstone himself.[80] He wrote to Mundella on 12 January 1880 that he was about to visit his sister, who was dying, at Cologne, and that he had referred his application to Lord Granville, and was waiting for the latter's advice. Mundella began to see that there was a real case for Hartington, and wrote a letter confessing his doubts:

'Query, is it for the best that there should be any change of leadership before the General Election? Much as I admire Gladstone, *I think not*. Let him take the chair at this dinner to Hartington, be *our Nestor* (what Lansdowne was to preceding Liberal Governments—what Bright has been to us of late), and he will give enormous strength to us, and bring the party into perfect cohesion; but a change from H to G before the election would endanger our success. . . . Gladstone *with* us, we shall have all the pronounced Liberals and all the Whigs, but *leading* us we shall have the former just alone. Morley, who is one of Gladstone's warmest friends, takes the same line. It is clear Adam is of my opinion, and both Granville and Hartington are impressed with the importance of utilising all our forces to *get rid of the government*.' [81]

But at the beginning of 1880 that still looked far off. On 5 February the Queen opened parliament with more state ceremonial than she had observed since the death of the Prince Consort. Argyle withdrew his motion of censure on the foreign policy of the government. Then Disraeli, his confidence buoyed by Conservative victories at Liverpool and Southwark, announced on 9 March that the government would be dissolved as soon as the budget had been introduced, and issued a programme in the form of a letter addressed to the Lord Lieutenant of Ireland. Ten days later Mundella's bill abolishing the property qualification for intending local councillors received the royal assent.

12

The election which followed gave a new complexion to the Liberal party. Radicalism was reinforced by a strange assortment of intelligence and vehemence, for James Bryce (Tower Hamlets) and Henry Labouchere (Northampton) were returned together with Henry Broadhurst (Stoke) and Passmore Edwards (Salisbury). Mundella himself was elected by a narrow margin, and reflected bitterly on the fact that his constituency had not returned another Liberal as well as himself.[82]

'Sheffield! Sheffield!' he wrote to R. Leader. 'That Sheffield should be the one and only great town in the Kingdom to desert the good cause goes to my heart. I am hurt and inconsolable, and every man I meet questions me in a note of reproach. Do let us understand the reason why?—and if it is in the power of man to change it, let us unite to do it.'

Gladstone's return for Leeds and Midlothian, coupled with the greatly increased Radical weight in the party itself, must have had its effect on Hartington, for when summoned by the Queen on

22 April to form a ministry he declined, and advised her to send for Gladstone.[83]

Gladstone did not forget one who had borne the heat and burden of six long years of opposition. On 27 April he sent a letter to Mundella proposing that his name should go forward to the Queen as Vice-President of the Committee of Council on Education. He added:

'One thing I will venture to say. The charge for education is enormous. When the object in view is of such value, it is apt to be assumed, taken for granted, that the money is all necessary and well laid out. I hope you will think that it is the duty of the official man representing the department to make vigilant inquiry, not only into augmentation, but into wasteful charges which may have crept in, and into charges also which having been originally necessary, may have become needless and therefore wasteful.' [84]

This characteristic Gladstonian approach should be borne in mind when the final assessment is made of Mundella's work in this office.

Mundella was delighted with his appointment and wrote to tell Robert Leader:

'Nothing could be more gratifying than the manner of this appointment. I have refrained even from calls of courtesy that I might not be considered *hunting or intriguing*. It seems as if I have been designated from the first as the right man for the Education Department. "It is close to the Cabinet" are Forster's words, "and practically you have your own way, are your own master, and have power to take part in other questions that may interest you." It has been my life's work and study, and I believe the appointment will command public approval.' [85]

When the Queen received the names, the same day as Mundella wrote to Leader, she noted in her diary: 'Another letter from Mr. Gladstone, submitting more unexpected names', and remarked:

'Mr. Mundella (one of the most violent Radicals) . . . and the equally violent, blind Mr. Fawcett. On my observing on Mr. Mundella's appointment, Mr. Gladstone praised him very much, saying he was a very religious man, very much for religious education, and never said anything offensive.' [86]

There were others, especially in clubland, who thought like the Queen. Lord Cranbrook, sauntering into his club on the last day of the month (which was bitterly cold), heard keen criticism of the appointments, especially those of Chamberlain and Mundella. 'The latter', he recorded, 'will do mischief, for he has pledged himself on some educational questions, especially as to teachers.'[87]

But his positivist friends were delighted. Frederic Harrison wrote :

'We are heartily pleased to hear of the place which you have accepted. Everyone recognises how well you will fill it. If you are too fond of certain old books to satisfy all of your friends we must still admit that as yet we are in a minority on that head. But I hope that old sore is done with.

'But no one in the Government, no one in the House perhaps, knows the real working of these schools or our poor children as well as you. And I know no one in the House or out of it, feels more truly for their poor little bodies and souls (or shall we say minds?).' [88]

He did not have to face re-election, but was returned un-opposed. On 8 May he came down to thank his constituents and to outline his programme. On the platform was the Rev. H. Sandford, the Sheffield School Inspector, whose pamphlet on labour and education in the Potteries, published twenty years before, had helped to kindle his interest in the task he was about to undertake. Mundella naïvely pointed out both the commercial and constitutional necessity of a well-educated nation, and how far the country was from it while full compulsion to attend school did not operate. For of the twenty-four million people in England, only seventeen millions were under bye-laws compelling their children to attend school. With his capacity for being morally earnest, even on a public platform, he declared that 'it may be God's will that I should complete the work'. It seemed so. Even Gladstone himself must have realised what a host of personalities he controlled, all bent on achieving something, for he wrote to Morley two days later:

'The new government will be tested by its acts. No doubt it will make changes that will be denounced as revolutionary, and then be recognised as innocent, or even good.' [89]

PART III
MINISTER OF STATE

CHAPTER ELEVEN

Vice-President of the Council, 1880–1885

JAMES BRYCE saw the aptness of Mundella's appointment, and wrote to congratulate him:

'Heartiest congratulations on appointment to an office in substance the most important of all our offices, one congenial to yourself, one in which hardly anyone could do so much for education and the well being of the working class altogether as yourself. For Gladstone to have seen this is perhaps the best omen for the new ministry.'

'His energy is irrepressible,' exclaimed a contemporary just before his appointment, 'and though he represents on pure principle a constituency which is pre-eminently the most rascally in England, he is withal fundamentally an able and honest politician'.[1] This industry, no less than this integrity, was the cause of delight amongst the enthusiasts on the school boards.

Lyulph Stanley, of the London school board, wrote:

'I am heartily glad of your appointment not only on personal but on public grounds. I feel now that education has a friend in higher place, and that we of the London School Board will no longer be thwarted by the department (to whom by the way far too much was referred in the late administration).'[2]

His friends all joined to wish him well: Henry Crompton, Sir Louis Mallet, Sir John Lubbock, P. W. Clayden and Henry Roscoe all stressed his suitability for the task that lay ahead. Significant were the remarks of political opponents like John Gorst, who wrote:

'I am sure that if anything would make me believe in the government it would be that you are in it. I hope you won't quite do away with Eton, although it is a conservative place, and I think the farm labourer class is far too much educated at present.'[3]

The administration of the education department which Mundella now undertook was only a part of his duties. The other part lay in the supervision of the veterinary functions of the Committee of the Privy Council: at this time just as important and pressing, in view of the plague that was infesting imported cattle. A rise in the price of meat was from one point of view as undesirable for the administration as a recrudescence of denominational strife.

Two other members of the department were concerned in policy.[4] The first was the *de jure* head, or Lord President of the Council. He was Lord Spencer, known as the 'Red Earl', from the colour of his beard, a man of forthright opinion. He allowed Mundella to have his way in the purely educational duties of the committee of council, and followed his lead.[5] This was noticed by both friends and critics of the pair. 'His Lordship has no notions at all on the subject of education', wrote the lecturer in education at Cambridge, 'and merely echoes what he has been told by Mundella.' [6] So too at South Kensington (where both were often seen in the first two years of the administration) a wag remarked, 'here come Lord Mundella and Mr. Spencer'.[7]

In addition to Spencer there was Sir Francis Sandford, the permanent secretary, who had succeeded Lingen (notorious for being in office when payment by results was instituted) in February 1870. Sandford had seen the board schools established, but was suspected of being in sympathy with the voluntary schools, a suspicion which his later career seems to confirm. His knighthood was seventeen years old, the result of particularly successful work in organising an international exhibition in 1862. He embodied 'the department' to the school boards, and was popularly supposed to control both ministers and inspectors.

I

But the impact of a new hand was felt in the department immediately. Mundella's first act was to crown the agitation of the last fifteen years and to complete the system of compulsion to attend school. It must be unique for a statesman to advocate, pass and administer a measure at first so controversial and so much opposed as compulsory education. The Mundella Act completed the machinery that was first set up in 1870 and tentatively expanded in 1876. Hitherto compulsion had been permissive—i.e. the school boards (set up in 1870) and the school attendance committees (set up in 1876) were allowed to make by-laws enforcing attendance at school. But many of them, fearing the loss in earning power of child labour, had still not done so. Mundella's Act declared they should do so 'forthwith'. If the local authority did not comply by the end of the year 1880, the department themselves would frame the by-laws. Moreover, it made the employer of any child between the ages of ten and thirteen liable to a penalty if that child had not a certificate of education as laid down by these by-laws.

The numbers of delinquent authorities were extensive. Four hundred and fifty out of the 2,000 school boards, twenty out of the 190 schools attendance committees, seven out of the sixty-seven urban sanitary committees had not submitted by-laws for approval, and 569 out of 584 unions had not got all their parishes covered. The administration of the act revealed the position. The flood of by-laws coming in for sanction, said the report of the committee of council led to 'a very heavy increase' of correspondence.

It was tackled with fierce energy. The Mundella Act became law on 26 August 1880, and two days later circulars were sent to all erring authorities. Within five months over 1,200 sets of by-laws were sanctioned, and by January 1881 only twenty-eight unions, eighty-one school boards, one school attendance committee and one urban sanitary authority had not complied. With these minute exceptions the whole population were compelled to send their children to school.[8]

It passed with such smoothness that Lord Sandon asserted that Mundella had taken advantage of a draft bill which he found prepared in the office in 1880. Mundella denied this with some heat. Sandon promptly wrote Mundella a letter of apology regretting that 'I should have thus misrepresented you, which is the last thing that I should wish to do'.[9]

It was another milestone in advance. For now the fifth standard was made the minimum standard for exemption of children over ten years of age from the compulsion to attend school. The Factory Act of 1878, it will be remembered, set up the fourth standard for such exemption. Moreover, the well-named 'dunce's certificate' was no longer available except for children of thirteen years of age, and even then the child was required to attend school half-time for another year.

His second act was to set in motion the reorganisation of technical education, especially that of the metropolitan institutions like the Royal School of Mines (in Jermyn Street) and the congeries of technical schools that were growing up in the wilderness of sheds and temporary buildings at South Kensington. The Director of Science under the Science and Art Department, Colonel Donnelly, was asked to submit a memorandum recapitulating the history of the establishments at Jermyn Street and South Kensington, and to elaborate a scheme for the reorganisation of the school. There was opposition to change, for the mining enthusiasts, like Warington Smyth, stood out against the proposals that would reduce the Royal School of Mines to the mere sub-department of a school for general science.[10]

Mundella and Spencer consulted the professors, and decided to concentrate all the science schools at South Kensington, where a school devoted to all branches of science applicable to industry could be formed.[11] In addition, they envisaged a special organisation as a training college for teachers. To placate the mining enthusiasts, they proposed to preserve the title of the Royal School of Mines for the special final-year course then being conducted in Jermyn Street.

Mundella wrote to Lord Frederick Cavendish at the treasury pointing out the significance of the change; underlining the fact that the new proposals were merely a return to conditions prevailing in 1853. What a typical argument for a reformer! He said it would be encumbent upon the professors to deliver once every two years a course of lectures to working men. He asked Lord Frederick Cavendish to give the decision of the treasury as quickly as he could, 'so as to allow the new arrangements, whatever they may be, to be settled and announced in time for them to come into force at the commencement of the next session of the school in 1881'.

But the treasury were not very co-operative. Lord Frederick Cavendish replied on 22 June 1881 that these 'very serious questions' had received the attention of the Lords of the Treasury, and they had decided not 'to concur in the merging of a strictly technical and professional school of mining knowledge in any more general scientific institution'. He expressed only limited agreement with the other proposals, 'on the understanding that now, nor within the near future, the Committee of Council do not foresee any serious increase of expenditure'.[12]

This parsimony, especially with regard to the ramshackle array of hutments that housed the central technical museums of the Empire, was bitterly regretted by Lord Spencer. Though he did manage to appoint Armstrong, and to add two courts to the South Kensington Museum, he said later to a royal commission:

'In 1881-2 we were continually applying to the Treasury for the completion of the buildings. We were always put off by excuses, they always said, "Well, we have got to build a new War Office, or a new Admiralty," and there was always one excuse after another, and I fancy those excuses and those difficulties have not yet been overcome.' [13]

But Mundella managed to secure the establishment of the Normal School of Science which, in October 1881, opened its doors with T. H. Huxley as dean. Officially it was a single institution organised in two divisions: the Royal School of Mines (constituting the departments of mining and metallurgy); and the Normal School of Science. Geology was the connecting link between them. But within the framework of these two divisions a vigorous individual development began.[14] A diploma or associateship of the Normal School of Science was set up for students who wished to qualify in pure science subjects, leaving the associateship of the Royal School of Mines for those who wished to qualify in metallurgy alone.

Meanwhile his third act had been to appoint a departmental committee to make inquiries and other recommendations on higher education in Wales. The names of this committee were announced a week before the Mundella Act became law. The committee produced one of the most influential reports of the decade, and its conclusions, though specifically Welsh, were applied by Mundella as part of a wider programme. Its report was in Mundella's hands within a year of its constitution. He said later:

'If there is one thing on which Lord Spencer and I have set our hearts, it is that we should make in this corner of Great Britain a model, a complete model, of educational organisation worthy of the imitation of the great English People.' [15]

As the committee was sitting, Mundella was encouraged to persevere in his reforms by the kind reception he had from his constituents, who, when he protested at their demonstrativeness, shouted: 'You're worth it.' He went abroad, and met Matthew Arnold, who was holidaying at Pontresina. Arnold took the opportunity to walk with Mundella in the rain and 'press several things upon him with regard to education'. So favourable a response did he receive that he wrote to his wife and daughter on consecutive days to express his delight at having 'more chance of influence with him than with any Vice-President we have ever had'.[16] This was high praise indeed, for W. E. Forster, vice-president ten years before, was Matthew Arnold's brother-in-law.[17] 'Mundella makes himself so pleasant,' Arnold continued, 'and I am sure, as I said to Sandford, that nowhere else in Europe is there to be found a minister exhorting his subordinate official to write more poetry.'

2

The needs of the time could only be satisfied by establishing a system of technical education,[18] for there were many symptoms that the existing public schools were producing the wrong kind of person. The efforts of Thomas Hughes (Mundella's old parliamentary associate of the seventies) to form a colony in Tennessee, where old public-school boys could find an outlet for their abilities, showed how badly balanced the educational system had become. Hughes acknowledged that 'little outlet of a satisfactory kind can be found for the swarming manhood of the English gentry and middle class', and confessed that the increasing number of this type of boy presented a very real social problem.[19]

Much the same thing was said by Lord Aberdare's committee on Welsh higher education which reported in 1881. Their hostility towards the existing public schools was balanced by their enthusiastic endorsement of the intermediate schools, part rate- and part state-aided. They urged that these schools should accommodate 15,000 instead of the existing maximum of 3,000, which they had not yet even approached.[20] They further suggested that these schools should be undenominational, with a revised curriculum, and with channels of exit and entry by means of a revised scholarship system. To crown the system the committee proposed the establishment of two university colleges. But the intermediate schools, they urged, should be established 'immediately'. It is not surprising that their report should have been called 'the educational charter of Wales'.[21]

Reinforcing this argument was the rapid progress of other countries in this matter. Technological progress was so important that Mundella declared, 'In the brains of the people lay the grandest mine of wealth and prosperity that this country possessed'. Germany and France had re-geared their educational machine to respond to the quickening tempo of the age. Germany, under Falk, had excused all who attended the *realschule* from two years military service. This *realschule* was educating from the age of nine for six years.[22] Falk also gave the teachers a new code. France, under Jules Ferry, had secularised her schools, and Ferry's work received an added significance in May 1881, when Tunis was occupied.[23] Mundella was aware of these foreign movements and what they portended. H. M. Felkin, his old business representative in Saxony, made a study of the efforts that the Chemnitz chamber of commerce had made to secure good technical education in the town, which was enabling the town to challenge the pre-eminence of the hosiery trade of Nottingham.[24]

Mundella took Felkin's work to Philip Magnus. Magnus was the head of the newly founded City and Guilds Institute, and was so impressed that he persuaded his committee to publish it as *Technical Education in a Saxon Town* in May 1881. It outlined the efforts that the citizens of Chemnitz had already made, and posed the burning question:

'It remains to be seen whether for increasing the industrial prosperity of this country, the people of England will be willing to make similar sacrifices.'

The publicity given to the topic was not in vain. Two months later a royal commission was appointed to examine the whole question of foreign technical education together with what was offered in England, and to compare the result. It was the first sign for fourteen years that the national complacency had been ruffled. Mundella's great ally in this matter, Bernhard Samuelson, was the chairman. So keen and anxious were the commissioners that they paid their own expenses on a tour of the continent that lasted for three years.[25]

By the end of August, Mundella was in great spirits. His plans were going forward in a fashion that could not have been better. An Irishman, reminiscing about these last few days of the 1881 session, relates how Mundella stayed in the house up to the very close, the only occupant of the front bench except Mr. Gladstone, and how his gurgling and basso laughter punctuated the dying hours of debate.[26]

3

As the Aberdare committee were taking evidence and the Samuelson commission were on tour, Mundella devoted his personal attention to the consideration of what was actually being taught in the elementary schools and what should be taught in the future. Hitherto the conditions of the government grant, awarded on the results of individual examination in the three R's, conditioned the growth of a soulless grind at the elementary skills of pen and tongue that form such a dark chapter in our educational history. Attempts had been made to encourage the teaching of specific subjects in the upper standards, 4, 5 and 6, but, owing to the viciousness of the system, the specific subjects lapsed into the same routine as the three Rs had done.[27]

On 2 August 1880 Mundella announced his intention of bringing in a new code. It was a tedious work. For the following year he devoted himself to the consideration of the proposals; they were then submitted to parliament. Eventually, by 1883, the money was voted to enable the code to operate. Perhaps even more significant than the changes he made was the way he made them, which marked the end of the autocratic tradition of Robert Lowe. For a newer code committee was set up. The permanent secretary of the education department later said before the Cross commission of 1886:

'It was a new departure as I understood it, to have a committee sitting round a table and deliberating as a committee. I do not remember being present at any such committee until this code. There was no code committee before this.'

This code committee was presided over by Mundella himself, and considered suggestions from school boards, the leading inspectors and other interested parties. After the preliminary sifting, a draft report was produced.[28]

In a year from the first announcement of his intention to modify the code, the draft report was hammered into a set of proposals ready to outline to the house. Mundella wrote to Leader on 1 August 1881: 'These will make or mar me. It will be a new era in elementary education. I have been at work on it for the past six months.' A week later he told the house:

'We simply submit these proposals to form the bases of the future education code of this country. We ask that it shall receive the fullest criticism. It is not a party question with us. What we want to arrive at, is sound educational principles, and we can deal with the money payments afterwards.'[29]

It was well received. He wrote to Leader again:

'I shall have to stand the fire of criticism till next spring, and then draft my proposals into a code, no light matter. Nearly all the press praised my scheme, the *Globe* gave the best and most intelligent article, the silly *Daily News* the worst. It actually ascribed my reforms to Sandford, who (although I praised him and all the permanent officials in order to secure their co-operation) I have dragged along with me.'[30]

The money was forthcoming. Lord Frederick Cavendish wrote on 4 March 1882:

'I shall write to you to-day accepting your proposed changes in the code as satisfactory. We should have been very sorry if we had been obliged to make any difficulties about a scheme which seems to have been worked out with great care and judgement.'

On the same day Mundella received what he called 'the most agreeable and distinguished honour that could fall upon me', for Henry Roscoe wrote to him from South Kensington:

'Your name was brought before the president of the council for election to the Fellowship of the Royal Society. The proposal was received with acclamation. Your certificate has been signed by the president and by every member of the council.'[31]

His work had been recognised.

The 'Mundella Code' blazed new trails. Though the core was still payment by results (an inevitable complement of state subvention), Mundella himself declared :

'I do not want the state to lay down a hard-and-fast line. There would be much less need of codes if the local authorities in every town and village were in earnest in carrying out their work. I want to decentralize in this matter of education. I hope the time will come when you will dispense with the committee of the privy council and insist on having no grants from them, but pay all out of your own resources as they do on the continent and in America. That is perfect freedom and perfect self-government.'[32]

But though this core remained, a great deal was done to moderate the rigours of the ordeal that is so well described in *Jude the Obscure*, where an examining inspector enters the room and the teacher falls on her face in a dead faint.

The most important changes were at the lower and upper ends of the elementary school. At the lower end, in the infant school, payment by results was moderated and manual employments and play were recognised, even though 90 per cent of the grant depended on examination. The inspectors noticed the immense improvement this effected in junior schools.[33] At the upper end a new standard 7 was introduced with a syllabus that made possible its separation into a school of higher grade. The code's more prominent feature, however, was the introduction of the 'merit grant'. Aimed at making teaching more intelligent, it eliminated the wasteful allotment of the government grant to mere elementary grind. Schools were to be classified as 'fair', 'good' or 'excellent' for the purpose of participating in the grant. For this purpose special instructions were issued to inspectors to guide them in their assessment:

'An excellent school is characterised by cheerful yet exact discipline maintained without harshness or noisy demonstration of authority. Its premises are cleanly and well ordered, its timetable provides a proper variety of mental employment and of physical exercise; its organisation is such as to distribute the teaching power judiciously, and to secure for every scholar, whether he is likely to bring credit to the school or not, a fair share of instruction and attention.

'Where circumstances permit, it also has its lending library, its savings bank, and an orderly collection of simple objects and apparatus adapted to illustrate the school lessons, and formed in part by the co-operation of the scholars themselves.' [34]

One more alleviation of the harshness of payment by results was the payment of the grant on the average attendance of the whole school, instead of on that of each individual. All children who had been on the register for twenty-two weeks could be examined, regardless of whether they had individual attendances of 250 or not. This meant that an increasing number of children, especially the backward ones, were presented for examination, and may in the end have led to a better appreciation of what was actually being taught in the school. The teaching of new subjects was encouraged by making them eligible for grants. Elementary science was recognised throughout the school. More attention to English and physical geography was ensured by a rearrangement of the list of class subjects. Specific subjects were extended to include electricity and magnetism; heat, light and sound; chemistry and agriculture. For girls, cookery appeared as a grant-earning subject. In the teaching of these the emphasis was to be on explaining the common objects of everyday life. Above all, the inspectors were to impress on managers and teachers that 'the more thoroughly a teacher is qualified for his position by skill, character and personal influence, the less necessary is it for him to resort to corporal chastisement at all'.[35]

But the most essential novelty about the Mundella code was that it was not unalterable. Arrangements were made through an administrative organisation of the inspectorate to ensure that a permanent code committee was created to modify such articles as were harsh or misunderstood.[36] For the first time, all the instructions to inspectors, together with all the requirements of the department, were made available in one volume, and it became part of the equipment of every school.[37]

The results of the code were far-reaching. Machinery had been devised by which it could be perpetually criticised and reconstructed. Moreover, it profoundly affected the status and work of inspectors, teachers and children. The inspectors felt the extra burden that this new code imposed upon them. One of them described the increase of work as 'somewhat alarming'.[38] Accordingly a reorganisation of the inspectorate into ten national districts, with a chief inspector in each reporting to the department, was instituted. A new class of sub-inspectors was recruited from men of special qualifications and experience.[39] The first woman inspector was appointed as a consequence of the introduction of cookery. One inspector, Willis, whose harshness was reported to Mundella, nearly lost his appointment, and it was only due to the intervention of Matthew Arnold that he retained it. In 1884 consideration for weaklings was urged upon the inspectorate, who should consider 'the health, age and mental capacity of the children' as well as their 'due progress in learning'.

The new code threw into heavy relief the inadequacy of teacher-training. The school boards in the van of advance had established pupil-teacher centres which pupil-teachers could attend. The London school board had come into conflict with the education department in 1875 because the code laid down that instruction to the pupil-teachers was to be given in the schools where they worked under the headmasters themselves. Now, however, central instruction was officially recognised, and the probationers who received such instruction were limited to a certain amount of teaching only, and were to attend these central classes for the rest of their time. Moreover, they were required to attend these centres in the day-time instead of in the evening. This official blessing to the pupil-teacher centres encouraged a number to spring up. In four years there were eleven in operation, with 1,636 pupils in attendance. Moreover, the efflorescence of the new local university colleges (the adjective describes their architecture) still further sapped the idea of 'apprenticeship' in the training of a teacher.[40]

This was the first proposal that was to disturb the hornets who were to rage about the code, as its provisions were seen to bear hardly on the voluntary schools. On 13 May 1882 the archbishop of Canterbury wrote a strong personal letter to Mundella on the question of limiting the number of pupil-teachers, stressing the strong feeling of the managers and teachers in the church schools against it. He pointed out that in the country schools, where there was only one pupil-teacher and no assistant teacher, 'the discipline and efficiency of the schools must inevitably be prejudiced'. He feared that the hours to be saved 'would all be taken in some cases from the time now devoted to religious teaching', and stressed the 'fear that the proposed changes may result in a diminution in the number of pupil-teachers employed'.[41]

Other aspects of the code came in for criticism as the nature of the provisions was more fully appreciated. Of all the misunderstandings it caused, perhaps the most blatant was the accusation of 'harshness'. A common ground of criticism was the cry of over-pressure which was paraded before parliament in language that verged on the extravagant. Mundella's attention was repeatedly drawn to deaths allegedly due to the strictness of the code. The most often quoted critic was Dr. Crichton-Browne, who declared:

'The infantile lip, that would curl with contempt at any reference to a witch or a ghost, quivers with anxiety at the name of a government inspector, and the examination day has appropriated to itself much of the foreboding that used to belong to the day of judgement'.[42]

But his views were not endorsed by the majority of the medical profession. The Lancet categorically declared: 'The educational system is not overworking children but demonstrating that they are underfed'.[43] This conclusion raised a new set of issues that Mundella was not slow to appreciate. He urged local authorities to follow the example of Rousden, a Devonshire village, and provide cheap meals for the children. This was itself a change of great moment.

4

By now a definite pattern of policy can be seen emerging from the welter of letters, reports and memoranda that surrounded

Mundella. The pattern emerges all the more clearly since he suddenly found himself untrammelled. Lord Spencer went to Ireland, and his translation, though it pushed Mundella 'very hard indeed',[44] enabled him to reinforce the claim that the *de facto* head of the education department should be the *de jure* head as well, with a control over all branches of the educational policy of the country.

He had secured compulsion in the elementary school. He had recast its code. He had a plan for higher education in Wales which needed action by the state. He had the preliminary report of the technical education commission. All pointed to the next step, a consideration of the existing means of higher education. In England this was the province of the endowed grammar schools, whose trust funds were being slowly and methodically surveyed by the charity commissioners, to whom he was to add radicals like Sir George Young and Mr. Anstey, to ensure that they worked with the vigour that he expected. For Wales he already had a plan. But for Scotland nothing existed. There, the rich Scottish endowments were as yet uninfluenced by the new ideas, and as yet untouched by the hand of government. Mundella conducted a bill through parliament to overhaul the Scottish endowments. It was a long one, with more than fifty clauses, and Mundella spoke over a hundred times during its passage, on one occasion leading the house in committee for twelve hours on a blazing June day. He experienced further opposition, for, as he confessed, 'nothing touches men like the administration of endowments'.[45] It was the most difficult and important measure he had yet dealt with. It set up a commission, under Lord Balfour of Burleigh, that was analogous to the endowed schools commission of 1869. This got down to work so quickly that within a year it had over 200 schemes before it. The remodelling of the trusts was carried out with especial regard to higher and technical education.[46]

But with regard to the Welsh programme the cabinet were not so quiescent. Mundella prepared a memorandum for Gladstone on 5 May 1882, which Lord Spencer signed, pointing out that by means of a loan, and without legislation, the essential parts of the Aberdare report could be implemented. It is worth reproduction.

'There should be established in the larger centres of population (say of 10,000 inhabitants and upwards) a class of elementary schools after the fashion of the higher schools at Bradford (see report of the Welsh committee, Vol. i, p. cxiii) in which only the (three) upper standards and specific subjects should be taught for a moderate fee not exceeding 9d. a week. These schools would afford thoroughly good education to poor but promising children, while they could prepare for the intermediate or grammar schools those who, from their family circumstances, or with the aid of scholarships, were able to continue their education beyond the usual limit of age in elementary schools. These schools would be established by the school boards of the districts, in premises provided *where necessary*, by means of a loan from the public works loan commissioners, sanctioned by the education department.

'*No Legislation is needed for this purpose.*' [47]

By July, however, Mundella was writing to Godley lamenting that the year's programme would not permit legislation on Welsh intermediate schools, but promising that grants for the establishment of the university colleges and the higher-grade elementary schools would be his especial care.[48] Mundella was as good as his word. In August he personally wrote to all the Welsh school boards asking that

'in places where there is a considerable population requiring education superior to that which can be provided in an ordinary elementary school, advanced elementary schools for boys and girls should be established, and that the instruction in such schools should be adapted as closely as possible to the characteristics of each place and to the educational needs of the inhabitants'.

He followed this up in November by sending all the boards a description of the Bradford higher-grade schools, with the comment that 'one or two more schools of the same character seem to be suited to meet some of the more pressing requirements of the Welsh districts'.[49] However, in the spring of 1883 the treasury was unwilling to grant money for Welsh intermediate schools, and the matter was shelved for another year.

5

Mundella's activity was watched by the opposition and the voluntaryists with the liveliest apprehension. His attack on the Scottish endowments was regarded as radical robbery. His attempts to encourage higher-grade elementary schools in Wales, supported by grants through the code, brought together the supporters of proprietary schools, who were even less reassured by the tone of his remarks towards them:

'I regret to say', said Mundella in January 1883, 'that there is nothing more meretricious in the whole of our education system than what is designated the middle class education of private venture schools, and more especially those miserable boarding schools, which are supposed to give both education and fine manners, but which turn out boys and girls utterly ignorant of what they might obtain at an elementary school at Birmingham for 2d. a week.' [50]

Two months later the *Sheffield Telegraph* commented on the local central (higher grade) school in the town; and the general principle of such schools:

'They offer a middle-class education at half the prime cost of the commodity to be supplied—they compete destructively with useful and honoured institutions which are based on honesty to pay their way without help from the rates.

'The Board are going outside the Act, outside the design of the legislature, outside any purpose for which a rate-levying power was bestowed on them.'

A leader of these outraged feelings and interests appeared in Cardinal Manning, a priest of striking personality. This was the chance for which Cardinal Manning had waited since the 1870 Act had been passed. Then he had been in Rome; now, as the second English cardinal since the reformation, he felt it was opportune openly to challenge the 1870 Act itself, declaring that its administration by the department was 'open to the censure of inequality and injustice'. Replies from its supporters merely stung him to further allegations. He was joined by Canon Gregory of the established church, who asserted with him that the 1870 Act 'has endowed with the school rate those who had done nothing and it has excluded those who have hitherto educated the people of England from participation in the school rate, to which they are also nevertheless compelled to pay'.[51] Mundella saw the motives behind the attack, and wrote to Leader on 10 December:

'I keep screwing up the quality of education and insist on the quantity being ample, and all this makes increased and increasing demands upon the voluntary system, and brings the poorer school gradually in the hands of the board. That is the real reason for Manning's outcry.' [52]

Mundella was busy in January, opening the large new grammar schools in Birmingham that had been built out of the remodelled King Edward VI foundation. He also went to Wales to assist in the arbitration between the claims of thirteen Welsh towns for the new university colleges. Ultimately the sites chosen were Cardiff and Bangor. This had the effect of rousing the feeling of nonconformists, who saw a cathedral in one town and near the other. As if the perils of the *via media* were not enough, Chamberlain chose this occasion to make a speech in favour of free education. Mundella privately disapproved, and commented, 'It is a much larger question than he seems to apprehend'.[53]

6

So, attacked by both churches and chapels, and prodded from the rear by the Birmingham group, Mundella began to cast about for a means whereby he could slough the veterinary functions of his office.[54] These occupied much of his time and involved endless wrangles. Earlier he had complained:

'This department is a very heavy one, and its demands incessant. Lord Spencer's absence throws everything on me. Lord Carlingford, who is nominally deputy Lord President, has not put in an appearance since Parliament rose.'

So in March 1883 he wrote a long and important letter to Gladstone:

'I am very reluctant to add to your heavy labours by troubling you with suggestions, especially such as may appear in the smallest degree personal to myself. I only do so because you requested me after our brief conversation on the treasury bench to put my ideas into writing. During my tenure of office I have obtained sufficient insight into the working of the veterinary department of the privy council to enable me to speak with some confidence on the proposal to set up a Department of Agriculture. The demand for this new department comes mainly from the opposition. Many of the leading country gentlemen sitting on the government side are averse or indifferent to it, although they do not venture openly to oppose it. That its establishment will be a concession to a sentiment which has grown up and increased of late years cannot be denied.

'The principal work which the new department will be called upon to undertake will consist in the administration of the acts relating to contagious diseases in animals, this and the collection of some additional statistics relating to agriculture appears to be all that will fall to the department at the outset. . . .

'I would suggest that the Lord President of the Council should also be minister of agriculture, assisted by a parliamentary secretary devoted to the interests of agriculture. The veterinary department should, if possible, be brought into the offices of the privy council and its name changed to that of agriculture department. . . .

'I am unwilling to trouble you with the views I ventured to express to you on Friday last that the time had come in my opinion when the education department should be severed from the privy council. I enclose a letter from the most experienced member of the department and, were I not in office, I could add much to enforce his views. I am convinced that without adding to the salary or status of the Vice-President, the work of his office and that of the chief permanent officials would be much simplified.' [55]

When Mundella returned from a fortnight's illness in April 1883, Lord Spencer had taken over the vice-royalty of Ireland, and Lord Carlingford had been appointed Lord President. He was a complete contrast to the picturesque and thorough Lord Spencer, and their correspondence reveals it. Lord Spencer could write a twelve-page business letter to Mundella on Christmas morning, whereas Lord Carlingford invariably wrote short notes. For Carlingford's position was due entirely to his wife, whose vigour and personality more than compensated for his own lack of quality and achievement.[56]

Mundella realised that the only reform to which he could expect Lord Carlingford to agree would be the severance of the veterinary functions from his department and the establishment of a committee of agriculture. After his return he wrote:

'It will relieve me of all the cattle business, which I shall be glad to be rid of. My own department ought to be cut adrift from the council the same as the Board of Trade has been, but while I have the control and do all the work I don't care about the personal question of my own title.' [57]

Three days later, on 17 April, Forster came to see him about the project to create a ministry of education. But once more Mundella was taken ill, on 29 April, and bills for extending compulsion to Scotland and intermediate education in Wales hung fire again.

Meanwhile, the irritation of the voluntaryists had been mounting, till in the sultry month of June the storm broke around his head. The National Society sent a memorial to Gladstone asking for assistance, reinforcing it with outside meetings. Mundella hastened to write to Carlingford on 4 June to warn him of the significance of their demands:

'I have felt now for more than a year past that this demand would be made. Cardinal Manning and Canon Gregory have struck up an arrangement (in which they have endeavoured, but unsuccessfully, to include the Wesleyans) to agitate for increased grants to voluntary schools. A series of articles have appeared in the *Nineteenth Century* from the pens of these two ecclesiastics making out the best case they can for their claims. These have been very effectively replied to by the Rev. R. W. Dale of Birmingham, who not only showed with great force and clearness the injustice of the demand, but also the consequences likely to follow upon it, *viz.* a renewed agitation for the abolition of all grants to schools set up by various religious bodies.

'I am sincerely anxious for educational progress and I believe we shall best secure this by the maintenance of the compromise of 1870. I am confident, however, that any attempt to depart from this compromise, any attempt to share the rates or differentiate the grants made to voluntary or board schools, would plunge us into a bitter agitation, *viz.* the complete severance of education from the control of the various religious bodies and the establishment of a system of national education under the management of the state. Already I find it sufficiently difficult to meet the attacks upon the weaker and less defensible portions of our present system, especially upon the training colleges. Lord Spencer thought the latter were hardly defensible in their present state.

Still, if those who have benefited most by the act of 1870 are so unwise as to attack it, or if the Government were so ill advised as to show a doubtful mind in dealing with the present demand, I am satisfied that serious agitation would follow, and that education would in all probability suffer until a final settlement was arrived at.' [58]

Mundella's friends in the house of commons saw that the only solution lay in a concerted demand for a minister of education. Lord Randolph Churchill took the opportunity to loose some finely-pointed barbs at Mundella's embarrassing position in listening to the debate on his own status. Gladstone publicly disparaged the proposed change, quoting Spencer and Carlingford as agreeing with him. W. E. Forster, now sitting below the gangway, who had raised the matter with Mundella two months before, said on this occasion: 'The real objection (i.e. to a minister of education) probably is that it is undesirable to make too much of education. If we were to have a minister for education, he might be pushing things on too quickly.' [59] Yet the debate had its results. A departmental committee was appointed on 9 August 1883, under the chairmanship of H. C. E. Childers, to 'consider how the ministerial responsibility under which the votes for education, science and art are administered, may best be secured'. Its composition was refreshingly liberal and favourable to the idea of a minister of education acting for both England and Scotland. As such they provoked further opposition from the Scots, who dreaded that they might come under an English official. Lord Dalhousie called on Mundella and, finding him out, left a note:

'I know you care a good deal about this question or I should not take the liberty of troubling you . . . if the report of the committee in favour of a minister of education is adopted, all you need to do to save education going to the Scotch Minister is to make a permanent head of the Scottish department who shall be in direct communication with yourself.'

It is little wonder that Mundella exclaimed to Robert Leader after such a year of trouble: 'I wish we could decentralise, and that the authorities cared more about education and less about imperial grants with the inevitable control which it entails'.[60]

7

His first act in the new year 1884 was to make a trip to Scotland to keep the Scottish boards strong in their enthusiasm. Here he could afford to use more advanced language than in England. He outlined functions to them that the recent revelations of the *Bitter Cry of Outcast London* provoked:

'In many cases local authorities must stand *in loco parentis* to children. If we are to reduce the misery we must leave to ministers the parents and adults but we must save the children. There is needed a great amendment to the law relating to parental responsibility to make them responsible for the care, the clothing and the education of their children.' [61]

His remarks were everywhere greeted with enthusiasm, as 'not the passing outburst of new-born zeal, but the logical outcome of a steady life purpose'.[62] He responded by loading the Burleigh commission with praise, declaring that he would walk barefoot to London if the English charity commissioners would be as active. It was a campaign to warn as well as praise, for 'of all the social problems that have to be dealt with in this generation there is none more terrible to be encountered than the ghosts of our old neglect'.[63] This was meat and drink to the radical party in Scotland. Members like George Anderson and James Cameron declared that it was the next best thing to the Midlothian campaign.[64]

But Mundella's English critics were not idle. Lord Norton (the former Sir Charles Adderley) appeared with another blast against Mundella's attempt to oust voluntary initiative in the sphere of higher education. Norton wrote in the February number of the *Nineteenth Century* condemning Mundella's 'independent educational experiments' and the school boards, who, under his inspiration, borrowed money for undertakings far outside his or any other parliamentary authority. Strong language was used. He accused Mundella of 'essaying a flight into continental bureaucracy', of having 'strongly avowed German preferences', and prophesied that he would fail in his attempts owing to the opposition of 'the English spirit'.[65] Mundella was under no illusions about the difficulties of the task that lay ahead. On 24 and 29 February he outlined them to Robert Leader:

'I have a tremendous lot of work on hand and now I am told that I must help with the cattle bill. I look forward to a good deal of opposition to my work this session. The denominationalists find the struggle to live growing harder. The increase of rates is pressing the needy and the greedy ratepayer. The enemies of education and the people who dread its influence, together with the lazy teachers, will all unite to make things uncomfortable for me. I shall fight it out, I hope, with courage and good temper.'

And five days later:

'I am in for a very heavy session. What with teachers, Tories, and sectaries, I can see that the whole educational system is going to be attacked all round and I shall have a tough time of it.' [66]

But, as often happens, the things he feared did not come to pass. The friction was provided by one in much closer contact with him than any of the people he mentioned—to wit, his own Lord President. For Carlingford was very averse to the way the Childers Committee was working, and had written on 13 February:

'What events! What next! I have just had a conversation with Childers by desire of Mr. Gladstone about the report of his committee. I am low at the prospect of being severed from the education department, and I am not satisfied with the new arrangements which seem to be working.' [67]

Mundella himself outlined his views before the committee on 1 April. He expressed disagreement with both Sir Francis Sandford and Lord Carlingford, who were in favour of a separate veterinary department. Mundella pointed out that things would be better if a Minister of Education were appointed, although he admitted that, as a *de facto* head of the education department, he had, with two exceptions, mainly got his own way to date. 'I care not how I might be called,' he declared, 'but whoever has charge of the education of the country should have a seat in the cabinet.' He went farther. He declared that the three separate departments of education, science and art, and museums should be merged under this one head, who should co-ordinate all policy. Furthermore, the minister should be able to exercise some control over the endowed schools, which hitherto were only subject to the re-modelling of their trust funds by the charity commissioners, and who remained free from any surveillance of the department in their operation, or any inspection of their curriculum.

Carlingford wrote the next day. He was still in favour of a board of agriculture, and asked Mundella to send him his ideas about it 'as soon as he could'.[68] The tension between them mounted. A month later Carlingford attempted to assert the prerogative of appointment which it had been agreed that the Lord President should forgo. The post was the key appointment of permanent secretary, made vacant by the retirement of Sir Francis Sandford after fourteen years' service. Carlingford's nominee was an inspector. Mundella's was Patric Cumin. Cumin was a former private secretary of W. E. Forster, and a known sympathiser with school boards, one who would strain *droit administratif* to its limits in their favour. Words ensued. Mundella threatened to send his resignation to Gladstone if his nomination was not approved. He won, and on 15 May Patric Cumin became the permanent secretary. He was an invaluable assistant.[69]

Childers' committee reported, recommending a minister of education who would act both for England and Scotland, with a board or committee of privy councillors to assist him. His duties should be equal to those of a secretary of state, and he should have a parliamentary secretary, together with a separate secretary for Scotland. Gladstone tried to overcome Lord Carlingford's opposition to the change by offering him the choice of two embassies. In a latter dated 7 September 1884 he wrote:

> 'Much to my dissatisfaction and a little to my surprise, I gathered from Childers a short time ago that there is to be a strong and practically unanimous report from his committee in favour of the appointment of a minister of education, with the intention, I apprehend, that he should be a member of the House of Commons.'

Carlingford refused, and continued to refuse as late as 21 February 1885, when he wrote to Gladstone:

> 'The change, I understand, is that in future Mundella would be called President of the Education Board, that he and I, inhabiting our separate rooms, would cease to confer together, and that the education department would lose its connection with the cabinet. I confess I fail to see what reforms this change would effect, and I am sure that a great many of those interested in education would think it a change for the worse.' [70]

Though this main proposal was not adopted, two most useful changes were made. The first was the creation of a separate secretary for the science and art department at South Kensington. This body, through a series of multiple activities, assisted the struggling higher-grade schools, the museums, and technical education generally throughout the country. Fortified by its semi-autonomy from the education department proper, it had begun to enlarge its power further, and to establish close relationships with the unofficial secondary schools that were growing up in the large towns under the ægis of the boards. The second change was the final separation of Scottish educational administration from English dominance. At the end of 1883 the Lord Advocate had been given a watching brief; later the duties became part of those of the new secretary of state for Scotland.[71]

A more important report came out in the month that Cumin

was appointed: May 1884 saw the publication of the long-awaited second report of the Samuelson commission. Its conclusions were given a wide publicity. Its most startling assertion was that technical education was not the province only of artisans and mechanics. Technical education was defined, as including languages, mathematics, history, and geography. The commission recommended that scholarships should be established from the higher-grade schools to the technical and local colleges.[72] Many northern school boards followed the recommendations of this report. They opened schools which operated as organised science schools receiving grants from the science and art department. Notable in this respect was the Manchester school board, under the chairmanship of Herbert Birley. When the Mundella code appeared, this school board had established a seventh standard and then an extra seventh. Now they made a radical change. The two leading board schools were merged into a large new building holding 1,200 pupils, with special provision for the teaching of science and art. It was so well equipped that it immediately drew upon the reservoir of ability that had been destined for Manchester Grammar School. This new school was called the Manchester Central Higher Grade School. It was opened, together with a new museum at Queens Park, Harpurhey, by Mundella on 5 July. The Manchester Central Higher Grade School was but a forerunner; within a year others had sprung up at Ardwick, Hyde Road, St. Lukes, Waterloo Road, Birley Street, Beswick and Ducie Avenue. The drain on the Manchester Grammar School became so heavy that S. Dill, the high master, wrote to Mundella, and, receiving no satisfaction, bitterly complained in 1885 that 'there are many signs of late that our place in the educational system is little recognised, and that our capacity of service to the community is quietly ignored'.[73]

The same opposition was visible in Wales, where the 'complete model of educational organisation' was taking shape with the opening of Cardiff and Bangor university colleges, each with a government subsidy of £4,000 a year. The headmasters of all the grammar and proprietary schools in the principality met at Shrewsbury to form a provisional committee for the protection of 'the old foundation schools which have borne the heat and burden of educational work in the past'. They passed a resolution that the age of admission to these state-aided colleges should be raised to seventeen, and that there should be an entrance examination 'as would effectually protect such colleges from the necessity of undertaking elementary instruction'.[74]

8

The new spirit now openly abroad and working in English education was epitomised in the first international conference on education to be held in the country. It was held in conjunction with the international exhibition at South Kensington from June to October 1884. With the co-operation of the foreign office, delegates from America, France, Germany, Belgium, Italy and Japan attended. The new ideas were on display. The British and Foreign Schools Society organised a kindergarten exhibition. Francis Galton initiated an anthropometric laboratory to show how intelligence could be objectively tested. The new scientific pedagogy, itself a product of the increasing teaching of science, was the subject of addresses. It was Heurism, the doctrine that knowledge cannot be presented as a ready-made parcel, but only as something that the student observed being gradually built up.[75] The triumph belonged to the science and art department, as the exhibition was held in their headquarters at South Kensington. In addition, the impact of foreign opinion gave added impetus to the new movement.

A touching ceremony took place on 9 August, when 80,000 factory workers, mainly women and children, presented Mrs. Mundella with a marble bust of her husband by Sir Edgar Boehm. They came by special trains from the distant parts of Lancashire and the dales of Yorkshire, and filled the Manchester Town Hall. Along the front seats were ranged 300–400 little half-timers who had enjoyed the benefit of the Factory Act of 1874, which they attributed to Mundella. 'As I and my wife walked along the rows and spoke to the little ones, I felt it was time to begin all over again as they were hardly big enough to be out of the nursery.' He did not make any party capital out of the scene. 'I am accustomed to attack and defence,' he declared, 'but I am not accustomed to returning thanks for so much kindness as I have received.' He added:

'Many of you know there is a constant conflict going on as to who shall have the credit for factory legislation, and both parties claim it. I think you may fairly repudiate it for both of them. It really is a question of social reform which forced itself by degrees on the best men of both parties, and it was opposed at first by the best men of both parties.'[76]

In September he went to Switzerland. On the journey he met the bishop of Gloucester, who had been the mouthpiece of a recent deputation of the National Society to the education department. The bishop introduced the subject and 'joked about it in the most amusing manner', confessing that the courtesy of the department 'bowed him out,' and made him withdraw with similar apologies, 'routed horse and foot, bag and baggage'. Mundella was delighted at the story, and wrote jubilantly to Leader:

'This shows what humbugs these people are in making their claims, demands and complaints, all with the hope of getting something.

'While Chamberlain is urging me to go in for free schools, the treasury is demanding a reduction of my estimates. Mine is a very difficult dish to carry even. Forster's compromise is not very easily worked, and I flatter myself that there are not very many on our side who would have carried the dish as long as I have with as little slopping over.'

So wrote Mundella to Leader on 21 January 1885, as Chamberlain vociferated from the inside and embarrassments accumulated abroad. The news of the fall of Khartoum reached England on 5 February, and eleven days later Mundella wrote:

'I am staunch as a rock to dear old Gladstone, but I feel the dangers of the situation acutely. I shall have a lively time about educational work. The voluntaries and the worst of the teachers are anxious to get rid of payment by results. The fact is they want more money for fewer and worse results, and they are ready to attack us on anything and everything that keeps them up to the mark. I don't mean to budge an inch.' [77]

9

To ensure that secondary education should respond to the urgent needs of the time, Mundella had made the interesting suggestion to the Childers Committee that endowed schools should be subject to inspection. This prompted J. Percival, the vigorous president of Trinity College, Oxford, to suggest that Mundella, together with three co-opted colleagues, should report on the whole of the endowed schools. Assistant commissioners to visit them would be paid for by means of a levy from the schools themselves, based on the number of pupils in the school. The idea was novel. The schools would pay to be inspected, and the cost to the state would be a 'mere bagatelle'. Sound as the scheme might be, its elaboration did not commend itself to Mundella. Perhaps it was unconscious irony that Percival's letter was dated 1 April. [78]

Far more practicable, and far more significant for the future of the secondary education of the country as a whole, was a measure for the promotion of intermediate education in Wales, which at long last Mundella found time to consider. It aimed at establishing secondary schools part rate, part state-aided, under a committee based on a county basis—an idea as fruitful as any that emerged at this time. The preliminaries of its introduction went on in the first three months of 1885, and in April, Thring, the official drafts-man, sent a copy to Mundella for amendment before it finally went to the cabinet. Here a hitch had to be overcome, for Mundella needed £15,000 for the state aid, which was refused by the treasury. Gladstone's fiat, 'Let this be done', smoothed the difficulties, and it went forward. But its presentation to parliament was delayed. By 20 April, Mundella was explaining to Viriamu Jones:

'You have no idea how difficult the situation is. We must pass redistribution bills and registration bills, and do all that is possible to meet the coming election. We must also provide all the means for carrying on the public service. And we must meet the periodic votes of censure. Government can do many things, but it has not yet reached the power of Joshua to command the sun and moon to stand still. Time is the sole difficulty. Be assured if I can steal a little I will deal with your bill.' [79]

His opportunity came a month later. On the 22 May, at two o'clock in the morning, he introduced his bill. But he was again baulked, this time by the perversity of an Irish member, who rose and moved that the house be counted out. With silent understanding the Irish members walked out of the house in Indian file. The delay left Mundella time to sketch only the main out-lines.[80] Two days later he was the victim of a bad bronchial attack. Gladstone wrote to warn him not to use his voice 'when the tubes are in a tender state', citing his own experience.

Outline as it was, the plan provoked criticism both from those who wanted all the church endowments confiscated, as well as from those who wished the proposed county committees to be entirely elective. Many, however, believed with Viriamu Jones that 'the great work you have taken in hand with regard to Wales, is bearing abundant fruit, which I know will be the best reward for all the thought and careful attention it has cost you'. The 'abundant fruit' was not for Mundella at this time. On 9 June 1885 Gladstone resigned, and Mundella left the education department. But the efforts of his opponents redoubled in intensity now that the general election was in the offing. Cardinal Manning declared that Christian education was in great peril, and argued that, since the state had entered into the matter of education, the clergy had a consequent right to enter into politics. A speech he made fifteen days after the government's resignation was a striking prelude to his entry into the election controversy. He warned his audience against allowing their children to become the children of the state, and expressed strong hopes that 'the middle class would rise up and say they did not want board schools for their children'. A further resolution was passed that the 1870 Act was 'unequal, unjust and dangerous to the voluntary schools of the country'. Mundella was furious. Manning heard of his wrath and wrote:

'I hear you are very angry with me for what I said at St. James' Hall as reported in *The Times*. I therefore send you a more full and correct report to make you more peaceful or more wrathful. . . . I shall hope to see you when the House meets again to find you pacified.' [81]

10

It was a position of great difficulty for Mundella. With Manning's picturesque leadership of the voluntary schools crusade against the godless, unjust and expensive board schools to contend with on one side, there was also the outrageous language used in Chamberlain's equally energetic campaign on the other. Mundella saw the yawning fissure that was developing, and wrote to Robert Leader ten days before the dissolution:

'I do not like the political outlook. We are all right as long as we stick together and are willing to defer somewhat to each other, but there is a tendency to force ultra radicalism down the throats of Gladstone, Hartington and others, which bodes mischief sooner or later. It means a bid for the leadership by the Birmingham section.'

Ten days after the dissolution he was even more emphatic:

'Chamberlain's language is very indiscreet, and unnecessarily alienates a number of *moderate and timid people*.' [82]

It was the balance between these two points of view that he endeavoured to strike in the coming election. Mundella himself was thus described in this year by Justin McCarthy:

'He brings with him an element of freshness of thought which is welcome. He is not a radical of the new school, it is true, but neither is he a radical of the old school. He represents only vaguely and faintly the new order to which the old is rapidly giving way. As an example of the rapidly decreasing section of what may be called the left centre of the Liberal Party, he possesses a peculiar interest of his own.'

In the summer, as the parties sparred for the general election that was to take place in October, Mundella went abroad. Before he went, he had declared his adherence to a policy of caution with regard to free education, for he argued: 'We cannot multiply free schools out of the rates under the present incidence of taxation or we shall produce a reaction against education'.[83] While he was abroad he looked into the free education systems of Germany as exemplified in Munich and Berlin, and was impressed. The British consul in Munich sang their praises, and declared he sent his own grandson to a free school. Moreover, the attendance was found to be extraordinarily high—an average of 97 per cent of pupils attended, as compared with the 75 per cent in the English elementary schools.

In Mundella's absence the rift between the right and left wings of the party on this, as on other questions, became embarrassing. Gladstone, in his manifesto published on 17 September 1885, reserved judgment on free schools, declaring: 'A contribution towards the cost of an article tends to it being more thoroughly valued by the receiver.' [84] On the other hand, Chamberlain, in a rousing campaign that was regarded as a triumph, was placing free primary education and county councils as part of his 'unauthorised programme', declaring that he would not rest until he saw 'this cruel and abominable tax abolished and until every national school is free throughout the length and breadth of the land'.[85] As October approached, Mundella had to make up his mind, before facing his new constituency of Brightside (the misnamed bowels of Sheffield, which was now one of the city's five parliamentary divisions). It was the home of the industrial workers who had enthusiastically supported him since 1868. It was obvious that he would have to make a pronouncement on the burning issues of the day.

Before he did so, he consulted both Matthew Arnold and Joseph Chamberlain. The latter was delighted, and wrote on 7 October:

'What a curious coincidence that we should have crossed letters on the same subject just at this time. I am glad you are coming to take your party in the fray. Can you come down for the night? In the hope that this will be possible I will not enter into a further discussion of free education. We shall sweep the country with free education and allotments, and the Tories will be smashed and the Whigs extinguished.'

Matthew Arnold wrote a week later:

'There is a good opportunity to speak on middle class education and nobody takes it. Look at my reports in the minutes for 1878–9, p. 468 and for 1882–3, p. 225. My foreign reports you know. Look also at my mixed essays, p. 143, and my Irish essay, p. 129. I shall be glad to give you either or both of these volumes if I have not given them to you already, which I ought to have done. To map out the ground, to determine what trust funds are properly available, is what might even now be put forward as fitting to be done by the state.' [86]

In this context Mundella's speech was extremely significant. It was a declaration of policy both with regard to primary education, which he wished to make free; and secondary education, which he wished to make more accessible. But as well as being an educational programme, it was an attempt to answer his old opponent Cardinal Manning, who in the same month had published advice in all the Catholic periodicals attempting to influence the voting of Catholics by advising them to put two questions to their prospective candidates. The first question was: 'Will you do your utmost to place voluntary schools on an equal footing with board schools?' and the second, 'Will you do your utmost to obtain a Royal Commission to review the present state of education in England and Wales, and especially the act of 1870 and its administration by the school boards?' concluding, 'As they answer "yes" or "no" let us decide'.[87]

Mundella's speech was delivered on 21 October 1885 in the Brightside Vestry Hall. It was a reasonable refutation of the objections to free education, with particular reference to the voluntary schools, which, he declared, would actually earn an increased grant by the improved attendance that would result. Nor would the teaching of the Bible suffer. His method was not a levy on the rates, but a grant from imperial taxes or the consolidated fund. The recipients of the grant would be the county authorities to be created in the wider programme of reform. Free schools, hitherto associated with the boards of guardians, would be a refining influence on the rest of the community, instead of a stigma. His programme went farther. He advocated state encouragement to continuation schools to keep pupils till they were sixteen, and some form of control of the endowed schools to make them more accessible to the lower middle classes.

It was a pity that this speech was not well circulated. Old Robert Leader, on his death-bed, was delighted at the way it read:

'It was a grand educational speech, and would look well in a pamphlet. You caused a panic on a small scale.' [88] Even more delighted was Chamberlain, who wished it to be more widely circulated:

'I have read your most excellent speech in the *Sheffield Independent* with great pleasure. Those d——d London papers have not given a single decent report. I feared it would be so but it is really too bad. I suggest you write a letter to *The Times*, recapitulating the chief arguments and drop a line to Buckle. It is really important that your view should be known and fairly considered. I see Shaw-Lefevre adopts free education and I suppose Trevelyan also.' [89]

The right wing of the party was drawn by the effect of the speech, and on 1 November Lord Hartington wrote a typical letter, showing the influence of Manning's article: 'I have said in my address that I am in favour of an inquiry into the working of the education acts as suggested I think by Childers, and I suppose that there is no particular importance to the inquiry being made by Royal Commission. What do they mean by placing voluntary schools on an equal footing with board schools?' and asking Mundella for a copy of the speech 'of which I hear such a good report'. Hartington himself had to rely for an actual report on Mundella's own account. Others, too, pressed Mundella for details. Ughtred Kay-Shuttleworth wrote, asking him how he met 'the objection of Socialism'.[90]

Mundella spoke at places other than Sheffield. He went to Bradford to help W. E. Forster, and earned the thanks of Matthew Arnold, Forster's brother-in-law, for doing so. He went to Wales, and from Hawarden came the invitation to spend the night on his way 'to and from'. But the last word was yet to be said. Lord Norton once more took up the cudgels for the voluntaryists in the November number of the *Nineteenth Century* with a telling criticism of the 'free schools' cry. In the same month the towns returned solid blocks of tory M.P.s at the elections.

II

Mundella himself was one of the few Liberals elected in the large towns, and H. C. E. Childers, who had himself suffered in the landslide at Doncaster, wrote to him:

'A young guardsman and ranting and roaring parsons, and bribery of 300 upset me. I congratulate you on your capital victory. I, too, had a habitation of female Primrose Leaguers to fight, but they did their cause more harm than good. I would do all in our power for our great chief, but his yielding to Chamberlain, and his uncertain sounds, have really destroyed us.'

The election was a stalemate. The Liberal majority of eighty-six, lowered by the umbrage that the 'schools question' had caused, could not withstand the Parnellite strength of eighty-six which was mobilised to support the Conservatives, who took office. The first act of Mundella's successor was to respond to the interests which had put the Conservatives in, by appointing a royal Commission. Lord Cranbrook wrote to Mundella asking him to serve on the commission, and enclosing a list of names, interspersed with denominationalists, and headed by Cardinal Manning and Canon Gregory. Mundella's response was a comment on the names, which, he said, were, with two exceptions, 'in favour of more money and less work', and declared, 'the whole composition of the commission will be regarded as highly denominational'. He suggested Sir Bernhard Samuelson, Roscoe or Lyulph Stanley to balance it, and warned Cranbrook that 'the religious question will become a burning one if not carefully handled'. The expostulation had its effect. Cranbrook enlarged membership of the commission from seventeen to twenty-two, and a more representative body was set up under Viscount Cross, Disraeli's old home secretary.[91] Mundella's contact with the Cross Commission did not end here. Matthew Arnold was again appointed as a travelling commissioner to investigate free education abroad. He wrote to Mundella telling him frankly: 'At the present I am against the abolition of school fees in this country, but this is not for the sake of the voluntary schools', and asking him what he should see abroad:

'I am going to Berlin first, then Saxony. I had already determined on Chemnitz because of what you had previously said of its schools. Then I shall go to Lucerne and of course Zurich. Do you think it really important for me to go to Bavaria if I am pressed for time?'[92]

This proved to be Mundella's last essay with Chamberlain. Gladstone, delphic, majestic and strangely fascinating, drew Mundella into the orbit of Home Rule, and all his emotions were caught up in the cult of the Grand Old Man. His bid for conciliation between the two policies had failed. An Irishman writing to one of the wilder, younger radicals sardonically observed as the year closed: 'Your party ought to set up a temple to Mundella and put his long nose in the tabernacle. It is sweet to know that he controlled the education of British youth.' [93]

12

Mundella's five years of office repeated the old story of reform. Certain obvious abuses, like payment by results and the lack of free schools, still remained. But to evaluate his work fairly, one must first define the four-fold circumscription of his freedom and the restricted context in which he operated.

To begin with, though he was *de facto* head of the department, he was not in the cabinet. In discussions on that level he had to depend on the Lord President. With Spencer this was successful, with Carlingford it was more involved, since Carlingford was cautious where Spencer was enthusiastic, weak where Spencer was adamant. Again, a further handicap was the parsimony of the treasury, inspired and regulated by the sound frugality of Gladstonian finance. 'They even complain of our giving a catalogue of South Kensington to a Royal visitor', Mundella wrote to Leader, explaining that, though he was vice-president, he himself had to pay for the report of the Royal Commission on Technical Education.[94] Indeed, he often referred to himself as 'the Oliver Twist of the Ministry', and the description was not inaccurate. Thirdly, with his belief in compromise, he had to balance a series of warring interests, all making strong representations, both to him and above his head. The great master-compromise, the 1870 act, he had to preserve from being itself attacked by the growing forces led by Cardinal Manning. Lastly, these five years witnessed some of the most deliberate attempts that had yet been witnessed to hold up the machinery of debate. Gladstone was forced to consider the introduction of the closure in order to secure the discussion of vital ministerial bills. Mundella was usually allowed the small hours of the morning for his departmental business, when sleep and obstruction prevented him giving of his best.

A typical scene is portrayed by Toby, M.P., of *Punch*, in his Diary for 27 July 1883:

'Lord Richard Grosvenor was fast asleep on the bench opposite. Mr. Cotes, with natural modesty, retired to a bench at the end of the gallery and was soon fast asleep. Lord Kensington was fast asleep at the bench at the door leading from the gallery. . . . Mr. Mundella was wide awake on the bench opposite. He had last night all to himself and his department, and a very pleasant evening it had proved. Of the many happy fittings of men and office which mark the present government, none have been more felicitous than the appointment of Mr. Mundella to the education department. An enthusiast on behalf of education, it might have been supposed that he would go too far, and incur the odium of the gentlemen sitting opposite, whose views on the working of the education act do not coincide with those of Liberal administrators. But the education department under Mr. Mundella works with unparalleled smoothness and success. Compliments coming from the opposite party are viewed with suspicion and are sometimes followed by complaints from the party amongst which the minister sits. It has been Mr. Mundella's good fortune to hear himself and his work extolled by Lord George Hamilton and Mr. Lyulph Stanley, Mr. Talbot and Mr. Henry Richard.' [95]

His success in overcoming these handicaps was due to his conciliatory approach to the thorniest of problems. His suppleness gained what a more histrionic adherence to principle would have lost. This suppleness enabled him to weather Manning's outcries, the expostulations of the teachers, the fanatical prejudices and the dormant apathies that education evoked, and to build for the future. He himself realised that his work had long-range effects which would not be immediately visible.

'We are only just on the threshold of the work. . . . We cannot undo the neglect of generations in seven years. One or two generations have yet to pass before we are in possession of an enlightened and intelligent people.' [96]

Friendliness underlay his observant regimen at the department. He was not too busy to take up the question of a pension for old Thomas Cooper, now seventy-six years of age and going out in all weathers to lecture, or to notice the abilities of his subordinates. J. S. Blackie confessed himself surprised that his musical talents, as well as his professorial work, had earned him praise. Henry Roscoe, whom Mundella consoled on the loss of a son, wrote: 'Of all the letters I received, not one has gone more to my heart or more truly represented my own feelings'. Social problems found in him a ready investigator. The housing of the industrial classes, and the Industrial Remuneration Conference, called at the beginning of 1885 'to consider how the profits of industry might be more equitably distributed', were two of the many of the marginal interests of his office.

With the inspectors he was firm and friendly. We have seen the reorganisation that was instituted in their office. He frequently toured their districts and made their personal acquaintance. With Matthew Arnold especially was he tolerant and sympathetic.

Arnold was rebelling in spirit against the 'dance of death in an elementary school', so Mundella released him from the ardours of inspection and secured him a pension of £250 a year. Arnold was grateful:

'I am sure I am not wrong in attributing in great measure to your good offices, the frank and full permission which I have received to take my desired leave of absence when, from what I had heard of opposition at the treasury, I had abandoned all expectation of it. Many, many thanks for this fresh proof of your active kindness.'

Arnold became a frequent visitor to the Mundella household. In one letter to Mundella's daughter he enclosed a copy of one of his books with the advice:

'Make your father read some of the essays, and do not be frightened at their ever-recurring topic of public schools for the middle classes. Think of the upper ten thousand of Sheffield and their wants.' [97]

Others like John Stainer, whom Mundella appointed as the music inspector of elementary schools in 1882, retained the friendship of their chief long after he had left office. When the political shadows had fallen round Mundella, Stainer sent him an account of his work, and added:

'I hope that the results will justify you in the confidence you placed in me by appointing me inspector, a confidence which will always make me feel bound to you by a debt of gratitude, as well as by that sincere respect and regard which all Englishmen owe to you as a man and as a statesman.' [98]

His record of achievement in these five years was impressive, judged by previous and subsequent activity. Full compulsion had been secured. A plan for Wales, which was avowedly to serve as a model for England, had been completed in all but the establishment of intermediate schools, and even here the kernel of future legislation is visible in the recognition of county committees.[99] Moreover, in the sphere of English education the report of Samuelson's Commission was to serve as the inspiration of school boards for initiating, on their own responsibility, the establishment of higher-grade schools, and a guide to legislators in the next half of the decade.

Not only in the structure, but in the working of the system had he made profound changes. The inspectorate was invigorated by a more open recruitment. The code was more amenable to alteration now that a permanent code committee was in being to consider suggestions. His own code virtually brought a type of education that was later to be designated 'secondary' into the reach of a vast new urban class by the stimulation of 'class' and 'specific' subjects. Infant schools were now recognised, and the local colleges had taken such firm root that the pupil-teacher system was becoming an anachronism. But all was done slowly and determinedly. Joshua Fitch, one of his chief inspectors, when he heard that Miss Mundella was contemplating a biography of her father, wrote:

'When you come to the chapter which deals with his administration at the council office, I hope you will give me the opportunity of contributing one or two facts. I have good reason to know intimately the nature of the reforms which he effected, and the high aims after further improvements to which he would have certainly given effect had he remained in office.' [100]

Neither the biography nor those one or two facts have hitherto been written.

CHAPTER TWELVE

President of the Board of Trade, 3 February to 10 July, 1886

THE tensions which were so patent in Gladstone's second ministry were possible only as there was loyalty from all sides to the personality of Gladstone. The Liberal party, realising this, had built the National Liberal Club, whose marmoreal fastnesses constituted a virtual temple to the Grand Old Man. Such feeling now became most intense, inspiring trade unionists and animating rich industrialists to work in harmony within the Liberal fold. It was a strange alliance, yet one of which Cobden and Hume would have approved. The events of the year 1886 were to shake it.

I

The results of the 1885 general election were fantastic. The Liberal majority in the house numbered eighty-six—the exact number of Parnell's own following. Parnell cast his die with the Conservatives, so Lord Salisbury remained in office. But, on 26 January 1886 Gladstone decided to turn him out. The pretext was the allotments question, the actual reason was that he had made up his mind to carry the Liberal party with him and grant Home Rule to Ireland. In that division (which took place at one o'clock in the morning of 27 January) seventy-six Liberals were absent,[1] while eighteen of the élite voted against him. Three days later, Argyll, crippled by gout, dictated a letter to his leader in which he complained:

'The parliamentary prominence which you give to a mere nostrum of the Radicals, distinctly outside your own programme, marks a decided patronage on your part of the Radical section as against the reasonable Liberals. I do not deny that the nostrum about allotments may be squeezed into reasonable dimensions, but that is not the question. There is not one of the peers whom I would trust to stand out for any principle of politics inconsistent with unity of the party. It is quite impossible for me to sympathise with this state of mind. I have seen what it leads to. It leads to the triumph of inferior men, who become the real leaders and movers of Liberal opinion. At this moment I cannot fee that we are under your independent and unbiased opinion.' [2]

On 28 January, Gladstone was cabinet-making. He listed 'five gone, two uncertain, and nine to be counted on'. In his letter to Lord Carlingford he seemed almost to confirm Argyll's opinions:

'The peculiarity of my work on this my third occasion of forming a government has been the necessity of mixing, in almost all cases, political explanations with the choice and distribution of offices.' [3]

With this explanation, Carlingford was dropped from the cabinet and the Lord Presidency of the Council. Among those scheduled to take his place in the cabinet was A. J. Mundella, who in the second ministry would have been promoted to cabinet rank in 1884 had not Carlingford proved intractable. Mundella had recently been on a fact-finding mission to Ireland for Gladstone, was now intensely loyal, and even evangelistic where Home Rule was at stake.[4] On Gladstone's first list, drawn up on 30 January 1886, his name appeared as a possible chancellor of the exchequer, while Chamberlain seemed destined to go to the Admiralty.[5] After toying with the idea of restoring Chamberlain to the board of trade, Gladstone wrote a fresh list of names, and this time Mundella was listed for it instead. On 3 February it was officially announced that Mundella was to be President of the Board of Trade, with a seat in the cabinet. With him in this small cabinet of fourteen were three other new members: Morley, Herschell and Campbell-Bannerman. *The Times* oracularly remarked that it was by no means a defect that the four newcomers had no previous cabinet experience. Lord Cranbrook, more hostile, noted in his diary: 'They may be workers, but will not add to the influence of the body, and will be echoes of their chief'.[6] But Gladstone confessed himself 'well satisfied', and writing to his son Henry on 12 February, remarked, 'It is not a bit more radical than the government of last year, perhaps a little less. And we have got some good young hands, which please me very much.' [7]

Four days earlier, Gladstone confessed to Chamberlain, 'As for me, I am like Lot's wife, solitary and pickled on the plain of Sodom'.[8] It would be hard to describe his complete insulation from the pressing problems of the day in a better manner. For on that very day a protectionist demonstration had clashed with another held by the Social Democratic Federation. The police asked the S.D.F. to hold their demonstration in Hyde Park. John Burns seized the red flag, and led his group off. As they went they broke windows in the Mall. Newspapers magnified these demonstrations, and the ringleaders of the riot were tried.[9]

Both these demonstrations were symptoms of a trade depression which had been recognised by the short-lived Conservative ministry of 1885-6, which had appointed a royal commission to ascertain 'how far the depression goes, and what it will lead to if nothing is done, also to examine critically the proposed remedies'. Gladstone recognised no such depression. On 24 October 1884 he had refused to appoint such a commission, and on 17 July 1885 he wrote to J. K. Cross (who had been asked to serve on the commission):

'I think the whole thing unsound at the core, appointed with an indirect motive, and having no legitimate purpose; and I would "touch not, take not, handle not". You will probably end in it as one of a protesting minority.' [10]

2

In these first weeks of office Mundella was able to undertake three important administrative reforms—all, in essence, collectivist.

The first was to provide the traders with an intelligence service. He told the Chambers of Commerce that British consuls were 'to be stimulated to greater activity . . . to furnish fuller reports of the trade and requirements of the different countries of the world'. *The Times* approved this 'noteworthy departure from the rules of red tape that have hitherto governed'.[11] From now onwards the consular reports were to be made available to the public at a low price, instead of being published among the general mass of foreign office papers. The number of reports so published soon mounted to over 250 a year.[12]

If statistics were made available for traders, they also had to be available to the labour world. Mundella was a great believer in the value of educating the working classes to see what the position of their country really was in the world picture. He had noted with approval the successful efforts made by the Americans to diffuse information among the working classes by means of labour boards—information which rendered the functioning of boards of arbitration easier than it was in England. So when Charles Bradlaugh suggested that the board of trade should undertake the collection and dissemination of labour statistics, Mundella immediately adopted his motion.[13] So the second administrative innovation took place. The labour department of the board of trade was set up, with an organ in which its findings could be published. As head of the department, Robert Giffen, a fortynine-year-old economist and statistician, who had served under Bagehot as assistant editor of the *Economist*, was appointed. To tighten still further the ties between the T.U.C. and the Liberal party, John Burnett was appointed as his assistant in the work of collecting statistics. But the trade unions looked upon the creation with no great enthusiasm, and a year later only eighteen of the 150 which were circularised took the trouble to reply.[14]

The third administrative reform was yet another expansion of the board of trade. This time it took shape in the fisheries department, established to take over the work hitherto done by three different government departments. The home office had looked after all questions dealing with salmon fisheries, the admiralty had dealt with all questions involving the naval reserve, and the foreign office had dealt with any statistical elements in the industry itself. But by 1886 the industry had outgrown its swaddling bands. Thirty-seven thousand vessels, 120,000 men and £15,000,000 worth of capital were involved, and disputes with other nationals made the fisheries more than ever a subject which required special treatment by a responsible government department.[15] Even more important was the backward condition of British fishing research compared with its foreign competitors. In ichthyology, as in industry, both the continental powers and America appeared to be far superior.[16] The writing on the wall had been seen at the International Fisheries Exhibition held in London three years earlier, and the organiser of that exhibition, Edward Birkbeck, advocated the necessity of a state-subsidised and state-controlled research department engaged in the scientific study of fish. There was no British counterpart to Spencer Baird of the United States of America, Mobius of Germany, Coste of France, Sars of Norway and Hubrecht of Holland; for T. H. Huxley, who might have been their peer, had resigned his appointment as Inspector of Salmon Fisheries in 1885, and his successor was not a specialist. Indeed, so great was the need for research that a deputation waited upon Mundella on 26 March, to voice the hope that he would obtain the experts needed to staff the fisheries department.

Ironically enough, the idea that the state should have anything

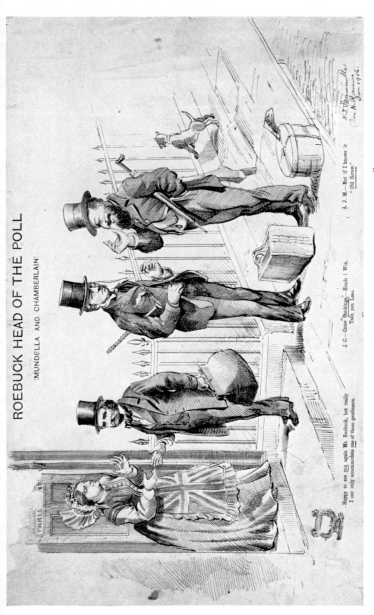

ROEBUCK HEAD OF THE POLL

(MUNDELLA AND CHAMBERLAIN)

"Happy to see YOU again Mr. Roebuck, but really I can only accommodate one of these gentlemen."

J.C.—Cease "Snarling."—Heads I Win, Tails you Lose.

A.J.M.—Not if I knows it "Old Screw."

THE PARLIAMENTARY ELECTION AT SHEFFIELD IN 1874

A Right wing forecast

to do with fisheries, even in the matter of promoting research, provoked Huxley's anger. He roundly asserted that the only body fit to be entrusted with research in this matter was the Royal Society, of which he was a past president. He wrote to *The Times* with heavy emphasis:

'I do not see what the Board of Trade has to do with such aid to science, nor why it is desirable that the gentlemen who are to be entrusted with this very considerable enterprise should have "the management of the fisheries" (which means the power of meddling with a great industrial interest) thrown in as a sort of *hors d'œuvre*.' [17]

Nevertheless, Mundella went ahead. As the Whitweek fishery conference drew to a close, he constituted the fisheries department of the board of trade. An assistant secretary, a chief inspector, with two other inspectors, were set to work. Office labour was supplied by the marine department. The new department was to look after both sea and inland fisheries. From this small nucleus soon developed a department which, united with the agricultural department formed three years earlier at Mundella's request, was to become a ministry.[18]

3

No such empiric administrative solutions could be found to the problem of railway freight rates.

A powerful section of the community, comprising manufacturers and farmers, had a very real conviction that one of the main causes of the trade depression was the unequal nature of British railway rates and freights compared with continental rates. Sir Bernhard Samuelson,[19] for long one of Mundella's chief political allies, published the results of an investigation which he had carried out for the Associated Chambers of Commerce. Samuelson's conclusions, based on close scrutiny and comparison of British and continental practice, pressed the need for prompt and thorough revision of British railway rates. Such a revision, argued Samuelson, should not be left to the railway companies themselves (as the Conservatives allowed them to do in 1885); nor should the unnecessary multiplication of trains be tolerated, for that had been one of the principal motives actuating the Prussian government when they assumed control of their railways. The body which should be entrusted with great power and direction over the railway companies, concluded Samuelson, was the existing Railway Commission, set up in 1873.[20]

The problem of high railway rates was focused for the new ministry by three things. Chamberlain, the previous Liberal President of the Board of Trade, had made some efforts to lower the higher railway freight charges, but had only succeeded in raising up a defensive association of shareholders.[21] Samuelson's report, with the imprimatur of the Associated Chambers of Commerce upon it, showed that the trading interest approved of its suggestions in principle. Lastly, the railways themselves had failed to effect, by private legislation in 1885, what was desired. It only remained for Gladstone's authorisation in cabinet of 15 February, plus the existence of a Conservative bill to combat the evil effects of high railway rates, to set the draftsmen working.

For the symptoms of the stranglehold which the railways maintained on the inland towns were many and various. Having bought the canals of the country, the railways could dictate the price which the inland trader or manufacturer had to pay. Moreover, they put him doubly at a disadvantage *vis-à-vis* his coastal competitor, for, in an attempt to capture sea-borne goods traffic, the railways offered preferential rates from coastal towns.[22] Under such handicaps, it was not surprising that many industries migrated coastwards.[23] To any demand for the voluntary reduction of their rates, the railways could, with much justification, point to their high wages bill and their heavy capital expenditure of the last fifteen years.

Manchester, one of the hardest-hit of all inland towns, determined to find a way out of the deadlock by building a ship canal to the sea.[24]

In a three years' war in the private bill committees of both houses (when two of their bills were rejected) they spoke long and vehemently of the high railway rates that were maintained by a conspiracy of the railways and dock interests concerned. Such words seemed justified by the subsequent actions of the railways themselves. For as soon as Mundella was able to deal with the question, on 23 February they organised a deputation to him maintaining that the proposed canal, if constructed, would do irreparable damage to the Mersey; that it would never obtain the capital it required; that the work would be left unfinished; and that it should not be considered a worthy project on which to find work for the unemployed.

The backbone of this deputation was provided by the London

and North-western Railway—the premier railway company in Great Britain, whose capital assets were nearly £100 millions. Leading the deputation was the fiery Lord Claud Hamilton [25] (who had helped Samuel Plimsoll in his agitation ten years earlier) and Sir H. Meysey-Thompson,[26] the former a Conservative, the latter a Liberal M.P. When the deputation failed, petitions from the L.N.W. Railway, the Liverpool Corporation and the Mersey Docks and Harbour Board were tabled for 1 April.

Mundella supported the ship canal projectors and the bill which they presented to enable them to pay to their backers interest out of the capital they had already received. Meysey-Thompson seconded the rejection of the bill, but Mundella, in a vehement speech, pointed out that it was only just to allow the bill to pass, since a canal, unlike a railway company, could not begin operating a section of their work to recoup themselves before the whole project was finished. Thanks to his official support, the bill avoided slow death in a select committee.[27]

4

But Manchester's particular solution would not fit the rest of England. Here some national measure was clearly indicated, and early in March Mundella introduced his Railway and Canal Traffic Bill, which was designed to secure a just and equitable re-assessment of railway freight charges over the whole of the British Isles. Although in the Queen's Speech the bill was referred to as one 'for extending the power of the Railway Commission in respect of the regulation of rates', it also gave considerable powers to the board of trade. For the draft envisaged the establishment of three new courts, one for England, and the other two for Ireland and Scotland respectively. These courts were only to hear cases of disputed rates between the public and railways; the effective lowering of the rates was to be the work of the board of trade itself. So, in the celebrated clause 24, all railway companies were required to submit revised schedules of rates and charges for approval within twelve months. Furthermore, a canal clearing house was to be established, to see that alternative rates for alternative routes were available.[28]

The introduction of Mundella's bill marked the end of a long period of suspense during which trading and agricultural interests on one side, and railways on the other, had been asking for changes.

The *Daily News* hailed it with approval, pointing out in an editorial that for years the traffic of the country had borne the deadweight of capital squandered by lawyers, landowners, surveyors and contractors. They praised the strengthening of the Railway Commission, as well as the admission of public bodies before it to prosecute complaints against the railways. 'Regulation of monopolies', they observed, 'is one of the functions of government', and concluded, 'There are many signs to show that we are entering upon a new era of railway management'.[29]

But other comment was not so favourable. *Herapath's Railway and Commercial Journal* pointed out that Mundella had 'not stolen Mr. Chamberlain's clothes', but rather seemed to have deferred to officialdom at the board of trade itself. 'The Railway Commissioners will be more or less a figurehead,' continued *Herapath*, 'the rates will be essentially the rates of the Board of Trade', and they doubted whether 'the drastic and autocratic powers conferred on the Board of Trade' would receive public assent.[30] *The Times*, though more cautious, held the same opinion. 'Mr. Mundella's proposals do not err on the side of timidity. It is evident that these proposals have travelled a long way beyond the somewhat tentative proposals of the last Parliament.'[31] The *Economist* was more outspoken: 'It appears to give the Board of Trade powers which are in excess of public needs, and which are scarcely likely to work to the public advantage'.[32] The *Bullionist* boldly forecast: 'The railway companies will be apt to press their own personal views to the utmost, especially as there is so formidable an array of railway men in the House of Commons'.[33]

The effect of the bill was explosive. Since the beginning of the decade most of the big companies had continued to issue capital at the average rate of half a million pounds a year. The Great Eastern (£40 millions), the Great Western (£44 millions), the Midland (£76 millions), the L.N.W. (£95 millions) and the Great Northern (£35 millions) could ill afford, in this time of falling prices, even a fractional reduction of their charges. The implications of the bill were even more onerous to the small railways, some of which had just been incorporated. Typical of the latter class were five small western lines. The Barry Docks Railway (£1,050,000) had only been incorporated in 1884, and was at the time undertaking the construction of a twenty-six-mile railway connecting the Rhondda Valley to a dock at Barry Island within the port of Cardiff. A similar project was incorporated in 1882 connecting the Rhondda Valley to Swansea, and was actually working a line from Cymmer to Port Talbot on which a dividend of 3 per cent was being paid. The Llangollen and Corwen was undertaking further extensions to connect Liverpool and Cheshire, and had just been granted the power to raise another half-million of capital. In Cornwall, the Helston Railway, incorporated in 1881, was not yet completed.[34]

For twelve days after its introduction these implications were hidden. *Herapath* on 20 March repeated its criticism of the bill:

> 'Its fatally weak point is the new jurisdiction to be given to the Board of Trade as regards the scheduling of rates at present and their revision in future. It would necessarily entail the enlarging of the department, and may materially affect its present high standing as an impartial commercial tribunal.'

But on the 23rd the Railway Defence Association met. On the motion of the chairman of the L.N.W., seconded by the chairman of the Midland, the railway companies were urged to summon emergency meetings of their shareholders.

It was a heaven-sent opportunity for the railway directors to establish control over the unruly element among their shareholders. Recently a number of the shareholders had been advocating a reform in railway management, and, under a chairman with the apt name of Paine, supported a periodical called *The Railway Shareholder*, which Paine edited. It was a fortnightly, devoted to the exposure of extravagance and directorial mismanagement. On 25 March it published an extremely favourable review of Mundella's bill, declaring that it 'would be glad to see it passed into law', and adding, 'The directorial power which is wielded is a *vested interest* and nothing else'.

As the largest railway in the kingdom, the L.N.W. set the pace. Free passes were issued to shareholders to attend an extraordinary general meeting to be held at Euston on 31 March. With the passes came a circular, pointing out four objections to the proposed bill: (i) the compulsory character of the revision as opposed to the hoped-for 'mutual agreement'; (ii) the conferment upon the board of trade of a power to intervene between traders and railway companies when rates were neither illegal nor unfair; (iii) the prohibition of any appeal on questions of undue preference; and (iv) the apparently unlimited powers which the board of trade would assume in being able to demand statistical returns from the railway companies.

The drum was loudly beaten by the other companies in circulars which, if anything, were even more vehement and flamboyant than this. The North-eastern declared : 'There is no adequate necessity for legislation of so novel and dangerous a character', for it would 'lead to a sense of insecurity in regard to all classes of private property'. The wealthy and eccentric Lord Grimthorpe petitioned the house of commons against the bill, objecting to every clause on behalf of the Railway Defence Association.[35] The Midland circular pointed to the fact that even if the revision of rates did come, it would give even less security than before:

'The revised and possibly curtailed rates upon which your revenue depends are not to be secured to you, but are to be exposed to further attack at any moment on the application of any local authority, association of traders, chamber of commerce, or agriculture.'

Herapath, giving the maximum space to these circulars, itself wound up with a strong editorial:

'The Board [of Trade] would verily be a Star Chamber of the most pernicious kind. Not only are all railways capitalists interested in frustrating this direct menace to their property, but trustees should especially rouse themselves, as the incomes of their beneficiaries and the value and security of their trust is likely to be seriously affected. . . . There is such a thing as being caught napping.'[36]

The chairman of the Regent Canal City and Docks Railway Company told his shareholders that 'if the bill passed in its present form, it would mean the entire cessation of railway enterprise in this country for years to come'.[37]

Formidable figures now emerged to thunder against Mundella. The chairmen of the main-line railways, on whose decisions many a middle-class household depended,[38] spoke out with one voice against him. For a week a heavy barrage of protest was sustained in crowded emergency shareholders' meetings throughout the country.[39] Sir Edward Watkin, director of ten railway companies and chairman of three, spoke of it as a major political issue, and forecast a fall in profits of from 25 to 50 per cent.[40] One of his fellow-directors was loudly cheered when he said, 'If the government will not withdraw the bill, then let us turn out Mr. Mundella'. At the Cannon Street Hotel, Sir Edward Watkin told the massed shareholders of the South-eastern that 'the Railway and

Canal Traffic Act might, for the first time, disgrace and dishonour the statute book of England'. Richard Moon,[41] addressing the L.N.W. meeting at Euston on 31 March, contended that railway shareholders were being dealt with in the same manner as Irish landlords, but pointed out that in Ireland land purchase was estimated to cost £200 millions, whereas the total amount of money invested in railways was four times that amount. Cries of 'Class legislation' were raised at the Midland meeting when the chairman, Mr. M. W. Thompson,[42] sardonically remarked that if the railway stock were held in small amounts by members of the working classes, they would not be faced with such legislation. At the Great Western meeting on 5 April, Chamberlain was quoted as saying that any revision must be a matter of arrangement with the companies. One director demanded that Mundella's bill should be made a test question at the next election, for confiscation was contagious.

These meetings certainly roused the shareholders. Mundella later confessed, 'I was deluged with letters from railway shareholders. Everybody believed, or affected to believe, that the measure which I introduced would destroy the value of railway property.'[43] Tacticians of the Conservative party were quick to realise the extent of the feeling, and advised the railway directors:

'There are more ways of intimidating governments than by openly speaking or voting against them. Railways M.P.s understand, quite as well as shipowners do, that even in cases where they dare not resist a popular measure, they can quietly combine to let down the government upon some vital question of a different kind, some question upon which the government has, by its pusillanimity, its vacillations, its delays, or its unseen misadventures, drifted into a position which invites attack, and which, if attacked by M.P.s of the same party, would be indefensible.'[44]

It was in that very position that the ministry now found itself.

5

It is necessary to retrace the story from 12 March to see what was happening to the rest of the cabinet. Gladstone was absent from the cabinet meeting of 8 March, and on 11 March the Channel Tunnel was the second item on the agenda. This, the cherished project of Sir Edward Watkin, was once again shelved, as it had been in 1882. But much more important was the third item on the agenda. Gladstone raised the question, 'Are we bound in honour or policy to do more than give to the landlords of Ireland fair optional terms of withdrawing from their positions?'[45] Chamberlain criticised, and opened the question of Home Rule. Gladstone stated his case, and noted: 'Spencer, Morley, Granville, Bannerman, Mundella, Rosebery, Ripon and Childers favourable'.

The cabinet meeting scheduled for 14 March was cancelled, Gladstone sending a paper to Spencer and Granville on which was written his scheme for the creation of a small proprietary class. 'In the meantime', he noted, 'the House would deal with the necessary finance, and with the Crofters Bill.' On 15 March he proposed to call in the draftsmen to draw up the Irish Land Bill, while he got his materials on Irish government 'a little into shape'. 'In the House of Commons', he added, 'I expect that necessary finance, and the Crofters Bill, will occupy the next two or three weeks.'

On 18 March the committee of the cabinet on the Irish question was set up. Gladstone wrote, 'Ask Harcourt if possible to find out absolutely Chamberlain's intentions'. He also noted:

'I have been considering whether it would be wiser to limit the possibility of the Land Transfer Act to 60m. instead of 120m.
   1. There would be less risk of its shocking the moneyed world and acting on the funds.
   2. There seems to be something not quite rational in putting out the mention of vast sums in an act when one cannot be certain of any operation at all—the whole being tentative.
   3. Open to Parliament to enlarge the sum.'

He was, as Brett says, 'plunging about like a child in its tub'.[46] Brett, who was in the Queen's private circle, held a dinner-party on 22 March, to which he invited Chamberlain, A. H. G. Grey, N. Rothschild and A. J. Balfour. Chamberlain discussed leaving the administration, and Rothschild said, 'A great city man, who has never gone against Gladstone before, came to me this morning to consult me about holding a big anti-Home Rule meeting in the city. I advised him not to do so at the present time.'[47] A day later, Gladstone held a full cabinet meeting, in which he consented to take the Irish Home Rule Bill first, and agreed that notice would be given for 29 March to introduce it.

On 26 March Chamberlain and Trevelyan resigned. This was at the very time that the railway companies were suppurating with dissatisfaction, and Chamberlain could enable many of these malcontents to salvage their independence by joining his cave. The cabinet, to judge by Gladstone's memoranda, were not cognisant of railway umbrage, for they did not discuss it. On 26 and 29 March Ireland was still the sole topic of discussion. It was temporarily ousted on 1 April by Bulgaria and Greece, but on 2 and 6 April it was restored to the exclusion of all others.[48]

But though the cabinet might not consider the umbrageous railway directors, the house of commons did. For on 8 April, on the momentous day when every member was in his place to hear Gladstone introduce his Home Rule Bill, Lord Claud Hamilton asked a question about the Railway and Canal Traffic Act. The house laughed as Mundella made a brief reply.[49] Then the motion to give Gladstone precedence was put and carried. But after the debate a member of Liberal county members met together to draw up a petition to Gladstone urging him to allow full discussion of the Railway and Canal Traffic Act. Co-secretary and energiser of the project was W. C. Quilter, a railway director who had been in the house for only five months.[50]

Quilter's petition found no fewer than ninety-eight supporters within five days, among them W. Bickford Smith, chairman of the Helston Railway, Sir J. St. Aubyn, a director of the Plymouth, Devonport and South-west Junction Railway.[51] Since these signatories embraced both members who might be in favour of the bill,[52] and others who might oppose it, Gladstone declared he would not forget 'the interest expressed by so large a proportion' of the house.

6

Gladstone, in estimating the chances of success on 18 March, was evidently of the opinion that he could give adequate compensation to the holders of Irish land by his Land Purchase Bill 'without shocking the moneyed world and acting on the funds'. But this hope was dashed. For one of the effects of the Railway and Canal Traffic Bill had been, as we have seen, to exacerbate a section of the 'moneyed world' which had particularly close links with the party which favoured a continuance of the union with Ireland.

The interests of the leading whig peers were also railway interests. The duke of Argyll, director of the Callander and Oban

Railway, categorically identified the Gladstonians and Parnel-
lites as 'potential abolishers of the decalogue, who would take
away the property of other men'.[53] His brother-in-law, the
duke of Sutherland, had a mania for railways which extended to
driving engines.[54] Sutherland had over a quarter of a million
pounds invested in the Highland Railway alone, while his son,
the marquis of Stafford, M.P., was a director of the London and
North-western and other railways.

Two of the leading Liberal peers in the house of commons were
similarly placed. The marquis of Hartington, representing the
Cavendish interests in the Furness Railway, also owned the Fer-
moy and Lismore Railway in Ireland. Lord Richard Grosvenor,
who had been the chief Liberal Whip, and Patronage Secretary to
the Treasury in the second ministry, was also a director of the
London and North-western Railway. Created a baron on 22
March 1886, his efforts were from now on to be entirely devoted
to railway administration, in which he made a name as chairman
of the London and North-western Railway from 1891 to 1911.

Similarly, among the commoners, A. H. G. Grey not only
managed the vast estates of the third Earl Grey, to which he subsequently succeeded, but was also a director of the North-eastern
Railway. Grey, as one of the triumvirate of the Liberal Unionist
Committee that met at Spring Gardens, was an important figure
in the formation of the anti-ministerial cave.

Gladstone himself put their motives clearly, in a letter he wrote
to R. H. Hutton of the *Spectator* at this time:

'I do think that the common ruck of your "Unionists" from Dukes down-
wards are warped by the spirit of class, but that comparatively few are aware of
it, and few consequently compromise their integrity. So among the opponents
of Peel there were some of the best men I ever knew—and the average were
men of respect. Am I warped by the spirit of anti-class? I cannot tell—my
dislike of class feeling gets slowly more and more accentuated, and my case is
particularly hard and irksome because I am a thorough-going inegalitarian.
For the fountainhead of my feelings and opinions in the matter, I go back to
the Gospels.' [55]

But on the Railway and Canal Traffic Bill he made no observation.

But others did, and continued to do so. On 28 April the Highland Railway convened a shareholders' meeting. The shareholders, meeting in circumstances which were described as 'very
exceptional', pledged themselves 'individually and collectively to

oppose the present attempts to reduce the value and security of their property'. They empowered the directors (who included the marquis of Stafford, M.P. for Sutherland, and Sir G. McPherson Grant, M.P. for Elgin and Nairn, to take all such measures as they might deem advisable in that direction. Within a fortnight the Railway and Canal Traffic Bill reached its second reading. On 6 May, when this took place, it was made abundantly clear where the rub lay. J. Bolton, chairman of the Caledonian Railway, moving the amendment to the second reading, declared that though the railways were anxious for a settlement of the rates question, they wished it to be done by mutual agreement, rather than by such arbitrary action on the part of the board of trade as was outlined in Mundella's Bill. Sir Richard Webster from one side of the house, and Sir J. Pease from the other, advised Mundella to withdraw this clause from the bill, in order to smooth its passage.

Such complaints against the arbitrary action of the board of trade received a piquant endorsement a week later. Sir T. H. Farrer resigned his position as permanent secretary of the board—an action not surprising in view of his opinions on radical legislation generally.[56] In his place Mundella appointed Henry Calcraft, the assistant secretary who had been in charge of the railway department for the past twelve years. Calcraft's place there was in turn filled by the appointment of Courtenay Boyle. It was upon this latter appointment that the *Economist* took the opportunity of remarking:

'It is not to his advantage that he is the son-in-law of a Scotch Earl. But we must confess that the appointment looks a little odd when viewed in conjunction with Mr. Mundella's Railway Bill. That Bill proposes to give large powers of control over our railways in the Board of Trade. It tends to confirm in their opposition (to his measure) those who object to have the Board of Trade officials authorised to interfere in matters of railway management, on the ground that they do not possess the special qualifications required.' [57]

The second reading was accompanied by the rumbling discontents of the journals. *Herapath* assumed its best jeremiad style to forecast:

'Cows far off wear long horns. Parliament is asked to sanction a gross act of plunder. When the mob is hungry it attacks bakers' shops. When trade is depressed, railways are looked upon as fair game. Will the process end here? If the example be set, where is the security for capital of any kind?' [58]

On the other hand, Ernest Moon, writing in the *Nineteenth Century*, looked back over the history of railway legislation to find consolation in certain principles which he extracted for the benefit of readers. They were: that parliament had never accepted the principle that it was justified in revising railway rates; that any such revision contemplated by the saving clause of the Railway Regulation Act of 1844 depended on the emergence of certain contingencies which (according to Ernest Moon) had not arisen in 1886; finally, that if any such set of contingencies or conditions were to justify parliament in revising rates, the only terms on which they should proceed would be such as to ensure to shareholders a fair interest on their investments. This last condition, concluded Ernest Moon, was not fulfilled by Mundella's bill.[59]

7

It was at this very time—12 May—that Chamberlain chose to break off relations with Gladstone by announcing that in future, negotiations between them would be conducted in public. He had taken the tide of umbrage when it was at its flood. So, when he summoned a meeting of the disaffected at his house at Prince's Gate, nine of the forty-nine M.P.s who attended had strong railway connections. There was his brother, Richard Chamberlain, chairman of a company which manufactured rolling-stock, together with Sir H. Meysey-Thompson and Sir J. J. Jenkins. Also present were J. P. Williams (M.P. for Birmingham South), director of the Midland Railway Carriage and Wagon Company, H. Wiggin (M.P. for Staffordshire), director of the Midland Railway, and Colonel Salis-Schwabe (M.P. for Middleton), who had spoken against the bill on its first reading. To these six must be added three who were directors of smaller concerns. J. Corbett (M.P. for Droitwich), of the Bishops Castle and Montgomery Railway, A. G. Kitching (M.P. for Maldon), of the Mersey Railway Company, and P. Rylands (M.P. for Burnley), director of the Bridgewater Navigation Company.

Disgusted by Chamberlain's opportunism, Mundella wrote:

'He has no sense of gratitude or loyalty; he cannot *serve* or *wait*. He hopes this time to give the Old Man a mortal stab. If he does not it will be because he regards it as too dangerous. . . . There is a good deal of heart searching among C.'s Birmingham friends, but C. is implacable in his hatreds, and unceasing in his intrigues.' [60]

On 22 May *Herapath* published the report of the Railway Commissioners *in extenso*, as a 'diatribe against the railway companies'. They accused the commissioners of 'wishing to pose as champions of popular claims, hoping that public opinion will vote for the retention of the Commission under the new state of things'.[61] On the same day, Lord Hartington's Liberal Unionist umbrella was covering Sir A. Fairbairn (M.P. for Otley), director of the Great Northern Railway and opposer of the Manchester Ship Canal project in early March; and also Sir Richard Anstruther (M.P. for St. Andrews), a director of the Caithness Railway, who died shortly afterwards.

The Railway Defence Association kept their steam up. On 25 May, at the Cannon Street Hotel, they found fresh fuel for their expostulations in a Railway Regulation Bill, which proposed to enforce better braking, continuous running-boards and other safety devices. With angry determination they made ready for yet another deputation to the board of trade.

On 27 May Gladstone was still not impressed by the likelihood that his Irish measures would be carried away by the force of the opposition now raised against his ministry. Just before the Liberal party meeting at the foreign office on that day, he jotted down what he considered would be the probable strength of the cave. It was

' 8 Chamberlain
66 Hartington
———
74
47 hopeful

'Upward progress since Lord Salisbury's speech.'[62]

On so fine an assessment, the slightest adverse influence would sway the waverers. Twelve days later, as the division bells rang in the early hours of 8 June, he knew that he had under-estimated the number of the cave by nineteen.

8

The ministry had undertaken too much. Saddled from the very beginning with such a huge obligation as Home Rule, it was goaded by the industrialists and farmers to set about a measure which would affect financial interests which were four times as great as those in Irish land. As Thorold Rogers said in the commons in this very year, railway shareholders were more widely distributed throughout the country than any other class except owners of consols. And this formidable class had been agitated and alarmed by the mass meetings of March and April. Whether it was an initial goad or a last straw, the Railway Rates Bill certainly attuned the ears of railway shareholders to the theme that Gladstonians were dangerous enemies to private property. We have seen how Huxley rose in anger at the modest suggestion that the fisheries department should undertake ichthyological research. His words were fundamentally the same as those of the railway directors. Both disliked the notion of collectivism.

The institutional strength of the railway interest had been built up over the previous forty years. Ever since they had been approaching parliament for permission to build lines, lawyers had been employed. These lawyers had devoured 25 per cent of the paid-up capital of railway companies, and in return had not only elaborated a network of case law, but had also assisted in the political sophistication of their clients. Other pressure groups, like the chambers of commerce and the various federations of industrialists and farmers, were learning political techniques by fighting the railways, who had developed a political technique of their own by fighting each other.

Mundella's bill afforded a useful weapon to the anti-Gladstonians. The 270,000 railway employees in the kingdom were carefully organised to protest against the bill, perhaps to distract them from their own grievances. A meeting was organised at Camden Town on 3 April to explain to the assembled workers that the bill would reduce their numbers, in addition to depreciating the present wages of those who were retained.[63] At another general meeting two days later at the Tolmers Square Institute it was categorically stated that 100,000 men would be thrown out of work. A petition was accordingly sent to various stations throughout the country. The organiser of these meetings was an ex-ticket collector named George Hare. In the same week he went to Doncaster, where he told an assembled meeting of the employees that 'this measure was introduced for the accommodation of merchants, who are trying to better their position and lower that of the working man. I look on it as a great attempt to crush the railways of this country out of existence.'[64]

At the other end of the social scale there were bodies like the city companies of London. These bodies, upon whose revenues the covetous eyes of the radical reformers had been cast for over a decade, were seriously threatened by both the Home Rule Bill and the Railway Rates Bill. They had already been pared of some of their revenues by the Parochial Charities Act of three years before. Now the security for their Irish rents was threatened on one side; while on the other those who had sold their Irish lands (like the grocers and cloth-workers) and invested their money in railway stocks were similarly threatened. Clock-makers, goldsmiths, ironmongers and shipwrights all held large blocks of railway shares. Naturally they infused some vigour into any anti-ministerial meetings held in the city, backing the efforts of bankers like Sir John Lubbock, G. J. Goschen and M. Biddulph.[65]

In between these two social extremes ran the propaganda of the Liberty and Property Defence League. Founded four years previously to 'resist legislation, to maintain freedom of contract, and to advocate individualism as opposed to socialism, entirely irrespective of party politics', their pamphlets cited railway regulation as a cardinal example of what they were fighting. The presence of Sir Edward Watkin and Lord Bramwell on their committee showed that the railway companies appreciated the work which the Liberty and Property Defence League was doing.[66] Their very assiduous pamphleteer was Wordsworth Donisthorne, who kept up an incessant fire against 'the philanthropic but inexperienced busibodies of the new school'.[67] The League maintained a wide circle of correspondents. Backsliding Liberals, like Lord Fortescue, assisted in their campaign.

As if to precipitate the issue, Gladstone had, on 1 May, issued his famous appeal to the masses as against the classes. This provided whatever justification was needed to convince the waverers that the legislation of his ministry was based on the desires of the masses. *Herapath* had no doubt that Mundella's measure fell into that category, describing it as 'a tentative hook to catch popularity'.[68] The *Economist* added of Gladstone's manifesto that 'of its effect upon the classes, that is, all who possess either property or intelligence, we have no doubt whatever. It will redouble their energy in resistance.' [69]

So when the testing time came on 8 June with the second reading of the Home Rule Bill it showed that Gladstone's calculations of 27 May had under-estimated the strength of outraged sentiment that had banded against him. He had anticipated a cave of seventy-four, but in the twelve-day interval it had grown to ninety-three. Of this number, twenty-six were directors of, or intimately connected with, railways. Excluding those who, like Hartington, Lord E. Cavendish, the marquis of Stafford and Viscounts Ebrington and Lymington, acted from whiggish rather than mercantile motives, there were still twenty who were more specifically of the 'railway interest'. Fifteen of the twenty directors have already been met in the foregoing pages. The other five were C. R. M. Talbot (M.P. for Glamorgan), director of the Great Western Railway (in which he held over £1,000,000 worth of stock), R. T. Gurdon (M.P. for mid-Norfolk), director of the Northern and Eastern Railways, H. C. Howard (M.P. for Penrith), director of the Cockermouth, Keswick and Penrith Railway, Sir J. St. Aubyn (M.P. for St. Ives), director of the Plymouth, Devonport and S.W. Junction Railway, and G. W. Hastings (M.P. for E. Worcester), director of the Worcester, Bromyard and Leominster Railway.[70]

It is not suggested that these twenty turned the scale against Home Rule. The political scene, with its sophistication of motive and cross-currents of opinion, does not admit of such simplification. But their very inclusion in the cave is significant. They show, by their presence, that the so-called 'threat of property' constituted by Gladstone's third ministry affected far more interests than those of the Irish landowner or the British taxpayer. It was the peculiar and particular misfortune of the Home Rule and Land Purchase Bills to be launched upon a political sea which, as we have seen, was already very agitated. Bifurcation, or fission, was implicit in the very structure of the Liberal party as constituted in the eighteen eighties. The structure could not stand three measures which together affected property worth £1,000 million —the Home Rule Bill in addition being charged with moral issues. But for the cult of the 'Grand Old Man' the fragmentation might well have been greater. As Spence Watson aptly observed of the seceders, 'If these men had not left us on Home Rule, they must have gone whenever any Liberal principle had to be put into practice'.[71] Well might C. Waring write at this time:

'Railway Companies have managed the state almost from the outset, and their authority over the convenience, comfort and prosperity of the community is now despotic. The limitations and exercise of the power of such a despotism are determined by one consideration alone—what will bring most money to the till.'[72]

Some glimmering of this lay behind Gladstone's words when he moved for the discharge of some bills and the passing of others: 'Of the more important bills I would at once state that the Railway Rates Bill is of such a magnitude which renders it impossible for us to prosecute it compatibly with the intention of winding up the business of the session.' [73]

As the decision to dissolve parliament was taken, the *Railway Times and Joint Stock Chronicle* declared: 'The advantage to be gained to the railway interest generally from an immediate dissolution of Parliament is sufficiently pronounced to make itself apparent'.[74] Gladstone, in spite of royal disapproval, stumped the country on yet another oratorical crusade. Mundella confessed: 'In all my forty years experience of elections, I have never passed through such a conflict as this. Bright and Hartington have damaged us most. Chamberlain has only damaged himself'.[75] He himself was ill. Incapable of bustling activity, he travelled round Sheffield wrapped in an Inverness.[76]

The issues were fused. The propertied classes had indeed united on a common platform against the ministry. Goldwin Smith, whose republicanism had once provoked Disraeli to call him a 'spouter of sedition', now came over from Canada to speak against Gladstone. Writing to the earl of Selborne, he said:

'The Irish difficulty, though bad, is not the worst of it. Worse still is the state of the House of Commons, which is now the only government, yet no more fit to govern than a street mob; worse still is the state of the nation, which is loose from its old moorings of principle, much shaken in moral fibre, and in a fever of revolutionary excitement. If you do not pull up you will slide into revolution.' [77]

Another radical, Mundella's old protégé Auberon Herbert, also came out strongly on the side of the individualists against the collectivist measures of Gladstone's ministry. In a series of articles in the *Newcastle Weekly Chronicle* (later reprinted as *The Right and Wrong of Compulsion by the State*) he exposed the collectivist implications of John Stuart Mill's *Essay on Liberty* and their working out in practice.[78] Scientists like Tyndall (whose wife was a cousin of Lord Claud Hamilton) and Huxley added their voices to those of men of letters like Matthew Arnold, Tom Hughes and R. H. Hutton to swell the anti-ministerial chorus.[79] In addition to the factor of outraged propertied interest, there were, of course, other factors mentioned by Morley: 'anti-Irish

R   257

prejudice, and the kind of influence exercised by the established clergy'. The country had been thoroughly awakened from end to end by the scares of March and April. Bryce, whose historical outlook was profound, confessed:

'Before the polling began, I felt, and I think most of my friends felt, that we were marching to defeat. The bulk of the influential local men, the men of wealth and standing in trade and manufacture, were mostly against us, and I do not speak of the landed gentry, for nearly all of them had left us before, some on the Eastern Question of 1876–8, and some, like the Duke of Argyll and Lord Lansdowne, on the Land Bill of 1881.' [80]

Bryce was right. But, though the Liberals were in a minority, Mundella still remained curiously optimistic, and wrote to Gladstone on 12 July:

'With very rare exceptions—and those not representative men—the general feeling is that we ought not to resign. This opinion has been so often and so passionately urged upon me during the last two or three days, that I feel it my duty to report it to you. Sir H. Thring came to me yesterday, and with tears in his eyes begged me to pray you to face the new house and die fighting. If the Liberal Unionists vote against us or abstain, they will damage themselves.' [81]

Gladstone replied:

'I share all your sanguine expectations, and am considering whether I shall counteract discouragement by an address. I think that the constitutional and political arguments show, as far as I can yet see, in favour of immediate resignation rather than meeting Parliament with our small, though crack, army of 200 men.

'I am above all things desirous that we should act on full discussion and conviction. I go up to town tomorrow, have asked you to a cabinet dinner on Saturday, and think of Monday for *the* Cabinet.' [82]

So, on 30 July, Gladstone went on to have his final audience with the Queen, and the third ministry came to an end.

9

'Fear of the 400,000 British Railway shareholders' was a very real thing. J. S. Jeans, secretary of the British Iron Trade Association, comparing the cost and conditions of working railway traffic in various countries, admitted that it was the one obstacle to any attempt to lower the capital burden of British railways. This capital burden made it essential for British railways to demand an average income of £1,968 per mile, as opposed to the £608 per mile demanded by the managements of the rest of the European railway systems. Jeans, as an alternative, could only suggest that heavier loads should be run. But in a discussion that followed he admitted that more serious remedies might have to be tried, since 'grave danger is threatened to English Industry by the fact that in future we shall have to compete with European rivals, whose railways, unlike ours, will be national property, and absolutely free'.[83]

That threat was now very real. The final report of the Royal Commission on the Trade Depression was published on 18 January 1887. The commissioners admitted that 'cheaper rates of carriage were enjoyed by our foreign competitors' and recommended:

(a) that greater facilities should be afforded to the public for ascertaining the rates which the companies profess to charge;

(b) that a cheap and effective procedure should be provided for obtaining a legal decision on any disputed point and for enforcing the decision when given;

(c) that greater attention should be paid to the development of communication of the country, and that no railway company should be allowed either directly or indirectly to control or own a canal;

(d) that every facility should be afforded by parliament for the construction of light railways and tramways in those parts of the country susceptible to further development in this respect.

Five of the eighteen commissioners expressed themselves more strongly:

'Preferential abatements made in the rates of railway carriage in favour of foreign goods shall be liable to compulsory revision by the proper tribunal on the ground of "undue preference" in the same way as preferential rates between one individual and another are now adjudicated upon.'

If the railway companies ever imagined that they would be protected by a Conservative government, they were soon disillusioned. As the *Stock Exchange* commented early in 1887:

'It might be supposed that with a Conservative Government in office, the railway companies would have little to fear in the way of unjust interference by Parliament, but the experience of the last session shows that, in these days, a Conservative Government is as ready as a Radical one to meddle with industrial undertakings.' [84]

For other, more vocal pressure groups, had coalesced against the 'protection of the foreigner' that was implied in preferential railway rates. Most hard-pressed by preferential rates afforded to foreign foodstuffs were the agriculturalists. To alleviate their several distresses, they were banding together to press various measures upon the government. Some of these measures were frankly protectionist. Others, like the demand for lower railway rates and the abolition of preferential charges, were more overtly so. The *Economist* supported them in their latter demands as 'putting an end to the bounties which now exist upon the introduction of foreign produce', since 'what is gained from low rates on foreign produce is gained at the expense of some other customer of the railways'.[85]

Open letters were exchanged between leaders of the farming interest and Lord Salisbury,[86] but Salisbury refused to countenance any form of protection. So, having formed an agricultural committee, a deputation of 100 M.P.s went to see Goschen. Led by Lord Elcho and Colonel Dawnay, they pleaded for another subvention from the imperial exchequer for making roads and the establishment of an agricultural department.

The railways, on the other hand, were in a better position than they were a year before, and could afford to be more tolerant of criticisms levelled against their charges. Prices had begun to rise even at the end of 1886, and a breath of optimism had begun to infect the trade reports.[87] Laing, speaking at a meeting of the London, Brighton and South Coast Railway at London Bridge on 26 January 1887, was able to declare: 'The improvement of traffic which we have been so long waiting for has come at last, and I must say that it has come with a suddenness which has rather surprised us.' Five days later, Mundella, speaking at Sheffield, admitted that the country had at last reached 'the bottom of the curve' and was 'turning upward'. He spoke of the railways and their susceptibility to state interference:

'You can hardly realise, when you have an interest as large as the railways of this country, how powerful that interest is, and how powerful its interests are to defeat almost any measure, however necessary and useful it may be. . . . You know capital is a matter which depends very much upon confidence, and is very susceptible if you touch it, and however justly you may deal with it, you will always find it a very difficult and responsible task to introduce any new measure in the interests of the public which affects capital.[88]

But it was going to be easier.[89] The North-eastern Railway admitted that their goods traffic had steadily increased in the previous three months, and were of the opinion that the improvement would go on.[90]

Coupled to the aggressive agricultural interest, whose cause was tainted by protection, were the equally vocal and powerful mining association and the iron trade. On 25 January 1887 they had sent a deputation to Lord Stanley (Mundella's Conservative successor) objecting to two aspects of the existing system of railway rates: the right of the railways to charge terminals (for loading, shunting, unloading, covering, uncovering, checking, invoicing, watching, marshalling and warehousing), which were 'almost destroying' trade in iron and steel; and secondly, the railway companies' arbitrary classification of the goods they carried. In face of these protests, the railways showed some willingness to co-operate. Two days after the deputation, a representative of the Great Eastern said that his company's attitude would be one of criticism rather than hostility. Just over a fortnight later, Richard Moon, chairman of the L.N.W., admitted that their classification of goods traffic required modernisation, but argued that the railways could not agree to anything that might prejudice their rights under act of parliament.[91] But he left the door ajar, by admitting that if the state guaranteed a dividend of 10 per cent to the shareholders, they would promptly deal both with preferential rates (for the farmers) and terminal charges (for the industrialists). Considering that at the same meeting the L.N.W. announced a dividend of 7 per cent, this was shrewd business on his part.

10

So, on this favourable and expectant sea of opinion, the Conservative Railway and Canal Traffic Act was launched at the end of February. Its similarity to that of Mundella dumbfounded the weeklies. *Herapath* wrote, 'Taken as a whole, it perpetuates the worst features of the bill introduced by Mr. Mundella, and is altogether unworthy to be classed with the well-meant attempt made by Mr. Chamberlain to settle the question', and expressed their 'astonishment and regret that the government should have thought fit to introduce, almost word for word, the clauses giving such extraordinary authority to the Board of Trade'.[92] The *Economist* shared this view:

'To introduce a new measure which retains all the objectionable features of the old one is simply to court defeat. It is a proceeding which can only be explained on the assumption that the permanent official of the Board of Trade have succeeded in dominating their successive presidents.'[93]

The offending clauses were soon whittled away in the house of lords, where the bill had originated under Lord Stanley's sponsorship. Clauses 2 and 4 were omitted, clause 5 withdrawn, clause

16 struck out, clause 20 postponed, and clause 24 amended. Thus the bill was shorn of the very clauses that gave it biting power—for the board of trade was now denuded of rights to receive complaints, to enter into communication with railway companies, and to publish any such correspondence. The Railway Commission were not to be given such full powers, and the damages they were entitled to award were scaled down. So the lords decided on 14 May.

But the leaders of the Conservative party were more 'constructive' in the Gladstonian sense of the term than were the rank and file. Lord Wemyss spoke out in the upper house against 'the upas-tree of Socialism planted by Mr. Gladstone in Ireland', which was now 'overshadowing the land, and attracting every kind of bird of prey to roost in its branches'. He deplored the marquis of Salisbury's cynical attitude to state interference, and accused the Conservative party of being 'a fifth wheel in the Socialistic coach'. He described the recent bills as 'drafted by a new Parliamentary firm, formed of Jack Sheppard, Dick Turpin, and Barabbas, under the guidance of the unjust steward'. He pointed to the ominous increase in the number of such 'constructivist' bills: 26 in 1885, 53 in 1886 and 107 in 1887. The Railway and Canal Traffic Bill he mentioned by name as 'taking away rights in a measure which would be impossible under the American Constitution'.[94]

The example of the United States, quoted by Lord Wemyss, was a singularly unhappy one with which to illustrate his case. For in that very year the Interstate Commission had been established to abolish discriminatory rates between individual shippers and localities.[95] The *Nineteenth Century*, in an article on 'Our Great Competitor', in June 1887, pointed out:

'The cost of transit of goods is very much heavier in Britain than in the U.S.A., and our governing powers seem to agree with our great railway companies that our competitors from the outside ought to have preference. To give a single case: goods can actually be sent from New York to London via Liverpool and Glasgow at less cost for freight and carriage than we, the British people, can send similar goods by the same rail from Liverpool or Glasgow to London or vice versa. . . . We must be up and doing while there is yet time to clear the decks of all unnecessary dead weight.'

The injunction to 'watch America' was taken up by the *Railway Times*, which by December 1887 was eulogising the Interstate Commission:

'It was popularly held in its inception to be the knell of many of the existing interests of the various railways, and the arguments which were assumed as most likely to favour that end, as well as the corresponding advantage of the trader, were pressed into the service of a similar crusade in this country'. [96]

Its results, they continued:

'have been beneficial at once in keeping down rates, and in increasing railway earnings through confidence in the stability and fairness of the charges stimulating the movement of freight'. [97]

II

By 1888 the hand of the government was definitely forced. The Fair Trade League, reorganised in 1886 on the lodge system throughout the country, captured the Conservative party conference in November 1887 by a dramatic vote of 1,000 to 12, which it took Lord Salisbury himself to reverse on the following day. Col. Howard Vincent, M.P. for Sheffield Central, the league's most intransigent mouthpiece, claimed to have captured fifty-two chambers of commerce throughout the country. Other organisations were springing up with the same end in view. The West of England Society for the Preservation of Agriculture and Other Industries, the West of England Association for the Defence of National Industry, and the Land and Labour Defence Association, were three of many which added their voices to the clamour for some form of protection for home industries.

These pressure groups united with others against the railways, and a steady stream of deputations flowed to the board of trade, headed by influential aggregates of M.P.s. The Railway and Canal Traders' Association, meeting at Eastcheap on 4 January 1888, resolved to fight a test case in the courts involving the vexed question of preferential rates, and arranged to levy a special fighting fund for the purpose. A fortnight later the National Sea Fisheries Protection Association met at Billingsgate under Sir E. Birkbeck and resolved to support a special bill to prevent preferential railway rates to foreign fish, rates which were causing their own catches to be either dumped in the sea or used as manure. Birkbeck voiced the general feeling of the assembly when he said that, since the association had been formed, no such vital subject had been brought before them. On 25 January 1888 a very influential deputation from the mining interests and the iron trade saw the president and permanent officials of the board of trade on the proposed bill and once more pressed the case against terminal charges. Finally, on 3 February, Lord Stanley was succeeded at the board of trade by Sir Michael Hicks Beach. The new president was himself a railway director, and had the confidence of the railway companies. A deputation from the companies came to see him on 18 April, led by the chairman, general managers and solicitors of the principal companies in the land, who, in addition to expressing that confidence, voiced their desire to see 'a fair and reasonable bill passed'. They endorsed the provisions of the government bill as sound on the reclassification of rates and allowing them sufficient room to appeal over decisions made by the commissioners in cases of undue preference. They expressed their horror at the provisions of two private members' bills on the subject that lay before the house. The first, Sir Bernhard Samuelson's, they objected to because it prohibited special rates for exports as well as imports, because it required them to carry goods at the same uniform rates over the whole of their systems, and because it prohibited them from appealing on questions of undue preference. The second bill, that of Sir E. Birkbeck, introduced on behalf of the fishing interest, they described as 'most objectionable in principles and confiscatory in its proposals'.[98]

The moral victory had been won. The railways had been brought to recognise that legislation was inevitable. The *Stock Exchange*, congratulating the government 'upon the disappearance of the heated opposition which Mr. Mundella had to contend with in 1886', mused:

'The ways of railway directors are indeed mysterious. This bill is substantially the same bill as that introduced by Mr. Mundella in 1886 and which created such a hubbub in railway circles. "Confiscation" was the mildest word applied to it, and at meeting after meeting incensed directors fulminated against its provisions. Now, not even Sir Edward Watkin has anything to say against it being read a second time, and, so far as we know, there has not been a single meeting held to protest against it.' [99]

When the bill was committed to the Standing Committee on Trade, it was the same story. As *The Times* noted, the committee 'dealt freely with the Bill, and not always in the way Sir Michael Hicks Beach and the Attorney-General suggested. It made many changes, not a few of them passed in the face of resistance on the part of friends of the railway companies'. It continued:

'The Bill has often been described as a farmer's measure. With greater show of reason it may now be termed. On almost all disputed points the Railway

Companies have been beaten. They have but feebly resisted: one cannot help remarking the contrast between the vigour with which they fought in former years and their present submissive or resigned attitude.' [100]

Mundella was jubilant. In the house of commons he gloated:

'The present Bill contains all that the former Bill did, and many other desirable provisions besides. It is the first step in the direction of state control of railways, and a very important step, showing how far we may be able to go in future'; [101]

while he wrote to the Leaders:

'The Railway Bill is *ours*, not theirs. We did the business in Grand Committee—it did not cost three hours in the House to get it through.' [102]

12

So, two years after he had introduced his measure, Mundella had the satisfaction of helping to amend the Conservative Railway and Canal Traffic Act to resemble his own. The powers which had been pared from the board of trade the previous year were restored to the measure when it was before the Standing Committee. This committee was given authority to draw up fresh rates for the railway companies, unless the companies had submitted proposals within six months from the passing of the act. Preferential rates were prohibited absolutely. Canals were to be released as far as possible from the control of the railways, to promote a healthy competition. By the time the act emerged, the board of trade was an informal court of arbitration. *The Times* commented:

'In 1886 this found little favour in any quarter. It was regarded rather as an amiable eccentricity little likely to produce much practical result. Further reflection, however, seems to have resulted in the formation of a considerable body of opinion in favour of the proposal. Mr. Mundella regards it with pardonable parental fondness as the most important part of the Bill, and without sharing his views, we may at least agree that it will tend to bring public opinion to bear upon the railway companies in a very salutary fashion.' [103]

The formation of that 'considerable body of opinion' was undoubtedly accelerated by agricultural distress. The *Sheffield Telegraph*, praising the 'disinterestedness of the Conservative party', unconsciously shed light on its well-springs: 'Magistrates are extinguished, and M.P.s whose incomes are derived from railway revenues are equally willing to suffer loss in the interest of the agricultural community'. [104] American example also stimulated the government, and Sir Michael Hicks Beach was loud in his praises of the Interstate Commerce Commission.[105]

But it was these very powers that were given to the board of trade which made the act extremely difficult to operate. *The Times* described the powers as 'vast—such perhaps as never before were lodged with any government department',[106] and expressed a pious hope that they would be exercised 'with a proper sense of responsibility'. The *Economist* was shrewder, and forecast that 'the companies would be one too many for the Board of Trade', and, by treating them properly, get their own way. Certainly the Railway and Canal Traders' Association thought so too, and they hurriedly set up a watching committee to protect their respective interests when the new rates and classifications were dealt with by the board of trade.

The *Economist* was right. The railway companies did as they were required, and submitted their revised schedules. But in the subsequent negotiations which led up to the thirty-five provisional orders they could not agree with the board of trade.[107] When the board submitted these provisional orders to parliament, the maxima were raised, and the companies secured themselves against any possible loss. By the time the fourth Liberal ministry took office, the problem had to be re-approached once more.

Such negotiating technique, coupled with their immense power and wealth, made the railway companies veritable states within the state.[108] It was against this power and wealth that Mundella stumbled during his tenure of the presidency in 1886. His misfortune had two consequences which were not fully appreciated at the time: it helped to precipitate the disruption of his party, and to provide yet a further illustration of the major antinomy facing the Gladstonians.[109] That antinomy—the conflict between Gladstone's own dislike of what he called 'construction' and the collectivist tendencies of the age—could be solved only by the formation of a new political party; and it is not without significance that in the formation of that party at this very time one of the major points of their creed was the nationalisation of the railways.

PART IV
ELDER STATESMAN

CHAPTER THIRTEEN

A Voice in Opposition, 1886–1892

URGENT and imperative as lower railway rates was the necessity of increased technical education among the work-people in Great Britain. The conclusions of the Samuelson commission were painted in darker overtones by the Royal Commission on Trade Depression, whose final report appeared in the year 1887. Mundella turned to it with the zest and eagerness that characterised his whole life. In January 1887 he went down to Wales to distribute prizes. There the wife of Viriamu Jones (formerly of Firth College, now principal of Cardiff University College) was much impressed by him as he spoke:

'Of commanding presence, tall and thin, with flowing beard grown grey, he stood, like a benevolent prophet of old, and in a deep resounding voice proceeded to establish friendly feeling between himself and his audience.' [1]

That 'friendly feeling' was absent at Westminster. For when he put a question to the chancellor of the exchequer on 7 March: 'Will Her Majesty's Government introduce or facilitate the passing of a measure authorising local authorities to establish and maintain schools and colleges adapted to the wants of their several localities, and will it recommend annual parliamentary grants?' he received an evasive reply. The problem, said the chancellor, was 'full of difficulties' and the annual grant 'could not be recommended'.

I

So once more the inevitable pressure group coalesced. Formed of politicians and scientists, it emphasised the imperative necessity of promoting technical education in Great Britain as soon as possible. Mundella had accompanied a deputation that had waited on the Conservative vice-president in February, and on 22 March himself led a deputation to the government in which he said:

'At present our industrial classes are like badly drilled soldiers fighting a battle with antiquated weapons. With the education that they had, it was like sending them into the field armed with Brown Bess to meet the best armed soldiers in Europe.'

269

The year of Jubilee seemed to afford a suitable opportunity to others like-minded. On 19 January, Lord Rothschild at the Mansion House advocated the establishment of an institute which would symbolise the marriage of science and industry: providing a Royal Society for the advancement of industrial knowledge. But Rothschild hoped that voluntary effort would build it. Huxley, who was present and seconded the resolution, sounded a more serious note. He deprecated a 'vast permanent bazaar' and wanted to see 'a port of call for all those who are concerned in the advancement of industry'.[2] He wrote to *The Times*:

'We are entering, indeed we have already entered, upon the most serious struggle for existence to which this country was ever committed. The latter years of the century promise to see us in an industrial war of far more serious import than the military wars of its opening years.'

He indicated that the great powers of the East (Germany) and the West (America) were both challenging us to this war, and concluded:

'We must be careful to organise victory. To those who remember the cotton famine and reflect how much worse a customer famine would be, the situation appears grave.'[3]

Others were not slow to respond. Hartington made a speech outlining the same arguments, and Mundella spoke at Sheffield on 12 April on the same theme. By 1 May Huxley was writing to Roscoe, telling him of the need for following up all this oratory with something more practical, and reporting a recent conversation he had had with Lord Hartington upon the subject. He pointed to Hartington and Mundella as the obvious people to take it up with Roscoe and then 'something would be done'.

Something was done. A month later to the day a meeting took place inaugurating the National Association for the Promotion of Technical Education. Aptly enough, they met in the room of the Society of Arts, Adelphi, home of so many earlier efforts to promote interest in industrial education.[4] The meeting consisted of delegates from school boards, trade unions, chambers of commerce, together with nearly forty M.P.s. The chair was taken by Lord Hartington, who, in a characteristic speech, advocated well-informed and deliberate consideration before a decision was taken.

So the association was constituted. The list of officers was imposing. Four leading Liberal peers were among the vice-presidents, together with the bishop of London and seven M.P.s.[5] Huxley and Tyndall were also among them. Mundella, himself a vice-president, moved that all those who were present should be invited to join the council, a motion which was seconded by Lord Rosebery. Sir Bernhard Samuelson and George Howell carried a resolution inviting the co-operation of the chief towns and industrial centres.

The aim of the association was to encourage educational reform and to improve (in a broad sense) all those who were employed in the national industries. The means were to be the same as those of other great pressure groups of the century—vigorous campaigning to educate public opinion, by the dissemination of information. To Mundella it was no new form of activity—it was but the Anti-Corn Law League and the Eastern Question Association working for a different end. The association was fortunate in getting the services of a brilliant young Oxford teacher who had recently carried through some successful administrative reforms in both Christ Church and Lady Margaret Hall. He was also M.P. for Rotherham, and was closely linked to the Co-operative Movement. His name was Arthur Acland. He chose as his assistant H. Llewellyn Smith, another young man of ability who was later to make a name for himself.[6]

Mundella, true to Huxley's opinion of him, opened the attack in the house of commons on 18 August 1887. The occasion was a debate on the estimates. Sir William Hart Dyke, as vice-president, talked of reviving the boards of guardians. Mundella, interrupted by emphatic negatives, then rose to attack the Cross Commission. 'If we do not get a good majority report we will get a report from some of its members which will be useful in the future,' he declared. He demanded further reforms: an independent education authority in the counties, a certain number of free schools, the complete abolition of the pupil-teacher system, and the doubling of the grant for the training of teachers. He protested against the exclusion of drawing ('the language of industrial art') for the sake of saving £50,000, and asked that cookery should receive a special grant. He sketched further extensions to the educational system, and specially stressed the need for continuation schools.[7]

In 1888, in the debate on the address from the throne, he spoke again. On 6 April he displayed the shameful state of the science and art department, declaring that its condition was a public scandal:

'The office accommodation and the examination rooms are altogether inadequate for the services which have to be performed. The servants there are working in passages, corridors, and cellars, and crowded up in unhealthy rooms in conditions under which no public or private servant ought to be asked to work.'

He urged the government to increase the size of the science school:

'This is our training school for scientific teachers. We talk about technical education in this House and on public platforms, we plead for it, and are all in favour of it—that is to say, we are all in favour of talking about it, but none seem to be in favour of spending money on it, and the result is we are about to diminish our supply of science teachers in consequence of lack of room in this department. There is no other country in Europe which has made such wretchedly small sacrifices for the training of scientific men for the purpose of giving scientific instruction, as our own.'

His eagle eye discovered in the same year that ideas he had put into practice earlier in the decade were now being dropped. One of them was an annual vote of £2,500 which he had secured for the purchase of objects of scientific or artistic interest for provincial museums: the local authorities meeting the cost half-way.

But the main brunt of the attack was shared by others. In particular did the two secretaries of the association, Sir Henry Roscoe and Arthur Acland, sustain the disappointments of introducing bills to give legislative form to the aims of the association. Above all, Arthur Acland was indefatigable in this way, and to his credit must go the grant to 'whisky money' in 1890.

This association was a tractive force behind all the educational reforms of the years 1886–1892, especially after 1889, when its aim was widened to include 'secondary' as well as technical education. By systematic propaganda, two acts were successfully carried through parliament. The first, passed in 1889 (the Technical Instruction Act), vested the county councils (established in the previous year) and other local bodies with power to supply or aid the supply of technical and manual instruction. The act's interpretation of 'technical instruction' was the same as that of the association. The wording of the act was also generously interpreted by the local authorities as meaning any kind of secondary education, and so far did some authorities go that they established scholarship ladders to grammar schools.

The second was more a gesture of the chancellor of the exchequer than an act. It was a direct result of the persuasion of Arthur Acland that Goschen allowed nearly three-quarters of a million pounds, intended to compensate publicans who had lost their licences, to go to the encouragement of technical education. This was a great and signal victory for the association, for the county councils used it both for grammar schools and for evening continuation schools. Mundella saw the tremendous social significance of it all:

'Technical education is a great social problem as well as an educational question. In a country like ours we can only feed the people by the people producing something they can exchange for food. So it is of the highest importance we should retain our commerce and our industrial superiority that we might be able to hold our own in the markets of the world.' [8]

He had spoken in this fashion twenty years before this, when the writing on the wall was less plain to see. Huxley was indeed wise in his outlook when he wrote to Roscoe that only he, Hartington and Mundella could get things done. The trouble was that Roscoe was too much of a professor, and Hartington was too indolent. It is a great pity that Mundella was left to talk in this fashion alone, for the language he used could be appreciated by ordinary men, had they but listened.

2

To advocate technical education, as Lyon Playfair discovered thirty years before, was to incur suspicions of secularism. So it is not surprising that the more vehemently Mundella and his allies argued on behalf of technical education, the more resistant did the voluntaryists and denominationalists become. For the voluntaryists and denominationalists were now in a strong position. They had forced the issue at the general election of 1885, and secured the appointment of the Cross commission to examine the working of the elementary education acts. Now, as the deliberations of the commission reached an end and the report emerged, Mundella rose to the attack once more.

He began with a question to Matthews, the home secretary, as to why the report of the commission had reached the newspapers before the house of commons had had a chance of seeing it. Matthews was at a loss to explain. The Code Reform Association, under its energetic secretary, Sonnenschein, declared that the report of the Cross commission 'could not be characterised by any other name than reactionary'.

The great division in educational outlook between the two parties at this time is well illustrated in the report. The late administrative head of the education department, Sir Francis Sandford, took the opportunity to voice sentiments which read strangely in view of the general line of advance in which he had participated as a civil servant from 1870 to 1884. For Sandford showed himself a greater supporter of the voluntary schools than even Cardinal Manning. Sandford condemned reforms which Mundella had undertaken during his vice-presidency, among them the central system for training pupil teachers, and the raising of the age of half-timers to eleven and full timers to thirteen.[9] He refused to under-rate or 'cast a slur' upon the system of 'payment by results'. Sandford's reactionary intransigence was matched by equally emphatic support for Mundella by Lyulph Stanley. An examination of the divisions that took place from 15 November 1887 to 8 May 1888 in the commission shows how violently party views coloured the report.

For so emphatic was the dissent of the Liberal members that they drew up a separate minority report, inspired by the energetic Lyulph Stanley, who, it will be remembered, was appointed to the commission to take Mundella's place. Lyulph Stanley's report advocated everything which the majority report did not, and the two statements of policy (i.e. the majority and minority report) became the programmes of the two political parties for the next decade. In particular did Lyulph Stanley remember the opposition of Sandford, for as late as 3 February 1893 he was writing to *The Times* pointing out that when Sandford objected to a review of the accommodation afforded by existing voluntary schools (on the grounds that it would prejudice their existence) he was the only commissioner out of the twenty-three who did so.

Many of the good suggestions of the majority report were overshadowed by its guarded attitude. It condemned, for instance (Sir Francis Sandford again dissenting), the system of 'payment by results' which still lingered in spite of the Mundella Code. But their condemnation was limited, for they wished it to be 'modified and relaxed', and acknowledged that 'the distribution of the parliamentary grant cannot wholly be freed from its present dependence on the results of examination without incurring the risk of graver evils than those which it sought to cure'. Mundella was not so blind to the good aspects of the report as to condemn it unreservedly, although some of his remarks outside the house were vehement:

'The majority report of the Cross Commission is just what I feared it would be. It wants to put back the clock and break up the compromise of 1870 . . . which if done would plunge us into a sectarian controversy and would undo much of the valuable work already done.' [10]

Fortunately for the Liberals, Lyulph Stanley, as a leader on the London school board, could ensure that his point of view was kept constantly before the public eye. [11] Stanley was also largely responsible for the formation of yet another pressure group, this time the National Education Association. It was launched at a meeting on 20 and 21 November 1888 over which Mundella presided; and was convened to protest against the 'reactionary proposals of the Cross commission'. At this meeting the National Education Association (a kind of revival of the National Education League of the seventies) was formed in order to promote a system of national education 'which shall be efficient, progressive, unsectarian and under popular control'. A. J. Mundella became the president and Lyulph Stanley the chairman of the executive committee. Offices were taken, and T. E. Minshall set about preparing a list of publications on the education question.

The constitution of this body illustrates the indignation with which the dissenters greeted the majority report of the commission, and their fear that the board school system might be jeopardised. The 'war' between the voluntaryists and the supporters of the board schools broke out as fiercely as before. Some speakers, like Handel Cossham, M.P., declared that the denominational party was seeking to build up a second church establishment and demanded that the schools should be managed not by 'parsons' but by an elected body over which the ratepayers had some control. The presence of Dr. Dale, Dr. Crosskey and the Rev. E. F. M. MacCarthy showed that the Birmingham dissenters remembered the act of 1870 and were coming forward in its defence. [12]

All this vigorous determination with which the National Education Association pressed for the rights of the school boards was largely responsible for the difficulties and anomalies which developed in the nineties to culminate in the Cockerton Judgement.

3

Nor had child labour been entirely abolished. The work that Lord Shaftesbury had begun was still unfinished. A considerable amount of feeling had been aroused over the 'pantomime waifs' or children employed in public entertainments. Miss Ellen Burke had published her book in 1884, and it had moved Lord Shaftesbury—then on his death-bed. The story runs that he summoned Benjamin Waugh, and ordered him to make an investigation and to 'right these wrongs'.[13]

Waugh did so, and he found that though Ellen Burke had exaggerated, some form of regulation was needed. So he persuaded Mundella to sponsor a bill for the prevention of cruelty to children. At the same time, the N.S.P.C.C. was formed to pressurise their point of view.

Mundella introduced the bill in 1888, but owing to the pressing measures of that year, he could not get it read a second time till 13 December. The M.P. for Camberwell appealed against it, and the attorney-general remarked on the debatable matter it contained. So it had to wait till the following year, 1889. It then went into committee on 19 June. To the accompaniment of a considerable amount of agitation in the country, Mundella worked hard in committee, speaking no fewer than sixty-five times. When the measure emerged it dealt with everything relating to the exposure, abandonment, neglect or ill treatment of children, as well as everything that related to their casual employment. Mundella declared that he looked to it to get rid of 'the breakages of civilisation which weigh so heavily upon the community.' [14]

As Mundella wrote :

'It is really a large, strong and comprehensive measure, larger than its name imparts. . . . I have had such laborious and incessant difficulties, such coaxings, wheedlings, and threatenings, such negotiations, conferences and complexities, that I am vowing I will never again, as a *private* member, attempt such a task. An old member remarked, as we returned home together, that he had never believed that I should get it through under ten years of work and agitation. I am the only member that has passed an important bill this session.' [15]

This Act of 1889 prohibited the employment of children under ten, and made it a misdemeanour punishable by imprisonment to neglect or ill-treat them. There was a struggle in the commons, and the ministry were defeated when they excepted children employed in theatres. The lords reversed this verdict, and allowed children to be employed from seven years and upwards, providing they had a magistrate's certificate.

4

A similar struggle took place at the end of 1889 and the beginning of 1890. This time Mundella was championing the board schools against the activities of the energetic bishop of Salisbury. His speeches show how he feared the denominationalists' desire to control the education of the young.[16]

This particular skirmish began on 6 November 1889, when Mundella introduced a deputation from the diocese of Salisbury to Lord Cranbrook. The deputation, representing the British and Foreign Schools Society, expressed the general disapproval of dissenters with the activities of Bishop John Wordsworth, whose administration of his diocese, they claimed, showed his open hostility towards them.

Bishop Wordsworth did not suffer this meekly. He immediately wrote a protesting letter to Mundella in which he declared:

'It is painful to be driven to conclude that many of those whose fathers had religious principles, and who taught and suffered for them, should be willing and often eager now to hand over the consciences of their children to be subjected to the training of a colourless and uncertain ratepayers' religion, provided only they can prevent the clergy of the Church of England from teaching in the elementary school, and make those whose principles are stronger than their own pay a double tax for education.'[17]

Mundella observed to young Leader on 30 December 1889:

'Pray look for my answer to the Bishop of Salisbury in the *Daily News* to-morrow. I have fired some heavy guns at him, from Bishop Frazer. This is going to be a serious business, and I want to show that whereas excellent religious instruction is now given, such intolerant conduct as this, sanctioned as it is by the Education Department, is likely to lead to an agitation for the secularisation of our schools.'

This he followed up with a long speech in the house of commons in the opening weeks of the 1890 session. He pointed out the growing influence of the denominationalists, and lamented the death of Patric Cumin, the one great bulwark against their influence in the education department.[18] There was a heated debate, but his motion was lost by 167 to 115 votes. It underlined, as one member pointed out, the problem of the next step in educational policy. Was it to be assisted education, or free education?[19]

Mundella was fighting the battle of the boards with half-hearted enthusiasm. He had already begun to think of the wider plan that was taking shape, and wrote to J. D. Leader asking him, 'What should you think of a scheme, if submitted by the government, to abolish school boards, and to transfer their powers to town councils and district councils?' So it is little wonder that Wordsworth imagined he had won a victory, and by September 1890 could write to Archbishop Benson:

'We opened the last of our schools yesterday in a quiet simple way, and since the collapse of Mundella's attack in the House of Commons have heard no recrudescence of dissenting feeling here.' [20]

5

The last decade of the century saw the clouds beginning to gather. He was deprived of his usual continental holiday (necessary to alleviate the rheumatism which made it increasingly difficult for him to sleep). He was being goaded by Sir William Leng, knighted for his Conservative sentiments in 1887, till he wrote to Leader: 'The man is an *utter cad*. I will not gratify him by treating him as an antagonist.' The newly imposed McKinley Tariff, which was compared by *The Times* to the Berlin and Milan decrees of Napoleon, gave points to Vincent's Fair Trade arguments.[21] Just now Vincent was doing all he could to draw Mundella into a public controversy. Yet at this very time it was particularly imperative that Mundella should refrain from all controversy, for he was appointed chairman of the trade and treaties committee. This was a consultative and advisory body appointed by Sir M. Hicks Beach on 1 April 1890 to consider the expiry of certain commercial treaties, and especially those embodying a 'most-favoured-nation clause'.[22]

The formal side of his work—the speech-making, the presenting of prizes—had to continue. At every public appearance Mundella insisted that the national life of the country was now committed to the people, who should become aware of their responsibilities and opportunities. He told school teachers that they were social missionaries 'doing a splendid work to prevent that social wreckage which at the present moment weighed so heavily on the minds of all thoughtful people'. Above all, he pointed to the opportunities afforded by the grant of 'whisky money' to the county and borough councils.[23]

He pressed Leader to let him distribute the prizes at the Sheffield

School of Art, 'as the next session will be an Educational Session'.
He remarked too:

'Have we not turned our curses into blessings? The taxation derived from
drink is going for higher education. I hope Sheffield will *at once* set up a commercial school at low fees out of the grants to the County Council, and help
the lower middle classes. Why should it not maintain a commercial side to the
Grammar School at, say, £5 a year?' [24]

He was nominated, with Lyon Playfair, to the committee which
advised the commissioners of the 1851 commission. An annual
sum of £5,000 was appropriated for scholarships to aid the
development of scientific education in the manufacturing districts
of the country. The committee submitted a report, and were subsequently entrusted with the duty of putting into operation the
scheme which had been devised. The scholarships were entirely
confined to research, and were limited especially to those branches
of science connected with the national industries of the country.
When awarded they were to be tenable at any approved institution
at home or abroad. His scientific partners in this enterprise reflect
the position he now held in the educational world. They were
Lord Kelvin, Professor Huxley, Dr. William Garnett, Sir Henry
Roscoe and Sir Norman Lockyer. [25]

It was in the midst of his round of speeches in Sheffield (this year
more than usual, since the National Liberal Federation had met
there) that he received news that his wife was seriously ill. He
hurried back to London, but efforts were of no avail: she died,
ending a partnership that had lasted for forty-six years.

She had been a great help to him. 'To look upon her was to
have a true revelation of all that a noble wife could be to a man
engaged in great and noble labours.' [26] In an age of happy
marriage she was a striking example. Frederic Harrison, agnostic
and outspoken, wrote to Mundella:

'Few men, unless it be your great chief, have made the nation know more
thoroughly how much their public life was supported by strength and happi-
ness at home.' [27]

Her circle of friends, curiously enough for one of Mundella's
outlook, was largely composed of the clergy—of all denominations. Even Cardinal Manning, who had not met her often,
wrote, 'I feel to share your loss. I have not been out of the house
for two months or I would come to you.'

His friends, Llewellyn Dillwyn, Broadhurst, Samuel Smith,

J. W. Pease and Thomas Burt, all rallied round with words of consolation. Thomas Burt's was brief and typical:

'My dear friend—I know how feeble are words—even those of sincerest sympathy in face of such a bereavement as yours. Deeply do I condole with you and pray that you may be strengthened and sustained in your sorrow.'

6

So it was a rather different Mundella who turned into the last decade of the century for a session which he had declared would be devoted to education. His manner was sharper and more intolerant, and L. J. Jennings, M.P. for Stockport, complained that when M.P.s began to speak on the subject of education, Mundella usually began his reply by 'telling them they did not know what they were talking about and ought to go home'.[28]

One can appreciate his testiness. New voices of social criticism were growing in volume. They had attracted William Morris, the treasurer of the Eastern Question Association, out of the radical camp ten years previously, and now they were attracting the growing unions of non-craftsmen that knew not arbitration. The great strike of the dockers in 1889 was a recent example of the discord that still existed between capital and labour. The superficial class congruence of the previous two decades was no longer possible.

For the earnest Gladstonian of the rank and file, the Grand Old Man had the explanation. He had said that social reform was like a walled garden full of fruit, which would be entered only when the Irish Question was satisfactorily settled.[29] But for Mundella the causes of the unrest lay deeper. He thought that a real educational policy could stem these evils, on the argument that 'you can make anything out of the child, but nothing out of the man'. Consequently in the eleven-point programme which he outlined in the *Review of Reviews* for April 1891 the first six points were devoted to educational matters. They were:

'1. Take care of the rights of the child and compel parents to fulfil their responsibilities.
'2. Assist the parents in educating the child, giving it free the best education that can be procured, including modern languages and drawing.
'3. Establish cheap and accessible intermediate schools in every town and in every country area where a first-class education can be had for £5 a year.
'4. Free children from labour till they are twelve and raise the half-time age to fourteen.

280

'5. Follow the German example and provide continuation schools, and look after the welfare of scholars after leaving school and train the blind.
'6. Feed starving scholars if necessary at the State's charge.'

Points 2 and 4 were to provide the interest of the 1891 session.

7

Opinion had been stirred by the publication of a series of reports by John Burnett, who, it will be remembered, was appointed in 1886 by Mundella to the labour bureau of the board of trade. Burnett had not wasted his time as a labour correspondent. His two reports on the *Sweating System in the East End of London* (H. of C. 331, London 1887) and the *Sweating System in Leeds* (C. 5513, London 1888) had provoked the appointment of a select committee of the house of lords to investigate his findings. The chairman of this house of lords committee, Lord Dunraven, tabled a bill at the beginning of 1891 to remedy this state of affairs.

Reinforcing Burnett's disclosures, a congress which met at Berlin in 1890 agreed that no child should be employed before the age of twelve. On the basis of these resolutions, both the government and the opposition framed bills. In addition to these, three more bills were tabled. One was in the hands of Mundella's old friend, Sir Henry James, and dealt with further regulation of the textile industry. Another was Lord Thring's, a draftsman's bill to tidy some anomalies in the law. The third was Lord Dunraven's bill arising from Burnett's disclosures.

The *Economist* was aghast at the plethora of regulations envisaged by five separate bills, and wrote: 'Far from having their hands tied tighter, our manufacturers have a just and reasonable claim that some of the restrictions be relaxed and their administration made a little more elastic',[30] and a little later, in the same vein, remarked:

'It is possible we can have too much of a good thing. It is hardly fair to make the staple industries of the country the target for amateur efforts in social and industrial legislation. We think they are fully justified in looking to the Government of the day to protect them from this vexatious and unnecessary interference in their business.'[31]

Mundella, who was in charge of the debate for the opposition at this juncture, wrote to J. D. Leader on 28 February 1891:

'The Government sent Gorst (with a strong delegation) to Berlin. They pledged themselves to the hilt to carry out to the full, if not to go beyond, the provisions of the Conference. They bring in their Bill—a weak flabby thing—they throw over the Conference—and expect everybody to welcome their miserable bantling with caresses. I knew beforehand the whole history. I knew that Gorst was in a state of disgust, and that the provisions of Berlin had first been considered, then placed in the Bill, then withdrawn to please certain employers, and finally Matthews had the face to declare themselves unpledged, that our assent had only been given *ad referendum*. But before finally signing the document Lord Salisbury twice telegraphed his entire assent, and authorised by a special dispatch the signatures binding Great Britain.'

As his opponent in this matter, Mundella found that he was fighting C. B. Stuart-Wortley, the M.P. for the Hallam division of Sheffield, who maintained that children would actually be worse off if the Berlin resolutions were carried out. But Stuart-Wortley was only acting under orders, and privately confessed to Mundella that the government were prepared to surrender in committee.[32]

When the most personal of the five factory bills came up for discussion Mundella was ill in bed at Folkestone. This bill (presented by Sir Henry James) dealt with the hours of labour in the textile industries. Mundella was very agitated at the thought that he would not be able to present his point of view. He wanted the debate to be postponed. On 27 May, Sir Henry James wrote to console him:

'Pray do not think of coming up. I went to the House last night and had a second interview with Goschen and urged him *earnestly* to give way, and you know how earnest I can be. I told him there would be motions for postponement, and the adjournment of the debate, and that the Bill would be injured by unnecessary amendments. I saw some signs of him giving way and the matter will be left for Smith to decide tomorrow morning. I have now written to both Smith and Goschen strong letters . . . Calmez-vous, calmez-vous mon ami. All will be quite right. Even if the Government will not give way your friends will maintain the debate until you can appear.' [33]

Henry James reinforced his private embassies with a stout public declaration the next day:

'There is no member of this House to whom the children employed in the manufacture of textile fabrics owe more than they do to the right hon. member for Sheffield who has taken the greatest interest in the question of the age at which children should be employed.

'When the question was raised in the standing committee, the rt. hon. Gentleman bore the burden of the debate, and I am sure that it will facilitate matters if he can be there when the Bill is discussed.' [34]

He was. Henry James won the day, and when the textile societies of the four northern counties presented him with an illuminated address, he wrote to Mundella describing how 'at the presentation the men cheered your name vociferously', adding, 'you know how much I owe to you for the success of the whole affair'.[35]

A fortnight later Mundella was stoutly resisting the home secretary's attempts to jettison the commitments of the Berlin Conference.[36] The home secretary declared that factory occupation could not injure the health of a child, and argued, 'We cannot expect the parent to keep his child doing nothing between the ages of ten and twelve'. Mundella acknowledged that though England held the supremacy over all the world, she paid a high price for it by wrecking her future population. He wanted standard 5 to be the minimum scholastic qualification for half-time employment.[37]

As might have been forecast, the result was a compromise. The age of eleven was agreed upon as the statutory minimum age for half-time employment in factories and workshops. But there were many misgivings on the Conservative side.[38] Most significant was the surrender of the Conservatives to the radical demand for 'local control', with the result that local authorities were given the supervision of sanitary conditions in all workshops, and the inspectors were obliged to co-operate with them in all matters. The domestic workshop had to keep lists of out-workers, which were to be available to both inspectors and local authorities. A final safeguard against 'truck payments' was provided by the 'particulars clause', requiring each employer to furnish in writing full particulars of the wages of his employees. As one turns the pages of *Hansard*, one sees the younger Liberals being entrusted with the duty of proposing certain motions in the debate. In this particular one, S. C. Buxton moved the age-raising amendments. But the effective thrust and parry of debate, no less than the strong support, came from Mundella, who caustically and characteristically declared that the speeches of those who opposed Buxton's amendment were 'the speeches of those who did not know what they were talking about'.

8

A stronger influence than international conferences or select committees of the house now began to affect the government, and that was the approach of the general election. Under this shadow, the government effected a remarkable conversion. In 1886 they had denounced free education. Now, in 1891, Sir William Hart Dyke could blandly inform the house, 'We have changed our minds'.[39] Some of the Conservative back-benchers were annoyed at the 'giants of the front bench deserting the position they occupied a few years ago', and moved a resolution against it.[40]

Even Mundella was incredulous, and wrote to Leader:

'You remember the howl that was raised against my free education speech in October 1885—it seems incredible that these same men should use it as a bribe; but mark what I say, these men don't mean free education after all; their plan when unfolded will be a mockery, a delusion, and a snare.'[41]

It meant in reality that the government made itself responsible for some £2,259,000 in fees, of which over 90 per cent had hitherto been paid by the parents, and less than 5 per cent been paid by the boards of guardians for parents who were too poor to afford it. As Professor Adamson has aptly commented, 'The movement for the abolition of school fees was almost exclusively political'.[42]

That it was a political move there can be no doubt. The *Economist* lamented the 'readiness with which both parties have engaged in competing for popularity to be gained by increasing the benefits which Free Education proposed on the labouring classes', and censured the government for yielding to 'the temptation to pose as benefactors of the working class'.[43]

Nevertheless Mundella led the Liberal opposition in their drive to extract the full pound of flesh which Sir William Hart Dyke's concession allowed. It affected children between five and fourteen in all schools. From 29 June to 2 July it was before a committee of the whole house, and Mundella spoke no fewer than forty-five times, and when it returned from the lords on 30 July he opened the debate, speaking nineteen times in one day. The scenes are as familiar as the themes. Midnight debates, persistent effort provoking passion, the odd and intermittent intrusion of the religious difficulty in every clause, the refusal of one amendment and diplomatic acceptance of another—all characterised the passage of the bill. But perhaps the strangest sight was to see Joseph Chamberlain, who, twenty years before had hoped to set the country on fire with his cry for free schools, now reduced to defending church schools in rural areas, and stalking out majestically before the time for a division.

Mundella's contribution to the measure was four-fold. First was his insistence on the dual aspect of factory and education acts, and his demand that the new half-time age for factories should be incorporated in the education act. The second was his amendment that the fee grant should be paid yearly by minute instead of by act. But his third, which was successfully wrested from the government, was that the grant should be available for all children from three to fifteen—i.e. to include the kindergarten as well as the boy who wished for another year of study. His least was a plea that went beyond the formal wording of the act, and was later addressed to the country at large. It was the very core of his political programme. It was a plea that the free schools should be good schools. It was a protest against the attitude that 'the existence of schools with fees calculated to keep out street arabs is of the utmost importance to the better class of parents'—a view held by the *Economist*.[44] For, as he told his constituents later in the year:

'There is a note being sounded up and down the country that it is not creditable to parents to have their children educated free, that it is not honourable, and that only the very poor ought to have them educated free. . . . I hope you working men will set a good example and have your children educated free. What we want to do is to raise the whole mass and to improve the condition of all our people by a better education. Don't let us have a division of classes within a class.'

He staked his faith on the great historical process which he saw taking shape around him:

'This is part of a drama which is not yet played out. It is a part of that great movement which began more than a hundred years ago in the uprising of the people. School life and the technical education of the worker are the means by which labour rises to a higher intelligence, and through higher intelligence to power and comfort. It is a favourite hobby of mine and when a man rides his hobby he rides it hard.' [45]

9

By now action in the administrative and legislative sphere had become a sophisticated response rather to reports of committees than to party histrionics. Consequently, the Liberal programme elaborated at Newcastle attracted little of Mundella's time and energy. Instead, he was immersed in the work of a standing committee and a royal commission, both on subjects in his special field.

As chairman of the Trade and Treaties Committee, he was

responsible for keeping the ministry informed on expiring commercial treaties and any new tariffs and duties. The committee sat from 1890 to 1892, and produced a number of reports dealing with tariffs and commercial relationships with France, Central Europe, the U.S.A., Spain, and other countries who were revising their tariffs: some of which were published and some not. Mundella, as chairman, spent a great deal of time and energy resisting the efforts of Colonel Howard Vincent and others to capture the committee's influence to promote tariff preferences within the Empire.[46] But, what was more important, it was an object lesson in the value of organised commercial intelligence—a fact which Sir Michael Hicks Beach recognised when he thanked Mundella for his services.[47] For Hicks-Beach himself often felt obliged to oppose Vincent in the house.[48]

His second interest was his membership of the Royal Commission on Labour, and in particular his chairmanship of Section C. This section dealt with conditions prevailing in the chemical, building, textile, clothing and miscellaneous trades,[49] and it was an appointment which he did not willingly accept at first. As he wrote to J. D. Leader:

'I was sounded about my willingness to serve, but having regard to the unusual amount of work that I have in hand I felt unwilling to add to it. Moreover I feel that however valuable the information which may be obtained by the Commission, it is only a convenient instrument for delay. This week, however, Mr. Gladstone has urged me to be one of two representatives of the Front Opposition Bench, and he was so kind in his appreciation of my usefulness and fitness, that I have left myself in his hands.' [50]

His work here was innovatory in several respects. He appointed four women inspectors to investigate the position of women in industry.[51] He sat and heard a variety of witnesses from every walk of life give their testimony in a series of meetings lasting from 1 May 1891 to December 1892, when the sections ceased to sit individually and the commission sat as a whole. He was impressed, and said as early as 7 November 1891, 'Every important witness who came to me, who had taken a wide survey of the field of labour, pointed to the value of the labour department'. [52]

Apart from witnesses, many people wrote to offer names or suggestions or to ask for information. Cardinal Manning wrote on 21 December 1891 recommending a sub-commissioner.[53] Applegarth, severed from parliamentary and trades union work since his expulsion from the Amalgamated Society of Carpenters and Joiners, was now interested professionally in diving apparatus, and wrote to Mundella asking if he could give a demonstration as to how by its use such dangerous work could be performed with absolute safety.[54] The Comte de Paris, hovering on the outskirts of any social experiment or inquiry in Britain, wrote yet another request for 'documents and publications' concerning the commission. [55]

10

The general election of 1892 saw Mundella leading the five Liberal candidates for the town on the platform at the Albert Hall on 13 June. When he rose, as the senior burgess of the town, to make his speech, the hall re-echoed with cheers and the gusty approval of the audience. With him on the platform were Sir Frederick Mappin, Bernard Coleridge, H. J. Wilson and J. H. Yoxall. As a representative group of the Liberal party in that year they could not be bettered. Mappin, a near millionaire, was the chairman of a great railway spring manufacturing company and M.P. for East Retford; Bernard Coleridge, a lawyer, was M.P. for the neighbouring constituency of Attercliffe; H. J. Wilson, chairman of the Sheffield Smelting Company, was M.P. for Holmfirth; and J. H. Yoxall, an ex-schoolmaster of the town, president of the National Union of Teachers, was M.P. for Bassetlaw. Fighting with them for one of the vacant Sheffield constituencies was R. E. Leader, son of his old friend of the *Independent*.

In addition to being catechised by the publicans, Mundella had to face two serious charges that might well have damaged him in the eyes of his constituents. One was his vote against the Naval Defence Bill; the other was his undoubted reluctance to surrender to the protectionist arguments of Howard Vincent. There was also a cry raised against him that free education would still have to be paid for out of the pockets of the working man.

He felt confident enough, however, to go over to Bradford and speak for his friend Shaw-Lefevre, who faced an even fiercer protectionist storm than he did. But by 30 June he was back to stump his constituency of Brightside: one of the most sprawling, ugly industrial spots in the whole of the West Riding. Against him ran a London barrister, Bargrave Deane, who energetically held meetings at street corners, attacking the fetish worship of the

Grand Old Man who, declared Bargrave Deane, was working for the disruption of the Empire. He made good play with some incautious remarks of Mundella's that the McKinley Tariff was a blessing in disguise. Posters were put about asserting that the Liberals, if they shut the public-houses and killed the beer trade, would most certainly kill much railway traffic too.[56]

The election itself was a mild one. Indeed, the local paper remarked, 'Judging by the example of Brightside, a marked and welcome change has taken place in the view which the average British elector takes of these events'. Gladstone might be hit in the eye by gingerbread elsewhere, but in Sheffield the utmost courtesy of behaviour marked the proceedings. There were, of course, minor incidents. On nomination day a small crowd assembled outside the town hall as the various candidates made their appearance; Howard Vincent, seeing them cheering as he came out, sought to take a photograph of his wife, sitting in the carriage, surrounded by cheering crowds. They quickly disillusioned him, however, by grimacing and cat-calling.

Enthusiasm for the Grand Old Man reached an apogee. His likeness stood proudly in every window of the dingy streets of Brightside, Grimesthorpe and Neepsend, side by side with those of Mundella. The inhabitants of those dingy streets obeyed the exhortations of the Liberal posters: 'BE EARLY AT THE POLLS AND WALK LIKE MEN', to such good effect that Mundella found himself returned with a majority of 1,227—a larger vote than ever before.[57]

But his party were not so lucky. Their majority (with eighty-one Home Rulers and one Independent Labour member) was only forty above the 269 Conservatives and forty-six Unionists. There was no resignation before the new parliament assembled. Only on 11 August did H. H. Asquith move a vote of no confidence to usher in the fourth Gladstonian administration.

THE CANDIDATES FOR PARLIAMENT IN 1874

Robert Leader is admonishing the kneeling Roebuck, while Leng looks on from the wings

CHAPTER FOURTEEN

President of the Board of Trade
11 August 1892 to 3 May 1894

WHEN, in August 1892, Mundella became President of the Board of Trade for the second time, Lord Harting-ton, now duke of Devonshire, wrote to congratulate him saying:

'I expect you will do a good deal of mischief collectively, but I have no wish not to see the individual members of the government trying to do as much as they can in their own departments.' [1]

Hartington, with his detached insight, saw the true structure of this administration. Individual members did try to do as much as they could in their own departments. As A. H. D. Acland, a newcomer who succeeded to Mundella's old post at the Committee of Council, wrote in his diary, 'We have no leader now—each man manages his own department'. For the leader was a legend: the lesson-reading, tree-felling, erudite darling of the party was failing. His features were still eagle-like, but the great eyes stared from a pallid face. Yet the old man could still call upon almost inexhaustible reserves, even though at eighty-three such calls were in the nature of overdrafts. All energy was given to the vigorous and effective prosecution of the Home Rule Bill. In this he likened himself to a galley-slave—'chained to the oar' as he told John Morley, and his metaphor, if taken to its conclusion, shows how far he was abdicating from his real position, which was to guide the ship of state.[2]

All this meant freedom for his subordinates—a fact which Mundella was quick to appreciate. The first years of his presidency of the board of trade were to place him among the successes of this administration. At the time Bernard Shaw mockingly compared the attitude of the rest of his colleagues to the social problems of the day with that of Mr. Snodgrass, who, seeing the disorder reigning in Ipswich and his leader seized by the authorities, took off his coat and announced he 'was going to begin'.

Unlike Mr. Snodgrass, or many of his colleagues, Mundella did begin.[3]

I

As might be expected, he began with the railway companies. The tangled negotiations to fix maximum charges that had followed the Railway and Canal Traffic Act of 1888, only ended in the passing of confirmatory orders by parliament, which laid down new charges to come into force on 1 January 1893. In accordance with the law, these new charges were posted up on all goods-stations a fortnight before the end of 1892.

But these new maximum charges were in many cases higher than the charges which had already provoked the outcry of the eighteen eighties. Naturally, there was an immediate outcry from the traders, who mobilised to get the help of the government against this aggressive action on the part of the railway companies. Mundella anticipated them. On 2 January 1893, the day after the new rates came into force, the board of trade wrote to the associated railway companies calling attention to the grievances of the traders, and asking whether the new rates were going to be reconsidered. Five days later, on 7 January, the associated companies replied reassuringly that they believed that many of the 'alleged grievances' would disappear by the end of February and 'that gradual completion of the revision by the goods managers, concurrently with meetings for full discussion between the traders and general managers, will best tend towards a settlement of differences'.[4]

The traders naturally thought that the last sentence implied that they would bear the burden of initiating such discussions, and that the maximum rates would be maintained wherever possible. They were quite justified in such beliefs. A contemporary American, writing on 'The English Railway Rate Question', declared categorically that 'the railways were the aggressors'.[5] So did a select committee of the house of commons, which was appointed to examine the question. This committee agreed that 'the companies were not justified in dislocating trade, and alarming so many interests, and in compelling traders to enter into long negotiations with them for the revision of rates'.

On the last day of February (when the railway companies had said that 'the alleged grievances would disappear'), the board of trade once more wrote to the railway companies, this time to suggest that they should return to the 1892 rates. The companies replied the following day that they were unable to accept the suggestion; but they left a loophole for withdrawal by adding that each company was at liberty 'to make such public announcements on the subject of railway rates as it may think desirable'. Through this loophole flowed a flood of letters from the chairmen of individual companies assuring the president of the board of trade that 'no rates would be raised that would interfere with trade or agriculture or diminish traffic'. Such increases as were made, continued the chairmen, would not exceed 5 per cent of the 1892 charges.

On 3 March the house of commons passed a resolution against the high railway charges which were still prevailing. On 12 April Mundella asked the railway companies to what extent they had managed to revise their rates. Sir Henry Oakley, in his reply, acknowledged that the revisionary mechanism 'had broken down'.

'To end the terrible noise and odium that exists', he continued, 'we had better revert as quickly as possible to our original classifications as voluntarily adopted, and set the stations right with the exception of the 5%, that is to say, they might not exceed 5% except in special cases.'

The traders, for their part, grew angrier and angrier with each fresh delay on the part of the railway companies. On 30 January they passed a resolution that the fixing of rates ought not to be left 'to the irresponsible discretion' of the railway companies. They proposed that an act of parliament, conferring yet more stringent powers on the board of trade, should be passed. These stringent powers would enable the board to fix the actual charges at something like the 1892 level. This was strong, collectivist language, and the traders were prepared to back it wholeheartedly. On 16 February a deputation numbering over 200 waited upon Mundella for this purpose. Mundella was sympathetic, and told them so. In the meantime, no fewer than seven private member's bills were printed for presentation to the house of commons: while the board of trade dealt with 'an unprecedented number' of complaints. By 17 March the board had forwarded to the associated railway companies (irrespective of deputations) 835 complaints of specific rate increases, and 211 resolutions in general terms. After his previous experience, Mundella was shy of dealing with the railways in a drastic fashion. Speaking to the traders, he said that the railway interest was so strong in parliament that it was impossible for him to do anything, even in his official capacity, unless the traders and farmers of the country were solidly united behind him. But even if he had the inclination, he most certainly had not the opportunity in the 1893 session; for time was burdened and mortgaged by the Home Rule Bill, which, introduced on 3 February, and rejected by the lords on 8 September, occupied eighty-two parliamentary days.

Moreover, he was already committed to a measure for shortening the hours of railway labour, which was calculated to annoy the railway directors.[6] Printed on 6 February, his bill empowered the board of trade to require for its approval full particulars of the hours of work performed by railway servants. *The Times* in a cautious editorial of 1 April 1893 warned the ministers that 'the great danger at the moment is that parliament should once more draw the legislative bow at a venture, and inflict yet another and more serious wound on the trade of the country'.

This bill was the only legislative measure of note passed by the ministry during the 1893 session. It was read a second time on 22 February, a third time five days later, passed the lords on 11 July, and received royal assent on 27 July. It might have passed through the house without any discussion whatsoever (since it embodied the report of a select committee) but for the persistence of G. C. T. Bartley, a Conservative member, who pointed out that it would become law without the house knowing anything about it.

As this bill got under way, Mundella yielded to the importunities of the traders and appointed a select committee to inquire into the manner in which railway companies had exercised the powers conferred upon them of fixing maximum rate charges. The committee had a wider scope: for it was 'to consider whether it is desirable to adopt any other means of settling the difficulties arising between companies and the public with respect to the rates and conditions of charges for the conveyance of goods'.

Under G. Shaw-Lefevre, it began to sit towards the end of May, and produced two reports by the end of the year.

Though the members of the Shaw-Lefevre committee rather vaguely proposed that increased powers should be given to the railway commission, they were specific, and unanimously agreed upon, the aggression of the railway companies.[7] As the *Spectator* (which was by no means a ministerialist organ) commented on 16 December 1893:

> 'The railway companies who put up so many of their rates to the maximum with the deliberate intention of teaching the traders not to go to parliament again for help, have only got themselves to thank.'

Even the *Economist* admitted that the railways had abused the powers conferred on them. This admission was a rebuke in polite language.

2

As usual, it was in the quieter, less sensational spheres of administration that Mundella achieved his greatest success. Here he took up and continued the work which he had begun in 1886. Then he had set up a statistical department of the board of trade, and founded the *Board of Trade Gazette* in order to provide an intelligence service for the world of commerce. Now he organised a special department of the board, complete with its own journal, also to serve as an intelligence service for the world of labour.

His conception owed much to American and to Fabian influence. Elgin R. Gould, who had been collecting statistics in Europe for the U.S. Bureau of Labour since 1887, gave evidence before the Royal Commission on Labour on 2 December 1892. A fortnight earlier the commission had heard Sidney Webb,[8] the energetic chairman of the London County Council technical education committee, giving his views as to how a labour department should be established.

Mundella took action long before the report of the labour commission was published. It was not easy. To begin with, Gladstone objected to Thomas Burt's appointment to a secretaryship to the board of trade. Someone had sent the prime minister the cutting of a speech made by Burt to the Northumbrian miners (whose secretary he had been for the previous twenty-seven years). The offending passage, underlined in red ink, ran:

> 'My new position will probably to some extent impose restrictions on me, but it need not, and shall not, stand in the way of my responding to any application on your part for such counsel and assistance as I can render.'

Gladstone had immediately written a letter of inquiry to Mundella in which he asked:

> 'It was certainly understood as I think when Burt took office he was to give up his secretaryship but was to be open for consultation from time to time as *amicus curiae*. Do you know anything of his intention, and if so, what is it?'

Mundella wrote to Burt, and was able to reply to Gladstone on 7 October, pointing out that the remark in question was not so much a speech as a circular, and assuring him:

'I feel sure that Burt's understanding is the same as yours and mine and that he will honourably adhere to it. He is so honourable and so judicious that I do not anticipate any disadvantage to the government from the exercise of this freedom. I hope and believe no difficulty will arise.'

He was more unlucky in his attempts to enlist prominent leaders of the labour world in his new labour department. He spoke to Tom Mann two days after a meeting of the labour commission, at which Mann had declared that he was favourable to the establishment of a labour department which should be charged with the duty of both obtaining and broadcasting information. Mann had especially stressed the necessity of having in each industrial centre a group of persons entrusted with the responsibility of collecting details concerning their own district, and the utilisation of such information to the best advantage. Yet on 19 November 1892 he turned down Mundella's offer, writing to say:

'I consider it of the very highest importance to the future good development of the nation that such a department should be established and take its rightful place in the government; and to be allowed to work therewith would be a great honour to any man who, like myself, is earnestly anxious for the success of such a department. At the same time, knowing that such a position limits one seriously from indulging in that general advocacy of reforms which I consider such an essential part of the conditions of progress, and without which healthy activity flags and dies, I have resolved that I will continue to organise, and if possible, to educate public opinion to enable the working classes to make use of such an institution, feeling sure that in this direction lies my proper sphere of action at present.' [9]

A similar reluctance was expressed by Fred Maddison, who wrote on the last day of 1892 to say:

'Allow me to consult a few of my colleagues at Hull, where I am pledged to fight the Tory member, which I do not feel at liberty to do while under the condition of strict confidence in your letter.' [10]

He found a third difficulty in the most unlikely place—among the permanent civil servants who would be called upon to work the new department. Robert Giffen protested on 22 December 1892 against the labour department being constituted outside the board of trade proper, and expressed his doubt as to whether the arrangement would commend itself to parliament. Mundella even offered to increase his salary, and though Giffen was grateful, he declared, 'I still dislike the idea of not being part of the Board of Trade proper, no matter what the terms'.[11]

Mundella tried hard to bribe Giffen by a higher salary—so much so that on 31 January 1893 Sir John Hibbert wrote to Mundella saying:

'I did not know you felt so strongly about a scale of salary for Giffen. . . . It will place him on an equality with the permanent secretary and would lead to a probable rise of salary all round. Is there not some half-way house to get out of the difficulty? Could you not call round on your way to the Cabinet?'

But evidently Giffen could not be bribed. On 23 May 1893 he wrote to Mundella, 'I must ask you to accept my excuses for declining the new post you offer me . . . and accept my resignation from this date'.

Nevertheless, in face of all these deterrents, he launched the department in January 1893. *The Times* saw in its establishment a political move 'due to the aggressive action of the Labour Party', and did not attach much importance to it. But Mundella forged ahead with the confidence of the inspired, and on the 29th of the month wrote to J. D. Leader: 'My labour department is a big thing, larger and more important in my opinion than the government itself apprehends. It will do a great work in the future.' He had some reason for confidence. He had formally announced the details of his plan: openly acknowledging it was based on the American model of Carroll D. Wright.[12]

The first activity of the labour department was to publish, in May 1893, the first number of *The Labour Gazette* ('a somewhat startling novelty', *The Times* called it) to popularise such information for the working classes. Its second was to provide for special inquiries into matters affecting the interests of labour. About the second of these innovations *The Times* was less enthusiastic, commenting:

'Good results are not to be attained by setting up without much care offices that are called Labour Bureaux, and appointing officers who are not trained statisticians to bring out volumes within a few weeks of their appointments under pain of losing their places.'

The opposition were not slow in raising the cry of 'radical jobbery' over the appointment of the local correspondents. Mundella was accused of making his own election agent in Brightside a local correspondent, and from March until May found himself facing criticism from C. B. Stuart-Wortley, Joseph Chamberlain,

Jesse Collings and, inevitably, Colonel Howard Vincent. But Bernard Shaw, watching events, praised him for 'having the courage to pick out in every town the right local correspondent, however advanced his opinion'.[13]

Slowly, in spite of further awkwardness from Giffen, the labour department was staffed. It was separated from the board of trade, with H. Llewellyn Smith as its head. This itself was an excellent appointment, for Llewellyn Smith [14] had done good work both as assistant secretary to the technical education association and at Toynbee Hall. To help him, a headquarters staff was appointed, consisting of a chief labour correspondent (John Burnett) and three assistants (Drummond of the Compositors, Dent of the Co-operative movement, and Miss Clara Collett). In addition to these at headquarters, thirty local correspondents were appointed in towns, at salaries of from £10 to £20 a year, whose reports on local conditions could be supplemented if necessary by inquiries from the central office. They celebrated their formation by producing the first set of statistics on strikes. At Sheffield, Stuart Uttley was appointed, and did good work.

A measure of the success of the new department was the changed attitude of the opposition. Mundella was alive to the change, and wrote to George Howell, now an M.P. himself, on 24 May 1893:

'I understand that Gorst and James Lowther are to make a vigorous attack on my administration of the Labour Department on Monday next. I hope that my old friends who represent Labour will deal with it themselves. *Privately*, they abuse their own people for not anticipating my work, publicly they wish to *depreciate it and minimise it*. Randolph at Liverpool bragged about it and claimed all the credit for it. They want to prove that neither by administration nor by legislation have we been able to effect any good thing. We shall do a good deal by both means.'

The attack, when it came on 30 May 1893, fell flat. Gorst moved to reduce Mundella's salary by £500 a year on the grounds that the labour department was 'a sham department possessing no administrative powers', and also that it was staffed by 'violent partisans'. Mundella found it no great difficulty to expose this as sophistry and idle rumour.

3

From the end of July to the middle of November 1893 the whole of the Midland coalfield was rendered idle by a vast lock-out of miners. Nearly 320,000 men were thrown out of work, and over 12,000,000 tons of coal were lost. Falling prices had made it impossible for the owners to continue the wages being paid at the beginning of 1893—wages which represented an increase of 40 per cent on those paid five years before. The owners asked that this 40 per cent increase be reduced to 25 per cent, declared that they would submit the whole question to open arbitration, and intimated that notices would be once at given to terminate contracts with the men by 28 July. The greatest industrial struggle of the century had begun.

There were ancillary struggles in other fields. South Wales miners staged a fortnight's strike, and then resumed work without obtaining any concessions. Northumberland yielded to the reduction without resistance. Durham fought long but with little success.

Anticipating a long fight, the men refused to accept dispute pay for the first two or three weeks. But blacklegs complicated the issue, and there were few excitements. A warm, dry summer enabled the consumers to forget that the coal was needed, and prices moved but slowly upwards. For nine weeks both parties in the dispute held doggedly aloof from each other. Then the dispute pay gave out, and the miners' families began to suffer. By this time stocks of coal were so low that some owners reaped a considerable harvest by restarting their pits at the old rates. On 10 October the associated owners called a meeting at Derby, and announced that, in view of the sudden rise in prices, they would modify their demands for a reduction from 25 to 15 per cent. Notices were posted on the collieries to this effect, but proved of no avail.

The struggle continued in the same dogged fashion till 3 November. After a conference lasting for more than two days, the negotiators left without arriving at a decision. The owners submitted their proposals. To these the men's representatives countered with a demand for the old rate of wages till 1 April the following year and a guaranteed minimum wage of not less than 10 per cent lower after that date. A fortnight later the two parties were brought together at the foreign office by Lord Rosebery, in response to a letter from Mr. Gladstone. The result was a temporary settlement on the basis of the men immediately resuming work without a reduction, and agreeing to the formation of a conciliation board, with an independent chairman, to settle wages after 1 February 1894.[15]

The march of events provided an apt commentary on the importance of Mundella's efforts towards lowering the railway rates and the necessity of establishing some machinery of conciliation. The first of these was manifest in the shortage (and consequent high prices) of coal that prevailed throughout the country after the first nine weeks of the strike. For although the South Wales, Durham and Northumberland collieries were working at full pressure (only the Midlands, Lancashire and Yorkshire pits were out of production), so high were the railway rates, that it cost as much to carry the coal from the Rhondda to North Dorset as to ship it to Alexandria—3,000 miles away.[16] The second, the need for conciliation boards, was satisfied by the strike itself. On 31 July Mundella had introduced a bill which proposed to authorise the board of trade to take the initiative in aiding by advice and local negotiations the establishment of volunteer boards of conciliation and arbitration in any district or trade, and to nominate, on the application of employers and workmen concerned, a board of conciliation to act when any trade conflict might actually exist, or be apprehended. Mundella announced the settlement of the great coal strike on the 17 August, and outlined just such a board under Lord Rosebery.[17] Yet so great was the prejudice against state intervention that *The Times*, though it acknowledged that the strike was 'the gravest and most disastrous this country has ever known', called the 'interference' of the ministry 'a doubtful step'.[18]

Though the credit for settling the strike is usually ascribed to Lord Rosebery, yet Rosebery himself acknowledged in a letter to Mundella, 'I know how hard you have worked and how unselfishly, and what relief it must be to you that the blight on our industries is now removed'.[19] Mundella had given of his best to secure an amicable ending to the crisis, and the success of the government was an apt endorsement of the creed he had professed for the past thirty-three years.

4

Three minor reforms also marked this year. The first was the simple administrative remedy to an evil to which his attention was drawn by the Rev. James Fell (chaplain of the Mersey Mission to

Seamen), who had been convinced that much of the evil commonly associated with seaports was due to the fact that seamen had to loiter in the dock area before they received their wages. Mundella, by swift liaison with Arnold Morley, the postmaster-general, was able to settle the matter so that he could announce jubilantly to J. D. Leader on New Year's Day 1893:

'I send you the transmission circular, the first completed bit of administrative work. It is a good thing done and is the result of what may be termed *combined effort*. It is so rare for one department to work harmoniously and *happily* with another that I wish the Post Master General's zeal and generosity to be acknowledged. He has acquiesced in all my proposals, and has agreed that no charge shall be made by his department for the work thrown upon them.'

As an attempt to prevent 'crimping' by providing facilities whereby the members of the mercantile marine need not draw their pay till they reached their home town, it was a great success. Officials of the board of trade, by witnessing the amount paid out, prevented any argument between employer and employee. The reform was such a good one that Mundella's inveterate political enemy, the editor of the Conservative *Sheffield Telegraph*, wrote to convey his 'hearty thanks for the great work so quietly done. To get them hurried home on landing is a good thing. To some of them the embraces of the printed petticoated pests that lie in wait for them are the embraces of slow death'.

The other two reforms were also maritime. The first was a North Sea Fisheries Bill to ratify the convention between the countries using the North Sea fishing areas (England, Belgium, Germany, Denmark, France and the Netherlands). It aimed at palliating the evils that sprang from the 'floating grog shops' which supplied the fishermen with liquor—a dangerous practice in the North Sea at that time. Up to now all the other countries had ratified the convention, but England had not. The second reform was to appoint a committee to investigate the undermanning of ships. A bill which stemmed from this had its first reading on 24 August and its second on 14 September. Since this was the longest session the house had had for forty years, Mundella was able to submit the bill to a joint committee of both houses on 7 November, and by 18 December, with the house still sitting, the report of the committee was heard.

Such vigorous individual action won him the applause not only of the Fabians but also of more official critics. By 18 July

1893 the *Sheffield Independent* was gloating with pardonable pride that 'while other Departments are bemoaning their inability to effect legislation, the Board of Trade, already enjoying the almost unique triumph of carrying the North Sea Fisheries Bill into law, has now got passed through both Houses the Railway Servants Bill'. Even the *Economist*, declaring that the session had been utterly wasted, qualified its condemnation by adding that Mundella had passed the one bill that would cause it to be remembered.[20] Gladstone, in a letter to Morley, wrote of Mundella, 'He is a very good fellow, and has done himself much credit in the present government'.[21] Nine days after he had resigned the premiership, his successor, Lord Rosebery, speaking on 'Social Problems' to the L.C.C. (then fast becoming the greatest exemplar of collectivist administration), showered praise on Mundella. Praising his attempts to lessen the working hours of railway servants, he declared that Mundella's labour department was 'the envy and imitation of continental nations, and the best equipped in the world'. He further declared, 'If this government had existed only for the purpose of producing the *Labour Gazette*, I venture to say it would not have lived in vain'.

Less than two months later, Lord Rosebery had lost him.

5

Ever since Mundella had been in parliament he had been closely linked with the New Zealand Loan and Mercantile Agency. In 1869, when he had joined the board, the managing director had been Falconer Larkworthy—a West-countryman eight years younger than himself.[22] Larkworthy, who had been then the managing director for three years (he was to remain so for another thirty years), was much impressed by Mundella's face and figure, his robust optimism, and his wide knowledge of blue books and consular reports. These qualities prompted him to invite Mundella to join the board of both the Bank of New Zealand and the New Zealand Loan and Mercantile Agency.

Ten years later, in 1879, there was a rapid expansion. Hitherto the trade had been in wool—the staple product of the colony. But in 1879 the *Strathleven* was sent on a trial voyage from New Zealand to England, fitted with the best-known refrigerating apparatus, and when she docked at London on 2 February 1880, the London representative of the New Zealand Loan and Mercantile Agency reported that the cargo of sheep carcases was in perfect condition.[23] To Mundella, who was in daily contact with the troubles that were continually being incurred by rises in the price of meat, this was the perfect answer. It was also a golden opportunity to Thomas Russell—an emigrant Irishman who had become one of the leading New Zealand lawyers. He was already involved in land adventures in New Zealand (among them a scheme for draining the Piako Swamp), and in 1879 he floated the Waikato Land Association, with a capital of £600,000, followed three years later by the Auckland Agricultural Association, with a capital of £1,000,000. In that same latter year, on 24 May, the *Dunedin* landed a shipment of 4,460 sheep carcases at London Docks.

By 1886 this had become a little financial empire, or, as the *Railway Shareholder* called it on 11 March of that year, 'a nice little family party'. The other participants in the control of these expanding companies were Sir James Fergusson, H. J. Bristow, Sir E. Stafford, W. K. Graham and Sir John Gorst. The extent of their responsibility ranged over the New Zealand Loan and Mercantile Agency, the Auckland Agricultural Company, the New Zealand Land Mortgage Company, the Bank of New Zealand, the Waikato Land Association, the Wellington and Manuwater Railway Company and the Commercial Bank of South Australia, and it embraced capital investments of £14,500,000.

Of these, the New Zealand Loan and Mercantile Agency was most encouraging. Started in 1865 with a capital of £500,000, it entered its thirtieth year with a capital of £4,500,000. It made advances to colonists on the security of their land and produce, and helped to market that produce in England. But in 1888 friction between the London and New Zealand boards resulted in Larkworthy going to New Zealand to investigate certain enterprises. On his return a fresh debenture issue was sanctioned by the directors. Unfortunately, all the previous debenture issues had been described in the prospectus as 'amply secured on the unpaid assets of the company, and upon investments and general assets of the company': now, in the 1888 issue, the word 'amply' was omitted. This omission on the part of the directors was to cost them dear. Mundella confided to R. E. Leader on 3 October 1888:

'It is very hard to suffer for the faults of others, and in this case we at this end have done so exceedingly well that it is doubly hard. For twenty-five years we have conducted the London branch with marvellous success, and our whole losses have been in all £1,000.

'The colony has suffered greatly from depreciation in values of land, and it seems they have not had the courage to write down the securities. However, it has now been done in a drastic manner, and new capital has come from the very first banking and financial firms in the city.

'I am sorry to say that I have not only suffered mentally but pecuniarily in this business, but I can stand the latter better than the former.'

On assuming office as president of the board of trade in 1892, Mundella, in accordance with Gladstone's directive, relinquished his directorships. At the time he did so the company was paying a 10 per cent dividend. But in 1893 there was an economic blizzard, which swept away a number of Australian banks. Some failures became notorious, like that of the Liberator Building Society in England, whose promoter, Jabez Balfour, was a Liberal M.P. When Balfour fled to South America and the government seemed somewhat slow in extraditing him, there were not wanting those who said that some ministers were less anxious than they ought to be to make him face the music.

On 11 July 1893 the New Zealand Loan and Mercantile Agency announced a temporary suspension of payments. The following day The Times announced that arrangements were being made to reconstruct the company, since, as it had been hitherto prosperous, there was no real cause for worry. On 21 July the order for the compulsory winding up of the company was issued. On 4 August 1893 a preliminary meeting of the creditors took place, presided over by C. J. Stewart, the official receiver of the board of trade. The only director of note whose name appeared at this time was Sir James Fergusson. Hopes of a satisfactory settlement still delayed the order for the compulsory winding up of the company.

Unfortunately, the receiver's reports were delayed for six months. When they did appear on 15 and 19 February 1894, they caught the eye of Mr. Justice Vaughan Williams in the Court of Chancery. He made his own name, and he ruined Mundella's.[24] For it was the extreme vigilance and probity of Mr. Justice Vaughan Williams that prompted him to order the public examination of the directors to take place in his court. The wording of this order was particularly unfortunate, since it amounted to a committal for trial, with the added implication of fraud.

It could not have come at a worse time. On 12 March 1894 Mundella announced in the commons that he wished to introduce two very important bills: one to settle the railway question, the other to promote boards of arbitration. Two days later he received a letter from Harcourt, which shows the effect of Vaughan Williams' words:

'I have just had a visit from Sir Henry James. I cannot tell you what a deep sympathy I have for you in this most unexpected and undeserved trouble that has come upon you. It did not need James' assurance that there is anything of which you had any cause to be ashamed. You may be sure all your friends will loyally stand by you for whom they feel the most sincere respect and regard.' [25]

From now on events moved swiftly to a climax. On 20 March Henry James pleaded for the directors, who by now were named, and though the Court of Appeal found that the implication of fraud was not proven, they ruled that the examination must go on. This was good copy for the newspapers. They seized on Vaughan Williams' statement that the board of trade had tried to repress the inquiry, and pointed fingers of accusation at Mundella, hinting that he, as president of the board of trade, who was himself compromised in the affairs of the company before 1892, should clear up the misunderstanding. *The Times* on 21 March 1894 worded its remarks with fine tact:

'The judges' remarks can hardly mean anything else [i.e. that Mundella had tried to suppress the inquiry]. Let us hope that Members of Parliament will not be withheld by mistaken considerations of courtesy of giving Mr. Mundella an opportunity of clearing the matter up by seeking a question in the House.'

The following day, Labouchere wrote:

'It seems as if you are being unfairly treated . . . judging from what I hear M.P.s say, there is a sort of idea that the official receiver is acting under you. This is absurd, but if you would like a friendly question to be put to you so as to make the matter clear, I will put it or get someone to. I hope you will understand I propose this as a friend, not as an enemy.' [26]

At the public examination on 9 April, Mundella went into the witness-box. He confessed that he did hold some debentures issued in 1892, although he had resigned from the board of directors. He admitted not only the sorry state of the company in New Zealand, but also that they had trusted the lawyers to draft the prospectus of 1888. This was an astounding admission for him to make. In the light of the delay in the presentation of the receiver's report, he was in a very unfortunate position, and the *Economist* pungently remarked on 12 May:

'There have been few sorrier records than that of the New Zealand Loan and Mercantile Company. It will be for those who invested in the Company to decide whether or not to take action against the directors, and also for the Board of Trade to say what further proceedings shall be adopted in view of the evidence adduced at the public investigation. In the latter case it is most unfortunate that the President of the Board of Trade, with whom the final decision must rest, is one of those most compromised in the inquiry.'

So he resigned. There was nothing else he could do. He followed this by a letter to H. J. Wilson, which was published in the *Sheffield Independent*. In this he wrote:

'Conscious that I am that not a single act of mine disentitles me to the confidence hitherto placed in me by those who have so generously supported me in public life, I felt that it ought to be my utmost care that the department of which I was head should run no risk of being crippled in its administrative action by my continuing in the position I occupied. If I had filled any other office of the Government, this reason for my resignation would not have existed, and I should have asked for judgement only on my personal act.'

Five days elapsed before he made his official explanation to the house of commons. He acknowledged his deep reluctance to resign, for he confessed that 'to leave unfinished a task a man has set himself to accomplish is a sacrifice I can scarcely exaggerate and certainly I was reluctant to make it'.[27]

On the day of his resignation, it was a bitter pill that *Punch* should publish a cartoon of *The Company Cormorant*, depicting such a bird in city dress, standing on shovel feet that gathered sovereigns as it walked, its mouth full to overflowing of the poor fish which it was about to swallow. But H. W. Lucy (who wrote 'The Diary of Toby, M.P.') consoled him in private with comforting words, and wrote in his *Punch* column of Mundella's speech in the house:

'The House felt that here was a good man suffering with adversity. That it was undeserved, had swooped down, and blighted temporarily an honourable career when it seemed to have reached its serener heights, made the calamity none the less hard to bear. Mundella comported himself with the dignity that commanded the respect of the House. Sat down amid cheering on both sides.'[28]

Even the *Economist*, which had been in the van of those who cried for his resignation, now moderated judgment after the event:

'It is quite right that he should resign, and we regret that he did not do so before public opinion had expressed itself in so exemplary a fashion . . . the business is a most unhappy one for Mr. Mundella, who is probably guilty of nothing but the carelessness characteristic of a guinea-pig director.'

While the *Illustrated London News* pointed a further moral:

'He has incurred no personal discredit . . . and is one of the victims of a commercial system which is certainly open to improvement. The custom by which public men join boards of directors, when they are unable to give the necessary supervision to complicated practical affairs, is sufficiently condemned by the resignation of one of the most competent administrators in the government. Mr. Mundella is an old and valued public servant and his misfortune should have the effect of rousing public opinion to demand a reform of this irresponsible system of directorships.'

It was more than a personal tragedy, for it helped to discredit the idea of which his life had been the testament. Liberalism, already suspect by labour groups because of the suspicion of 'vested interest' which it embodied, now lost one of its strongest contacts with the labour world. It is no coincidence that in this very month of his downfall the Independent Labour Party should adduce, as one of its arguments for the establishment of an industrial commonwealth, that 'to members of the Independent Labour Party, plutocratic Liberalism, which takes £250 millions per annum in the form of interest, is in every way as bad, as wicked, and as harmful, as aristocratic Toryism, which takes a similar sum in the form of rent'.

Giving point to their arguments was the report of the labour commission, which appeared at this time. As the most costly and elaborate official investigation yet undertaken, something more than the issue of sixty-six blue books was expected. The recommendations showed a radical fission in the opinion of the commission itself. The majority were not prepared to recognise the state as an industrial arbitrator; the minority wanted it to be something more. This fission was eagerly seized upon by the Fabians, and Beatrice Webb wrote a telling article called 'The Failure of the Labour Commission' in the *Nineteenth Century* for July 1894. For many of the immediately practicable suggestions of the labour commission were by now stale, as Mundella had, during the previous year, tried to carry them out.[29]

CHAPTER FIFTEEN

The Last Phase, 1894–1897

I

MUNDELLA'S wretchedness at having to relinquish office was yet further aggravated by his inability to meet his constituents. The critics howled that he was afraid, that he could not put up an adequate defence, and that he would be accorded the same hostile reception as in the days of the Eastern Question agitation. Sir Henry James, from now on a faithful friend, wrote to H. J. Wilson on the day Mundella made his parliamentary statement:

'In reference to our conversation as to the propriety of Mr. Mundella forthwith holding a meeting of his constituents for the purpose of stating his position in connection with the affairs of the New Zealand Loan Company, I have thought it right to discuss the matter with the Solicitor-General.

'He and I agree in thinking that such a meeting ought not, and with propriety cannot be held until it is ascertained if any further legal enquiry into the affairs of the Company is to take place.

'If such should be the case, Mr. Mundella would be open to censure if he anticipated that inquiry by now holding a meeting and thereat making a statement upon the subjects to be hereafter inquired into.

'Mr. Reid and I have, therefore, advised Mr. Mundella that, however strong may be his inclinations to meet constituents with the object I have above referred to, he must for a time delay in doing so.'

Gladstone wrote him a letter sympathising with him in his great misfortune; Lord Rosebery, speaking at Birmingham on the day after he had resigned, paid tribute to 'the scrupulous sense of honour' which Mundella displayed 'in quitting the government until the affairs of the company with which he was connected are cleared up'.

He nursed his sorrows for six months; till the time came for him to make a statement to his constituents. Before he did so, he asked Sir R. T. Reid, who had just been made Attorney-General, what he should say. Reid replied on 1 December:

'I think I should say about the New Zealand Case, if I were you, merely this. That you quitted office because a Company in which you had been a director had failed in the panic of '93 and your position as President of the Board of Trade required you to take some part in liquidating companies. Therefore your interest might, to the public, seem to be in conflict with your duty.

'That really there was no such conflict, for during the years you had been a director you had done your duty, and were conscious of it—that this company had paid large dividends for 27 years till the Bank failures of '93 caused its temporary suspension, and now it is again at work and prospering, you believe.

'That you had refrained from saying anything before because some proceedings were possible against other directors, not against you, and you were advised it would be improper to discuss pending matters.

'That those proceedings had been abandoned—none had been threatened against you. The best answer you could make to any reproaches that uninformed persons might advance against you is this: the Law Courts are open— if I have done anything worthy of blame it is impossible I should have been able to say—no one has ever attempted to make me answer for it in a court of Law.

'I would say this and no more.' [1]

A fortnight later, in the Burngreave Vestry Hall, Mundella faced his constituents to explain why he had resigned. The way was made easier for him by the formal presentation to him, on the 11th, of his portrait and a cabinet of cutlery and silver goods, by the citizens of Sheffield. Irrespective of party, they rallied to subscribe 'in grateful recognition of the very valuable services rendered by Mr. Mundella to the trade and commerce of the city during the past twenty-five years'. His Brightside constituents greeted him with 'Kentish fire', a rolling, disciplined clapping that they reserved for occasions when the speaker needed sympathy. His speech, unlike his formal statement in the house seven months before, was in his best informal style.

His protests were less emotional, and the passage of time had enabled him to infuse a more detached and objective note into his statement.

If anything were needed to show he had suffered in the affair, it was the fact that he was left without much money. He had to apply for a second-class pension of £1,200—which was only granted to high public servants whose necessities were considerable. Here again Henry James proved a tower of strength, and wrote on 14 January 1895:

'I am delighted to be able to tell you in confidence that it is all right about the pension without you having asked for it or mentioned it. Whether you do or not—Hallelujah!'

The opposition papers pelted him with abuse, led by the *Sheffield*

Telegraph. Some of the more scathing articles he cut out and sent to Henry James, who replied:

'Can I set George Russell at work upon Ashmead-Bartlett to see that the *Telegraph* attacks shall be stopped. G. R. will do anything I ask him.'

Five days later he again wrote:

'My advice to you is not to enter on any controversy on the subjects referred to. Writing as a very old friend and therefore knowing your true character well, and also being acquainted with the facts relating to the New Zealand Company, I strongly advise you to take no notice of these attacks.

'I recall Edmund Burke's saying to the electors of Bristol

'I am sensible that no endeavours have been left untried to injure me in your opinion but the use of character is to be a shield against calumny.'

And I am equally sure that the estimation in which you are held by your many friends is a perfect shield to you and that there is no act of yours in connection with the New Zealand Company or otherwise which should cause any political friend to refrain from supporting you.' [2]

2

He took the advice. By March 1895 he was back to his old form again—arbitrating in the Hanley Pottery dispute. His personal advice to William Owen, the men's leader, to show a more friendly spirit, and to Thomas Twyford, to deal with the men direct, instead of leaving it to the manager, bore fruit. Both were grateful. Both not only wrote individually to say so, but more formally expressed their 'gratitude for your disinterested labours in connection with the matter. The manner in which you conducted the arbitration was perfectly satisfactory to both employers and men and their representatives.' [3]

As an accompanying gift they presented him with an afternoon-tea service adorned with figures emblematic of arbitration.

He was also busily occupied with a task which had been given him during the dark aftermath of his resignation. This was the chairmanship of the committee which was examining the condition of the poor law schools in London. Poor law schools, as they existed in the last decade of the century, were a disgraceful survival of an age when to be poor was to be evil. Many of these pauper children were herded into large barracks, where they were subject to the iron discipline of the officers. In this unregulated community life, little care was taken to prevent scourges like ringworm and ophthalmia afflicting the children. Over half the total of 18,000 children in poor law schools lived in institutions of the barrack type and there were deeper, more spiritual diseases than ringworm and ophthalmia. Through the mists of official secrecy leaked information of cases like that of Ella Gillespie, an officer in the Hackney pauper schools. Her treatment of delinquent children was found to vary from beating them with stinging-nettles, to making them kneel against hot-water pipes. She was known to bang their heads against the wall until the blood flowed. Her punishment was five years imprisonment. Another, even more scandalous case, arose in 1894, when 141 children in a barrack school fell ill through eating meat from the officers' waste. Investigations showed that the officers had been taking the meat, and having themselves consumed the best, allowed the children to have the rest.

This latter case provoked the inquiry. With Mundella on the committee were Sir John Gorst, Lyulph Stanley, the Rev. Brooke Lambert, Mrs. Barnett, Sir J. Russell Reynolds and Mr. W. Vallence. Later, Dr. E. Nettleship came in place of Sir J. Russell Reynolds, since it was found that the numerous cases of ophthalmia and ringworm made the services of a doctor necessary.[4] Joshua Fitch, too, was called in. Mundella wrote to him:

'I am satisfied that a report from you upon these schools would be a great national advantage. The opportunity is too good and too important to be lost, and I should be grateful to you if you would confer with me upon it.' [5]

Throughout the year 1895 the committee continued its work. It sat fifty times, interviewed seventy-three witnesses and asked 17,566 questions. Each member inspected schools as he (or she) pleased. Towards the end of 1895, after the general election, Gorst became vice-president of the council, Mundella's old office from 1880 to 1885. This did not make for the harmonious working of the committee. As Mrs. Barnett wrote on 7 December 1895, 'Gorst is so able and so hasty that the elements soon make a blaze'.[6] The day before this, another member of the committee, the Rev. Brooke Lambert, wrote to sympathise with Mundella at Gorst's conduct:

'The conduct of that particular member of our committee who caused all the unpleasantness last Wednesday has seemed to me throughout undignified, and very near ungentlemanly. Certainly it is not what one expects of a man who has had to deal with big questions.'

Mundella's own conduct was praised by Brooke Lambert some time later, who found his conduct as chairman so impressive that he wrote:

'What I knew before of his industry, his great kindness, his tact and courtesy, and above all his genuine sympathy with all who needed help was especially brought home and magnified by what passed on that committee.' [7]

The report bore Mundella's impress. It dealt with the moral issue. Condemning the barrack schools because their very nature led to cruelty and injured the full development of pauper children, the report recommended that a new metropolitan authority charged with a minute supervision of all poor law institutions should replace the existing one. The education department should inspect the schools themselves. But the very publication of the report was launched into a sea of controversy. Up to the last month of his life Mundella had to press for the implementation of this report.[8]

3

At the general election on 2 July 1895 he was returned unopposed for Brightside. The day after the election Henry James wrote to him:

'Your unopposed return met my newly opened eyes this morning. Now I want you to look back just a year ago, when I used to tell you that everything would necessarily come right. Now has not my prediction come aright?

'Here you are unopposed for Sheffield with the goodwill and good opinion of every human being who knows you—not a soul has been able to point to one act of your life you need be ashamed of.

'There you are once again back on the front opposition Bench just as you would have been if there had been no breeze. It must have pleased you too from one point of view to see Gorst in the Government and George Russell trusted not only by the South Eastern people but by lots of different sorts and classes.

'No my dear A. J. every cloud has passed and here you are as ready again for office as you would have been if that little brute Vaughan Williams had never devilled for Halsbury.

'We shall win at these elections but I doubt of the government having a long life, and then, back you are.' [9]

It was some consolation to know that in the same election both Morley and Harcourt, whose quarrels had done so much to weaken the Liberal party after Gladstone's retirement, were unseated. The Conservative majority of 152 sustained a Conservative ministry which the *Economist* called 'the most powerful of the century'. In it his two old offices were held by C. T. Ritchie and Sir John Gorst, both of whom had ideas fundamentally opposed to his own. It was in opposition to the translation of these ideas into practice that Mundella once more found his tongue.

Ritchie at the board of trade had, in the previous Conservative ministry, been responsible for the highly successful experiment of setting up county councils. These county councils, throwing off technical education committees to levy the technical education rate and administer the whisky money, were encroaching more and more on the domain of the school boards. Thus there were two authorities now in the field of local educational administration. To the county councils the Conservatives were prepared to lend all their assistance; here they could fight the battle against the school boards on behalf of their clerical supporters.

This was seen by Sir John Gorst, now holding the office of vice-president of the council. He was well aware of the fact that the Conservative victory at the polls was, as Lord Cranborne said, largely due to the supporters of the voluntary schools. The primate voiced the general feeling of the established church on 15 January 1895, when he had publicly attacked the board schools as not giving sufficient religious education, and complained that the voluntary schools (who did) were pinched to the point of extinction by the insensate demands of the education department.

In response to this pressure, and fortified by Ritchie's administrative precedents, Gorst, in 1896, proceeded to introduce a bill which would not only aid the voluntary schools, but aid them through these county authorities: thus undercutting and undermining the very roots of the board school system. That this bill was but a prelude to the complete uprooting of school boards all over the country, Mundella was convinced. To him it represented the complete reversal of the policy to the construction and maintenance of which he had devoted much of his political life. Such a bitter pill he refused to swallow. The attempt to make him do so aroused him from his quasi-retirement and brought him back into the parliamentary arena.[10]

He saw grave dangers in Gorst's bill besides this: dangers of denominational warfare being revived; the 1870 compromise being overturned; the principle of community control of local schools abandoned for administration by a soulless bureaucracy of a county council. He described the bill as 'a revolutionary, reactionary and insidious measure', and went to Sheffield to stir up his constituents on the subject. The decentralisation which Gorst claimed as meritorious, he re-labelled as 'disorganisation'. He accused Gorst of throwing to the winds the accumulated experience of a generation:

'The whole object of the bill', he vociferated, 'is to subordinate school boards to county councils with a view to the gradual extinction of the school boards. Some of the clauses are astounding in their audacity, and we will fight them tooth and nail.

'The practical extinction of school boards is something too disastrous to contemplate. One of the most audacious clauses in the bill is the enabling of parents to insist on special religious instruction suitable to a religious denomination being taught. Let this clause pass, and there will be immediately a propaganda of Primrose dames and Kilburn sisters, and every description of proselytising bodies urging parents to claim for their children some special religious instruction.' [11]

His clamour roused others. In spite of the enormous Conservative parliamentary majority, they were forced to drop the bill, which, as the *Economist* acknowledged, was the major measure of their first session.[12] Its abandonment was not at all unwelcome to certain Liberal Unionist elements in the government itself: Devonshire is said to have remarked with a certain laconic satisfaction, 'Gorst, your damned bill's dead.'

The duke was wrong. The following year, a similar measure of aid to the voluntary schools was introduced without the direct attack on the board school system which the measure of 1896 had contained. This aid—five shillings per child—once more stung Mundella into violent opposition. It would, he declared, remove the desire of the voluntaryists to contribute to maintain their own schools: it would preserve schools that were already inefficient, and, most heinous of all, by being paid through an association of voluntary schools, it would remove such schools from popular control.

'Surely', he asked, 'the hon. member does not mean that the state is to pay the cost of secular education in denominational schools without either the ratepayers or the taxpayers, or the parents of the children who are compelled to attend them, having a voice in the manner in which the money is to be spent, or in the management and control of the schools?' [13]

Mundella defended the religious education given in the board schools. 'It is not given by little pupil teachers,' he said, comparing such instruction to that given in the voluntary schools. 'It is not suspended for five or six months at a time, but is given regularly, systematically, by certificated teachers who are capable of instructing children in religion.' [14]

He fought and hacked away at the bill as it passed clause by clause through the house of commons. He supported an amendment which aimed at restricting such a grant to all needy voluntary schools then existing, not to those which might come into existence after the act became law.

'The argument of the clergyman will always be "Do not take a board school, but rent our Sunday school, for then you will get a grant of 18/- or 19/- per head, 10/- fee grant, and, in addition, this 5/- bonus." This means keeping down the quality of education. The object of all this is to stop the growth of the board schools and prevent the extension of that education which the board schools give; in short, it will be a bonus for the provision of schools which will just fulfil the demands of the department but nevertheless be inferior schools.' [15]

He concluded one speech amidst ringing cheers when he said:

'Is it not deplorable that we should be discussing this question of sectarianism, that we should be fighting for clerical domination and clerical schools when everything round us warns that the greatest danger that Englishmen have to encounter today is the tried and proved intelligence of those who have had greater educational advantages than we have given to the British people? If we mean to do justice to our people, if we mean to equip them so that they may fairly discharge their duty in life, be good subjects, and fit to govern the Empire, we must make them as intelligent as any other people in the world. This bill is not the way to do that. This bill is a retrograde step and it is deplorable that at the end of the nineteenth century, instead of improving and raising our education, we should be lowering it.' [16]

The upshot was that a free gift of £615,000 was made to the voluntary schools, by giving a bribe of £154,000 to the board schools.

The fumblings of these two years; the half-hearted attempts to overturn the compromise of 1870 which Mundella had done so much to preserve; the continued frustration of all attempts and suggestions to improve the quality of national education; all wrung a bitter cry from Mundella in the debates on supply in 1897. He spoke with some vehemence, pleading for more effective compulsion to get rid of the daily absenteeism of nearly one-fifth of the school population. In the rural districts, he declared, the compulsory clauses of the Education Act were scarcely ever enforced, since many magistrates had evidently made up their minds not to do so. Nor could the school board officer, overworked and badly paid as he was, enforce attendance in the towns as it should be enforced.[17] The results of all this were that illiteracy was still widespread amongst those who were of school-leaving age.

To combat this, Mundella urged that higher standards should be imposed; that half-time labour should be abolished; and that compulsory continuation schools should be established; as he had also urged on the government when they had brought in their Factories and Workshops Bill two years earlier:

'Half time labour is not cheap,' he told them, 'as some people think it is. It is against the interest of the nation, who, of course, desires to see a race of strong and healthy people, and altogether wrong to put children of eleven, as the case is now, or of eight, as was the case down to 1874, into a mill at six in the morning to work for six hours.' [18]

He believed that the effective provision of a national system of education would render much legislation unnecessary. In that belief he opposed both the limitation of the import of foreign cattle and the compulsory labelling of foreign goods. He also opposed any attempt to set up official courts of industrial arbitration, believing that the interested parties 'should formulate their own methods'.

As the protagonist of these ideas, he chaired the meetings of the National Education Association. But he felt that 'he was not helping on the work, but fighting to maintain it as it is'. He saw mighty forces combining to sweep away all that his political career had been devoted to building up. Especially was this true in the sphere of secondary education. The new county councils, with their control over technical education, were a real threat to his beloved higher-grade schools. These higher-grade schools, which Mundella had done so much to encourage by his own code of 1882, were now attacked from two sides. On one hand Cardinal Vaughan insisted that they were 'completing the de-christianisation of a great many Englishmen', on the other the Fabians saw in them only an unwarranted trespass by the school boards into a field which they were not entitled to enter. Moreover, the collectivist administration of Sidney Webb, who, as chairman of the London technical education board, was creating the greatest civic capacity-catching machine yet seen in the world, was a powerful illustration of the Conservative argument.

4

So the denunciations sounded hollow: the spectres were hard to conjure up. He himself realised that he was fighting to keep things as they were, rather than moving forward for a fresh change.

Just as his black bushy beard became a white silken mane, so his rolling bass tones had mellowed too. There were others in whose voices rang a greater fervour: younger men like Acland and Lloyd George who were being acknowledged as the fighting supporters of the board schools. His own public utterances were deploratory rather than exploratory; diffusive rather than effusive; ripe rather than rip-roaring.

Yet in 1897 he was as active as ever. March of that year saw him fighting to amend Gorst's second education bill as it passed through committee, but in April and May he waned. Henry James, ever a cheering friend, wrote on 1 April, gently rallying him:

'W. V. Harcourt is really *very ill*. I am sorry for this. I fear he will never hold on to reap another harvest. I was much amused when last night the Duke of Argyll referred to your description of the Scotch system of education: "a more inaccurate description is impossible to conceive and I am astonished at Mr. Mundella giving it. He ought to know better. Of course my Lords I am quite aware that taken in its literal sense the description is perfectly accurate." '

'I observed to Lansdowne who sat next to me "Antony John is seldom as right as that".'

'Do get well soon.'

He did, and wrote a disclaimer to Argyll's imputations which was published in *The Times*. His advancing years and lonely spirit evidently came to the ears of Queen Victoria, for Henry James wrote on 12 May:

'Ever since Thursday there has been a complete upset at Windsor. *She* says you remind her so much of John Brown.... Ponsonby was quite alarmed when she heard of someone having sat on your hat at the Board of Trade. She declared you must be protected and ought to stay at Windsor always. Don't do that, but ask Harcourt how you can please her most.' [19]

On 8 June he had picked up enough strength to go to Newton Abbot, in Devonshire, and speak for his friend Charles Seale-Hayne (who had been paymaster-general in the previous Gladstone ministry). This theme was that England need not fear the capital nor the resources of other countries, only their intelligence. He quoted Denmark as an example to the farmers, to whom he was speaking; as a country which, by exercise of trained intelligence, had overcome the threat of competition in agriculture and was now exporting her farm produce. 'Unless Englishmen wake up,' he warned his audience, 'and shake off their lethargy in educational matters, to make themselves as intelligent as every other nation in Europe, this country will suffer'.[20]

He was in good company. Seale-Hayne agreed with him so much that by the terms of his will he left over £90,000 to found an agricultural college, which has, since then, become a reality.

Eleven days later, he was urging the house of commons that:

'The time has come for a new advance in our educational school system. In Germany children are compelled to attend at school until they are fourteen years of age after which they have to attend continuation school until they were eighteen.'

As Sir William Hart-Dyke observed: 'These are remarks of a very serious nature'. Pointing to a significant change that had taken place in public opinion, he continued:

'Many members on both sides are looking to a vast change . . . the only one is for the State to supply all the education from the primary school to the University.'[21]

On 13 July he told a friend, 'I have never felt better in my life'. He was then busily engaged in promoting a deputation to the chancellor of the exchequer on behalf of Firth College, which was seeking the status of a university college.[22]

He went home, ate a hearty meal, and retired to bed. The following morning, when his manservant, Henry Herbert, went to wake him, he was found insensible.

For eight days he remained paralysed, recognising his two daughters by the merest flicker of the eyes. His strong spirit did not give up without a struggle. On the 21st he died. He was then seventy-two years old. All that week a constant stream of visitors had left their cards at 16 Elvaston Place, among them the Duchess of Teck, A. J. Balfour and Sir John Gorst.

5

Even his burial was the subject of criticism. On 31 July an unsigned letter appeared in *The Times* urging that the proceedings which had taken place should not form a precedent. The writer referred to the three services which were held: one at St. Margaret's, Westminster, another at St. Mary's, Nottingham, and a third at the cemetery. 'I have not recollected any cases', wrote the correspondent, 'where the whole service was read twice over in the presence of the family and the coffin.'

Society mourned conventionally, for an elder statesman had

died. But there were many who saw, as Lord Edmond Fitz-maurice did, that 'a gap was left in the old fighting force of Liberalism'. His old fellow fighters wrote with deep feeling of their old ally and leader. Among them G. J. Holyoake, Lyulph Stanley, Henry Crompton and G. Shaw-Lefevre spoke with deep emotion. Shaw-Lefevre especially. Writing to Polly Mundella on 22 July 1897, he declared:

'Your father was one of my oldest political associates and friends and there were few men of our contemporaries with whom I more generally agreed, and with whom I had more constant relations, and you know how deeply I sympathised with him in his trouble three years ago when I thought he was most hardly treated by the government of which he was a member. I thought this must have undermined his strength and contributed in the end to his death.

'It must have been a satisfaction to you and to him that his friends rallied so generously to him so that the verdict of the nation completely exonerated him from the slightest slur on his character. His loyal and noble character shines out the more brilliantly and his death will be deeply felt by the whole country.' [23]

'To know him was to love him.' So Lord Brassey epitomised the feeling of a host of sympathisers. That warm, impulsive Italian strain in his nature peeped out in many directions: in his multi-coloured socks, his embarrassing enthusiasm, his optimism, and his invariable readiness to believe the best in anyone. Herbert Gladstone called him 'guileless', and that epitomises him. He was no sinister character, nor even a shifty politician, but a man with one idea, the constant reiteration of which tried the patience of his friends and (it seems) of posterity.

CHAPTER SIXTEEN

His Place in the Period

THE collisive elements in Victorian society prompted Marx to evolve his theory of the class war, and challenged Mundella to promote class peace. One, watching the struggle from the British Museum, suspected the British working-class leaders. The other, a practical industrialist, co-operated with them.[1] Naturally enough, in doing so, Mundella has received considerable attention from orthodox marxist historians. He has been labelled as one who tried to permeate the minds of the trade union leaders with bourgeois ideology, a practitioner of the 'subtle art of fostering and shaping the opportunist ideology of the English proletariat'.[2]

Such a label is unjust. The 'fostering and shaping' in which Mundella indulged was of a different order. Early nineteenth-century unionism, when Mundella was young, had a tradition of antipathy to machine production. Nottingham and Leicester were previously notorious for anti-machine riots, and much the same spirit pervaded Sheffield. Nor did the opportunism of the mid-century unionists need shaping. They saw in capitalism a necessary order, and proclaimed in the T.U.C. of 1877 their intention of making the 'workers themselves capitalists'. Mundella was unique, even in the sixties, even among advanced employers, in his friendly attitude to the unions. Others of the middle class with social consciences as acute as his condemned the unions out of hand. Charles Reade, for instance, a novelist who used his craft for the exposure of social abuses, spent nine years in the composition of Put Yourself in His Place, a novel which thinly disguised the fury he felt against the unionists. Every press cutting which his secretary Saunders could obtain on the trade union congresses was labelled under the title of 'the dirty oligarchy', and Charles Reade himself paid a visit to Sheffield to collect material for the book.[3] The opening passages of this book evoke a fine atmosphere of the town as it existed when Mundella first came to seek its suffrages. Others were equally hostile. The

Quarterly Review lamented the 'expensive machinery' of union-ism, with its 'infinite mischief and ill-feeling'.[4] Frederic Harrison, one of the few friends of their dark days, acknowledged their tendency to become 'exclusive, hidebound, and retrograde, slaves of their own investment'.[5] Even the Parliamentary Committee of the T.U.C. felt the lack of 'a missionary spirit' [6] before another decade had ended.

I

In 1860, when Mundella perfected the technique, the very word arbitration had no meaning, for previous boards were mere shadows. Though he himself wrote: 'I never claimed that my plan was strictly novel and original',[7] both his own contemporaries and ours have insisted that his responsibility for the practice cannot be denied, however great the evidence for previous attempts. Henry Crompton, writing at the time with no prejudice in his favour, called Mundella 'the inventor of systematic industrial arbitration': [8] while over half a century later J. R. Hicks wrote categorically:

'The history of Conciliation begins at Nottingham in 1860 . . . he was the father of arbitration . . . his grip on the conditions of industry and his extra-ordinarily sane judgements led him to the root of the matter.' [9]

The Nottingham board was the pattern from which others were developed. Its aim—the promotion of social peace—became the gospel of a generation. It was imitated in the Nottingham lace trade, traditionally one of the most quarrelsome in Europe. It spread to the basic iron trade after a lock-out of four months, and the joint board established as a result of a visit to Nottingham has functioned ever since, extending its jurisdiction to England, Wales and Scotland.

'Search the pages of history,' said the trade unionist William Trow, 'and you will not be able to find in those pages a parallel case where any system has been of so much advantage to the workmen, to the employers and to the trade of the district as arbitration has been to our workmen in the North of England.' [10]

The practice not only spread to other industries, but it afforded to many political leaders a valuable training in the management of economic questions, and a unique apprenticeship in a sphere of political life which was to become more common as the century drew to its close. Joseph Chamberlain, in spite of his later disparaging remarks on the 'rough arbitrament of strikes and lock-outs', gained stature from his presidency of the South Staffordshire Mill and Forge Wages Board, set up in 1876, for whom he arbitrated till he joined the Liberal cabinet in 1880. Similarly, Henry James was able to utilise the sense of sportsmanship which made him president of the M.C.C. to establish a great reputation in the labour world by participating in similar industrial arbitraments; while James Frazer's tenure of the episcopal see of Manchester was made all the more notable by his arbitraments of the disputes in the painting trades of his diocese in 1874 and 1876.

But the chain reaction consequent on Mundella's establishment of the first working board at Nottingham is implicit in the industrial history of the rest of the century, and prepared the way for the one beyond. It foreshadows the Whitley Councils of 1917, the National Industries Conference of 1919, and the Turner–Melchett Conference of 1929. Indeed, the resemblance of the spirit animating the Nottingham board to that animating the Whitley Councils can be seen from Mundella's evidence to the Royal Commission on Trade Unions in 1867:

'One of the most evident results of this interchange of thought and opinion is that the workman becomes better acquainted with the laws which govern trade and commerce and with the influence of foreign competition, and the master learns how to appreciate the difficulties of the workman and to sympathise more with his trials and struggles to maintain and improve his position.' [11]

It is this wider significance of arbitration which constitutes Mundella's contribution to the practice and thought of his time. For his success at Nottingham in 1860 set two very important ideas in motion. The first was that trade unions were a help, not a hindrance, to business: 'We could have done nothing', he told the royal commission, 'without the organisation of the unions'.[12] This generous and unqualified recognition both of the ideas animating and the structure sustaining the workers in their fight for better standards was unique among employers of the time, and undoubtedly helped many of the economists to abandon their adhesion to the Wages Fund theory.[13] The second idea was even more novel: that discussion between employers and labour, equally represented, on such a basic question as wage rates, could not only be allowed, but deliberately promoted. These discussions, moreover, were not to consist of a deputation of workers meeting the masters at the end of a table, but were to be carried on round a table, with every person treating his neighbour as an equal, and agreement being reached without the necessity of the chairman having to give a casting vote.

In the thirty years that followed, Mundella's original board waxed, waned and disappeared, but the idea behind it persists even today in the Wagner Act and Taft–Hartley laws in the United States of America.[14] By the end of the century it was being promoted by such diverse political figures as Lord Randolph Churchill, Joseph Chamberlain and James Bryce.[15] Also, in those thirty years the symbiosis between capital and labour constituted the strength of the Liberal party. The labour groups, though they might pass resolutions about labour representation, led the Liberal middle classes along collectivist paths. In their pilgrimage, the Liberal party lost the propertied interests, first in land, then in railways. These men of property hastened to cross the road to board the Conservative coach, hoping that it would take them back the way they came. But, as one disappointed traveller observed, the Conservative coach did not run that way. It travelled, if anything, even faster along the collectivist road than did the Liberals.

2

No Liberal statesman better illustrates this collectivist trend than Mundella. Two new ministries of the crown can trace their origin to reforms initiated by him when he was in office. The Department of Agriculture, established in 1889, partially due to his casting off the veterinary functions of the Committee of Council in 1884, and the Fisheries Department of the board of trade set up in 1886, were both in turn merged into the Ministry of Agriculture and Fisheries in 1919. Similarly the Ministry of Labour, when it was created in 1916, took over the duties of his Labour Department, first set up as a Bureau of Labour Statistics in 1886, and later given stature by his administrative reforms of 1893. The skeletal framework of the system of labour exchanges was but a logical extension of the functions of the local labour correspondents whom he first appointed in 1893.[16]

Not only in the formal pattern of the machinery of government did he make changes, but also in the spirit in which it was carried out. He ensured that the bureaucracy was responsive to the party in power. At the Committee of Council, his Code Committee was quite a new thing. For the idea that either the vice-president or his inspectorial mandarins could ever need advice was quite alien to the traditions of a department once presided over by Robert Lowe. In this Code Committee we are justified in seeing the prototype of the present Consultative Committee which is recruited from outside the bureaucracy to advise the minister of education on matters of policy. Mundella's regimen, both at the Committee of Council and at the board of trade, was marked by excellent appointments: Patric Cumin and Sir Courtney Boyle being two among many. His ever-active wish to recruit his inspectors from the ranks of experienced teachers and his labour correspondents from experienced trade unionists, showed that he was a realist as far as administration was concerned. Not for him the bureaucracy of a caste which would paralyse the working of the machine.

Lastly, in his attitude to the over-mighty pressure group he acted in the best traditions of English government. Factory employers, railway shareholders, closed scholastic corporations: all had to surrender to the over-riding claims of the public's real needs. This was Matthew Arnold in practice, the new idealist theory of the state which was to be so brilliantly expounded by T. H. Green and Bernard Bosanquet. The state, as the embodiment of the best selves of all its members, was to regulate railway rates, compel children to attend school, support local colleges of technology. All this was done quietly and without ostentation.

As he himself wrote early in his administrative career:

'My success is really due to *hard work*, and a certain shrewdness, or common sense, or instinct, *whatever you like to call it*, which keeps me out of blunders. My versatility is inherited, so is my elasticity; but while I know I am not a genius, I am conscious of a power and love of hard work; and though I say it, I am sincere and honest.' [17]

He was a Fabian before the Fabians, even in name. [18]

3

His activity was pressurised by one of the most difficult constituencies in England. 'Sheffield! Sheffield! Damn bad place Sheffield!' George III had growled as his ministers prepared to arraign the local newspaper editor on a charge of high treason. This radical tradition had buoyed up such later agitators as Harney and Holyoake: the former famous as the first English marxist, the latter notorious in his day and age as an evangelical secularist. Nor was this the only contact which the town had with the doctrines of Marx. One Sheffield editor and politician, Isaac Ironside, printed Marx's comments on foreign affairs. The *Sheffield Free Press* had a brief but vigorous life, and its editor was still alive to plague Mundella when he first appeared to solicit the votes of the Sheffield workmen.[19]

Not only was this radical tradition solidly behind him, but he was also forced to trim his sails to nonconformist winds. Though he never showered money on their chapels, as Hadfield did, he was forced to lend an ear to their dislike of brewers and clergy. Their little chapels, once embellished with names like Mount Zion, Zoar and Bethel, are today being rapidly converted into furniture repositories, cinemas, repertory theatres, factories and schools. Then, however, they were active cells of Liberal sentiment. J. H. Barber in his Quaker Adult Schools,[20] Walter Lenwood at Nether Chapel,[21] John Manning at Upper Chapel,[22] John Calvert at Zion Chapel in darkest Attercliffe,[23] James Stacey at the Methodist New Connexion College among the mansions of Ranmoor,[24] all kept the moral sense of their congregations alive. In the congregations were men like Robert Leader with his two sons: and H. J. Wilson, whose enthusiasm nearly upset the Liberal cause in 1874.

It was this emotive element in the Liberal party of Sheffield which provided the force behind Mundella's public utterances. Their moral horror at the Bulgarian atrocities was a far more effective agent in the revival of Liberalism than all the mathematical calculations of Schnadhorst and the National Liberal Federation.[25] And to the working men of the congregations there seemed to be a curious analogy between the downtrodden Hebrews of the Old Testament, and the exploited working-men of the new industrial dispensation. Such men learnt their oratory in the lay preachers' pulpit, and exercised it in the Trades Council.

Mundella himself had led a Liberal group in Nottingham, where the experience he had won with 'Number 30' enabled him to guide the fortunes of its unhappy Sheffield counterpart. The adjective is almost inadequate to describe the state of perpetual disorganisation which obscured so much abundant life. The roots were divided. On one side were the manufacturers like Mappin and Firth, whose frail Liberalism had to be cosseted and nourished; on the other were the hardy spokesmen for the trade unions, like

Rolley and Uttley, whose capacity for causing umbrage varied directly with the economic winds of the times.[26] Making sure that they were divided, and taking good care that any division should be permanent, was one of the ablest editors of the day— W. C. Leng—whose *Sheffield Telegraph* never failed to garner a rich harvest for its columns from Liberal discords. As Mundella wrote with feeling after the disappointment of the 1880 election: 'The *Telegraph* is the real source of the mischief'.

Mundella did his best to preserve a united front. He was in constant touch with Normansell of the miners, Dronfield of the Amalgamated Trades, and later Uttley of the Federated Trades Council. He urged them to move for political objects like the county franchise in 1873, and eleven years later could privately exult to Leader after it had been secured:

'We are passing quietly through a great revolution, which will have a powerful bearing on the future destinies of the country. We are going straight for Democracy, and I am glad of it. The days of "Stout Earls" who are little better than *stupid fools* are numbered.' [27]

He also urged Leader to cultivate the industrial oligarchy of Sheffield:

'We must strengthen ourselves with people of social standing and moderate views in the locality. I know it is not a pleasant doctrine for our Radical friends. . . . I think if Mr. Mappin were to throw himself into public life and be liberal with his purse in promoting organisation, and in helping to establish clubs in all the outlying districts, he would render us the service of which we stand in most need . . . he would either bring to us, or neutralise, many of those timid but influential people who turn the scale at any election.' [28]

And when Leader found it even beyond him, Mundella remarked:

'I think the middle class of Hallamshire—well, I had better not say what I think. There are just enough good men like yourself and Mappin to save them from the fate of Sodom and Gomorrah.' [29]

4

His strong feeling sprang from the indifference of that middle class towards his efforts on behalf of the commercial interests of the borough. From January 1871, when he first attended a meeting of the chamber of trade, he was an active agent in the promotion of their causes. One has only to riffle the pages of *Hansard* to see how patient and persevering was his attendance at all discussions which bore on the trade of the town. Especially was this so in the matter of the trade-marking of goods—a matter which affected them with increasing intensity as German cutlery began to flood the markets which Sheffield had hitherto monopolised.

For this competition, some Sheffield cutlers were partly to blame. In the heyday of the trade, when orders flowed in so fast that it was impossible to execute them, certain cutlery firms had subcontracted German firms to manufacture goods for them, marking them with Sheffield marks, and importing them as being of their own manufacture, and possibly re-exporting them again. Such trade, while it lasted, was a profitable one, but it ran counter both to the best interests and traditions of the town. For the 350-year-old Cutlers' Company, as a collective conscience, was endowed with the right, not only of granting marks, but of inspecting the works to which they were granted and burning unworthy products. To many of its members such sharp practice was very damaging, since German manufacturers, eager to learn from their rivals, turned to the manufacture of cutlery on their own account, marking the inferior wares as made in Sheffield, and the best with its proper place of origin. Thus the traditional character of Sheffield cutlery was prejudiced, and the reputation of the town suffered.

Mundella was particularly active on behalf of the Cutlers' Company. In 1872, in the Customs and Inland Revenue Bill, he secured the insertion of a clause prohibiting the importation of falsely marked goods. Three years later he was responsible for the insertion, at the very last moment, while the bill was in the committee stage, of clause 9, which protected the ancient power of the Cutlers' Company in the matter of giving trade marks. As he wrote to Leader on 31 July 1875:

'The last week has been the heaviest of my life. The Trade Marks Bill introduced from the Lords at an early hour in the morning practically extinguished the Cutlers' Company, and rendered more than half the Sheffield Marks worth millions of pounds, non-registerable. From that hour to this I have had nothing but anxious negotiations and fightings. We were three days in Committee and I have made Sheffield secure on every point; how I did it, and how much labour, tact and energy it required to do it, Nixon and the Sheffield deputation will tell you. I never saw men more gratified or more grateful.'

By 1883 the matter was once more raised, when Joseph Chamberlain was at the board of trade. Again the whole question of the registration of Sheffield trade marks was under review, for the Cutlers' Company were found to be powerless in the matter of their infringement. Since it was impossible to introduce a private bill, Mundella prevailed upon Chamberlain to include the necessary clauses endowing the Cutlers' Company with further powers in his own patents bill.

'He did this for my sake,' wrote Mundella on 8 August 1883, 'but all the time grumbling at the company which he curses very heartily for old remembrances, saying they deserved no consideration from him or myself. I kept him and all parties in good humour, however, and heaved a sigh of relief last night when I heard the Speaker put the question. . . .'[30]

The problems of falsely marked goods assumed even more frightful dimensions by 1886. Before the Royal Commission on Trade Depression the labour representatives, like Stuart Uttley and R. Holmshaw, were direct in their accusations that it was part of the general employers' technique to overcome the rising costs of Sheffield labour. 'Where there are so many practising the manufacture of inferior goods,' Uttley continued, 'you have to attack a great many, and it would require a strong force to carry it out.'[31] Holmshaw produced more spectacular evidence: with a knife of real shear steel he began to actually hack away a blade which had been falsely marked as shear steel. The *Independent* ran a series of articles on the 'Trading Treason' which could so wilfully damage the products of the town. Such revelations were given due prominence by the American press.[32]

When Mundella first became president of the board of trade in 1886 he took action. Two representatives of the Cutlers' Company were sent to the Industrial Property Convention held at Rome in that year: a convention at which Germany was represented. He told J. D. Leader: 'So the facts will be brought out. Now in making this statement, handle it delicately. We don't want to frighten the Germans at the outset.' Leader was so delicate that Leng rushed in to claim for the Cutlers' Company the entire credit for taking the initiative in the matter. But the necessary legislation had yet to be passed, and in this Mundella played as great a part as he had in the Railway and Canal Traffic Act.[33] The Conservative bill was merged with a private one which Mundella had tabled, and the consolidated bill became law that year. Stringent customs duties prohibited the importation of any goods that could be even remotely conceived to be of British origin, while the whole onus of proof, which hitherto had lain with the complainant, was now transferred to the defendant. Well might the *Independent* crow: 'At length we have got a Merchandise Marks Bill on which we are able to look with unprecedented satisfaction'.

The increasing pressure of foreign competition and the loss of the world market led to the rise of a strong protectionist element in the town. As a devout free-trader, Mundella was horrified at the thought of the labour movement succumbing to such a sorry expedient. By 1889 he was lamenting that Broadhurst had been to see him with disturbing news:

'The Trade Unions have been *got at* for the first time. Money has been lavishly spent in paying for delegations to London, hotel expenses, etc., and Shipton has been the organ of demoralisation. Nothing, however, can be said of this, as it would only make matters worse. *Uttley is bitten with the thing*, and I have had resolutions from all the unions. Uttley is a good fellow of very narrow intelligence and bad judgment, and is ready to embrace protection in every form. It is pure nonsense to suppose that because we prohibit fraudulently marked merchandise, indecent literature, and other baneful things, that we are to treat cheap food in the same manner.' [34]

Not for nothing did he ask to give the prizes at a Sheffield school in the following year, adding that he had a hundred copies of the *Life of an English Hero*, and asking: 'Would it be right to give a single copy, on my own account, to each of the prize-winners? Would it be deemed political? If not, how many copies would be needed for the prize-winners?' [35]

The hero in question was, of course, Richard Cobden.

5

Mundella's positive answer to all the critics was a simple one: cultivate the national intelligence. 'The grandest mine this country possesses', he repeated, 'lies in the intelligence of its inhabitants.' It was this that made him independent of both the old Education League and Union. 'A sound logical theory would never set up existing denominational schools, but there they are, and the nation has paid a large proportion of the cost,' he remarked not long after he had entered parliament. And again, 'I want enough schools and sufficient pressure to bring the children to them; but I don't care how this is accomplished if it is done in fairness to all classes and all creeds.' [36]

This animated his attitude to primary education. He tried to persuade Forster to adopt some measure of compulsion in 1870.[37] He urged that the best factory schoolmaster was the inspector, and pressed for the steady raising of the age at which a child could begin half-time labour. Yet he was more than Shaftesbury's spiritual legatee. For Shaftesbury the 'all-conquering march of intellectual power' was a cause for lament, but for Mundella it was a matter for exultation. Not without reason were the doors of the grammar school, which had been slowly opened by the work of the commission appointed by Forster, suddenly slammed by Sandon. Mundella lamented Sandon's act as 'converting the school of the community into the dead school of the sect'. It was in fighting this attempt of Sandon's that he stayed in the house for twelve hours, from three in the afternoon till three in the morning, and emerged as the foremost Liberal protagonist of education.

The final deliverance of the children from the factories owed much to him. When he first took up the question in Parliament, he told Leader:

'I have been consulted about the Factories Acts whenever an amendment has taken place for the last fifteen years. . . . I am in constant communication with Mr. Baker, the ablest of the two chief inspectors, and we are agreed on a remedy. . . . His *heart* is in his work. Redgrave "entre nous", discharges his duties in a perfunctory spirit, and I know his superiors think so.' [38]

This was in 1869. Nine years later, after his own measure for the relief of children in factories had been adopted and passed by Cross as a Conservative measure, he found himself still at odds with Redgrave, who was now sole chief inspector. 'He is disposed to ride the high horse,' Mundella wrote, 'but I brought him down the other day by insisting I was going *straight to Cross*.' [39] The presentation he received in 1884 from the Lancashire factory operatives was itself a testimony of his work for them.

Nor was this the only step which Mundella took to enhance the status of the schoolmaster in society. He was as able an advocate for the N.U.T. as he had earlier been for other trade unions. He pressed for the diminution of official returns required by the education department, for enlarged schools on American lines with modern furniture, for the establishment of a regular system of promotion for teachers to the inspectorate. This above all was most needed, since the old system of recruitment from the universities tended to make the clubs rather than the schools the real centre of inspectors' activities. Even Matthew Arnold, great as he was, seemed to spend much of his time at the Athenæum. The effect of de-classing inspection was not unnoticed by Mundella's critics, who published warnings against the 'prussianising' of the schools.

For Mundella's outlook was modern. His technique of social investigation—intelligence test, personal visit and report—sounds curiously familiar. So does his argument for the endowment of more power to the state: 'The adoption of a new principle—the establishment of a new idea,' as the duke of Argyll called it in 1867. Mundella wrote in 1873:

'An argument which is freely advanced against the interference of the state with relations of Capital and Labour is that it tends to undermine the independence and self-reliance of the class which it seeks to protect, and teaches them to look to the State rather than their own exertions to remedy evils requiring redress.'

Adding:

'My answer to this is that the factory operatives of Lancashire and Yorkshire have made greater advances in self-reliance and independence during the past fifty years than any other class of English operatives. Building and Benefit Societies, Co-operative Associations, both for distribution and production, have taken their rise and flourish among them on a scale of magnitude unknown in any other part of the United Kingdom.' [40]

At the same time as he successfully campaigned for the emancipation of the children from the factories, he urged the establishment of vocational institutions in the large towns. His first public address after he had been adopted as the parliamentary candidate for Sheffield was devoted to education. In January 1869 he was exhorting Leader to extend the scope of the Sheffield School of Science and Art: 'Sheffield ought to have not less than 800 students and under the new science minutes, chemistry, metallurgy and mechanics ought to be taught to as many more. This is reckoning very moderately. . . .' He offered to get Ruskin or Henry Cole to come down and speak, and indicated that government grants were available for extensions. But by February the truth was made known to him, and he lamented: 'Schools of art will not prosper if they are made the vehicles of party displays. I am very sorry to find that Sheffield school ranks so low.'

When a real opportunity came five years later to help in the establishment of a college for adult education, he was eager to co-operate. 'That university movement is a grand one,' he told

Leader on 1 December 1874, 'but pray keep Miss Lucy Wilson out of it. Let it be done by men. Get Stuart and a deputation from Cambridge, and Morse and a deputation from Nottingham. If you have any difficulty, let me help you.' He thought so much of the movement that he left London at a time when there was a great need of his presence in order to speak at the inaugural meeting.

At the same time he had been active in securing the establishment of provincial patent museums throughout the country in order to stimulate technological education. Twice, as the estimates for the British Museum vote lay before the house of commons, he referred to this need, and told Leader, 'I hope to live to see Sheffield well supplied with duplicates . . . and aided by a parliamentary grant for lectures on science, natural philosophy, mechanics, etc.' This 'great and congenial work', as he liked to describe it, was undertaken at the same time as he was trying to help the London artisans to found their own Trades Guild of Learning, which was launched at a meeting on 14 June 1873, when Morley and he took turns in the chair. Its successor, the Artisans' Institute, he also helped by subscription.[41]

Subscription seemed to him an admirable basis on which to found Firth College. He just could not believe that Mark Firth was as liberal as Leader insisted, and wrote: 'I would not give a shilling to Firth College, and I hope Mr. Mappin will not: let it stand on subscription and not endowment. It is far healthier.'[42] But as the college got under way, and the buildings in Leopold Street, next to the Central Higher Grade School as it then was, were formally opened by the prince whose name the street bore, so Mundella moderated his distrust of Firth as a political opponent, to concentrate on making the college a centre of industrial education. He considered Bentley, the first principal, to be 'a first-rate man . . . better for the post than Moore-Ede . . . a good Liberal [who] means to make the College a success and keep it clear of politics'.[43]

But it was as a nursery of potential industrial workers that he envisaged its future. 'We are rotting in ignorance as far as the industrial training of our people is concerned,' he told Leader on 10 December 1882, 'and I am sure if you had seen what I have recently seen you would wonder how long we could hold our own against the intellectual forces that will shortly be brought to bear against us.' Not even higher-grade schools were enough: provincial colleges must go forward even more rapidly. Spurred by this sense of imminent industrial war, he implemented the provisions of the Aberdare Report, and established two university colleges in Wales. He tried, and succeeded in getting Ruskin's Museum for Sheffield. In May 1883 he went to the City Guilds of London, then disbursing money for technical education under the fear that foreign competition was real and Liberal confiscation was imminent. Thanks to Philip Magnus, whom Mundella had appointed to the Royal Commission on Technical Education, he obtained a grant of £300 a year for Firth College. This pleased F. T. Mappin so much that he intimated that if the name were changed to Hallamshire College he would endow it. Retailing this story to Leader, Mundella asked, 'What do you think of that?' [44] Mundella, however, prevailed on Mappin to give another £2,000, although the name Firth College still remained unchanged. He groaned: 'If a new church wanted building, some ignorant snob would fork out the money, although it were twenty or thirty thousand pounds'. [45]

As a member of the royal commissioners of the 1851 Exhibition fund, he was instrumental in securing a further grant of £300 a year from that body to sustain two science students at Firth College: one to be elected for two years each year. [46] The original proposal was to allot them conjointly to Sheffield and Nottingham, but Mundella fought the proposal, and secured both for Sheffield against the arguments of Lyon Playfair. The following year he was the bearer of even more good news. He had long pressed for enlarged government grants. On 28 February 1891 he could say with confidence: 'We shall get another £15,000 for University Colleges from Goschen . . . it is given to placate Chamberlain, and to strengthen him in Birmingham. Never mind, we shall be glad to get it.' [47]

So the college grew. Eighteen years after it was first opened, the last act of Mundella's political career was to promote its elevation to the status of a university college.

6

To a generation familiar with the T.U.C., organically connected both with government departments and outside bodies, fortified by a total membership of some eight million workers, the puny, almost furtive congress of 1868, with its miserable total of 118,367 members, offers a strong contrast. In 1951 the T.U.C. is an equal member of the National Joint Advisory Council with the British Employers' Federation and the Federation of British Industries. The National Joint Advisory Council functions at cabinet level, advising the party in power on questions affecting policy and administration. It also has parity of representation with the British Employers' Federation on the Joint Consultative Committee to the Ministry of Labour. It nominates representatives to serve on numerous educational bodies of both a national and international character, like the Railway Rates Tribunal and the United Nations Organisation. It is closely knit into the fabric of the British Labour Party through the National Council of Labour.[48]

When this powerful organisation writes its hagiography, Mundella will take a prominent place. For as Henry Broadhurst, as we have seen, wrote to him:

'We owe more to you than to any other single man in the House of Commons, but in addition to what you have done publicly we owe to you perhaps more for what you have done quietly for our relief and benefit.'

This, written at a time when a Conservative ministry was in power, showed that the leaders of the unions realised that the security of their funds and their right to picket in a strike were in a very real sense due to Mundella's watchfulness, enterprise and advocacy.

It represents something more. Mundella was well aware that his educational plans implied the opening up of new avenues between class and class, whereby the rigid barriers that had hitherto separated them could be dispensed with, and capital and labour could, by associating, work for the national benefit. His efforts, not so much for the direct alleviation of working-class conditions, as for the raising of their status and the equalisation of their opportunities, were continued when he assumed office at the education department, and at the board of trade.

He was as alive as Charles Booth to the evils which flourished in the proliferating slums of the industrial towns, where the dignity of human existence was outraged and blighted before it could even flower. Not for nothing was Applegarth co-opted to the royal commission to investigate the working of the Contagious Diseases Acts. For though his union expelled him for accepting office, their action could not hide the dreadful incidence of the venereal diseases in the towns. Mundella's courageous and enlightened stand for a more rational treatment of these matters and a suspension of the techniques of a police state earned him little credit at the time.

For three years he patiently presented his bill to secure for working men the right to take their seats as elected represent- atives on local bodies—a right which has since been exercised with such vigour that now they almost dominate them. By such means the dignity and responsibility of the working classes were advanced, and his own party of middle-class Liberals supplanted.

In that party he was never of the inner core. In the first genera- tion he was too conventional for Chamberlain, too radical for Lowe. In the second he was too crude and prosy for Morley, too commercial for Acland and Asquith. They were never quite sure whether he was a rogue or a fool, but they were convinced that he was a bore. In the twilight of the century his star never shone with anything like the intensity of those of lesser men. In Sheffield itself he was eclipsed by men like Sir Howard Vincent, whose baleful influence on the Conservative party congress in 1887 took all Lord Salisbury's authority to counteract. That year symbolises Mundella's eclipse in the political firmament. Robert Leader had died: and of his two sons, one was perpetually yearning to retire from journalism to cultivate his antiquarian interests,[49] while the other nourished political ambitions of his own, in which Mun- della did not figure.[50] Others of his former supporters and advisors also entered Parliament for themselves: H. J. Wilson for Holmfirth, and F. T. Mappin for East Retford, and later for Hallamshire. Mundella himself recognised the re-distribution of loyalties: 'Let the others fight, I am too old', he told one of the young Leaders. For old he was. Rheumatic gout—the first attack in his lifetime—came soon afterwards, and he had to take once more to his bath chair.[51]

But he still had strength enough to pave the avenue when he took office for the last time in 1892. There, his establishment of the Labour Bureau, with its network of correspondents, fore- shadowed the more ambitious creation of a ministry of labour twenty-three years later.

7

Though he was never resident in Sheffield, as Chamberlain was in Birmingham, he did much to enable its corporation to promote their control over the public utilities of the town. A firm believer in the value of municipal loans, he invested £12,000 in Nottingham Corporation Stock. His two political agents before 1885 were intimately connected with the Sheffield corporation, W. J. Clegg and J. W. Pye-Smith both filling the mayoral chair. Often, the mayor, even though not an avowed Liberal, would preside at Mundella's annual address, as a token of the great debt which the town owed its energetic burgess.

During his twenty-nine years' representation of the borough it rose to the status of a city, and it was as mayor that W. J. Clegg laid the foundation-stone of its town hall. Those years witnessed a considerable aggregation of corporation responsibilities for the acquisition of which Mundella's help was often sought. Apart from the educational powers with which they were endowed (powers which Dicey saw were more collectivist than any of the century), six other acts of parliament deserve some comment. They were collected in book form by J. W. Pye-Smith, after he became town clerk in 1887. The first, the Sheffield Improvement Act of 1871 (34 & 35 Vict. cap. lxxix), increased the council to sixty-four members and delegated to them powers over the drivers of carriages and omnibuses. The second, a year later (35 & 36 Vict. cap. cxliii), extended those powers to tramways. The third, in 1875 (38 Vict. cap. x), yet further extended them for street improvements, and the manner in which this act was used can be seen in the number of Victorian street names in Sheffield. The fourth, in 1883 (46 & 47 Vict. cap. lvii), conferred upon the corporation the power to raise money by the issue of stock, as well as further powers for sanitation, police, licensing and the administration of justice. The fifth (50 & 51 Vict. cap. clxxviii) enabled the long-suffering citizens to take over the local water-works in 1887, a problem which had much exercised Mundella seventeen years before. The sixth, in 1890 (53 & 54 Vict. cap. ccxxv), gave additional powers, which included the collection of all the municipal rates and a further power to increase the library rate and levy one for town improvements.

Thus, though it was only water socialism (for the gas company

334

successfully defied all attempts to be taken over, even with 9 per cent debentures), it worked wonders. From being the filthy town of Horace Walpole and Engels, Sheffield became the fifth provincial city in Great Britain, and the first in Yorkshire.

8

His strength lay in his power to take the tensions of his time. He was the pre-eminent Lib.-Lab. of his generation, though he would have scorned the title. His nature made it inevitable. Supple, diplomatic, humane, he had few interests outside the blue books, except they be in the sunny heights of Monte Generoso. With a Roman Catholic father, a Church of England school-master, a Baptist apocalyptic as his adolescent mentor, and adult association with the foremost rationalists of the time, he was not qualified to be a doctrinaire. His early chartism, nourished in the shadow of the whiggery of the Duke of Newcastle, was trans-muted by Gladstonian caution to a political outlook which won the support of such vociferous labour leaders as Odger of one generation and Uttley of the next. His house at Elvaston Place, though it never attained the celebrity of nearby Gore House, entertained such diverse representatives of his generation as Browning, Frederic Harrison, Sir Henry James and R. H. Hutton. Hutton, as editor of the *Spectator*, had the entry to most Liberal houses of his time, and openly acknowledged that the Mundella family 'were nearer the exact mark politically, socially, and in all points of feeling than almost any'.

Mundella's views had never the abrasive rub of either Morley's or Labouchere's, though he could express himself as firmly as either. Though borne along by the same wind as filled the sails of the Liberation armada, he never wantonly railed against the vested interests of the clergy, though he felt strongly about them. On the vexed question of disestablishment he parted company with Thomas Hughes, and once confessed to Leader:

'I believe that the connection to the state is most injurious to the Church and prevents the free development of Christian life within it. I am wearied and disgusted with the wrong headedness of the clergy, produced, as I believe, by their dread of the loss of the predominance and social prestige which the Establishment gives them. This connection has made them the allies of the brewers, and the enemies of the school boards, and there is no Liberationist living who sighs more for Disestablishment than I do.'

The general election which took place two years before his death put an end to those hopes. 'Down goes the middle class radicalism and the nonconformist conscience', wrote Scott-Holland at the time. 'They lie smashed in ruins. How shall we do without them? It will be an immense and perilous shifting of centres.' [52] Indeed, it was a good thing for Mundella's own peace of mind that he did not live to see his precious boards swept away and his higher-grade schools transformed into grammar schools.

But the long-term effects of his work are around us all. The fully fashioned stocking (for which he has never received his full share of credit and praise), the secondary technical school (a twentieth-century variation of the higher-grade school) and the local college have justified his vision and redeemed his lost reputation. So, too, the trade unions and the integration of consultative councils with the industrial machinery of society have developed along lines which he so shakily sketched a century ago. Well might Stopford Brooke write of him:

'He led a very noble life, and all that he could do, he did. I wish the thousandth part of us could say the same when our time comes. He was always on the side of just and loving causes, and he never lost his ideals. No higher thing can be said of a man. England is the better for his work, and we all, man by man, are the better for his life.' [53]

BIBLIOGRAPHICAL NOTES

The manuscript sources are in the Sheffield University Library, the Bishopsgate Institute and the British Museum. In the Sheffield University Library the Mundella Correspondence (abbreviated as M.C.) consists mainly of letters written to Mundella; and the Leader Correspondence (L.C.) of letters written by Mundella to Robert Leader and his two sons. Typed transcripts of the latter were made by Mundella's daughter, Maria Theresa, and presented by her niece, Lady Charnwood, to the university. Dr. Sidney Peyton has been very kind in affording me facilities to use them. In the British Museum there are the Bright Papers (Add. MSS. 43383–92 and 44877), the Cobden Papers (Add. MSS. 43647–78, and 43807–8), the Gladstone Papers (Add. MSS. 44086–835) and the Dilke Papers (Add. MSS. 43874–967). In addition to the staff of the Manuscript Room for help in locating material, I would like to thank those in the Reading Room who tracked down numerous nineteenth-century blue books. The Bishopsgate Institute houses the Howell Correspondence (H.C.), in addition to a matchless collection of pamphlets and working-class newspapers. To the manager and governors I am indebted for permission to quote from them.

The public libraries of Leicester, Nottingham, Manchester and Sheffield have supplemented the gap left by the destruction of so many provincial files at Colindale during the war. To the patient staffs of these four civic libraries, who so willingly bore many files up from their basements, I am much obliged.

Specific obligations are listed in the notes. But I would like to mention those who undertook the thankless task of surveying the work while it was on the stocks: Sir Fred Clarke, Professor Richard Pares, Professor G. P. Jones, and the late J. L. Hammond all made suggestions. Conversations with John Danby and Professor G. R. Potter, and encouragement from Professor A. V. Judges have helped me considerably. But perhaps my chief debt is to my friend and colleague, Professor G. H. Turnbull, who made it all possible. Both publisher and printer have been most helpful beyond normal obligations in these matters.

Permission to utilise previous articles in the *English Historical Review* was kindly given by Messrs. Longmans Green and Company, and for helpful criticism of one of these articles I am obliged to Mr. P. M. Williams, lecturer at Trinity College, Oxford.

CHAPTER ONE

[1] Michelet, *History of France*, trans. W. K. Kelly (London, 1844–6).
[2] *The Huguenots* (London, 1880), 355.
[3] For a general picture of the activities of these Italian immigrants see Max Beer, *History of British Socialism* (London, 1920), i, 71; W. C. W. Wicks, *The Italian Exiles in London 1816–1848* (Manchester, 1937); and E. R. Vincent, *Byron, Hobhouse, and Foscolo* (Cambridge, 1949). To balance the picture, it must be remembered that in 1825 the restrictions on the emigration of English skilled artisans were swept away, and that tide began to flow outwards to the

United States of America. See *Queen's Quarterly*, lvi (Canada, 1949), 418–24, and *Select Committee on Emigration* (1827), 4.

[4] Davidson, *Eminent Radicals* (London, 1880), 126–7.

[5] Lady Charnwood, *An Autograph Collection* (London, 1930).

[6] *D.N.B. Supplement*, iii, 209.

[7] M.C. 23 Sept. 1883.

[8] As, for example, when he once said in the house of commons, 'No man could have a greater love and admiration than I have for my country', a heckler cried, 'Which country?' At elections he was often caricatured as a German Jew, intent on the ruin of honest British working men.

[9] Bates, who was the same age as Mundella, later went to work in Allsopp's offices at Burton-on-Trent. Mundella was proud of his friend, and referred to him in the house of commons—e.g. *Hansard*, cclv, 1982.

[10] *Hansard*, cc, 239; A. Mursell, *J. P. Mursell* (London, 1886).

[11] W. Felkin, *A History of Machine Wrought Hosiery and Lace Manufacture* (1867), 454–8.

[12] T. H. Ward, *The Reign of Queen Victoria* (London, 1887), ii, 51. In an article in this Miscellany, Mundella describes how adults took opium to still the cravings of hunger, and administered Godfrey's Cordial to keep their children quiet.

[13] J. H. Clapham, *An Economic History of Modern Britain* (Cambridge, 1939), i, 563–4.

[14] Felkin, *op. cit*, 459.

[15] T. Cooper, *Autobiography* (London, 1872), 164–70. He sent a copy with a covering letter to Mundella referring to 'the bold way you introduced yourself when young'.

[16] When Cooper died in 1892, his nephew offered Mundella a choice of his uncle's effects 'as a souvenir of the bond of brotherhood and lifelong interest which existed between them', M.C. 2 Aug. 1892.

[17] See Chapter Two, n 41.

[18] See Felkin, *op. cit.*

[19] *ibid.*

[20] R. B. Prosser, *A List of Patents compiled from Official Sources 1817–1852* in Leicester Public Library.

[21] The round frame was invented by Brunel the elder (1769–1849), but the genius who made it practicable was Luke Barton. See Quilter and Chamberlain, *Framework Knitting and Hosiery Manufacture* (London, 1867), 26.

[22] Felkin, *op. cit.*, 473.

[23] M.C. 1865 (no date).

[24] Felkin, *op. cit.*, 472.

[25] *ibid.*

[26] *D.N.B. Supplement*, iii, 209.

[27] T. Lomas, *R. Harris, A Memoir* (Leicester, 1855). He returned from the Napoleonic War (in which he had been a corporal in the British Army) to build up a firm with warehouses at King Street and Braundstone Gate.

[28] *Leicester Chronicle*, 22 April 1848, and G. R. Searson, *Liberalism in Leicester 1826–1850* (Leicester, N.D.), 139.

[29] The bill received Royal Assent on 30 June 1845, and William Vickers, a shrewd City Father, said that it had altered the whole aspect of the town (*Nottingham Review*, 12 Oct. 1860).

[30] *The Times*, 2–9 Jan. 1852.

[31] *Nottingham Review*, 3 Oct. 1851.

[32] *Edinburgh Journal*, 20 Dec. 1851.

[33] T. C. Hine, *Diary of Events in Nottingham; Knitters' Circular*, July 1897.

[34] W. H. Wylie, *Nottingham Guide* (1852), 75.

[35] *Eliza Cook's Journal*, 15 May 1852.

[36] *Nottingham Review*, 3 Oct. 1851.

[37] *Hansard*, ccii, 753.

[38] Quilter and Chamberlain, *op. cit.*, 29.

[39] *Hansard*, cxcvi, 914.

[40] J. H. Clapham, *An Economic History of Modern Britain*, ii, 86.

[41] *Hansard*, cxcviii, 645.

[42] L.C. 6 Sept. 1868.

[43] *Nottingham Review*, 5 Feb. 1855.

[44] *op. cit.*, 17 Sept. 1860.

[45] *op. cit.*, 4 Feb. 1859.

[46] The others were an oil refinery (30 March 1848), a wholesale confectioners (30 Sept. 1849), a lace factory (6 Dec. 1849), the goods station (6 Sept. 1850), a warehouse (21 May 1851), Berreys' (18 Feb. 1857), a match factory (18 June 1858), and Latters (14 July 1858).

CHAPTER TWO

[1] 1834–1924, a former student at the School of Design who began with William Cope before entering the service of Heymann. Sixty-seven of his oil- and water-colours were acquired for the Castle Museum.

[2] Lewis Heymann married Julia Alexander, daughter of a Hamburg capitalist, and was the manager of A. J. Saalfeld before setting up on his own. Mellor, *Men of Nottingham* (1924), 221, says of him, 'No man did more to extend the lace trade of Nottingham'. He kept his designers together as a team where he could personally inspire them, and in the *1862 Exhibition Catalogue* his productions were declared to 'surpass those of France'. He died in 1869.

[3] 1825–78. He entered into partnership with William Cope, whose mechanical genius, coupled to his own commercial ability, enabled them to buy up the firm of Robinson, Son, and Sissling of New Basford, where he moved the firm. He was a sheriff in 1859, and in 1860 he gave great assistance to Mundella's efforts for social peace.

[4] Both of whom were also pioneers in social reform, which they found necessary in view of the aggregation of large numbers of workpeople in one area. Owen died in 1858, after spending his fortune. Salt became M.P. for Bradford in 1859, and contributed to radical reform movements.

[5] The money was actually given by his son, anonymously.

[6] H. Cole, *Fifty Years of Public Work* (London, 1884), i, 354–6.

[7] He was preceded by W. Page, and succeeded by W. V. Copeland.

[8] Apart from the Luddite riots, which made the town notorious, there had been food riots (1812), framework knitters' riots (1837), chartist riots (1839) and election riots (1841). For a fuller picture of turbulent Nottingham at this time see J. D. Chambers, *Transactions of the Thoroton Society* (Nottingham, 1944), xlvii, 29–43; and the novel by J. C. Street, *Kester Lane* (1862).

⁹ Charles Paget, 1799–1873, became a J.P. in 1839, and High Sheriff in 1844. He organised a milk supply to the town from Ruddington Grange, and gave his half-time juvenile workers a good schooling by getting William Spencer to come and teach them. He represented the Liberals at three subsequent elections, and when the Nottingham school board was created, he was placed second out of the forty candidates who stood for election. He was washed off a rock at Filey and drowned on 13 Oct. 1873.

¹⁰ William Felkin, 1795–1874, was the agent for the firm of Heathcote of Taunton, lace-manufacturers, and a great agent whose interest in the trade led him to write his classic history from which I have already quoted. He was in great demand before parliamentary committees, and did such good work that his friends purchased an annuity for him. He was mayor in 1851–2.

¹¹ *Nottingham Review*, 16 Oct. 1857.

¹² *op. cit.*, 5 Aug. 1859.

¹³ To combat the teachings of G. J. Harney (the first English Marxist, who Marx himself derisively called 'citizen Hip-Hip-Hooray') and G. J. Holyoake (the noted secularist), a young Congregational minister, R. S. Bayley, proposed the establishment of a People's College in 1842. It soon had 300 students, and when he left the town in 1848 it was continued by a students' committee until 1879. Some of these became famous: Samuel Plimsoll (1824–98) we shall meet later in these pages; James Moorhouse (1826–1915), who as Bishop of Melbourne drafted the constitution of the Australian Church; James Wilson (1825–1902), who became a newspaper editor in India and a friend of Lord Ripon; E. Birks (1829–99), who became manager of the Sheffield Banking Company; and Thomas Rowbotham (1827–98), who sustained the teaching at the college after Bayley's departure, were the most outstanding. As well as Nottingham, Leicester and London set up similar colleges, and as F. D. Maurice acknowledged, they were 'plagiarists from the Sheffield people'. The college at Nottingham began in 1846 to 'ensure the mental and moral improvement of the labouring population, clerks, warehousemen and others receiving wages for their services' and later developed into the University College. See E. M. Becket, *The History of University College, Nottingham* (Nottingham, 1928), 13, and *Sheffield University Gazette* (1950), No. 7, 2–3.

¹⁴ No. 2, 1 Sept. 1860.

¹⁵ No. 2, 6 Nov. 1861.

¹⁶ *Nottingham Review*, 20 May 1859.

¹⁷ White was a veteran of the storming of Ghuznee (23 July 1839) and Khelat. The others were J. G. Simpkins, Robert Evans, J. M. Perry, George Hine, W. J. Johnson, T. R. Starey and Dr. Ransom. By 25 Aug. 1859 (i.e. within three months) they held their first field day in the mayor's presence, when six companies paraded, mustering some 400 volunteers. On 4 March the following year they held their first uniformed church parade, and Canon Brooks preached on the text, 'Put on the whole armour of God.' On 13 June 1860, at the National Review in Hyde Park, with the Queen present, they were acknowledged to be 'the best corps on the ground . . . their marching was perfection'. By this time White had become the adjutant. See Mellor, *Men of Nottingham*, 257.

¹⁸ *Nottingham Review*, 12 Oct. 1860.

¹⁹ Cobden's American diaries were printed for the first time in *Journal of the Illinois State Historical Society*, xliii (1950), 187–203. In them Cobden reveals his

enthusiasm for American education ('I hereby dedicate myself to the task of promoting the cause of the infant school in England where they may become an instrument for ameliorating the fate of children working in the factories whose case I fear is beyond the reach of all other remedies') and his fervent belief in the Illinois Central Railway, in which he invested most of the capital he possessed. It was to examine the affairs of this undertaking that he went to the United States for the second time in 1859, where he was even more impressed by the schools.

[20] J. Bright and J. E. T. Rogers, *Speeches of Richard Cobden* (London, 1878), 609.

[21] Morley, *Life of Cobden* (London, 1881), ii, 396.

[22] Speech, 4 July 1884.

[23] He gave at least four accounts of the origin of this board which supplement that given in the *Nottingham Review* at the time: to the Trade Union Commission of 1868, to the Social Science Association at Birmingham in the same year, to a meeting at Bradford, which was printed as *Arbitration as a Means of Preventing Strikes*, and to the *Economist*, 18 Jan. 1868.

[24] Besides Mundella, the leading employers were Ward, Lee and Ashwell; the leading workers being Pickard, Hayes and Nettleship.

[25] Nettleship, reported in the *Nottingham Review*.

[26] J. R. Hicks in *Economica* (London, 1930), 24–39. Mundella was most anxious that the two should not be confused, and wrote, 'Some people keep writing about the Conseils des Prudhommes and identifying them with courts of arbitration. There is no resemblance between the two. The former are merely third parties constituted as a court to settle disputes that have arisen out of past transactions. The latter consist of the parties themselves, not merely settling past questions, but arranging the rates of labour and all questions arising therefrom for the future.' L.C. 3 Sept. 1868.

[27] *Nottingham Review*, 5 Sept. 1860.

[28] *op. cit.*, 7 Dec. 1860.

[29] 1832–69. He succeeded to the family estates in 1852, and, like Lord George Bentinck, the subject of Disraeli's biography, devoted himself to the racing world. Liberal cartoonists delighted to portray him lying on a couch, surrounded by empty bottles and betting slips.

[30] Then twenty-eight years old, an inevitable choice in view of the fact that his father, the fifth duke, was colonial secretary at the time, and owned the shell of the castle which overlooked the town.

[31] Whose zeal, alleged the Liberals, was so notorious that he had been sentenced to four months' imprisonment at York for libelling the corporation of Hull.

[32] *Nottingham Review*, 17, 18, 20, 21 and 24 Dec. 1861.

[33] It sat from 1862 to 1866, and produced six reports. In March 1861 H. S. Tremenheere reported that many employers were in favour of a general education act (*Parliamentary Papers*, 1861, xxii, 538).

[34] *1st Report*, 274–87.

[35] *Capital* (3rd edition, ed. Engels, London, 1908), 482.

[36] Nassau Senior at the 1863 Social Science Congress. See Report, etc., 63–4.

[37] Autobiographical letter, L.C. 11 Oct. 1875.

[38] Evidence to the Trade Union Commission.

[39] M.C.

40 Morley, *Life of Cobden*, 860.

41 Speech 28 Aug. 1868.

42 1820–77, 'By far the ablest mid-century politician' (R. C. K. Ensor, *England 1870–1914*, 1936, 132); 'the beautiful and virtuous mean of our present working class' (Matthew Arnold, *Culture and Anarchy*, Cambridge 1935, 90); 'the idol of Metropolitan Radicalism' (S. and B. Webb, *Trade Unionism*, 1920, 237–8). He was, like Southwood Smith, William Lovett and George Howell, a West-countryman, and succeeded the last-named as secretary of the newly formed London Trades Council, and made it a very efficient pressure group. He tried to establish a newspaper to challenge the dominance of the working-class *Beehive*, then edited by George Potter, a sectionalist whose main strength 'lay in pub-crawling' (R. W. Postgate, *The Builders' History*, 1932, 196). For Odger's activity at the time of Garibaldi's visit, see Carl F. Brand in *American Historical Review*, xxx (1925), 251–70, for the most up-to-date account of his life see the *University of Toronto Quarterly*, xviii (1948), 68–75, and for the London Trades Council see its *History* published in 1950 with a foreword by Julius Jacobs.

43 1833–1924. Born in Hull, he had emigrated to America, but soon returned, and built up the Amalgamated Society of Carpenters and Joiners. He was the moving spirit of the 'junta' in the sixties. See his *Life*, by R. Humphrey (London, 1915).

44 1833–1910. A chartist who later took a prominent part in the 'nine hours' struggle. Joined the 'junta' in 1860, and became a director of trade union affairs. He became a close student of politics, and his correspondence with men of affairs is now preserved in the Bishopsgate Institute, London.

45 24 April 1864.

46 1803–87 had been made an hon. LL.D. at Trinity College, Dublin, in 1863 for his technological discoveries. See 'The Genesis of American Engineering Competition, 1850–1870' by D. L. Burn in *Economic History*, ii (1931) 292–311.

47 1800–83, who issued the encyclopædia bearing his name in 1859, crowning a great series of popular educational works. In 1853 he had visited America, and confessed that the idea of settling there 'was not without its allurements'. For his observations see *Ohio State Archaeological and Historical Quarterly*, lix (1950), 139–49.

48 J. Morley, *Life of Gladstone* (London, 1903), ii, 127.

49 Marx to Engels, *Selected Works* (London, 1942), ii, 603. Garibaldi's adjutant, Major Wolff (Thurn Taxis), was present. Marx himself, who acknowledged Odger's part in organising the meeting, did not attend the meetings of the council, the first time because he was ill, the second time because he was late.

50 Samuel Morley (1809–86) used the great wealth he had amassed from his connection with the firm of I. and R. Morley to promote such movements as administrative reform, temperance and disestablishment. He was a supporter of George Howell in a literal sense, for when the Reform League was founded, with Howell as secretary, he contributed to his salary.

51 In this he was helped by W. R. Cremer (1838–1908), who in 1865 was secretary of the International Working Men's Association, which was intended, not for world-wide revolution, as Marx hoped, but to stop English employers from bringing in numbers of foreign workmen to break strikes. As such it

was part of the 'junta's' plan. See his *Life*, by Howard Evans (London, 1911).

[52] See the file in Nottingham Public Library.

[53] Mellor, *op. cit.*; *Date Book of Memorable Events in Nottingham*.

[54] 23 June 1865.

[55] Extra police had been already drafted to the town: 100 from Derby, and twenty from Newark and Lincoln.

[56] Mundella's account of the whole affair, given to the Lord Mayor after the event, is in the Nottingham Public Library.

[57] E. Hodder, *Life of Samuel Morley* (London, 1889), 157.

[58] L.C. 15 Dec. 1872.

[59] W. H. Ransom (1824–1907). Since 1854 he had been physician at the Nottingham General Hospital. He had once been a fellow-student of Huxley's, defeating him in an examination, Huxley as a consequence going into the navy (L. Huxley, *Life and Letters of T. H. Huxley* (London, 1900), ii, 133). Ransom was Mundella's close friend and family doctor.

[60] He previously sat for Middlesex (1847, 1852), Dover (1857–65), and Liskeard (1859–65).

[61] For a full account of this election as seen by the contestants see Bertrand and Patricia Russell, *The Amberley Papers* (London, 1937), i, 488–502.

[62] The results were :

R. Bernal Osborne	2,518	} Elected
Lord Amberley	2,494	
Sir G. Jenkinson	2,411	
Handel Cossham	2,307	

[63] M.C.

CHAPTER THREE

[1] Sanitary conditions were bad : there were nearly 40,000 back-to-back houses crowded together. Children played near open middens, with the result that typhus, diarrhoea and scarlatina were rife. In spite of the compulsory Vaccination Act of 1867, vaccination was not only ignored, but the agitation against it led to the election of guardians who had no intention of carrying it out. The Chief Sanitary Inspector reported a death rate of forty per thousand. Heeley Brook was described as 'an elongated cesspool', and many houses contained stagnant water with the foundation walls soaked with sewage. For further examples see J. M. Furness, *Record of Municipal Affairs in Sheffield, 1843–1893* (Sheffield, 1893) 151–77.

[2] 1821–1910, head of his father's cutlery business, 1841–59; senior partner in the firm of Thomas Turton and Sons, 1859–85, director of Midland Railway, 1869–1900. He began life as a nonconformist, and ended as a tolerant churchman. He became one of Mundella's most valuable supporters as Mayor 1877–8, a founder of the Sheffield Technical School in 1885, and himself a Liberal M.P. for East Retford 1880–5, and for Hallamshire 1885–1906. J. H. Stainton, *The Making of Sheffield 1865–1914* (Sheffield, 1924), 345–7.

[3] 1810–79, began life in Sheffield at Ibbetson's fileworks in 1832, set up on his own in the same trade in 1837, and in 1845 built one of the first foundries east of the Wicker. From then onwards it grew with the railways. In 1861 his Cyclops works began to roll rails, in 1863 armour plate, and in 1865 (the year after it

became a limited liability company), it embraced the iron and steel works at Penistone, and after 1873 the Oaks collieries. When he died, his interests covered 1,157 acres of land, all industrialised. Stainton, *op. cit.*, 249; *Cammell Laird and Company* (Sheffield, N.D.).

⁴ 1816–96, after apprenticeship to a factor in Fargate, he became a manager in 1831, inventing the conical steel spring buffer for railway waggons in 1848. In 1856 he opened the Atlas Steel Works near Cammell's, adopting the Bessemer process when others were sceptical as to its value, and, by concentrating on the manufacture of armour-plate, won the Gold Medal of the 1862 Exhibition. His partner in the limited liability firm set up in 1864 was J. D. Ellis (1824–1906), who succeeded him as chairman, 1870–1906. See Sir Allan Grant, *Steel and Ships* (London, 1950).

⁵ 1819–80 started business with his father in a humble way, and in 1849 opened the Norfolk Works, which, like Cammells and Brown's, were in Savile Street. He supplied steel for Armstrong, Vavasseur and Whitworth, and by 1871 was the leading gun-forger of the world, his 'Woolwich Infant' being famous. A. C. Marshall and H. Newbould, *The History of Firths', 1842–1918* (1924), 736–7. See Chapter Fifteen, n. 22.

⁶ *op. cit.*, 25.

⁷ Stuart Uttley (1827–1911), a file-cutter since 1850, left the trade in 1869 and migrated to the Atlas Steel works of John Brown. He later succeeded William Dronfield in the secretaryship of the Organised Trades of Sheffield— or the Federated Trades Council, as it came to be called. *Notes and Queries*, 193 (1948), 279–80.

⁸ Joseph Mather, 1737–1804, the poet of the filesmiths, a collected edition of whose songs was published in Sheffield in 1862. *Notes and Queries*, 195 (1950), 320–2.

⁹ 1826–69, rose to the secretaryship of the saw-grinders after 1849. He died two years after an unsuccessful attempt to rehabilitate himself in America.

¹⁰ Marshall and Newbould, *op. cit.*, 24.

¹¹ See his evidence before the Royal Commission, reported in *Sheffield Independent*, 21 June 1867.

¹² 1826–94, helped to form the Typographical Association out of the ruins of the National Typographical Society in 1849, and from 1861 onwards was a leader of the conciliation group among the trade unionists of the town as secretary of an anti-rattening committee formed after an outrage at Acorn Street in 1861. He was a founder and secretary of the Trades Council, and took a leading part in trying to settle the strikes of the filesmiths after 1865, for which see *Notes and Queries*, 193 (1948), 145–8.

¹³ Reported in *Sheffield Independent*. Dronfield was made the secretary of this National Alliance.

¹³ᵃ It might be regarded as the real precursor of the T.U.C.

¹⁴ Comte de Paris, *The Trades' Unions of England* (trans. T. Hughes) (London, 1869), 5.

¹⁵ Which, according to Cobden, an anti-trade-unionist, was what they ought to do if dissatisfied with conditions at home. The Staffordshire Potters acquired a large tract of land in Wisconsin, U.S.A., and established a district called Pottersville to relieve their unemployed fellow workers. The movement was not as successful as anticipated. J. C. Wedgwood, *Pottery and its History* (1913).

¹⁶ All trade-union historians, from the Comte de Paris to the Webbs and

G. D. H. Cole, point out the fact that in this the unions were victims of an unjust interpretation of the law.

[17] In the *Spectator*, 26 Oct. 1866, he took great pains to point out that (i) the outrage against Fearneyhough was not countenanced by the Association of Organised Trades, (ii) the association had been largely successful in preventing such crimes, (iii) the joint committee of masters and men of which Dronfield had been appointed secretary in 1861 had failed through the masters' refusal to attend; (iv) unionists were often blamed for outrages which they did not commit.

[18] W. T. C. King, *History of the London Discount Market* (London, 1936), 242–56.

[19] Quoted by D. L. Burn, *The Economic History of Steelmaking* (1940), 4–5.

[20] April 1868, 435–7.

[21] Burn, *loc. cit.*

[22] 1820–1905, who, after establishing a railway works at Tours in 1846, began the manufacture of agricultural implements at Banbury in 1848, and iron at Middlesbrough in 1853, later transferred to Newport in 1863. His Britannia works at Middlesbrough produced many by-products from tar, and he spent much in trying to make steel from Cleveland iron ore, a problem ultimately solved by Gilchrist Thomas. He was M.P. for Banbury 1859, 1865–85, and for North Oxfordshire 1885–95. His enthusiasm for technical instruction will be encountered later in these pages, Chapter Eleven, n. 25.

[23] *Select Committee on Technical Education*, QQ. 4561–795.

[24] Quoted with approbation by J. W. Adamson, *English Education 1789–1902* (Cambridge, 1930), 320.

[25] 21 Oct. 1867, reported in the *Independent* the following day. Mundella said that he had been in correspondence with the promoters of the scheme 'since the beginning of the year'. The editorial called attention to such boards as 'mitigating the evils of trade unions', but Mundella himself went farther, and insisted that without unions such arbitration boards could not work. He called attention to the bill which Lord St. Leonard had passed in that very year for establishing boards, elected by the ratepayers, but gave it only guarded approval.

[26] 1831–1923, who, while at Oxford, absorbed the positivism of Richard Congreve, was called to the bar (Lincoln's Inn, 1858), and became a great friend and ally of Mundella's.

[27] 1822–96, entered Lincoln's Inn 1844, and became a barrister at the Inner Temple three years later. His Christian Socialism drove him to enlist the services of the unions for co-operation. He defended them, secured them powerful patrons like Lord Goderich (later Lord Ripon) and put at their service the pen which had written *Tom Brown's Schooldays*. But he was not in favour of the Ballot, as he told Howell (1 June 1865, H.C.), and was only a lukewarm supporter of the Reform League (23 July 1865, 9 Feb. 1867, H.C.), because both were political and purely secular aims. His help at this juncture was to be counterbalanced by a similar coldness later.

[28] *Sheffield Independent*, 8 and 15 Feb. 1868.

[29] Margaret Higginbotham, 'A. J. Mundella and the Sheffield Election of 1868', in *Hunter Society Transactions*, v (Sheffield, 1943), 285–93, part of a larger study on A. J. Mundella and his Sheffield connections, which is now deposited in typescript form in the library of the University of Sheffield.

³⁰ See *Seventy-Three Years Progress: The Story of the Sheffield Independent* (Sheffield, 1892). Leader's effective control of the paper lay during the years 1833–75, after which time his two sons, J. D. and R. E. Leader, took over. The last named wrote a biography of Roebuck published in 1897.

[31] *The Times*, 17 and 18 Jan. 1868.

[32] ibid.

[33] *Report of an Educational Conference at Birmingham* (Birmingham, 1868).

[34] Monthly Report of the A.S.C. & J., Oct. 1869, quoted Humphrey, *Life*, 30.

[35] Organised by J. Normansell, for whom see Chap. 4, n. 6. Sheffield had its own colliery owners, like sixty-seven-year-old William Dunn, who was one of the foremost Liberals of Sheffield, and who had been seriously considered as a possible candidate for the representation of the borough.

[36] Professor H. W. McCready of McMaster University, who is writing a study of the Positivists, kindly showed me this letter from the Harrison Papers.

[37] 1787–1879, one of the original founders of the Anti-Corn Law League, and a crusader against all forms of religious tests for offices.

[38] R. Humphrey, *Life of Applegarth* (London, 1913), 66. Gladstone was also urged to go to Sheffield by T. D. Acland, but wrote back a decided negative, which, nevertheless, showed that he had no sympathies with Roebuck: Morley, *Life*, i, 604–5. Mundella, however, had the confidence of Glyn, who was the real organiser of the party at this time. See A. F. Thompson, 'Gladstone's Whips and the General Election of 1868', *English Historical Review*, lxiii (1948), 199: 'Glyn's actions with the Reform League were conspiratorial throughout'. Of Glyn, Mundella wrote: 'I met Glyn by accident. He threw off all reserve and was full of congratulations, and told me that Mr. Gladstone was much pleased and desirous for my success. He even went so far as to say that there were not half a dozen men in England that Mr. Gladstone so much desired in the next Parliament as myself. I turned a deaf ear to all this sort of thing' (L.C. 24 July, 1868).

[39] *Proceedings*, etc., 1868, 868.

[40] This was itself a symbol of the union of employer and working-class interest that secured Mundella's election. Mundella had written to Leader on 19 July: 'The more I reflect on the course which matters are taking, the more I am convinced of the desirability of being supported at the meeting by such gentlemen as Mr. Dunn and yourself . . . let me have such men as Mr. Dunn, yourself, Mr. Askham, and as many as possible of that type to support me, and I shall have no difficulty in placing the saddle on the right horse.'

[41] Broadsheet in the Nottingham Public Library.

[42] *Nottingham Express*, 20 Nov. 1868.

CHAPTER FOUR

[1] *Sheffield Independent*, 10 Oct. 1868.

[2] L.C. 3 Jan. 1869.

[3] M.C. 8 Jan. 1869.

[4] 'Search the pages of history', its secretary W. Trow told the Royal Commission on Labour in 1894 (QQ. 15182–3), 'and you will not be able to find a parallel case where any system has been of so much advantage to workmen,

to the employers, and to the trade of the district.' See Chapter Sixteen, n. 10.

⁵ L.C.

⁶ J. Normansell (1830–75), described by the Webbs as 'second only to Mac-Donald' (for whom see Chapter Seven, n. 12.), entered the pit at the age of seven, and became a national leader of the miners. In the eight years from 1864 (when he became secretary of the South Yorkshire Miners' Association) to 1872 he raised the membership from 2,000 to 20,000.

⁷ L.C. 21 March 1869.

⁸ Henry Crompton (1836–1904), son of a judge, became an ardent positivist in 1859. He was appointed clerk of assize on the Chester and North Wales Circuit the previous year. L.C. 2 and 7 May 1869.

⁹ Economist, 10 July 1869.

¹⁰ G. Howell, Labour Legislation, Labour Movements, and Labour Leaders (London, 1902), 176, places the turning-point in the negotiations as a breakfast given to Bruce and the Union leaders.

¹¹ Sixty-seven years old, he had been sitting for Carlisle since 1861. As an employer who had profited greatly from technological changes, he believed in compulsory education, and published an open letter on the subject in 1867. But at the same time he was very hostile to the trade unions: 'the least educated, those possessing the least thought for the future and employed least on ma-chinery, are the most violent and thoughtless employees'. J. G. Hurst, Edmund Potter and Dinting Vale (Manchester, 1948).

¹² Sheffield Telegraph and Sheffield Independent, 25 Aug. 1869.

¹³ M.C.

¹⁴ M.C.

¹⁵ Humphrey, Life of Applegarth, 221.

¹⁶ L.C. 28 Dec. 1869.

¹⁷ Hansard, cc, 242.

¹⁸ L.C. 3 Jan. 1870.

¹⁹ The publication of Matthew Arnold's Culture and Anarchy at this time, with its powerful strictures on the hebraistic elements in nonconformity, undoubtedly helped to discredit Baines. For Arnold's contacts with Cobden in this matter see Review of English Studies, xxv (1949), 249–54.

²⁰ His son, Lord Sandon, who later succeeded him in the title, later became vice-president of the council from 1874 to 1878.

²¹ Quoted by J. L. and B. Hammond, Lord Shaftesbury (Pelican Books, 1939).

²² The League published a fully indexed report of all the Parliamentary debates.

²³ Economist, 12 March 1870.

²⁴ J. L. Garvin, Life of Chamberlain (London, 1932). 111–14.

²⁵ L.C. 10 March 1870.

²⁶ Keighley Snowdon points out that this made a great impression on Sir Swire Smith, then beginning public life.

²⁷ Hansard, 11 March 1869.

²⁸ ibid., 8 June.

²⁹ ibid., 6 April.

³⁰ ibid., 9 May.

³¹ ibid., 10 May.

³² ibid.

³³ M.L. 25 March 1869.

³⁴ J. McCabe, *Life and Letters of G. J. Holyoake* (London, 1908), ii, 98.

³⁵ M.L. 21 Nov. 1869.

³⁶ For Cobden's American diaries, see *Illinois State Historical Society's Transactions*, xliii (Springfield, 1950), 187–203.

CHAPTER FIVE

¹ L.C. 5 July 1870.

² L.C. 24 July 1870.

³ L.C. 31 July 1870.

⁴ L.C. 27 Aug. 1870.

⁵ 'New Light on the English Background of Thomas Hughes' Rugby Colony in Tennessee,' *Publications of the East Tennessee Historical Society* (1949), 69–85.

⁶ As vice-president of the council from 1880 to 1885, he was to play a great part in the encouragement of the Higher Grade School, for which see Chapter Ten.

⁷ U.S. Grant (1822–85) had been President of the United States for two years, and was just recovering from the disastrous appointments of the first flush of office.

⁸ Secretary of the Treasury, who was not interested in civil service reform.

⁹ Significant in view of later findings of the Playfair Commission in England. The radical dislike of patronage had already begun to take effect in Gladstone's first ministry.

¹⁰ The leading spirit in these civil service reforms in the U.S.A., who resigned not long afterwards.

¹¹ An Indian, who was driven from office a year later.

¹² Speech at Sheffield, 17 Jan. 1871.

¹³ Lady Charnwood, *An Autograph Collection*, 206.

¹⁴ L.C. As president of the board of trade in 1886, Mundella was to assist and support the International Trade Marks Conference in Rome. His constituents were much exercised over the question for the rest of the century.

¹⁵ A. S. Hewitt was in the chair. The title of the lecture was 'Strikes, Arbitration, and the Civil Service in Great Britain'. L.C. 27 Nov. 1870.

¹⁶ *Sheffield Independent*, 29 Nov. 1870, the *Beehive*, 3 Dec. 1870.

¹⁷ Reported in *The Times*, 15 and 18 Dec. 1870.

¹⁸ M.C. 20 March 1881.

¹⁹ *Great Britain from Adam Smith to the Present Day* (London, 1937), 376.

²⁰ M.C. 30 Jan. 1871.

²¹ M.C. (with the reports).

²² Report of the proceedings in the *Sheffield Independent*, 11 Jan. 1872.

²³ M.C. 16 Jan. 1871.

²⁴ L.C. 27 Nov. 1870.

²⁵ L.C. 3 March 1871.

²⁶ *Sheffield Independent*, 17 Jan. 1871. Two years later, when J. F. Moss, clerk to the Sheffield school board, went to Germany, Mundella facilitated his passage by introductions.

²⁷ L.C. 11 Dec. 1870.

CHAPTER SIX

[1] See his speech at a National Conference of Repealers 9 Feb., and in the house of commons, 14 Aug. 1871; 22 July 1872; 23 May 1873, and whenever the Repeal was discussed.

[2] Dilke was engaged in promoting universal instruction in arms. Gwynn and Tuckwell, *Life*, i, 36.

[3] *Hansard*, 21 March 1871. As late as 30 Oct. this year, McCullochs the bankers were sending him statements of the pay rates of the U.S. Army.

[4] The occasion was Sir John Lubbock's motion for modification of the Code on 21 July 1871, which Mundella seconded.

[5] L.C. 11 March 1871.

[6] The first part of the bill became law on 21 June, the second part was finally defeated two days earlier, when a sudden deluge of white-shirted members fresh from dinner, outvoted the champions of the unions, in spite of Bruce's protests.

[7] Howell, *Labour Leaders*, 183.

[8] M.C. 11 July 1871.

[9] For John Scott Russell, see F. Boase, *Modern English Biography* (Truro, 1901), iii, 352-3. His *Systematic Education for the English People* (1869) was quoted by Mundella with approval.

[10] *Observer*, 17 Oct. 1871. A day later, one of the signatories to the alleged pact, wrote to the *Exeter Gazette*: 'All that has passed, as far as I am aware, is that some peers and members of parliament have expressed their readiness to consider any suggestions for legislation on questions affecting the well-being of the working classes, and to discuss them in a friendly spirit.'

[11] *Economist*, 18 Nov. 1871, in a special article, called it 'a pompous preparation for a public fiasco'.

[12] L.C. 25 Sept. 1871.

[13] S. Hutchinson Harris, *Auberon Herbert* (London, 1943), 129-30.

[14] L.C. 18 Nov. 1871.

[15] 29 Oct. 1871.

[16] M.C. 10 Nov. 1871.

[17] M.C.

[18] L.C.

[19] L.C.

[20] This established Burnett's reputation. Four years later he became secretary of the A.S.E.

[21] 2 Nov. 1871.

[22] 29 Oct. 1871.

[23] H.C. 28 Dec. 1871.

[24] L.C. 12 Aug. 1871.

CHAPTER SEVEN

[1] L.C. 25 Nov. 1869.

[2] S. Harrison, *The Great Sheffield Flood 11 and 12 March 1864* (Sheffield, 1864), W. Terrey, *The Sheffield Water Works* (Sheffield, 1908).

[3] In June 1869 the Sheffield Corporation appointed a special committee to consider the propriety of their purchasing the Water Works Company, and in

the following month a gas committee was requested to give a similar report on the Gas Works. Counsel's opinion was taken, and with his favourable report, the Corporation decided by a majority of twenty-eight to four to purchase the Gas Works in September. Meanwhile, the Water Company, having failed in their case before the borough Justices, sought parliamentary powers to be exempted from giving a constant supply of water under pressure. Parliament rejected the Corporation Water Bill in March, and their Gas Bill in April 1870. Then the Water Company obtained their order from the Court of Queen's Bench restraining the Council from recovering the £1,526 costs from the rates. J. M. Furness, *Record of Municipal Affairs in Sheffield* (Sheffield, 1893), 157–9.

⁴ Thomas Moore (1809–80), mayor from 1868 to 1871, was a brewer who had been expropriated by the duke of Norfolk.

⁵ John Yeomans (1823–87) was Town Clerk from 1859 until 1887, the year in which the corporation finally obtained possession of the Water Works.

⁶ L.C. 24 July 1871. He was an old political friend of Mundella. L.C. 5, 13, 24 July 1868; *York Daily Herald*, 27 Feb. 3 and 6 March 1882.

⁷ A landowner of Saltley, near Birmingham, who in 1858 became vice-president of the council, and in 1866–8 under-secretary for the colonies. He later became president of the board of trade 1874–8, and from then onwards, ennobled as Lord Norton, he continued as a critic of Mundella's policy. He died in 1905, aged eighty-nine. The autonomous constitution of New Zealand was drafted at his house. See Chapter Twelve, n. 65.

⁸ L.C. 25 July 1872.

⁹ For which see Chapter XI, 'The Great Citizen in Action', 1873–76 in J. L. Garvin, *Life of Chamberlain* (London, 1932), 185–214.

¹⁰ Earl Fitzwilliam (1815–1902), who died worth nearly three million pounds, petitioned against the Sheffield Corporation's Improvement Bill of 1871, and the mayor wrote to him (Furness, *op. cit.*, 167) pointing out that his objections were almost identical with those tabled by the Gas and Water Companies. Thirteen other petitions were lodged against it, with the result that a bill of 318 clauses was whittled down to one of forty-eight clauses. The duke of Norfolk also refused to sell his market rights in 1874, even though offered £267,450. Much was, however, due to the narrow outlook of the city fathers. Mundella was fond on complaining to Leader in the vein he used on 13 Oct. 1871: 'I see a pretty state of affairs in your Municipality. Everything is mean, petty, and narrow in the extreme. What a contrast to Leeds! Sheffield would do well to spend half a million in improvements. A better Town Hall might be followed by better Town Councillors, and more public spirit. I am grieved when I hear such unfavourable comments made upon my constituency. . . . I wish you would preach the duty of the wealthy intellects of Sheffield, taking their share in the elevation of the town.' Matthew Arnold thought much the same, and told Mundella's daughter so. *Review of English Studies*, xxiii (1947), 355–7 and Chapter Sixteen, n. 27.

¹¹ Humphrey, *op. cit.* 242, 264; L.C. 13 Oct. 1871, 'Applegarth works for Glyn whenever needed, and is always willing to help the Government'.

¹² 1821–81. G. D. H. Cole asserts that he was more responsible than anyone for building up the trade unionism amongst the miners, and acknowledges that the Coal Mines Regulation Act of 1872 'laid the foundation of modern mining legislation'. *Short History of the British Working Class Movement* (London, 1927), ii *passim* and Chapter Four, n. 6,

[13] L.C. 18 June 1872. Lord Elcho (1818–1914), who had carried through the Master and Servant Act of 1867, was an opponent of the Reform Bill in that year (the so-called 'Adullamites' had met at his house). He was constantly clashing with Mundella over the latter's alleged disrespect for the rights of property. For Mundella's opinion of him see *Hansard*, 12 April, 1870.

[14] G. Howell, *Labour Leaders*, etc., 197.

[15] T. Rothstein, *From Chartism to Labourism* (London, 1929), 268.

[16] *Sheffield Independent*, 16 July 1872.

[17] *Hansard*, 23 April 18 and 25 July 1872.

[18] Joseph Irving, *Annals of the Time* (London, 1875), 54. Henry Richard (1812–88) was the apostle of arbitration in international affairs, promoting numerous peace conferences. He was elected in 1868, with a majority of over 4,000, M.P. for the Merthyr Boroughs, and as such was the first real exponent of the puritan and progressive life of Wales in the house of commons; the father of that 'Celtic fringe' which was later to throw up such men as David Lloyd George.

[19] Edward Miall (1809–81), also an ex-nonconformist minister, learnt his journalism on the *Leicester Mercury*, and, as editor and founder of the *Nonconformist*, swayed his co-religionists so much that he was returned for Bradford on 12 March 1869. He was an advocate of disestablishment; a pillar of the Liberation Society.

[20] Even such an anti-government bishop as Dr. Magee of Peterborough was moved to say in the house of lords (*Hansard*, 19 Feb. 1872), 'These vigilance committees are rapidly becoming a dangerous ruling power in the Church instead of the Bishops. . . . A nice state of things for the clergy, the Church Defence Association swooping down on them from above, the Church Union rushing on them from below, while every now and then they find themselves hooked by a neat turn of the episcopal wrist.'

[21] M.C. 20 Jan. 1872.

[22] L.C. 4 July 1872, also 12 Aug. 1871.

[23] See *East Tennessee Historical Society's Publications* No. 21 (1949) for the estrangement which developed between Hughes and the Unions.

[24] Stemming in part from the influence of John Stuart Mill, whose contacts with Comte helped to popularise the philosophy, then found so congenial by the middle-class allies of the unions.

[25] L.C. 7 Jan. 1872.

[26] S. Hutchinson Harris, *Auberon Herbert*, 133.

[27] Only nineteen days before, he had also lamented to Leader that Hughes' activity on behalf of the Church wearied him. 'I walked out when Hughes' motion was put. I am sick of these attempts at Church reform. They all come to nothing.'

[28] *Daily News*, 20 March 1872; L.C. 22 March 1872.

[29] L.C. 6 June 1872.

[30] L.C. 29 April 1872.

[31] L.C. 6 June 1872.

[32] L.C. 19 April 1872.

[33] *Manchester Guardian*, 4 April 1872.

[34] 1826–1919, later Liberal M.P. for West Norfolk 1885–6, 1892–1902. He was a Primitive Methodist preacher at the time. R. F. Wearmouth, *Some Working Class Movements* (London, 1948), 292.

[35] H.C. 7 April 1872. The first meeting of labourers took place on 14 Feb. of that year.

[36] A very good date. Jacob Bright's attempt to secure the franchise for women had been rejected the day before by 222 votes to 143, and the Licensing Bill was read for a second time on that day in the lords.

[37] M.C. 29 April 1872.

[38] L.C. 23 July 1873 (a year later).

[39] L.C. 1 April 1869.

[40] Lord Amulree, *Industrial Arbitration in Great Britain* (Oxford, 1929), 87–9 and App. III.

[41] Report in *Sheffield Independent*, 13 Aug. 1872.

[42] L.C. 24 Nov. 1872. He was now a director of John Brown's, the Sheffield steelworks, which, with his active interest in the New Zealand Loan and Mercantile Agency, enabled him to live moderately well.

CHAPTER EIGHT

[1] It was in this very year that F. W. Maitland was senior in the moral science tripos at Cambridge. Later, as Downing Professor of Law, he was to popularise the teachings of the great jurist Gierke, who regarded the state, not so much as an association of individuals in pursuit of a common life, but as a congeries of groups, dialectically reacting on each other to give life to the state.

[2] *Law and Opinion in England* (1905) places the beginning of the collectivist period at 1865, the year in which Mundella returned to political life.

[3] S. and B. Webb, *History of Trade Unionism*, 311; but see F. Keeling, *Child Labour in the United Kingdom* (London, 1914), 9–11, and J. Dunlop and R. D. Denman, *English Apprenticeship and Child Labour* (London, 1912), 106–33.

[4] L.C. 3 Jan. 1872.

[5] *Sheffield Independent*, 22 March 1872.

[6] See, for instance, Matthew Arnold's castigation of the worship of machinery and Americanisation in *Culture and Anarchy* (1869).

[7] Fitzjames Stephen had been secretary to the Newcastle Commission on Education, 1859–61, and had just returned from being chief legal member for the Council in India. Edward Jenkins criticised his 'Bismarckism' in the *Contemporary Review*, June 1873.

[8] For the text of Mundella's correspondence from Fitzjames Stephen at this time, see *Times Literary Supplement*, 18 Dec. 1948.

[9] E. von Plener, *English Factory Legislation* (London, 1873), with an introduction by A. J. Mundella. Mundella's forthright advocacy of the necessity of state action won the approval of Charles Bradlaugh (*Labour and Law*, 40) as late as 1891 and the Webbs in 1920 (*Problems of Modern Industry*).

[10] M.C. Jan. 1873.

[11] L.C. 14 Jan. 1873.

[12] L.C. 20 June 1873.

[13] L.C. 30 June 1873.

[14] L.C. 2 Feb. 1873.

[15] L.C. 18 June 1873, 'The Nonconformist Committee has taken quite the corner I expected, and with such inflammable elements as you have in Sheffield, a conflagration sooner or later seems inevitable'.

[16] Francis Adams, *The Elementary School Contest* (London, 1882), 275, points out that the year 1872 'marks a new period in the growth and direction of the agitation against the 25th clause'. Adams went to Bath with the agent of J. C. Cox (later to win fame as an antiquarian, but at this time an ardent supporter of Arch and Chamberlain) to examine the Liberal candidate on his attitude.

[17] H. J. Wilson (1833–1914), director of the Sheffield Smelting Company, who had come to Sheffield in 1869. He was a supporter of Josephine Butler, as well as being an ardent Nonconformist.

[18] *Fortnightly Review* (1873), 287–305.

[19] L.C. 20 June 1873.

[20] M.C. 8 Aug., 25 Nov. and 2 Dec. 1873.

[21] Referring to the debate on the Contagious Diseases Act, which had been heard by H. J. Wilson. Afterwards Mundella pressed him to consider the adoption of Allott as a potential Liberal candidate.

[22] *Hansard*, 11 June and 30 July 1873.

[23] *The Times*, 12 June 1873.

[24] Howell, *Labour Leaders*, etc., 318.

[25] L.C. 2 Aug. 1873.

[26] L.C. 6 Aug. 1873.

[27] *Economist*, 27 Dec. 1873.

[28] L.C. 5 Oct. 1873.

[29] H.C. 30 Dec. 1873.

[30] L.C. 7 Jan. 1874.

[31] *Sheffield Telegraph*, reporting the conference.

[32] Howell, *op. cit.* 338. His circular to the working-class electors asked them to demand 'straightforward replies' to the ten-point labour programme.

[33] See illustrations.

[34] M.C.

[35] L.C. 7 Feb. 1874.

[36] Lord Halifax summed up popular feeling when he wrote to Gladstone: 'People are frightened—the masters were afraid of their workmen, manufacturers afraid of strikes, churchmen afraid of the Nonconformists, many afraid of what is going on in France and Spain—and in very unreasoning fear have all taken refuge in Conservatism. Ballot enabled them to do this without apparently deserting their principles and party' (Morley, *Life of Gladstone*, ii, 75).

CHAPTER NINE

[1] L.C. 7 March 1874.

[2] Morley, *Life of Gladstone*, ii, 80.

[3] L.C. 25 June 1874. Mundella was also perturbed about Disraeli's ministers. 'Adderley is a country gentleman incompetent to buy two sticks of toffy, and Cavendish-Bentinck a little mean drunken aristocrat, without the slightest capacity for business. He is notorious in the House of Commons for his unsteady gait after dinner.' L.C. 28 March 1874.

[4] Originally published in 1845, it was republished in 1853 and again in 1871.

[5] R. A. Cross (1823–1914), M.P. for S.W. Lancashire, close friend of the Queen. See Chapter Eleven, n. 91.

[6] Henry Higgs, *Political Economy Club* (London, 1921) 350. Goschen said that Mundella's appointment seemed to violate 'the strictly *economic* character of the club'.

[7] G. A. N. Lowndes, *The Silent Social Revolution* (Oxford, 1937), 5.

[8] G. R. Parkin, *Life and Letters of Edward Thring* (London, 1898), ii, 175 and 181.

[9] Written at the conclusion of the debate.

[10] *The Times*, 21 and 22 July 1874.

[11] A token of reward for the labour support which he had received in the election.

[12] e.g. Frederic Harrison in *The Times* 14 March, and George Potter on 30 March. Potter wrote, 'I believe the Commission to be altogether unnecessary. Its result, an indefinite postponement of most earnest legislation upon questions on which Parliament already possesses the fullest information. It effectively relieves members of parliament from definite pledges for immediate legislation given at the recent general election. It will give opportunities for prejudiced persons to resuscitate obsolete charges against Trade Unions; and it will weaken, to a most serious extent, the confidence placed in those who govern us.'

[13] L.C. 14, 18, and 21 March 1874. MacDonald's adhesion to the Commission was not announced even at the congratulatory dinner given to him and Burt at Anderton's Hotel on the 18 March. Rolley (1839–1912) was a Sheffield labour leader, who in this year was president of the T.U.C. He later became a Conservative agent. See Chapter Sixteen, n. 26.

[14] G. Howell, *Labour Leaders*, 344–9, admits that 'the expressions we used then could not be justified' in the light of later events.

[15] W. R. Cremer (1838–1908) was a promotor of Applegarth's Union (the A.S.C. and J.) in 1860, and secretary of the British Section of the International Working-men's Association from 1865. His advocacy of arbitration secured him the Nobel Peace Prize in 1903.

[16] Henry Broadhurst in *Sheffield Independent*; dated 29 June 1876 and published a fortnight later.

[17] L.C. 8 Oct. 1874.

[18] Morley, *Life of Gladstone*; Fitzmaurice, *Life of Granville* (London, 1905), ii, 134.

[19] Bernard Holland, *Life of the Eighth Duke of Devonshire* (London, 1913), i, 143–4.

[20] *Life of Granville*, ii, 142.

[21] L.C. 15 Jan. 1875.

[22] L.C. 16 June 1874.

[23] L.C. 15 Jan. 1875.

[24] M.C. 21 Jan. 1875.

[25] G. O. Trevelyan (1838–1928), nephew of Lord Macaulay, whose life he was at this time writing, was an enthusiast in the cause of Italian freedom. M.P. for the Border Burghs, he was the chief advocate of the county franchise being widened. His life, by G. M. Trevelyan, was published in 1932.

[26] G. M. Trevelyan, *Life of John Bright*, (1913), 406–9.

[27] Gwynn and Tuckwell, *Life of Dilke*, i, 86.

[28] M.C. 26–30 Jan. 1875.

[29] *ibid.*

[30] Humphrey, *Life of Applegarth*, 188.

[31] L.C. 12 April 1875.

[32] F. T. Mappin (1821–1910), a millionaire manufacturer of railway springs, who became Mayor of Sheffield 1877–8. See Chapter Three, n. 2.

[33] M.C. The writer was one of those who worked with Mundella for a common platform with the Dissenters in 1872.

[34] *The Times*, 9 Oct. 1875. Other Commissioners were Lord F. Cavendish, Sir Charles du Cane, H. M. Brand and T. Knowles, M.P.

[35] *Hansard*, 31 July 1875.

[36] *ibid.*, 14 Feb. 1876. L.C. 17 April 1876.

[37] *ibid.*, 15 June 1876.

[38] L.C. 26 June 1876.

[39] *Hansard*, 2 July 1876.

[40] *ibid.*, 10 July 1876.

[41] *ibid.*, 13 July 1876.

[42] *ibid.*, 21 and 25 July 1876.

[43] *ibid.*, 3 Aug. 1876. The debate adjourned at 4 a.m.

[44] L.C. 8 Aug. 1876.

[45] L.C. 17 April 1876.

[46] F. Adams, *The Elementary School Contest* (London, 1880), 319.

[47] J. McCabe, *Life and Letters of G. J. Holyoake* (London, 1908), ii, 177.

[48] To Lady Bradford, 5 Aug. 1876 (Monypenny and Buckle, *Life of Beaconsfield*, London, 1929), ii, 825.

CHAPTER TEN

[1] L.C. For the diplomatic history see Mihailo D. Stojanovic, *The Great Powers and the Balkans 1875–1878* (Cambridge, 1939).

[2] He accused the Liberals of wishing to 'create a cry against the Government' (Monypenny and Buckle, vi, 43).

[3] W. T. Stead (1840–1912), in his *Reminiscences and Correspondence of Madame Novikoff* (London, 1909), 276, pays a tribute to the activity of both Mundella and Leader at this time. 'Birmingham,' he continued, 'which in educational matters justly prides herself on being the first, was not disposed to take the lead on this occasion.' Stead received his reward in 1880, when he went to London as assistant editor of the *Pall Mall Gazette*. Three years later he became its editor. As an inveterate seeker after sensations, he spent a term in prison for a technical offence while collecting material for a series of articles on the White Slave Traffic.

[4] Twenty years later he admitted he was 'slow to observe the real leanings of the Prime Minister, his strong sympathy with the Turk, and his mastery in his own cabinet. I suffered others, Forster in particular, to go far ahead of me' (Morley, *Life*, ii, 118).

[5] A. G. Gardiner, *Life of Sir W. V. Harcourt* (London, 1932), i, 312.

[6] Gwynn and Tuckwell, *Life of Dilke*, i, 209, 216, 217.

[7] He protested against the whole idea of such a Conference, as being detrimental to the unity of the Liberal party (Holland, *Life*, i, 183–6).

[8] M.C.

[9] M.C.

[10] M.C.

[11] May Morris, *William Morris, Artist, Writer, and Socialist* (London, 1936), ii, 12. P. Henderson (ed.), *Letters of William Morris* (London, 1951) 103 ff.

[12] M.C.

[13] M.C.

[14] H. Broadhurst, *From Stonemason's Bench to Treasury Bench* (London, 1901), 79–88.

[15] Gladstone Papers, Add. MSS 44258 ff. 123 *et. seq.*

[16] *ibid.*, ff. 136–7.

[17] W. P. Adam was Liberal whip from 1884 to 1880.

[18] Gladstone Papers, f. 138.

[19] L.C. 30 Nov. 1876.

[20] M.C.

[21] M.C.

[22] L.C.

[23] For the general diplomatic history, see R. W. Seton-Watson, *Disraeli, Gladstone and the Eastern Question* (London, 1935).

[24] *Annual Register* (1876), 118–20.

[25] *The Times*, 9 Dec. 1876.

[26] E. A. Freeman's *History of the Norman Conquest*, just being finished at this time, shows his enthusiasm for democracy.

[27] Morley, *Life*, ii, 125.

[28] *Hansard*, 16 Feb. 1877.

[29] M.C.

[30] P. W. Clayden, *England under Lord Beaconsfield* (London, 1880). P. W. Clayden (1827–1902), an active unitarian minister who became secretary of the newly founded Free Church Union in 1868, at the same time assuming the assistant editorship of the *Daily News*. His leading articles did much to increase its influence as a Liberal nonconformist organ. An old fellow campaigner with Mundella.

[31] H. A. L. Fisher, *Life of James Bryce* (London, 1927), i, 67.

[32] Auberon Herbert (1838–1906) organised the breakfast. It was his last attempt to walk in the same political path as Mundella.

[33] From which address they issued the twelve pamphlets on the Eastern Question.

[34] Gladstone Papers, *op. cit.*

[35] R. W. Seton-Watson, 182.

[36] L.C.

[37] L.C. 14 May 1877.

[38] Seton-Watson, 77.

[39] *Fortnightly Review* (1877), 127.

[40] J. L. Garvin, *Life of Chamberlain*, i, 258.

[41] Seton-Watson, 191.

[42] L.C. 2 June 1877.

[43] L.C.

[44] Gladstone Papers.

[45] *ibid.*

[46] S. Hutchinson Harris, *Life of Auberon Herbert*, 192.

[47] H. C. F. Collier, *Diary of Lady Monkswell* (London, 1946), 29.

[48] Seton-Watson, 272. Many future agitators, like Maltman Barry and John Burns, received their first taste of such activities in these meetings.

[49] M.C. Chamberlain published the letter which Gladstone wrote to him in *The Times* of 5 Jan. 1878.

[50] M.C.

[51] Herbert wrote to Leader suggesting that a new meeting be held 'immediately'.

[52] M.C.

[53] L.C. 15 June 1878.

[54] L.C. 19 July 1878.

[55] Henry Broadhurst (1840–1911) first settled in London in 1865 and by 1872 was chairman of a committee agitating for increased pay. The following year he was elected chairman of the Labour Representation League. He persuaded his union to establish their headquarters in London, and delegate powers to the officials of the central committee for negotiating in the name of the whole body.

[56] John Burnett (1842–1914) was later to be appointed by Mundella to the Labour Department of the board of trade. See Chapters Twelve and Fourteen.

[57] Mundella, as a member of the Select Committee on Workmen's Compensation, did them great service by making a vigorous stand against the doctrine of common employment. Even the unions were not aware of this, and attacked him for not doing so (see his telegram to the T.U.C. at Bristol 10 Sept. 1878). Recent historians of this question have accorded him his rights, e.g. Wilson and Levy, *Workmen's Compensation* (Oxford, 1939), i, 32.

[58] Reprinted in *Sheffield Independent*, 19 Aug. 1876.

[59] L.C. 27 July 1877.

[60] I am indebted to Mrs. B. Hammond for this story.

[61] *Statistical Journal*, xli (1878), 87–134.

[62] *Hansard*, 5 Aug. 1878.

[63] *Sheffield Independent*, 19 Jan. 1875.

[64] *Hansard*, 3 May 1877.

[65] M.C. July 1886.

[66] J. F. D. Donnelly (1834–1902), Director of Science at South Kensington, and later to be head of the Science and Art Department, told a Royal Commission on Technical Education (1884) how manufacturers feared to allow workmen to attend technical classes, fearing loss of their trade secrets (vol. v, QQ. 2862–3).

[67] Fawcett, as irreconcilable as ever, used the occasion to browbeat the Liberals who were originally responsible for the Cattle Bill.

[68] As published in the *London Gazette*, 25 Sept. 1879. Alexander Redgrave was made Chief Inspector of Factories under this act.

[69] When Normansell stood for the Barnsley Town Council, his union deposited £1,000 at the bank in his name. This act sought to abolish that fiction. *Times*, 3 Aug. 1879.

[70] For this, and other letters, see *Journal of the British and Germanic Philology*, xlix (Illinois, 1950), 566–9.

[71] Harcourt only came under direct orders from Hartington, who told him, 'Damn it, you must go' (L.C. 10 April 1879). Mundella was disappointed in Harcourt not only from his past record, but also because he insisted on staying in the best local hotel, instead of accepting one of the numerous local invitations. Later, after yet another brilliant oratorical effort on Harcourt's part, Mundella wrote, 'He has excelled himself, yet withal I distrust his Liberalism. If ever he gets into a commanding position, he will turn out a very poor reformer. He may help us to turn out the government, but he will be slow to deal with great reforms' (L.C. 5 Oct. 1879).

[72] L.C. 24 Nov. 1878.

[73] Especially at one meeting on 18 Dec. 1878 when interruptions were frequent. Waddy was returned by 14,062 votes to Stuart-Wortley's 13,584.

[74] P. W. Clayden, *England under Lord Beaconsfield* (London, 1880), 541.

[75] *Life of Granville*, 183.

[76] *op. cit.*, 188 and 190.

[77] L.C.

[78] M.C. 9 Jan. 1880.

[79] M.C. 14, 16; and 17 Jan. 1880 L.C., where Mundella writes, 'I have been closeted twice at Devonshire House, where the freest conversation has been entered into on the whole question of leadership, etc.'

[80] He adduced five considerations against the thought of his leading the party once more (Morley, *Life*, ii, 156).

[81] L.C. 17 Jan. 1880.

[82] Mundella (17,217) and C. B. Stuart-Wortley (16,546) were returned. S. D. Waddy polled 16,506 to come third.

[83] The Queen sent for Hartington because of her 'confidence in his moderation', Morley, *Life*, 174–6.

[84] Gladstone Papers.

[85] L.C. 28 April 1880.

[86] *Letters of Queen Victoria*, ed. G. E. Buckle (2nd. Series), iii, 89.

[87] A. E. Gathorne Hardy, *The First Earl of Cranbrook* (London, 1910), ii, 138.

[88] M.C. 1 May 1880.

[89] Morley, *Life*, ii, 178.

CHAPTER ELEVEN

[1] Davidson, *Eminent Radicals*, 125–6.

[2] M.C. 20 April 1880. For Mundella's friendliness to school boards see J. H. Bingham, *The Sheffield School Board* (Sheffield, 1949), 9, 35.

[3] *ibid.*

[4] L. A. Selby-Bigge, *The Board of Education* (London, 1927), 2–10, for a history.

[5] John Poyntz, fifth Earl Spencer (1835–1910), called by J. L. Hammond 'a man of good critical judgement, but without constructive forces' (*Gladstone and the Irish Nation*, 439).

[6] F. Storr, *Life and Remains of R. H. Quick* (Cambridge, 1899), 81.

[7] H. E. Roscoe, *Life and Experiences*, written by himself (London, 1903), 288.

[8] *Report of the Committee of Council on Education for 1880–1*, xxvii.

[9] Sandon had accused Mundella in the house on 8 Aug. 1881, and wrote this in apology.

[10] Huxley and Donnelly were particularly keen on the establishment of a Normal College of Science to train Science teachers.

[11] Huxley's letter, showing the impression which the French model had on him, is among the Mundella letters.

[12] *Correspondence between the Science and Art Department and the Treasury as to the Organisation of the Normal School of Science and the Royal School of Mines*, c. 3085, P.P. 1882.

[13] *Committee on Science and Art Buildings* (1897), QQ. 4996–5024. This committee recorded their sorrow at not being able to hear Mundella's own testimony before he died.

[14] By 1890 the name had changed to the Royal College of Science, and by 1910 it had merged with the Royal School of Mines and the City and Guilds College: for which see *Imperial College of Science and Technology, A Short History* (London, 1945), 12–20.

[15] Speech at the opening of University College, Bangor, 18 Oct. 1884, when he referred to Wales as 'my happy hunting ground for educational experiments'.

[16] *Letters of Matthew Arnold, 1848–88*, ed. G. W. E. Russell, ii, 174–6.

[17] For his relations with Mundella see *Review of English Studies* (Oxford, 1947), xxiii, 355–7, and W. F. Connell, *The Educational Thought and Influence of Matthew Arnold* (London, 1950), 282–7.

[18] For previous efforts see *The Vocational Aspect of Secondary and Further Education* (Manchester, 1950), 6–21.

[19] Hughes' attempt to found a settlement for the supernumerary Tom Browns has been well described by M. B. Hamer, *Tom Hughes and his American Rugby* (North Carolina, 1928); as well as by himself *Gone to Texas, Or Letters from Our Boys* and *Vacation Rambles* (London, 1896).

[20] The actual number was 1,600.

[21] T. I. Ellis, *The Development of Higher Education in Wales* (1935), 36–54.

[22] Dr. Falk was appointed to the Ministry of Public Worship and Instruction in 1872 and issued his general regulations on 15 Oct. in the same year. The *mittleschule* (a higher-grade school with an industrial bias that evolved during the *aufklärung*) was encouraged by allowing its pupils remittance of two years military service. F. Paulsen, *German Education Past and Present* (1908), 251–8 (trans. T. Lorenz), 251–8.

[23] Jules Ferry, minister for public instruction, 1879–82, re-organised the whole educational system. A positivist like Harrison and Crompton, he carried the secularisation of education against the opposition of the clerical party. Symbolic of resurgent France was the occupation of Tunis in May 1881. See *Life* by A. N. Rambaud (1903).

[24] H. Felkin, *Technical Education in a Saxon Town* (1881). Felkin was a student of educational theory, and translated Herbart for English readers. He was the representative of the Nottingham Manufacturing Company in Chemnitz.

[25] Bernhard Samuelson was the general editor, and emphasised apprenticeship systems and workshop training. Dr. Henry Roscoe inquired into foreign research. Philip Magnus visited schools. Swire Smith reported on social conditions. John Slagg and William Woodall kept a watching brief for industry as a whole, and Gilbert Redgrave was the secretary. William Mather went to the U.S.A., and H. M. Jenkins reported on agricultural education. For a good summary of their report see John Leese, *Personalities and Power in English Education* (Leeds, 1950), 219–23.

[26] T. M. Healy, *Letters and Leaders of My Day*, i, 133.

[27] Initiated by W. E. Forster in the code of 1871.

[28] He described the composition of the committee in parliament, 8 Aug. 1881. It consisted of Sir Francis Sandford (the permanent secretary), J. Sykes and P. Cumin (two of the three assistant secretaries), Warburton, Sharp and Fitch (three inspectors), presided over by Mundella himself. 'We had', he said,

'many a long and laborious day before we arrived at the scheme which we have now submitted to the house.' The draft report was put through a finer sieve, and Matthew Arnold, Moncreiff, Oakeley and Blakiston, inspectors of four large towns, were called in for consultation.

[29] *Hansard*, 8 Aug. 1881.

[30] L.C. 14 Aug. 1881.

[31] M.C. Lord Frederick Cavendish to A. J. Mundella, and Henry Roscoe to A. J. Mundella, 4 March 1881; Mundella to R. Leader, 15 March 1882.

[32] Speech at Manchester, 8 July 1884.

[33] *Report of Committee of Council on Education*, 1883–4; 1885–6, 280, 'beyond question the code which came into force in May 1883 has effected an immense improvement in schools and classes for infants' (Tremenheere in 1886). Mundella's interest in infant schools is seen in Oct. 1880, when the British and Foreign Schools Society received the anonymous offer of a new college, and approached Mundella for advice; he suggested that it be used for training infant-school-mistresses, and they followed his advice (H. B. Binns, *A Century of Education*, 207).

[34] *Report of Committee of Council*, instructions to Inspectors, 1882–3, 158.

[35] *ibid.*, instructions to Inspectors, 1882–3, 158.

[36] The code committee whose working was so well described by Patric Cumin before the Cross commission; see *1st Report*, Minutes of Evidence, 41. A good modern appreciation is by John Leese, *Personalities and Power in English Education* (Leeds, 1950), 138–9.

[37] *The Times*, 18 June 1885, has a good appreciation of the part this codification played in enabling teachers to understand what was actually required of them.

[38] J. A. Willis (of Middlesex) in his report of 1882–3, 476.

[39] G. Balfour, *Educational Systems of Great Britain*, 27. John Bright wrote three letters to Mundella, imploring consideration of his son-in-law for a vacancy.

[40] R. W. Rich, *The Training of Teachers* (Cambridge, 1933), 237.

[41] M.C. 13 May 1882.

[42] His report was printed as a parliamentary paper.

[43] The controversy can be followed up in the pages of *Hansard*, the *Nineteenth Century* and the correspondence columns of *The Times*. Mundella's speech on 26 July 1883 for school meals, the *Lancet's* opinion, expressed 4 Aug. 1883, and S. C. Buxton's article in the *Nineteenth Century* for Nov. 1884 (especially p. 825) seem to clinch the matter in favour of the view that the pressure was not caused by the code. Mundella became president of the Central Council for Promoting Self-Supporting Penny Dinners, which circulated details of the Rousden experiment in the spring of 1885.

[44] L.C. Mundella to Robert Leader, 29 April 1882.

[45] *ibid.* Mundella to Robert Leader, 28 July 1882: 'You can have no conception of what my daily and nightly life is and will continue to be until this session ends; the Scotch Endowment Bill is a stiff task.'

[46] Scottish Education Department, *Smail Report on Technical Education* (1946), 4–5, points out the great significance of the commission in the evolution of Scottish technical instruction. See also J. Kerr, *Scottish Education*, 301 and 370.

[47] British Museum, Gladstone Papers, Add. MSS. 44258, ff., 190.

[48] *ibid.*, no. 191 (6 July).

[49] *Report of the Committee of Council*, 1882–3, 107. Both letters were signed, not by Sandford, the permanent secretary, but by Mundella himself. It caused

comment, e.g. Evans and Claridge, *J. Hirst Hollowell and the Educational Movement* (1911), 276.

[50] Speech at Birmingham, Jan. 1883.

[51] Cardinal Manning (the Cardinal Grandison of *Lothair*) wrote, 'Is the 1870 act a just law?' for the December issue of the *Nineteenth Century* in 1882; R. W. Dale replied in Jan. 1883; and Canon Gregory joined forces with the Cardinal in Feb. 1883 in an article entitled 'Religion and the Rates'. On 6 Feb. 1883 Lord Ripon wrote from India to T. W. Allies, secretary of the Catholic Schools Association, condemning Manning's 'Grave want of political judgement'. 'His Eminence', continued Ripon, 'knows nothing of the forces which he is about to array against him, or of the sleeping dogs which he is about to awake. If this policy is maintained by His Eminence when I return to England, it will be impossible for me to resume the chairmanship of the Poor Schools Committee. . . . The system is one which the Catholics of most countries in Europe would give their eyes to have introduced among them. If the Cardinal's scheme is taken up and pressed by the Catholics, it will, I am convinced, be productive of the most serious injury to Catholic education' (Ripon Papers : British Museum Add. MSS. 43598).

[52] L.C. 10 Dec. 1882.

[53] L.C. 23 Jan. 1883. It is significant that the Independent Schools Association was formed at this time.

[54] Sir Henry James nicknamed him 'Trichinosis' at this time.

[55] M.C. 19 March 1883.

[56] Countess Waldegrave, whom he married in 1863 and who died in 1879. She was a famous hostess who, though married three times before, devoted her abilities and fortune to the success of his political career. She reopened Strawberry Hill, Horace Walpole's old residence, and it became one of the chief meeting places of the Liberal party.

[57] L.C. 13 April 1884.

[58] M.C. 4 June 1883, Sandford also enclosed a statement.

[59] *Hansard*, 29 June 1883.

[60] L.C. Mundella to Robert Leader 18 Oct. and 10 Nov. 1883.

[61] At Edinburgh, 15 Jan.

[62] *Glasgow Herald*, 15 Jan.

[63] At Edinburgh, 15 Jan.

[64] L.C. To Robert Leader 22 June 1884.

[65] In the *Nineteenth Century*, Feb. 1884 ('On Examining in Elementary Schools').

[66] L.C. Mundella to R. Leader, 24 Feb. 1884.

[67] M.C. 13 Feb. 1884, also *Hansard* 29 June 1884, when W. E. Forster threw light on these new arrangements, commenting, 'It has been adopted in the last few weeks that the president should consult the vice-president in the case of appointments'.

[68] M.C. 2 April 1885.

[69] G. W. Kekewich, *The Board of Education and After* (1902), 27.

[70] Gladstone Papers, Add. MSS. 44123.

[71] L. A. Selby-Bigge, *The Board of Education*, 5–12.

[72] On 2 July Mundella opened the technical institute which Bernhard Samuelson gave to Banbury and announced that a knighthood had been conferred upon him for 'his services to the education of the people'.

[73] A Mumford, *Manchester Grammar School*, 1515–1915, 373–4.

[74] K. Viriamu Jones, *Life of J. Viriamu Jones*, (London, 1915), 203, who himself received letters from one headmaster saying what an adverse effect the opening of a higher-grade school had on his own grammar school.

[75] It was advocated by Professors Meiklejohn and Armstrong.

[76] *Manchester Guardian*, 10 Aug. 1884. To R. Leader, 17 Sept. 1884.

[77] L.C. Mundella to Leader, 6 and 10 Feb. He had earlier referred to Gordon as 'a little mad'.

[78] M.C. J. Percival to Mundella, 1 April 1885. Percival had created Clifton College since 1862, and as a president of Trinity College, Oxford, was a pioneer of university extension and women's education.

[79] *Life of Viriamu Jones*, 204. Nine days later a meeting of London Welshmen took place in the memorial hall, Farringdon Street.

[80] *ibid.*, 206, and *Hansard*, 22 May 1885.

[81] *The Times*, 25 June 1885. M.C. 29 June 1885.

[82] L.C. To Robert Leader, 29 May and 19 June 1885.

[83] Speech on a hillside outside H. J. Wilson's house in Sheffield on 9 July.

[84] Address to the electors of Midlothian.

[85] Garvin, *Life of Chamberlain*, ii, 69, and *Radical Programme*, 22, 162, 218.

[86] M.C. Chamberlain to Mundella, 7 Oct.; Arnold to Mundella, 14 Oct.

[87] C. H. D. Howard in *English Historical Review*, lxii (1947), 45.

[88] *Sheffield Independent*, 22 Oct. 1885, M.C. Leader to Mundella, 23 Oct. 1885.

[89] M.C. Chamberlain to Mundella, 23 Oct.

[90] M.C. Chamberlain to Mundella, 23 Oct. See also C. H. D. Howard in *English Historical Review*, lxv (1950), 479–91.

[91] *ibid.*, Cranbrook to Mundella, 17 and 20 Dec. 1885, Mundella to Cranbrook, 19 and 21 Dec. 1885. Cranbrook originally suggested the bishop of London as chairman, with Cardinal Manning, Canon Gregory, Dr. Rigg, Rev. C. D. Morse, Alderson, T. E. Heller (of the N.U.T.), Rev. R. W. Dale, Sir John Lubbock, Lord Harrowby (lately Viscount Sandon), and Lord Beauchamp. To these he later added Sir Francis Sandford, Sir Bernhard Samuelson, S. C. Buxton, Samuel Rathbone, Henry Richard, Lord Norton, G. W. Shipton, B. F. Smith, J. G. Talbot and B. C. Molloy, with a new chairman Lord Cross. Mundella, who was on the original commission, withdrew the following year in favour of Lyulph Stanley.

[92] M.C. Arnold to Mundella, 6 Nov. 1885.

[93] A. Thorold, *Life of Labouchere* (1913), 257.

[94] C. 31 May 1884: 'I cannot get copies of the report of the Technical Commission without payment. My secretary has tried but in vain.'

[95] H. W. Lucy, *A Diary of Two Parliaments* (1886), 359.

[96] Speech, 20 Nov. 1883.

[97] M.C. Arnold to Mundella, 4 Aug. 1883; Arnold to Miss Mundella, 6 March 1882.

[98] *ibid.*, John Stainer to Mundella, 1895.

[99] A. H. D. Acland and H. Llewelyn Smith, *Studies in Secondary Education* (1892) 118.

[100] M.C. Sir Joshua Fitch to Miss Mundella, 17 April 1898. He himself played no small part in educational advance at this time, being prominent in the infant school movement; see A. L. Lilley *Sir Joshua Fitch* (1906).

CHAPTER TWELVE

[1] Including Courtney, Goschen, A. Grey, Hartington, Henry James and Lubbock.

[2] Gladstone Papers, Add. MSS. 44016, 29 Jan. 1886.

[3] *ibid.*, 44123, f. 251.

[4] Gladstone had wanted Carlingford to accept an embassy in 1884, to allow Mundella to take over his work, but Carlingford had been very unwilling to leave his office, and Gladstone did not press the matter. *ibid.* 44123, 7 Sept. 1884, 44258, 30 Dec. 1885.

[5] The papers are in Add. MSS. 44771, ff. 13 and 38. 'Hartington, Goschen, *Mundella*, Courtney, and Campbell-Bannerman' are listed for the Chancellorship, with Hartington and Mundella underlined.

[6] A. E. Gathorne Hardy, *Gathorne Hardy, first Earl of Cranbrook*, ii, 241; J. A. Spender: *Life of Campbell-Bannerman*, (London, 1923), i, 97. This loyalty is confirmed by a letter in the Gladstone Papers of 15 Dec. 1885, where Mundella expressed his anger that 'any other member of the party should presume to determine the course to be taken by the Liberals in view of the present state of affairs'. The same day, John Morley wrote to Spence Watson, 'Much dirty intrigue going on. I won't be a party to snubbing the old man' (F. W. Hirst, *Life and Letters of John Morley* (London, 1927), ii, 272). So Mundella's loyalty was no more vocal than Morley's.

[7] Morley, *Life*, ii, 402. Sir Henry Slesser, *A History of the Liberal Party* (London, 1944), 112, saw the presence of Mundella and Broadhurst in the government as a symptom of 'the advent of democracy'.

[8] Add. MSS. 44126, 8 Feb. 1886. He wanted 'a good long exposition' from Chamberlain.

[9] The Fair Traders had been growing in strength since 1877, and they had recently been reinforced by Colonel Howard Vincent, the remodeller of the C.I.D. at Scotland Yard, who was now their official spokesman in the house. The Cobdenites refused to listen to any suggestion that adherence to a free-trade policy might be a cause of the depression : see Benjamin H. Brown, *The Tariff Reform Movement in Great Britain* (New York, 1943). The demands of the S.D.F., on the other hand, were expounded in *Socialism Made Plain* (1883). They urged an extensive programme: housing, free education and school meals, an eight-hour day, progressive taxation on all income over £300 a year, the establishment of national banks, the nationalisation of railways and land, and the organisation of the unemployed under state projects. Gladstone refused to see the existence of a crisis: 'There is no crisis at all in view. There is a process of slow modification and development mainly in directions which I view with misgiving' (to Acton, 11 Feb. 1885, Morley, *op. cit.*, ii, 310).

[10] 17 July 1885: quoted by B. H. Brown, *op. cit.*, 63.

[11] *The Times*, 1 March 1886.

[12] Palgrave, *Dictionary of Political Economy*, i, 853; Tilley and Gaselee, *The Foreign Office*, 241.

[13] Bradlaugh, in a speech at Northampton on 7 Jan. 1886, declared his intention of moving for such a board. When he did so on 2 March, Mundella declared (*Hansard*, 2 March) that he adopted the motion 'with a deep sense of the urgency and importance of doing all that is possible'.

[14] C. Bradlaugh, *Labour and Law* (1891), 200.

[15] There were disputes between the Canadians and Americans: see *Correspondence Relating to the North American Fisheries*, 1884-6 (London, 1887).

[16] Especially America, where Wood's Hole was established by Spencer F. Baird in 1871. His successor, G. B. Goode, executed a survey of all the coasts and inland waters of the country.

[17] *The Times*, 30 March 1886.

[18] Sir F. C. Floud, *The Ministry of Agriculture and Fisheries* (1927), 275-7.

[19] Bernhard Samuelson (an ironmaster at Middlesbrough and Newport) had been chairman of the parliamentary committee on railways in 1873, from whose report the act of that year had emerged, setting up a railway commission. He had been employed in an investigation of technical education abroad for Mundella in which he had earned his baronetcy. *See* Chapter Eleven, n. 25.

[20] Samuelson's report received full publicity in the *Economist*, 9 Jan. 1886. A week later the *Railway Times* devoted a considerable amount of space to a discussion of its main provisions, concluding, 'It means State control and management of private enterprise which would be as objectionable as it is uncalled for'. It is significant that the problem of railway rates and their regulation was engaging the attention of young A. T. Hadley, then an instructor at Yale, whose classic on the subject was first published at this time, and noticed in the *Economist* of 16 Jan. 1886.

[21] Under the guiding genius of Mr. (later Sir) Henry Oakley, who utilised in this sphere the experience he had gained in fighting the war of rates against the Midland Railway Company (see C. H. Grinling, *History of the Great Northern Railway, 1845-95* (1898), 369-71.

[22] Case-histories are many. Wilson Cammells, the second largest steelworks in Europe, moved from Dronfield (in Derbyshire) to Workington on the coast, and thereby saved £60,000 a year in railway charges. This was in 1881.

[23] At the Social Science Congress in 1884 it was reported that six important firms in the Black Country were transferring to the coastal regions in order to save transport costs. G. C. Allen, *The Industrial Development of Birmingham and the Black Country 1860-1927* (1929), 234; R. Stainton, *The Making of Sheffield 1865-1914* (1924), 269.

[24] *The Times* on 18 Oct. 1882 declared that the five and a half million inhabitants of Manchester were at the mercy of a combination of port, dock and railway authorities, which they likened to those of mediaeval robber barons. The citizens could not use any of their existing five lines of canal, since they had been either bought up by the railway companies, or else they had become receptacles for sewage. It was in these circumstances that Daniel Adamson had embarked on his project for a Manchester Ship Canal: a project described by its historian, Sir Bosdin Leech, as 'an attempt to stem the current that was reducing Manchester to the position of a second rate city' and to give her 'as cheap carriage as her competitors'. Bosdin Leech, *A History of the Manchester Ship Canal* (1907).

[25] Lord Claud Hamilton, who had entered Parliament twenty-one years earlier, when he was twenty-two years old, had been member for Liverpool since 1880. His eldest brother, who had become duke of Abercorn in 1885, before the official head of the Irish landlord class, and in 1888 president of the Irish Landlords Convention. Three of his younger brothers were M.P.s, and his six sisters married into the nobility. His own railway directorships included

the Great Eastern, the Downham and Stoke Ferry, the King's Lynn Docks and Railway, and the Tottenham and Hampstead Junction Railways. Owing to these claims, he retired from parliament in 1888.

[26] Sir H. Meysey-Thompson was a colleague of Lord Hartington's father on the board of the Furness and Cockermouth, Keswick and Penrith Railways, in addition to being a director of the North-East and the Forth Bridge Railways.

[27] Lord Claud Hamilton and Sir H. Meysey-Thompson managed to find seventeen Liberal M.P.s (in addition to Meysey-Thompson himself) to support their objections to the bill by voting against the ministry. They included: the Hon. H. R. Brand (M.P. for Stroud), A. H. Brown (M.P. for Wellington), L. H. Courtney (M.P. for Bodmin) and two other railway directors—Sir A. Fairbairn and Sir H. H. Vivian (M.P. for Swansea).

[28] It took a fortnight to alter the railway companies.

[29] 14 March 1886.

[30] 13 March 1886.

[31] 12 March 1886.

[32] 13 March 1886.

[33] This 'array' was a well-organised pressure group. *Bradshaw's Railway Shareholders Guide* for 1886 lists eighty-four railway directors as members of the house of commons, and forty-six as members of the house of lords. Their importance has been indicated by J. A. Thomas, *A Study of the Economic and Functional Character of the House of Commons 1832–1901* (1939).

[34] For details of this and similar railway expansion during the first half of the decade see *Bradshaw*. But *Bradshaw* (p. 145) omits to give W. Bickford-Smith his correct suffix of M.P., nor does it include him (p. 601) as belonging to the railway interest, which he did, since in 1881 he promoted the Helston Railway. H. Robertson, Liberal M.P. for Merioneth, was heavily involved in much of this expansion: as director of the Llangollen and Corwen; the Seacombe, Hoylake and Deeside; the Vale of Llangollen; the Wellington and Severn Junction; and the Wirral Limited. As a Scots railway contractor, he had migrated to Wales, where his Brymbo iron and steel works lived largely on such business. Other Liberal M.P.s similarly affected were D. Davies (M.P. for Cardigan), who was vice-chairman of the Barry Docks Railway; Sir J. J. Jenkins (M.P. for Caermarthen), director of the Rhondda and Swansea Bay and the Llanelly and Mynydd Mawr Railways; and Sir H. H. Vivian (M.P. for Swansea), director of the Rhondda and Swansea Bay Railway.

[35] Raised to the peerage in February, he was described by *The Times* (5 Feb. 1886) as 'in his time the autocrat of the Parliamentary Bar . . . the terror of weak committees, and the master of a powerful and pungent controversial style'. Grimthorp's petition objected to nearly every clause of Mundella's bill. He declared it was the largest commercial question that had ever engaged the attention of the country. His letters to *The Times* (19 and 30 March 1886) were widely quoted.

[36] 27 March 1886.

[37] J. S. Forbes on 26 March 1886.

[38] Thorold Rogers warned the government (*Hansard*, 6 May 1886) that 'the railway interest is more widely distributed throughout the country than any other property except Consols'. Other speakers stressed this at the time. 'If this bill passes, we shall have nothing to live on. There are millions of people in the United Kingdom whose means are invested in railways, and who have not other

means of support whatsoever. What is to become of us and those millions dependent upon us if this bill passes?' (C. Watson reported in the *Sheffield Telegraph*, 1 April 1886).

[39] Full reports of all these meetings were given in the daily papers like *The Times*, *Manchester Guardian*, *Sheffield Telegraph*, and *Sheffield Independent*, and the *Glasgow Herald*; the weekly *Herapath's Railway and Commercial Journal*, the *Railway Review*, the fortnightly *Railway Shareholder* and the monthly *Railway Office Gazette*. The *Daily News* was not so generous in allotting its columns to these protests.

[40] His chairmanships were of the Manchester, Sheffield and Lincolnshire, the South-eastern and the Metropolitan Railway Companies. His directorships, those of the Blackpool; Cheshire Lines; East London; Manchester, South Junction, and Altrincham; Oldham, Ashton-under-Lyne, and Guide Bridge; Sheffield and Midland Joint; and the Wigan Junction. He spoke of Mundella's bill as a political issue, and warned the government that he spoke for 400,000 voters.

[41] Now seventy-two years old, he had been director of the L.N.W. since 1847. See Pendleton's *Our Railways* (1894), i, 194–6.

[42] Now sixty-six years old, he had been chairman of the Midland Railway Company since 1865.

[43] Speech at Sheffield, 30 March 1887.

[44] *Sheffield Telegraph*, 6 April 1886.

[45] Gladstone's cabinet memoranda for the 1886 ministry are collected together in B.M. Add. MSS. 44647.

[46] *Letters and Journals of Reginald Viscount Esher*, ed. M. V. Brett (1934), 123–4. Chamberlain's disaffection was known to Morley as early as 5 Feb., for when he was asked, 'What is Joe playing at?' he gave the answer, 'Fast and loose'. It was at this dinner-party that Balfour saw important omens for the Conservative party, and wrote the long letters to his uncle two days later telling him that Chamberlain could count on seventy or eighty members. He also told his uncle of Chamberlain's avowed intention (according to Fowler) to break up the Liberal party. Mundella had been convinced of Chamberlain's boundless powers of intrigue ever since they had contested Sheffield together in 1874, and Chamberlain, the night before the election, had put out posters asking Liberal voters to 'plump' for him (i.e. vote for him solely).

[47] *op. cit.*

[48] B.M. Add. MSS. 44647.

[49] P. W. Clayden, *England under the Coalition* (1892), 37.

[50] W. C. Quilter was a stockbroker, a founder of the National Telegraph Company (where he had previously met state intervention) and director of two railway companies—the Central Wales and Caermarthen Junction, and a year later, of Felixstowe and Bawdsey Ferry.

[51] *The Times*, 20 April 1886.

[52] This petition was also signed by George Howell and Charles Bradlaugh, which shows that discussion of the bill was desired by the radical wing.

[53] Parliament rose for a fortnight on 19 April. Morley compared the heat of political passion to that of a furnace. Argyll's speech opened the fortnight, being delivered at Glasgow the day after parliament rose.

[54] Like his grandfather, the third duke was a 'leviathan of wealth', much of which was tied up in railway and canal enterprises.

⁵⁵ Gladstone Papers (British Museum Add. MSS.), ccclxiii, 181.

⁵⁶ Farrer, permanent secretary to the board since 1885, wrote to Goldwin Smith on 29 Aug. 1885: 'I am not happy about the future of politics. I am afraid of promising to do for the workers more than laws can do.' He had told the Railway Rates Committee of 1881 that unequal rates were good for trade, and was quoted as an apologist for the existing system by J. B. Pope, *Railway Rates and Radical Rule* (1884), 184–204. This is confirmed from Farrer's evidence to the *Royal Commission on Trade Depression* (3rd Report, c. 4749, QQs. 14952, 14984 and 14995). On 16 May 1886 Mundella wrote to Granville asking for a peerage for him (Gladstone Papers, 44179, f. 106).

⁵⁷ 15 May 1886.

⁵⁸ 8 May 1886.

⁵⁹ May 1886, 771–8.

⁶⁰ L.C. 13 May 1886.

⁶¹ This, was, of course, an unjustified gloss.

⁶² Gladstone Papers, B.M. Add. MSS. 44647.

⁶³ Mundella wrote to the Society of Railway Servants acknowledging that he had received complaints that these meetings were staged.

⁶⁴ 6 April 1886, *Sheffield Telegraph*.

⁶⁵ *Royal Commission Report on the London Livery Companies*, xxxix (5 vols.), 1884. The Clothworkers sold their Irish estates for £87,000 in 1871–5 and the Grocers for £112,401. The Goldsmiths had £6,300, the Clockmakers £5,405, the Ironmongers £7,850, the Shipwrights £2,250 in railway stock. Others, in their returns, grouped Consols and railway stock together.

⁶⁶ The chairman, Lord Wemyss, had, as Lord Elcho, been a moving spirit in an earlier cave—that of the Adullamites. Their pamphlets—*Socialism at St. Stevens* (1883), *Overlegislation in 1884* and *Liberty and Law* (1884) were reinforced by meetings.

⁶⁷ Sir Ernest Barker, *Political Thought from 1848–1914*, 235, refers to his gospel of *let be*.

⁶⁸ 12 June 1886.

⁶⁹ 8 May 1886.

⁷⁰ Chamberlain's brother Richard has been excluded from this list, as has Sir E. Watkin, who by now was so independent a Liberal that in the voting against the Home Rule Bill he was not included in the ninety-three. The fifteen directors who have been already met are: Sir H. Meysey-Thompson, Sir A. Fairbairn, Sir R. Anstruther, Sir H. H. Vivian, Sir G. McPherson-Grant, W. Bickford Smith, J. Corbett, D. Davies, Sir J. J. Jenkins, A. G. Kitching, W. C. Quilter, H. Robertson, P. Rylands, H. Wiggin and J. P. Williams. Apart from the *D.N.B.*, biographical details abound in Boase: *Modern English Biography*, *Dod's Parliamentary Companion*, *Who Was Who* (1897–1916) and (1916–28) and the obituaries in *The Times*.

⁷¹ R. Spence Watson, *The National Liberal Federation 1877–1906* (1907), 55.

⁷² *Fortnightly Review*, June 1886, 737–70.

⁷³ *Hansard*, 11 June 1886.

⁷⁴ 12 May 1886, adding, 'Mr. Mundella's Bill fully justifies all that has been said of it by its opponents'.

⁷⁵ 12 July 1886, Gladstone Papers 44258.

⁷⁶ On 13 May 1886 *The Times* reported that he was confined to his house with an affection of the throat, and on 22 June 1886 that he had been confined to

his house 'for some time'. He rested in Hertfordshire before commencing his campaign.

⁷⁷ A. Haultain, *Letters of Goldwin Smith* (1913), 186. For Goldwin Smith's earlier relation with Mundella and the advanced Liberals see *Queen's Quarterly*, liv (1947), 452–60.

⁷⁸ S. Hutchinson-Harris, *Auberon Herbert* (1943), also cites Herbert's letters to *The Times* for 2 and 7 July 1886, which argued that Gladstone's Irish legislation was purely opportunistic.

⁷⁹ Arnold, in 'The Nadir of Liberalism' (*Nineteenth Century*, May 1886, 661), asserted, 'On the reasonableness of the Conservative Party our best hope at present depends . . . our pressing danger at the moment is from the Liberal Party and its leader. If they cannot be stopped and defeated, the thing is over'. Hughes and Hutton brought over the *Spectator* to the Unionist side.

⁸⁰ H. A. L. Fisher, *James Bryce*, i, 215.

⁸¹ Gladstone Papers 44258.

⁸² M.C. Gladstone said that the adverse result of the election was completely unexpected, and told G. W. E. Russell, 'The experts assumed we should sweep the country', *One Look Back* (1912), 262.

⁸³ *Statistical Journal*, lxix (1886), 693–735.

⁸⁴ 11 Feb. 1887.

⁸⁵ The various protectionist societies formed by H. J. Pettifer, S. W. Poynter, James Hunt and, above all, Sir Howard Vincent also helped.

⁸⁶ On 17 Feb. 1887 on behalf of the Suffolk farmers written by Lord Bristol; and 17 March on behalf of the east of England generally. The deputation went on 21 March.

⁸⁷ W. W. Rostov, *British Economy of the Nineteenth Century* (Oxford, 1948), 84.

⁸⁸ To the Sheffield Chamber of Commerce, 30 Jan. 1887.

⁸⁹ C. D. Campbell, *British Railways in Boom and Depression 1878–1930* (1932), pointed out that the average rate of dividend, which was 6·79 in 1880 and —10·45 in 1886, had begun to climb back once more. In 1887 it was 2·09, and in 1888 it had risen to 9·39. His conclusion was that the shareholder bore the burden of the cyclical depression (p. 44).

⁹⁰ 5 Feb. 1887.

⁹¹ Reported in the *Stock Exchange*, 18 Feb. 1887, which regarded it as an omen that he should have made this speech.

⁹² 5 March 1886.

⁹³ 5 March 1887. In this connection it is worth noting that T. H. Farrer wrote a letter to the *Economist* on 29 Jan. 1887 pointing out that he and three other members of the Royal Commission on Trade Depression (Ecroyd, Muntz and Lubbock) had argued in favour of letting the railway companies alone.

⁹⁴ *Hansard*, 15 Aug. 1887, 462.

⁹⁵ The act was passed on 4 Feb., and five days later *Herapath* was describing its activities. Started in the north and middle west by J. N. Reagan (from Texas) and S. M. Cullom (from Illinois), it not only kept down rates, but increased earnings. See also *The Times* 18, 24, 25 and 31 Jan.; 7, 8, 10 Feb.; 3, 9, and 24 March; 1, 8, 22, 25, 26, 27, and 28 April 1887.

⁹⁶ 3 Dec. 1887.

⁹⁷ It was the resolute action of the Railway and Canal Traders' Association Council, meeting monthly to report progress on the Conservative Bill of 1887,

that did much to ventilate the question of terminals and undue preference. They declared that they would oppose the retention of such powers in the hands of the railways 'by all means in their power'. The railway companies maintained complete silence till the deputation of 18 April 1888.

[98] *Railway Times and Joint Stock Chronicle*, 21 April. The deputation, commented the paper, appeared 'a submission to the inevitable'.

[99] 12 May 1888.

[100] 26 July, 1888.

[101] *Hansard*, 25 July 1888.

[102] L.C. 12 Aug. 1888.

[103] 11 May 1888.

[104] A reference to the Local Government Act of the same year.

[105] *Hansard*, 10 May 1888.

[106] 26 July 1888.

[107] During 1888 and 1889 Courtney Boyle and Lord Balfour of Burleigh sat for eighty-five days to consider the companies' proposed rates, and the 4,000 objections tabled against them. After the Provisional Orders were drafted they were laid before a Joint Committee of both houses from 1891 to 1892, where the rates were raised once more. When the new rates did come into force on 1 Jan. 1893, they were higher than the old ones already in force.

[108] They were so described by T. C. Farrer in *Economic Journal*, i, 358.

[109] The article by C. Waring in the *Fortnightly* (1886), 737–70, realised the implications of Mundella's bill: 'It cannot fail to have momentous results not contemplated by its authors in the near future. It opens the entire question of the relations between the public, the state, and the proprietors in such a manner that they cannot be settled within the compass of the Bill.'

CHAPTER THIRTEEN

[1] K. Viriamu Jones, *Life of J. Viriamu Jones*, 209.

[2] *The Times*, 27 Jan. 1887.

[3] *ibid.*, 21 March 1887.

[4] *Life and Letters*, iii, 9; Sir H. T. Wood, *History of the Royal Society of Arts* (London, 1913), 15, 464.

[5] Lords Granville, Ripon, Rosebery and Spencer; Mundella, Broadhurst, Lubbock, Lyon Playfair, Samuelson, Stuart, and R. Temple.

[6] A. H. D. Acland, the thirty-nine-year-old M.P. for Rotherham, had been the first secretary of the University Extension movement at Oxford. With Sir Henry Roscoe, he was a very effective co-secretary of this association.

[7] With Lyulph Stanley, J. H. Gladstone and Frederick Leighton, Mundella had formed the Drawing Association to secure 'the simple linear training of the hand and eye, and of the mind generally' in every school in Great Britain.

[8] 1 Dec. 1887.

[9] See *Bulletin of the John Rylands Library* (Manchester, 1948), xxxi, 110–19.

[10] 16 Oct. 1888.

[11] For his work at the London school board see Graham Wallas, *Men and Ideas* (London, 1940), 81–5.

[12] *Report on the Conference at Exeter Hall 20 and 21 November 1888* (pamphlet) shows that twenty M.P.s and 170 delegates were present.

[13] Rosa Waugh, *Life of Benjamin Waugh* (London, 1913), 148–9; Gertrude Tuckwell, *The State and its Children* (London, 1844), 118–26.

[14] *Hansard*, 10 Nov. 1889.

[15] L.C. 13 July 1889. He complained bitterly about both Waugh and Stead in another letter on 21 Aug. 1889, 'Stead . . . assumes that some vague and unworkable clauses would go through Parliament in a breath. This is the sort of new journalism of which Stead is the pioneer. Waugh and he are bosom friends. They keep up a certain amount of prurient sensationalism between them. They both pose everlastingly as Christians of a new type, they call it unconventional Christianity, and a pretty vulgar, prurient, blasphemous muddle it is.'

[16] F. A. Channing was much impressed by a speech which Mundella made on this topic at Wellingborough at the close of 1888 (*Memories of Midland Politics*, 89).

[17] M.C. 28 Nov. 1889.

[18] See *Bulletin of the John Rylands Library*, xxx, 271–7.

[19] *Hansard*, 25 March 1890.

[20] E. W. Watson, *Life of Bishop Wordsworth* (London, 1915), 203.

[21] The increasing menace of German cutlery and cheap imitations of Sheffield ware made many of Mundella's constituents very anxious.

[22] M.C. for Hicks Beach's letter of invitation.

[23] A triumph for A. H. D. Acland, who on 10 June 1890 challenged the government's proposal to allot some £700,000 (the proceeds of a liquor tax) to publicans scheduled to lose their licences. As secretary of the Technical Education Association, he urged that the money be earmarked for that purpose. After six weeks, the government acceded to his request, to the great displeasure of *The Times*, which commented, 'It seems as if ministers have resigned themselves to following the line of least resistance'.

[24] L.C. 24 Aug. 1890.

[25] T. M. Lockyer, *Life and Work of Sir Norman Lockyer* (London, 1928), 141.

[26] The editor of the *Liverpool Daily Post* to Mundella.

[27] M.C. 1 Dec. 1890.

[28] *Hansard*, 3 July 1891.

[29] Morley, *Life*, ii, 487 described the great interest felt in the Parnell case.

[30] 17 Jan. 1891.

[31] 28 Feb. 1891.

[32] L.C. 28 Feb. 1891.

[33] M.C.

[34] *Hansard*, 28 May 1891.

[35] Henry James, as a lawyer and M.P. for Bury, was entrusted with the bill. Mawdsley, who compared Mundella's work in 1874 with that of Shaftesbury in 1848, gave a third reason why Henry James was entrusted with it: 'This work (i.e. the 1891 Bill) was of such an arduous character, involving such an amount of untiring attention to detail and other things, that we felt it would be unfair to ask the same man to undertake work of that character a second time in his life.' *Lancashire Echo*, 6 June 1891.

[36] *Hansard*, 18 June 1891.

[37] He pointed out that eleven was both the age recommended by the Cross

Commission, and agreed to in the Berlin Resolution, as early enough to begin half time work.

[38] Not till 1893 was this embodied in an Education Act.

[39] *Hansard*, 8 June 1891.

[40] G. C. T. Bartley (once an examiner in the Science and Art Department, a founder of the National Penny Bank and an advocate of old age pensions) moved, with E. C. Baring, an amendment against it. They deplored the increasing supplementation of individual initiative.

[41] L.C. 9 May 1891.

[42] *English Education 1789–1902* (Cambridge, 1930), 381.

[43] 4 July 1891.

[44] 13 June 1891.

[45] Annual address to his constituents, 7 Nov. 1891.

[46] J. E. Tyler, *The Struggle for Imperial Unity* (London, 1938), 191. L.C. 2 Sept. 1890.

[47] M.C. Hicks Beach acknowledged that the success of the committee was 'largely due' to Mundella's personal influence as chairman.

[48] 'The question of the Treaties, Fair Trade, etc. was raised, as you see, by Lowther and Vincent, on the Address. Here was an opportunity for unlimited discussion and a test vote. Lowther (who avowed himself a Protectionist of the old school) made a Protectionist speech. Vincent talked of his travels, and of his statesman friends in far countries. Beach followed promptly, and smashed them utterly. I was ready, if necessary, but the whole thing was beneath contempt.' L.C. 10 Feb. 1892.

[49] Mundella at first held no high opinion of the Commission when it was first mooted: 'The Labour Commission is a dodge to stave off difficulties. No doubt much useful knowledge will be accumulated, but its real purpose is to postpone a number of pressing matters till after a General Election,' L.C. 28 Feb. 1890.

[50] L.C. 21 March 1891. He said the same thing to his constituents, 7 Nov. 1891.

[51] Miss Orme, Miss Collett, Miss Abraham and Miss Irwin. Miss Emily Faithful recognised the innovation in *The Times*, 19 Feb. 1891. Their success was a prelude to the appointment of Miss Abraham and Miss M. Paterson as factory inspectors under the home office. T. K. Djang, *Factory Inspection in Great Britain* (London, 1942), 62.

[52] In the *Review of Reviews* for April 1891 Mundella outlined an eleven-point social programme. The first six were educational reforms, the remaining five included an eight-hour day, the establishment of a Labour Bureau, temperance and land reform, progressive income tax on the Swiss model, and heavier death duties.

[53] M.C. 21 Dec. 1891.

[54] Humphrey, *Life of Applegarth*, 271.

[55] M.C.

[56] The *Sheffield Telegraph* issued a manifesto urging the 'men of Brightside' to 'remember that Mundella voted against the Naval Defence Act'. It continued: 'remember that he is a champion of foreign manufacturers who dump their cheap labour products down here while denying to you the right to compete with them except under the disadvantage of a hostile tariff'.

[57] The figures were: Mundella, 4,938; Bargrave Deane, 3,661.

CHAPTER FOURTEEN

[1] M.C. 21 Aug. 1894.

[2] Morley, *Life*, ii, 248. The MS. of Acland's diary is in the possession of his grandson, Sir Richard Acland, who kindly permitted this quotation to be made.

[3] *Fortnightly Review*, liv, (1893), 569.

[4] *Select Committee on Railway Rates and Charges* (2nd Report, 1893), v–vii.

[5] E. Mavor, in *Quarterly Journal of Economics* (Boston, 1894), 280–318.

[6] F. A. Channing had moved a resolution on 23 Jan. 1891, supported by 124 members (only 141 were against him), which had led to the appointment of a Select Committee. For giving evidence before this committee some men were victimised, and the Committee reported that too.

[7] *Hansard*, 16 May 1893. Shaw Lefevre's committee reported twice in c. 385 and c. 462. In the second they tried to answer the question, 'Did the railway companies break faith in January 1893?' and came to the conclusion 'It is difficult to understand the explanations afforded . . . and still more difficult to understand what they do understand of them' (xiii *et seq.*).

[8] Sidney Webb proposed that the existing Statistical Department (set up by Mundella in 1886) should be amalgamated with the Factory and Mining Section of the home office, and that the separate department so created should be represented by a cabinet minister, armed with powers to obtain statistics. *Report of Royal Commission on Labour* (c. 7421), 88.

[9] Tom Mann, one of the leaders of the great strike of the dockers in 1889, had just made an unsuccessful bid to become secretary of the rich and powerful A.E.U. He was later to become a leading spirit in the London Reform Union and the I.L.P. This letter is historic, marking a definite refusal to share in Liberal administration. For his life see S. and B. Webb, *Trade Unionism*, 370.

[10] Fred Maddison, editor of the *Railway Gazette*, who had contested Hull as a Liberal-Labour candidate, was, ironically enough, to succeed Mundella as M.P. for Brightside.

[11] Sir Robert Giffen (1837–1910) became chief of the statistical department of the board of trade after serving as assistant editor of the *Economist*. Both the commercial (1882) and labour (1892) departments were subsequently made subordinate to him. He was a strong Liberal Unionist from 1886, and criticised Gladstone's Home Rule finance in 1893.

[12] Carroll D. Wright (1840–1909) was the first commissioner of the U.S. Board of Labour.

[13] *Fortnightly Review*, liv, 582.

[14] H. Llewellyn Smith had been a Cobden prizeman at Oxford in 1886, and had subsequently acquired a great knowledge of London's East End.

[15] *Economic Journal* (1893), 650–7; R. Page Arnot, *The Miners* (London, 1949).

[16] R. C. K. Ensor, *England 1870–1914*, 299.

[17] At the inauguration of the London Chamber of Arbitration on 23 Nov. 1892, it was specifically stated that the example of the arbitration clause in the 1888 Railway and Canal Traffic Act led to its foundation.

[18] *The Times*, 17 Aug., commenting on Mundella's announcement.

[19] M.C. 18 Nov. 1893.

[20] *Economist*, 19 Aug. 1893.

[21] Gladstone Letter Book for 1894, Add. MSS. 44549, f. 371, written 11 Feb. 1894.

[22] Falconer Larkworthy (1833–1928) went to Australia when he was twenty-two, and in 1861 went to New Zealand to wind up the business of the Oriental Bank. Later in the same year he opened a branch of the Bank of New Zealand to provide currency for the new gold-fields. At the end of the year he returned to England, where for almost thirty years he was managing director of the Bank of New Zealand. He helped to float the New Zealand Loan and Mercantile Agency (of which he was managing director from 1866 to 1890), the Waikato Land Association, and the Auckland Agricultural Company. See his *Ninety-One Years* (London, 1924).

[23] Critchell and Raymond, *A History of the Frozen Meat Industry* (London, 1912).

[24] Vaughan Williams was known for his frankly expressed detestation of 'the earnest Liberal who claims that he alone is right', and this trial must have afforded him particular enjoyment. E. Moberly Bell, *Flora Shaw* (London 1942), 43.

[25] M.C. 14 March 1894.

[26] M.C. 22 March 1894.

[27] *Hansard*, 24 May 1894. Sir Algernon West, *Private Diaries* (London, 1922), 293, recorded how he had met 'poor Mundella', who said he hoped 'I should not think he had done anything dishonourable which was the last thing I should think of him'.

[28] *Punch*, 19 May 1894, also M.C.

[29] As the *Report of the Labour Commission* says on 101–3, 'several suggestions which we should have desired to make . . . have been anticipated with the publication of the *Labour Gazette*'.

CHAPTER FIFTEEN

[1] M.C. R. T. Reid (1846–1923) was knighted in 1894 in the same month as Mundella resigned from the government. He was at first solicitor-general, becoming attorney-general in October of this year.

[2] Henry James (1828–1911), Mundella's old friend, became a Liberal Unionist and Attorney-General of the Duchy of Cornwall. M.C. 14, 23, 28 Jan. 1895.

[3] M.C.

[4] S. and B. Webb, *English Local Government* (London, 1929), viii, 29; Gilbert Slater, *Poverty and the State* (London, 1930), 159; Sir William Chance, *Children under the Poor-Law* (London, 1897), though a general indictment of Mundella's committee, admits on p. 121 that 'aggregation of children in great numbers in large barracks cannot be good for them'.

[5] Fitch had previously been appointed by Mundella in 1883 to be chief inspector of schools in the Eastern Division.

[6] Dame Henrietta Barnett, *Canon Barnett* (London, 1921), 685. She formed 'The State Children's Association' to campaign for amelioration.

[7] Brooke Lambert (1834–1901), anticipator of the scientific social researches of Charles Booth. After a visit to the West Indies, he returned to assist in the promotion of the London University Extension Society. He had been vicar of Greenwich since 1880.

[8] On 17 June 1897 Mundella was urging that the poor law schools should be broken up.

[9] M.C. Both Gorst and George Russell were implicated in the New Zealand Loan and Mercantile Agency.

[10] See Halévy, *History of the English People* (Pelican Books), Epilogue, ii, 94–9, for an account of Gorst's motives.

[11] 27 April 1896 at Sheffield.

[12] *Economist*, on the withdrawal of the bill.

[13] *Hansard* (4th series), xlvii, 315.

[14] *op. cit.*, xlvi, 545.

[15] *ibid.*, 1375.

[16] *ibid.*, 550.

[17] *op. cit.*, l, 304.

[18] *op. cit.*, xxxi, 187.

[19] M.C.

[20] *The Times*, 9 June 1897.

[21] 17 June 1897.

[22] Firth College, founded by the great steelmaster whose name it bore, had applied for admission to the Victoria University of Manchester, but had been refused. Mundella had long assisted it: he secured it a grant in 1883, and another in 1890.

[23] Obituary notices were in all the major papers. A large number of letters were written to Miss Maria Theresa Mundella which are still preserved among the Mundella Correspondence.

CHAPTER SIXTEEN

[1] Marx complained bitterly to Engels about Odger and his associates, declaring that at the next meeting of the International he 'would personally deal these fools . . . the finishing blow'—*Selected Works* (London, 1942), ii, 614. See especially Mundella's paper to the Social Science Congress at Birmingham in 1868, in which he called Odger 'one of the most intelligent trade unionists of the country'. *Proceedings, etc.* p. 526. He quoted Odger's remarks on strikes with approval.

[2] T. Rothstein, *From Chartism to Labourism* (London, 1929), 266.

[3] M. Elwin, *Charles Reade* (London, 1931), 203, 208, points out that Reade first toyed with the idea in 1859, and began collecting newspaper cuttings in 1862, and says, 'On none of his subsequent novels did he spend half the time and trouble which this book cost him'. It was first published in the *Cornhill*, March 1869–July 1870, and in the latter year Reade put it on the stage as a play.

[4] Oct. 1867. Compare also *Blackwood's Edinburgh Magazine* for Feb. 1867, which called every member of a trade union 'either a slave or a tyrant, or a combination of both, like an Eastern visier', and *Punch*, 26 Jan. 1867, quoting Charles Markham's speech on the 'idle, thoughtless men who were unable to raise themselves to the same level as the superior working men'. Markham was a Chesterfield industrialist, who wrote letters to the *Sheffield Independent* against Mundella's candidature in 1868, signing them 'Voices from the Hive'.

[5] *Nineteenth Century*, Nov. 1889, 724.

[6] See especially the Report of the Tenth Trade Union Congress of 1877, and the excellent article by Irving Garbati in *University of Toronto Quarterly*, xx (1950), 69–84.

[7] L.C. 1 April 1869.

[8] *Industrial Conciliation* (London, 1876), 33.

[9] *Economica*, March 1930, 27.

[10] Secretary to the Association of Iron and Steel Workers to the Royal Commission on Labour (c. 6795, iv), QQ. 15182–3. See also MacDonald's apostrophe twenty years earlier, 'Look at the glorious state of things in England and Wales. In Northumberland the men now meet with their employers round the common board. In Durhamshire a Board of Arbitration and Conciliation has also been formed and 75,000 men repose with perfect confidence in [its] decisions. . . . There are 40,000 men in Yorkshire in the same position', J. R. Raynes, *Coal and its Conflicts* (London, 1928), 32. To do Mundella justice, he did not approve of Lord St. Leonard's Act of 1867 (which provided that interested persons might establish a Council of Conciliation on permission being granted by the Crown, the council to be elected on a local trade basis), for he wrote to Leader on 1 April 1869, 'One would not like to speak disrespectfully of anything so well-intentioned, but a more absurd piece of legislation was never effected'. Nor was he any more hopeful as to the prospects of his own act passed in 1872, which contained the unique feature for ensuring agreement between the parties by the exchange of a printed copy of articles between masters and men. He only presented the bill at Howell's insistence.

[11] Pointed out by Lord Amulree, *Industrial Arbitration in Great Britain* (Oxford, 1929), 83.

[12] J. R. Hicks, *op. cit.*, 30.

[13] It was in the years 1866–9 that F. D. Longe, Cliffe Leslie, Fleeming Jenkin and W. T. Thornton published their articles attacking the wage-fund theory. The latter's views influenced John Stuart Mill, who in the *Fortnightly Review* gave currency to the doctrine that unions could gain at an expense other than that of their fellow workers. Mundella knew Mill (L.C. 24 July 1868), and accompanied him when he spoke at St. James' Hall in that month.

[14] There were, according to the Royal Commission on Labour, no fewer than sixty-four boards of arbitration existing in 1893. For the consecutive development of the idea (and gloss on Mundella's Board) see D. Knoop, *Industrial Arbitration and Conciliation* (London, 1905); A. C. Pigou, *Principles and Methods of Industrial Peace* (London, 1905); S. and B. Webb, *Problems of Modern Industry* (London, 1920); J. R. Hicks, *The Theory of Wages* (London, 1935); J. H. Richardson, *Industrial Relations in Great Britain* (Geneva, 1938); Dorothy Sells, *British Wages Boards* (Washington, 1939), and John T. Dunlop, *Collective Bargaining: Principles and Cases* (Chicago, 1950). From 1910 to 1924, 72 per cent of labour disputes involving cessation of work were settled by conciliation.

[15] *The Times*, 23 Feb. 1891, *Hansard* debates on arbitration bills, in 1892, 1893, 1894 and 1895.

[16] Their work was only discontinued in 1909.

[17] L.C. 8 Feb. 1883.

[18] Apart from his Italian ancestry, he also used the term in letters, e.g. *ante* p. 161.

[19] Isaac Ironside (1808–70) was such a plague to Mundella, that the latter wrote to Leader, 'I think he ought to have his head shaven. He writes letters to Hadfield and myself, abusing everybody from Castlereagh to John Bright.' L.C. 13 March 1869. 'He is such a goose I fear he will be always hissing at somebody', L.C. 10 April 1869.

[20] H. M. Doncaster, *J. H. Barber* (Sheffield, 1905), ii, 346–70, for his letters in support of Mundella's candidature in 1868.

[21] Walter Lenwood was at Nether Chapel from 1872 to 1885.

[22] At Upper Chapel (whose history he published in 1900) from 1889 to 1902.

[23] John Calvert was such a success when he came to Zion Chapel in 1857 that his congregation, poor as it was, built him a bigger one in 1863. There he remained till 1895, having been twice refused permission to retire. He was a great school builder.

[24] W. J. Townshend, *James Stacey, D.D.* (London, 1891), quotes on p. 163 a remark he made in the Potteries, 'Capital and Labour are not, and cannot be, in conflict, though they are at times made to appear so'.

[25] They were nourished by such national nonconformist magazines as *The Revival*, the *Christian Herald*, the *British Weekly*, *Good Words*, the *Nonconformist*, the *British Quarterly Review*, the *Congregationalist*, and the *Baptist Messenger*: all a rich quarry for the student of their ideas.

[26] He also had to contend with artisans like William Rolley (1839–1912), who, after a varied career as policeman, engine-driver, steel melter and farrier, became president of the Trade Union Congress held in Sheffield in 1874. He ended his life as a Conservative political agent. John Wilson (1820–90), a working cutler and supporter of Mundella in Brightside, which he represented on the Town Council from 1874 till his death. He was a confirmed opponent of trade unions, and told the Social Science Congress so in 1865.

[27] L.C. 3 Dec. 1884. His view of Earl Fitzwilliam (1815–1902), one of the twenty-eight noblemen recorded in 1883 as possessing above 1,000,000 acres of land in England, and Lord Lieutenant of the West Riding (where he owned 22,192 acres) from 1857 to 1892. He came in for a good deal of bitter comment from Mundella for the management of his collieries. 'He has set a bad example to the whole district', Mundella wrote (L.C. 30 May 1873). 'Now he will either have to loose the profits of his colliery or knuckle down to the Miners' Association. He had a fine opportunity for doing a gracious thing, and reading the workmen a good lesson, but he objects to their acting reasonably and honourably at Normansell's bidding. Lord Halifax and myself were at great pains over this business, and you see the result. I am tired of hereditary legislation and legislators, they are at the root of a good deal of our social mischief.' Mundella also felt strongly about the other hereditary landowner of Sheffield, the duke of Norfolk. 'Why should he take £100,000 a year out of Sheffield on which he pays only income tax?' he asked Leader on 8 Feb. 1885. 'All your local expenditure, in the meantime, going to improve his property.' See Chapter Seven, n. 10.

[28] L.C. 2 Feb. 1878.

[29] L.C. 9 July 1883.

[30] 'There are too many corns on the foot for the boot to be allowed to pinch very tightly,' continued Uttley, *Royal Commission on Trade Depression* (c. 4715, 1886), and Samuel Osborne, head of the great steel firm which bore his name, agreed that the seriousness of false marking could hardly be exaggerated (Q. 3268).

[31] *Sheffield Independent*, 6, 12, 20 and 27 March 1886.

[32] *Chicago Tribune*, 8 March, carried headlines, 'Great Cutlery Manufacturers playing havoc with their country's reputation. Importing inferior German goods and re-exporting them as home manufactures. Some revelations that American dealers would do well to ponder over.'

[33] In the midst of his seemingly endless representations to the Conservative president of the board of trade, he wrote to Leader, 'Much as I love you, I wish you and your merchandise Marks Bill were at . . . Monte Carlo. We may be hoist with our own petard', L.C. 14 Jan. 1887. He was thinking, of course, of the thin boundary between this and protection.

[34] L.C. 28 April 1889.

[35] L.C. 27 Aug. 1890.

[36] L.C. 20 Feb. 1870.

[37] Acknowledged by Forster when he opened the first Sheffield Board Schools on 18 August 1874.

[38] L.C. 12 Sept. 1869.

[39] L.C. 25 Jan. 1879. The occasion was Redgrave's too literal interpretation of the act (which bore hardly on many of Sheffield's small 'mesters').

[40] Ernst Edler Von Plener, *English Factory Legislation* (London, 1873), viii. Misdated by the Webbs (*Problems of Modern Industry*, 1902, 114) as written in 1893.

[41] C. T. Millis, *Technical Education, Its Development and Aims* (London, 1925), 39, 42.

[42] L.C. 6 Sept. 1879.

[43] L.C. 28 Oct. 1879.

[44] L.C. 2 and 21 May 1883.

[45] L.C. 30 June 1883.

[46] L.C. 31 July 1890.

[47] 28 Feb. 1891. He also urged Leader to so 'work' the Technical Act (which endowed the country and borough councils with power to levy a penny rate for technical education) that the moneys obtained by it should go to the support and extension of continuation schools, then coming into favour. For the full blessing of the Committee of Council, the country had to wait till the next Liberal ministry, when A. H. D. Acland, by his evening school code, made it possible for such councils to earn government grants by establishing classes for adults over twenty-one years old. Attendance at such schools had been compulsory in Saxony since 1873 (F. H. Dale, *Special Reports on Educational Subjects*, i, 484), and were common in the rest of Europe by the end of the century (M. E. Sadler, *Continuation Schools in England and Elsewhere* (Manchester, 1908), 483–576).

[48] P.E.P.

[49] L.C. 28 May 1895 : 'I hope you see your way clear to a life of learned leisure, free from the responsibilities of daily journalism'.

[50] He did not want Mundella to contest Brightside, but to challenge the Conservatives in the new Central Division of Sheffield after the redistribution of seats in 1885. Mundella replied, 'I have had three pretty stiff contests, and I am willing that others should have the opportunity of *winning their spurs*'. Leader himself stood for Ecclesall, another parliamentary division of the city, but was defeated, both in 1892 and 1895.

[51] He told J. D. Leader in 1879 (L.C. 10 March), 'I can hardly drag about the house from sheer debility. I am afraid I am wearing bodily. I am very deficient in that wiry vigour which distinguishes such men as Gladstone and Forster.' Ten years later he was repeating 'I am warned that I must go softly, else I may break up.'

[52] L. E. Elliott-Binns, *Religion in the Victorian Era* (London, 1936), 407.

[53] To Miss Mundella 23 July 1897.

Index

A

Abyssinia, 81
Abraham, Miss, 371
Accrington, 163
Acland, A. H. D., 271, 272, 273, 289, 315, 339, 362, 369, 370, 372, 377
Acland, James, 36, 341
Acland, T. D., 346
Adam, W. P., 156, 172, 179, 197, 356
Adams, F., 353
Adderley, Sir Charles (Lord Norton), 94, 109, 221, 350, 353, 362
Agriculture, 218, 222, 321
Allies, T.W., 361
Allon, H., 174
Allott, 76, 131, 353
Allsop, Rebecca, 15
Amberley, Lord, 44–6, 118
America, United States of, 14, 38, 50, 55, 78, 81, 83, 84–91, 94, 108, 163, 187, 195–6, 225, 240, 262, 266–7, 293, 321, 344, 352, 359, 368
Anderson, G., 169, 221
Anstruther, Sir, 101, 253, 367
Anti-Corn Law League, 18, 172, 175, 271
Applegarth, R., 39, 40, 50, 53, 54, 55, 57, 58, 59, 60, 62, 71, 72, 75, 82, 99, 100, 102, 110, 111, 120, 129, 158, 286–7, 332, 346, 347, 350, 354
Arbitration, 32–4, 53, 58, 67, 88, 102–4, 121, 265, 297–8, 318–20, 375
Arch, Joseph, 119–20, 351, 353
Argyll, Duke of, 173, 237–8, 249, 258, 315, 329
Armstrong, H. E., 362
Armstrong, Sir W., 103–4
Army, 93–4
Arnold, Arthur, 176
Arnold, Matthew, 77, 207–8, 229, 230, 231, 232, 234–5, 257, 322, 347, 350, 352, 359, 360, 362
Ashmead-Bartlett, Sir E., 308
Ashworth, Henry, 134, 136
Askham, 346
Asquith, H. H., 288, 333
Astley, G., 182
Aubrey, W. H. S., 135

B

Bagehot, W., 146
Baines, E., 76
Baird, S., 240
Balfour, A. J., 248, 316, 366

Balfour, Jabez, 302
Balfour of Burleigh, Lord, 215, 221, 369
Ballot, 82, 87, 119
Banbury Technical Institute, 361
Bangor University College, 217, 359
Barber, J. H., 323, 374
Baring, E. C., 371
Baring, F. T. (Lord Northbrook), 23
Barnett, Mrs., 309, 373
Barry, P., 98
Bartley, G. C. T., 292, 371
Barton, Luke, 22, 29
Bates, H. W., 15–16, 19, 20, 21, 38, 338
Bath, election at, 130
Bath, marquis of, 176
Baxter, S., 49
Bayley, R. S., 340
Bazley, Sir T., 132, 134, 135, 136, 144
Beaulieu, M., 191
Beckton, gas producer strike, 126, 128
Beehive, 96, 99, 126, 135, 195, 342
Beer retailers, 28, 100–1, 140
Beesly, E. S., 40, 58, 68
Belgian iron girders, 225
Bennet, H., 32
Bentinck, Cavendish G. A. F., 147, 353
Berlin, conference at (1890), 281–2
Berlin, Congress of (1878), 185
Bentley, 330
Bickford-Smith, W., 249, 365, 367
Biddulph, M., 255
Birkbeck, Sir E., 240, 263, 264
Birks, 121
Birley, H., 224
Birmingham, 57, 72, 73, 75, 76, 170, 178, 195, 215, 218
Birtwhistle, T., 133
Bismarckism, 129
Bitter Cry of Outcast London, 221
Blackie, J. S., 234
Blakiston, J. R., 360
Board of Trade, 82, 237–66, 289–305
Boehm, Sir E., 225
Bolton, J., 251
Booth, Charles, 332
Borough Funds Bill, 108–10
Bosanquet, B., 322
Boston, Mundella's interests in, 38; visits, 86
Boyle, Courtenay, 251, 322, 369
Bradford, 14, 30, 216, 231
Bradlaugh, C., 117, 123, 186, 329, 352, 363
Bramwell, Lord, 255
Brand, H. B. W., 44
Brand, H. M., 355

379

Brand, H. R., 364
Brassey, T. (Lord Brassey), 71, 102, 317
Brett, Justice, 126
Brett, R. (Viscount Esher), 248, 366
Bridges, Dr., 92, 125, 135, 165
Bright, Jacob, 352
Bright, John, 68, 82, 89, 142, 153, 155, 156, 157, 177, 178, 195, 257, 360, 375
Brightside, 48, 229, 230, 307, 371
Bristol, 45, 130
British Association, 33, 46
British and Foreign Schools Society, 360
Broadhead, W., 48–9, 53, 344
Broadhurst, H., 152, 170, 172, 174, 185–6, 198, 279, 327, 332, 354, 356, 357, 363, 369
Brogden, A., 155
Brooke, Stopford, 173, 336
Brooke-Lambert, Rev., 309, 310, 373
Brooks, Canon, 340
Brown, A. H., 365
Brown, B. H., 363
Brown, Sir John, 47, 344, 352
Brown, John, 315
Browning, Robert, 173, 180–1, 195
Bruce, H. A. (Lord Aberdare), 56, 70, 71, 72, 96, 100, 208, 210
Brunner, J. T., 125
Bryant, W. C., 87
Bryce, James, 173, 175, 198, 203, 258, 321, 356, 368
Bulgarian atrocities, 168–9, 249
Bullionist, 244
Bunce, J., 84
Burke, Edmund, 308
Burke, Ellen, 276
Burnett, John, 102–3, 186, 240, 281, 296, 349, 357
Burnley, 102
Burt, Thomas, 138, 149, 280, 293, 294
Butler, Josephine, 92, 353
Buxton, C., 92
Buxton, S. C., 283, 360, 362
Buxton, Sir T. F., 67, 174

C

Cairns, Lord, 72
Calcraft, H., 251
Caldecott, Dr., 130
Caldecott, Randolph, 195
Calvert, John, 376
Cameron, James, 221
Cammell, Charles, 37, 76, 343–4
Campbell, Sir G., 175
Campbell-Bannerman, H., 248, 363
Cannon Street Hotel, 117, 246
Canterbury, archbishop of, 214
Cardiff University College, 217, 269
Carlingford, Lord, 218, 219, 222, 223, 233, 248, 363
Carlyle, Thomas, 172, 175, 180

Carnarvon, Lord, 99, 182
Cavendish, Lord E., 256
Cavendish, Lord F., 171, 173, 206, 211, 355, 360
Cattle plagues, 186–8, 203, 219, 221
Central Council for Promoting Penny Dinners, 360
Central Nonconformist Committee, 122
Chamberlain, Joseph, 57, 72, 78, 109, 129, 130, 131, 138–40, 152, 155, 159, 160, 166, 167, 170, 177–8, 179, 180, 183, 187, 199, 217, 226, 228, 229, 231, 238, 242, 248, 252, 253, 257, 284, 296, 319–20, 321, 325, 326, 331, 333, 334, 350, 353, 356, 362, 363, 366
Chamberlain, Richard, 252, 367
Chambers of Commerce, 32, 181, 239, 241, 242
Chambers, William, 40, 342
Channing, F. A., 370, 372
Chaplin, H., 175
Charity Commissioners, 147, 215
Charnwood, Lady, 337, 338, 348
Chartists, 17–18
Chemnitz, 209, 232
Chicago Tribune, 376
Childers, H. C. E., 119, 220, 222, 223, 226, 231
Churchill, Lord Randolph, 220, 296, 321
Civil List, 117, 118
Clapham, Sir John, 17, 338, 339
Claussen, Chevalier, 21
Clayden, P. W., 175, 196, 203, 356
Clegg, W. J., 121, 334
Clifton, Sir Robert, 34–6, 41–5, 341
Coal Mines Regulation Act, 110, 114, 350
Cobden, Richard, 18, 20, 30–2, 38, 40, 41, 76, 82–3, 124, 134, 237, 344, 347, 348, 363
Code committee, 210, 213, 235–6, 322
Code Reform Association, 273–4
Cole, G. D. H., 345, 350
Coleridge, B., 287
Collett, Miss C., 296, 371
Collings, Jesse, 72, 296
Committee of the Privy Council on Education, 52, 199, 203–36
Contemporary Review, 112, 129
Continuation Schools, 271, 281, 316, 377
Conscience Clause, 78
Contagious Diseases Acts, 90–3, 332, 349, 353
Cooper, Thomas, 17–8, 102–4, 186, 234, 338
Co-operative Movement, 82
Co-operative News, 116
Cope, W., 339
Copeland, W. V., 339
Corbett, J., 252, 367
Cossham, H., 45–6, 275, 343
Coste, 240
Courtney, L. H., 363, 365

County Courts Bill, 81
Cowen, Joseph, 103, 169
Cox, J. C., 122, 130, 131, 156, 353
Cremer, W. R., 117, 123, 150, 342, 354
Crichton-Browne, Dr., 214
Crimean War, 23, 26
Criminal Law Amendment Act, 96, 117, 127, 128, 134, 148, 150-1, 349
Crompton, H., 68, 69, 116, 117, 127, 136, 137, 150, 203, 317, 318, 347, 359
Cross, J. K., 239
Cross, R. A. (Lord Cross), 142, 144, 145, 150-1, 164, 193, 210, 232, 271, 274, 275, 353, 360, 362
Crosskey, Dr., 275
Crossley, Sir F., 134, 136, 145
Cullom, S. M., 368
Cumin, P., 165, 222-3, 277, 322, 359, 360

D

Daily News, 70, 101, 117, 168, 211, 244, 351, 356
Dale, David, 68, 104
Dale, Rev. R. W., 130, 219, 275
Dalhousie, Lord, 220
Dana, R. H., 86, 87, 88
Darlington, 104
Davies, D., 365, 367
Dawney, Col., 260
Deane, Bargrave, 287
De Grey (Lord Ripon), 90, 248, 361, 369
Denison, Speaker, 68
Denmark, 315-6
Departmental Committee on Metropolitan Poor Law Schools, 309-10
Departmental Committee on Welsh Education, 207
Dent, J., 296
Derby, Lord, 169, 183
'Derby Lad', 196
Dilke, Sir C. W., 77, 78, 93 101, 102, 118, 123, 142, 155, 169, 170, 349, 354, 355
Dill, S., 224
Dillwyn, L., 279
Disestablishment, 120, 167, 335
Disraeli, Benjamin, 70, 93, 119, 128, 133, 142, 148, 157, 167, 168, 169, 171, 184, 185, 198, 257
Dixon, George, 67, 72, 78, 84, 109, 120, 130-1, 140, 141, 156, 162, 163, 167, 179
Donisthorne, W., 255
Donnelly, (Major later Sir) J. F. D., 193, 206, 357, 358
Drawing Association, 369
Dronfield, William, 49, 50, 53, 58, 61, 62, 324, 344
Drummond, C. J., 296
Du Cane, 355
Dunn, T., 62, 346
Dunraven, Lord, 281

E

Eastern Question Association, 175-6, 177, 181, 182, 183, 185, 258, 271, 280
Eaton, John, 85
Ebrington, Viscount, 256
Eccarius, J. G., 117
Economist, 71, 77, 95, 136, 147-8, 240, 244, 251, 255, 260, 261, 266, 281, 284, 285, 293, 300, 303-4, 310, 312, 341, 347, 349, 353, 368, 372, 374
Edinburgh *Journal* 21, *Magazine*, 374, *Review*, 51, University, 163
Education Act, 1870, 77-80, 217, 219, 228, 353; 25th clause of, 128-9, 130, 136
Education Act, 1876, 164-7
Education Act, 1880, 204-5
Education Act, 1891, 283-5
Education Act, 1896, 311-14
Education Code, 94, 210-14, 349, 359
Edwards, Passmore, 198
Elcho, Lord (Wemyss), 111, 114, 123, 127, 260, 262, 351, 367
Eliza Cook's Journal, 21, 339
Ellicott, Bishop, 122
Elvaston Place, 121, 195, 316
Emerson, 86
Employers' Association, 133
Endowed Schools Act, 1874, 146-8
Engels, F., 335, 342
Evans, Robert, 340
Examiner, 155
Exeter Gazette, 349
Exeter Hall, 182, 370
Exhibition of 1851, 31, 331
Exhibition of 1854, 22
Exhibition of 1862, 339
Exhibition of 1867, 51, 52
Exhibition of 1878, 193
Exhibition of 1883, 240
Exhibition of 1884, 225
Extraordinary Gazette, 29

F

Fabians, 293, 299, 305, 314, 322
Factory legislation, 37, 56, 74, 124, 125, 131, 133, 137, 138, 143, 144, 161, 162, 163, 164, 193-4, 225, 314, 328
Factory Acts Reform Association, 123, 143
Factory Workers Short Time Committee, 122, 133, 145-6
Fairbairn, Sir A., 253, 365, 367
Fair Trade, 286, 327, 363
Farrer, T. C., 369
Farrer, T. H., 251, 367, 368
Fawcett, Professor Henry, 74, 102, 115, 118, 119, 130-1, 132, 134, 140, 144, 145, 148, 154, 156, 169, 174, 193, 199, 357
Fearneyhough, T., 49-50
Felkin, H. M., 209, 359

Felkin, W., 19, 27, 33, 338, 340
Fell, Rev. J., 298–9
Fergusson, Sir J., 162, 301, 302
Ferry, Jules, 209, 359
Firth, Mark, 48, 56, 323, 330, 344
Fish Stall Gazette, 29, 41
Fisheries Department of the Board of Trade, 240–1, 299, 321
Fison, W., 132, 144
Fitch, Sir J., 236, 309, 360, 362, 373
Fitzmaurice, Lord E., 179, 317
Fitzwilliam, Earl, 350, 376
Forster, W. E., 30, 56, 73, 75–6, 77, 79, 89, 90, 103, 122, 123, 145, 153, 154–7, 163, 165, 167, 170, 176, 177, 183, 184, 186, 187, 196, 197, 208, 220, 222, 226, 231, 328, 355, 359, 377
Fortescue, Lord, 255
Fortnightly Review, 67, 128, 129, 150, 155, 156, 177, 369, 375
Foscolo, Ugo, 14
Framework Knitters, 14–6, 19, 21, 32
France, 84, 98, 209, 225, 240
Frazer, Bishop James, 171, 320
Freeman, E. A., 174–5, 180, 356
Freshwater Fish Protection Act, 188
Froude, J. A., 180

G

Galton, F., 225
Game Laws, 81
Garnett, Wm., 279
Gathorne-Hardy, G. (Lord Cranbrook), 99, 151, 199, 232, 248, 277, 358, 362
George, D. Lloyd, 315
Germany, 74, 79, 84, 94, 104, 119, 208–9, 221, 225, 229, 240, 280, 281, 283, 348, 370
Giffen, Sir R., 240, 294–5, 372
Gillespie, Miss E., 309
Girdlestone, Canon, 122
Gladstone, H., 317
Gladstone, J. H., 369
Gladstone, W. E., 40, 60, 63, 68, 77, 78, 89, 93, 100, 113, 117, 118, 125, 128, 134, 142, 146, 147, 150, 152, 153, 157, 169, 172–3, 175, 176, 177, 178, 180, 181, 183, 184, 196, 197, 198, 199, 200, 203, 209, 222, 223, 226, 227, 228, 229, 232, 233, 237, 238, 247–9, 250, 252, 253, 254, 255, 256, 257, 258, 266, 280, 288, 289, 293, 294, 297, 300, 302, 306, 346, 353, 355, 358, 363, 367, 368, 372
Glasgow Chamber of Commerce, 145
Glasgow Herald, 85, 366
Glasgow University, 196
Gloucester, Bishop of, 226
Globe, 185, 211
Glyn, G. G., 110, 346, 350
Godfrey's Cordial, 338
Gorst, Sir John, 179, 203, 296, 301, 309, 310, 311, 312, 315, 316, 374

Gould, Elgin R., 293
Goschen, G. J., 109, 146, 153, 154, 167, 254, 260, 282, 331, 353, 363
Graham, W. K., 301
Granville, Lord, 154, 176, 178, 196, 197, 354, 367, 369
Green, J. R., 173
Green, T. H., 322
Gregory, Canon, 217, 219, 232, 362
Grey, A. H. G., 248, 250, 363
Grimthorpe, Lord, 246, 364
Grosvenor, Lord R., 233, 250
Guile, D., 62, 99
Gurdon, R. T., 256

H

Hadfield, George, 59–62, 131, 375
Hadley, A. T., 364
Haldane, R. B., 195, 346
Half-Timers, 56–7, 122–5, 131–6, 193–4, 204–5, 281–3
Halifax, Lord, 353, 367
Hamilton, Lord Claud, 127, 243, 249, 257, 364–5
Hamilton, Lord George, 127, 192, 234, 364
Hamilton, Lord John, 127, 364
Hanley, labour troubles at, 80, 308
Harcourt, Sir W. V., 114, 119, 128, 138, 149, 150, 152, 153, 170, 176, 195, 248, 303, 310, 315, 355, 357
Hare, G., 254
Hare, T., 146
Harney, G. J., 322, 340
Harris, Richard, 19, 20, 338
Harrison, Frederic, 54, 58–9, 67, 68, 116, 126, 137, 141, 195, 200, 279, 319, 335, 345, 346, 354, 359
Hart Dyke, 271, 284, 316
Hartington, marquis of, 142, 153, 154–7, 159, 170, 171, 176, 183, 196, 197, 198–9, 228, 231, 250, 253, 256, 257, 270, 273, 289, 312, 354, 355, 357, 358
Hastings, G. W., 256
Havelock, Sir H., 174
Headmasters' Conference, 146
Healy, T. M., 209, 359
Heller, T. E., 362
Herapath, 244, 246, 251, 255, 261, 366, 368
Herbert, Auberon, 55, 82, 97, 101, 117, 118, 128, 173, 180–1, 184, 186, 193, 257, 349, 351, 356, 357, 368
Herbert, Henry, 316
Herschell, Lord, 238
Heurism, 225
Hewitt, A. S., 348
Heymann, Lewis, 25, 26, 34, 339
Hicks Beach, Sir M., 184, 264, 266, 278, 286, 371
Higher grade schools, 212, 216, 217, 224, 235, 314, 330, 331, 336

Hine, B. H., 20, 38; George, 340; Jonathan, 20, 22; John, 20, 38; T. C., 21, 26, 339
Home Rule, 197, 248, 249 ff, 255, 292
Homes, Oliver Wendell, 86, 87, 88
Holmshaw, R., 326, 327
Holyoake, G. J., 74, 167, 317, 322, 340, 348, 355
Hornby v. Close, 50, 54
Howard, H. C., 256
Howell, George, 41, 55, 59, 105, 111, 113, 119, 123, 133, 136, 137, 138, 143, 149, 150, 151, 170, 173, 174, 186, 270, 296, 342, 345, 347, 349, 351, 353, 354
Hubrecht, 240
Hughes, Thomas, 51, 86, 71, 72, 82, 85, 96, 97, 101, 116, 140, 148, 149, 208, 257, 335, 345, 348, 351, 359, 368
Hutton, R. H., 194, 250, 257, 335, 368
Huxley, T. H., 46, 163, 240, 241, 254, 257, 270, 271, 279, 358

I

Independent Labour Party, 266, 305
Illustrated London News, 25, 304–5
Industrial Remuneration Conference, 234
Ingelow, Jean, 195
Inspectorate, 213, 322, 328
Intermediate education in Wales, 207, 208, 227
Inventions, Mundella's use of, 21–4
Intelligence testing, 76, 225
International Working Men's Association, 75, 117, 342–3, 354
Irish, 140, 227, 232, 247–9, 253, 280, 289
Ironside, Isaac, 323, 375

J

James, Henry (Lord James of Hereford), 114, 150, 281, 282, 283, 303, 306, 307, 308, 310, 320, 335, 361, 363, 370
Jeans, J. S., 258–9
Jenkin, Fleeming, 378
Jenkins, E., 129, 130, 142, 352
Jenkins, H. M., 354
Jenkins, J. J., 252, 367
Jennings, L. J., 280
Jevons, S., 192, 365
Johnson, W. J., 340
Johnstone, Sir H., 101
Jones, E., 55
Jones, J. V., 227, 269, 363, 369
Jones, Lloyd, 59
Jude the Obscure, 211

K

Kay-Shuttleworth, Sir U., 231
Kempson, W., 16

Kendall, G., 53
Kettle, Sir R., 112
Kitching, A. G., 252, 367
Knowles, T., 355

L

Labouchere, Henry, 198, 232–3, 303, 335, 362
Labour Bureau of Statistics, 239–40; Department of, 293–6, 305, 333, 371; *Gazette*, 295, 300; Representation League, 357, Royal Commission on, 286–7, 305, 371, 372, 373, 375
Laing, S., 260
Lancashire Coal Strike, 57–8; *Echo*, 370
Lancet, 214
Land Purchase Bill, 248–9, 253 ff.
Land Tenure Association, 117
Lansdowne, Lord, 258, 315
Larkworthy, Falconer, 300, 373
Lavaleye, Emile de, 191, 193
Lawson, W., 142
Leader family, 323, 337, 344, 345, 346, 348, 350, 352, 357, 361; J. D., 265, 277, 278, 281, 286, 299, 300, 304, 333, 369, 377; Robert, 55, 58, 60–1, 68, 69, 74, 76, 78, 79, 84, 86, 89, 96, 98, 99, 101, 105, 106, 111, 117, 121, 125, 127, 129, 130, 134, 136, 139, 140, 145, 146–7, 152, 153, 156, 158–9, 160–1, 163, 165, 168, 169, 176, 177, 178, 179, 180, 181, 183, 187, 189, 195, 197, 198, 199, 210, 221, 226, 228, 233, 324, 330, 333, 344, 345, 346, 348, 350, 352, 353, 360, 361; R. E., 287, 295, 301, 326, 327, 333, 377
Leatham, 142
Leach, 189, 190
Lecky, W. E., 173
Leeds, T.U.C. at, 216
Leeman, G., 108, 350
Leicester, 15–20; *Chronicle*, 338; *Mercury*, 351
Leighton, Baldwyn, 120
Leighton, Frederick, 369
Leng, W. C., and the *Sheffield Telegraph*, 61, 127, 151, 182, 196, 217, 247, 265, 278, 299, 307–8, 324, 326, 347, 371
Lennox, Lord Henry, 99
Lenwood, Walter, 323, 376
Leslie, Cliffe, 375
Liberation Society, 160, 351
Liberty and Property Defence League, 255
Lichfield, Earl of, 55, 99
Liddon, Canon, 174, 180
Lincoln, Lord, 35–6, 341
Lockyer, Sir N., 279, 370
London, Bishop of, 362; Chamber of Arbitration, 372; East End slums, 79, 125; School Board, 89, 161, 173, 203; *Standard*, 90; *Telegraph*, 39, 70, 185; Trades Council, 55, 95, 342

Lowe, Robert, 67, 135, 142, 145, 146, 151, 154, 157, 310, 333
Loughborough, 73, 124
Lowell, J. R., 87
Lowther, J., 296, 371
Lubbock, Sir J., 145, 203, 255, 349, 363, 368, 369
Lubez, 117
Lucy, H. W. ('Toby, M.P.'), 233, 304, 362
Lymington, Viscount, 256

M

MacDonald, A., 110, 112, 123, 138, 148, 149, 150, 186, 354, 375
McPherson, Grant, Sir G., 251, 367
M'Weeny, W., 133
Maddison, Fred, 294, 372
Magee, Bishop, 351
Magnus, Sir Philip, 209, 331
Maitland, F. W., 122, 331
Mallet, L., 82
Maltby Common, 189–90
Manchester, 58, 76–7, 119, 224, 225, 242–3, 351, 364, 366
Mann, Tom, 294, 373
Manners, Lord John, 73, 99, 101
Manning, Cardinal, 217, 227–8, 230, 231, 232, 233, 234, 274, 279, 286, 361, 362
Manning, Rev. J., 323
Mappin, F. T., 47, 159, 160, 161, 287, 323, 324, 331, 333, 343, 354
'Mary Ann', 53
Mather, Joseph, 48, 344
Mather, Wm., 359
Maurice, Rev. F. D., 92, 340
Marx, Karl, 37, 40, 88, 117, 318, 323, 342, 374
Mason, Hugh, 144
Mellor, John, 34
Meysey-Thompson, Sir H., 243, 252, 315, 367
Miall, E., 155, 118, 351
Midland Counties Illuminator, 17
Mill, John Stuart, 44, 51, 70, 146, 194, 257, 351, 375
Mines Regulation Act, 112–14
Molloy, B. C., 362
Monkswell, Lady, 182, 356
Moon, Ernest, 252; Richard, 247, 261
Moore, T., 107–8, 350
Morley, 97
Morley, Arnold, 299
Morley, John, 79, 128–9, 156, 181, 238, 248, 258–9, 289, 300, 310, 333, 335, 341, 342, 370
Morley, Samuel, 41, 43–4, 117, 123, 130, 174, 330, 342, 343
Morris, William, 171–2, 174, 176, 280, 355
Moss, J. F., 348
Mundella, A. J., see table of contents, v–vi

Mundella, Antonio, 14, 374
Mundella, Maria Theresa, 86, 104, 140, 236, 377
Mundella, Mrs. Mary, 19, 279–80
Mundella, Mrs. Rebecca, 15
Muntz, 167, 368
Murphy, Rev. G. M., 174

N

National Association for the Promotion of Technical Education, 270–2
National Education Association, 274, 314
National Education League, 75, 72–3, 74, 76, 77, 129, 131, 167, 178, 327, 347
National Education Union, 76, 327
National Federation of Associated Employers, 132–4, 136
National Liberal Club, 237
National Liberal Federation, 178, 179, 279, 323
National Society, 15, 219, 226; for Prevention of Cruelty to Children, 276–7
Naval Defence Act, 371
Nettleship, Dr. E., 309
New Social Movement, 98-100
Newcastle nine hours strike, 102–4; Chronicle, 257
New York Tribune, 85; Working Men's Union, 88
New Zealand loan and Mercantile Agency, 300–5, 306, 308, 352, 373, 374
Nineteenth Century, 221, 231, 252, 262, 305, 360, 368, 374
Nonconformist Revolt, 115, 129, 275, 277, 323, 352
Normansell, John, 53, 69, 112, 324, 346, 347, 357
Northcote, Sir S., 99, 175
Northrop, B. G., 89, 111
Norwood, C. M., 158
Norfolk, Duke of, 376
Nottingham Board of Arbitration, 32–4, 319; Corporation stock, 334; Express, 42, 346; Enclosure Act, 21; Liberal Party, 28–9, 41–6; Manufacturing Company, 38, 80, 105–6, 124, 359; Parliamentary Elections, 26, 34-6, 41–6; Review, 21, 38, 338, 339, 340, 341; T.U.C. at, 105, 112–4; University College, 26, 340

O

Oakley, H., 291, 364
Odger, George, 39, 40, 49, 53, 62, 71, 95, 96, 112, 117, 123, 150, 335, 342, 374
Ogilvy, Sir John, 132
Oldham, 118
Osborne, R. Bernal, 45–6, 90, 343
Overend and Gurney, 51
Owen, Robert, 25, 339; William, 308

P

Paget, Charles, 26, 27, 34, 41, 43, 340
Pakington, Sir J., 99
Pall Mall Gazette, 126, 149, 355
Paris, Comte de, 126, 286, 344
Parnell, 232, 237, 370
Patents, 19, 21–3, 81, 87
Pease, J. W., 251, 280
Percival, J., 226, 362
Percy, Lord Eustace, 93–4
Peto, Sir M., 35, 51
Pickard, W., 53
Playfair, Sir L., 154, 155, 157, 273, 279, 331, 348, 369
Plener, Ernst Edler von, 352, 377
Plimsoll, S., 59, 70, 71, 127, 128, 138, 157–9, 340
Political Economy Club, 146
Poor Law Commission, 308–10
Positivists (*see* Bridges, J. H., Crompton, H. and Harrison, F.)
Potter, George, 46, 96, 98, 100, 342, 354
Potter, Edmund, 70, 72, 73, 135, 347
Potteries, 18, 308
Price, E. P., 60, 62
Pye-Smith, J. W., 334

Q

Quick, R. H., 358
Quilter, W. C., 249, 366, 367

R

Railways, 26, 241 ff, 291 ff.; and Canal Traders Association, 368 ff; Defence Association, 242, 245, 246, 253; *Review*, 366; *Shareholder*, 245, 301, 366; *Times*, 262–3, 369
Ransom, Dr., 46, 340, 343
Reade, Charles, 318, 374
Reagan, J. N., 368
Redgrave, A., 328, 357, 377
Reform Club, 75, 140, 154, 155, 156, 157, 179
Reform League, 73
Reid, R. T., 306–7, 376
Reports: Children's Employment Commission, 36–7, 40; Committee of Council on Education, 203–236, 360; Labour, 305, 371, 372, 373, 375; Metropolitan Poor Law Schools, 308–10; Select Committee on Technical Education (1867) 52; Royal Commission on Technical Education, 224; Welsh Education Committee, 207, 208.
Review of Reviews, 280–1, 371
Reynolds, J. Russell, 309
Richards, H., 115, 160, 161, 174, 177, 234, 351, 362
Richmond and Gordon, Duke of, 99, 175, 186, 187
Riots, 189, 239, 339

Ripley, W. H., 145
Rigg, Dr., 362
Rigg, A. T., 195
Ritchie, C. T., 310–11
Robertson, H., 365, 367
Robin Hood Rifle Corps, 29–30
Roebuck, J. A., 55, 59–62, 69, 87, 131, 346
Rogers, J. E. T., 74, 173, 253–4, 365, 376
Rolley, Wm., 324, 354, 376
Roman Catholic Schools, 361
Rome, Industrial Convention at, 326
Roscoe, Sir H., 203, 211, 232, 234, 270, 272, 273, 279, 359, 360
Rosebery, Lord, 196, 248, 297–8, 300, 306, 369
Royal College of Science, 359
Royal Commission on Trade Unions, 53–4, 68
Royal Society, 211, 241
Ruskin, J., 173
Russell, Lord Charles, 149 ; Lord John, 169
Russell, John Scott, 98–9, 117, 349
Rylands, P., 167, 252, 367

S

St. Aubyn, Sir J., 249, 256
St. James' Hall Conference, 173–5, 228
St. Leonards, Lord, 277–8
Salisbury, marquis of, 173, 175, 247, 253, 260, 262, 333
Salisbury School Board, 277–8
Salis-Schwabe, Col., 252
Salt, Titus, 25, 134–5, 136, 339
Samuelson, Sir B., 52, 97, 101, 153, 209, 224, 232, 235, 241, 264, 271, 345, 359, 361, 362, 364, 369
Sandford, F. R. (Lord Sandford), 204, 218, 274, 359, 360, 362
Sandford, Rev. H., 200
Sandon, Viscount (Earl of Harrowby), 145, 146, 161, 165–7, 192, 328, 347, 362
Saxony, 38, 52, 73, 75, 76, 124, 209, 232, 377
School Boards, 77–80, 117, 161, 164, 165–8, 194, 204, 210, 220, 221, 224, 228, 270, 277–8, 311–3, 336, 348, 377
School meals, 214, 281
Scotland, 215, 220–1, 223, 315, 360
Seale-Hayne, C., 315, 316
Seton Watson, R. W., 182, 356
Shaftesbury, 77, 97, 123, 127, 144, 145–6, 166, 172, 173, 174, 175, 176, 276, 328
Shaw, Bernard, 280, 296
Shaw-Lefevre, G. J., 287, 292, 317, 372
Sheffield, Acts relating to, 334–5; Association of Organised Trades, 49, 59; Brightside, 48, 229, 230, 307, 371; Chamber of Commerce, 90, 196, 368; Filesmiths, 48; foreign steel in, 51; Gas Company, 107; Liberal Association, 159–61, 178; non-conformists, 128, 131, 323, 376; out-

rages, 48–50; Paradise Square, 121, 183, 189 ; parliamentary elections : (1868) 59–63, (1874) 138–141, (1879) 196, (1880) 198, (1885) 231, (1886) 257, (1892) 287–8, (1895) 310; School Board, 358, 377; Trades Council, 188; T.U.C. at, 136–8; Trading Treason, 376; University College movement, 154, 192, 329–331, 316, 340, 374; Water Company, 107–9, 349–50

Shipton, G. W., 327, 362

Smith, B. F., 282, 362

Smith, Goldwin, 59, 87, 137, 184, 257, 367, 368

Smith, H. Llewellyn, 271, 296, 362, 372

Smith, R. Blakelock, 107, 109

Smith, Samuel, 279

Smith, Sir Swire, 247, 359

Social Democratic Federation, 248–9, 363

Social Science Congress, 49, 102, 103, 341, 346, 364, 374

South Kensington, 51, 147, 204, 205–7, 223, 225, 272

South Yorkshire Miners' Association, 57, 114, (see also Normansell, J.)

Spectator, 62, 90, 149, 194, 250, 292–3, 344

Spencer, Lord, 204, 206–7, 215, 219, 233, 248, 358, 369

Spencer, Herbert, 115, 193

Stafford, marquis of, 251

Stainer, J., 235

Stainton, Rev. R., 54, 121

Stanley, Lord, 260

Stanley, Lyulph, 45, 118, 174, 203, 232, 234, 274, 275, 309, 317, 362, 369

Stansfeld, James, 140, 142, 160–1, 167, 174

Statistical Society, 191, 357

Stephen, Fitzjames, 126, 129, 149, 352

Stead, 168, 172–3, 355, 370

Strikes, 18, 32, 58, 126–8, 296–8

Stuart-Wortley, C. B., 196, 282, 295, 358

Stuart, James, 330, 369

Switzerland, 73, 75, 162, 227, 232

Sybil, 99, 143

T

Talbot, C. R. M., 256

Talbot, J. G., 234, 362

Taylor, P. A., 169

Technical Education, 193, 206, 269–73, 285, 314, 329–31, 343, 345, 370, 377

Thring, E., 146

Thring, Lord, 227, 281

The Times, 23, 56, 57, 71, 99, 132, 135, 147–8, 155, 160, 161, 162, 174, 183, 194, 228, 231, 238, 239, 241, 244, 264, 265, 266, 278, 292, 295, 298, 303, 315, 316, 339, 348, 353, 354, 356, 363, 364, 365, 366, 367, 371, 372, 374

Trade Depression, Royal Commission on, 239, 259, 326

Trade Unions, 23, 53, 95–6, 97, 105, 110–12, 116, 121, 122, 123, 126–7, 128, 136–8, 150, 151, 152, 157, 173, 186, 194, 318, 331–2, 374

Trades Guild of Learning, 330

Trevelyan, G. O., 15, 153, 154, 155–6, 174, 248, 354

Turk, George, 113, 114

Twyford, Thomas, 308

Tyndall, John, 257, 271

U

University extension, 26, 154, 192, 213–4, 217, 224, 316, 329–31, 340, 373

Uttley, Stuart, 296, 324, 326, 327, 335, 344, 376

V

Vaughan Williams, Justice, 302, 303, 310, 373

Victoria, Queen, 198–9, 258, 315, 359

Vincent, Col. H., 263, 278, 286, 287, 288, 296, 333, 363, 368, 371

Vivian, Sir H. H., 365, 367

W

Waddy, S. D., 160, 196, 358

Wages Fund Theory, 51, 320, 375

Wales, 207–8, 215–6, 217, 219, 224, 227, 230, 231, 235

Wallace, A. R., 21

Ward, W. G., 25, 26, 31, 105, 339

Waring, C., 256, 369

Watkin, Sir E., 246, 247, 255, 264

Watson, R. Spence, 256, 363

Waugh, B., 276, 370

Webb, S. and B., 123, 293, 305, 344, 352, 372, 373, 377

Webster, Sir R., 251

Wells, D. A., 87, 89

West, Sir Algernon, 373

Westminster, Duke of, 175, 176

Westminster Palace Hotel, 125, 128

Whiskey money, 273, 278

White, J. E., 36–7

White, Jonathan, 31, 340

Whiteing, R., 55

Whitworth, H., 135

Whitworth, Sir J., 40, 343

Wiggin, H., 252, 367

Williams, J. P., 252, 367

Willis, J. A., 213, 360

Wilson, H. J., 92, 129, 131, 159, 160, 161, 184, 287, 304, 306, 323, 333, 353, 362

Wilson, James, 340

Wilson, John, 376

Wilson, Lucy, 330

Workmen's Compensation, 138, 357

Wright, C. D., 372

Y

Yeomans, John, 108

Young, Nelson W., 88

Yoxall, J. H., 287